RACIALIZED MEDIA

Racialized Media

The Design, Delivery, and Decoding of Race and Ethnicity

Edited by Matthew W. Hughey and Emma González-Lesser

NEW YORK UNIVERSITY PRESS
New York

NEW YORK UNIVERSITY PRESS
New York
www.nyupress.org

References to internet websites (URLs) were accurate at the time of writing.
Neither the author nor New York University Press is responsible for URLs
that may have expired or changed since the manuscript was prepared.

Library of Congress Cataloging-in-Publication Data
Names: Hughey, Matthew W. (Matthew Windust), editor. | González-Lesser,
Emma, editor.
Title: Racialized media : the design, delivery, and decoding of race and
ethnicity / edited by Matthew W. Hughey and Emma González-Lesser.
Description: New York : New York University Press, 2020. | Includes
bibliographical references and index.
Identifiers: LCCN 2019041704 | ISBN 9781479811076 (cloth) |
ISBN 9781479814558 (paperback) | ISBN 9781479807826 (ebook) |
ISBN 9781479859924 (ebook)
Subjects: LCSH: Mass media and race relations. | Mass media and minorities.
Classification: LCC P94.5.M55 R35 2020 | DDC 302.23089—dc23
LC record available at https://lccn.loc.gov/2019041704

New York University Press books are printed on acid-free paper,
and their binding materials are chosen for strength and durability.
We strive to use environmentally responsible suppliers and materials
to the greatest extent possible in publishing our books.

Manufactured in the United States of America

10 9 8 7 6 5 4 3 2 1

Also available as an ebook

For Menaka, Bianca, Noa, and Liev

CONTENTS

Introduction

The "Labor" of Racialized Media

Stuart Hall and the Circuit of Culture

MATTHEW W. HUGHEY AND EMMA GONZÁLEZ-LESSER

In September 2018, the tennis star Serena Williams lost the final of the US Open to Naomi Osaka after receiving three code violations from the chair umpire. Williams was outspoken and expressive during the match, accusing the chair of unfair and biased calls and calling him a "thief." Depicting the event, the veteran Australian cartoonist Mark Knight drew a cartoon showing Williams stamping on her racquet, with a baby's pacifier on the ground nearby, and the umpire asking Osaka, "Can you just let her win?" The cartoon was published in the Australian-based *Herald Sun*. There was an eruptive response around the globe. The *Irish Times* asked, "Outrage-mongering or old-fashioned racism?" (O'Connell 2018). A *Washington Post* article said the cartoon used "dehumanizing" facial features, while Brenna Edwards, a Black journalist who reports for *Essence* magazine, said that the cartoon "dates back to the Jim Crow era. . . . You have Serena in the foreground as a hulking mass, not even looking like a human" (ABC News 2018). Knight rejected such characterizations and stated, "I find on social media that stuff gets shared around. . . . It develops intensity way beyond its initial meaning. . . . No racial historical significance should be read into it" (ABC News 2018).

The incident reveals the social import of the concept of "race" and its relationship to varied mass media. From streaming broadcast tennis matches to newspaper cartoons, from journalism to social media debates, meaning-making and contestation over race and racism are pressing concerns of the media world (Hunt 1997). Such constructions and discourses are additionally imbued with notions of difference, identity, representation, inequality, power, agency, and ethics, gesturing toward how unsettled and uneasy the place of race is across a media-saturated globe.

For decades now, scholars have empirically investigated the influence of media exposure in issues related to race and racism and have cataloged how media impacts our thinking, emotions, and behaviors. Importantly, ample evidence shows how the manner of ethnic and racial representation in the media can result in either harm or benefit for different groups. For example, Patricia Hill Collins's notion of "controlling images" in *Black Feminist Thought* (1990), John Downing and Charles Husband's *Representing "Race"* (2005), Stephanie Greco Larson's *Media and Minorities* (2005), and Elizabeth Ewen and Stuart Ewen's *Typecasting* (2011) are all landmark studies that concentrate on the frequency of racial depictions that litter the mediascape. Yet much less scholarship and fewer conclusive takeaways have been generated concerning the media production, regulation, and consumption of these representations. As such, the authors of the chapters in this book directly address the social dynamics that underpin the design, delivery, and decoding of the intersection of "race" and "media."

What Is "Race"? What Is "Media"?

We take the social scientific constructionist approach that "race" is a meaningful category of human difference by virtue of the social significance with which it is imbued. That is, the concept has no biological validity, essence, or inherent ability to determine our lives (Morning 2014). From sociology to biology and from genomics to anthropology, experts in these fields do not deny that clusters of human populations carry particular genetic information. But clusters of genetic material do not provide the basis for social distinctions that society recognizes as "race." As the sociologists Karen Fields and Barbara Fields (1994, 113) put it, "Anyone who continues to believe in race as a physical attribute of individuals, despite the now commonplace disclaimers of biologists and geneticists, might as well also believe that Santa Claus, the Easter Bunny and the tooth fairy are real, and that the earth stands still while the sun moves." Even Craig Venter, one of the first scientists to map the human genome, stated, "The concept of race has no genetic or scientific basis" (Weiss and Gillis 2000, A1).

Race is, however, a "social fact" (Bonilla-Silva 1999). It operates over myriad social dimensions as powerful ideologies and dominant and central social institutions, through group interests and personal identities, and within the scope of everyday interactions (Hughey 2015; Roth 2016; Morning 2017). What we recognize as "racial" depends on arbitrarily selected and defined phenotypes, as well as practices, beliefs, customs, and many other random criteria we use as evidence. Importantly, the concept of "race" was birthed in the service of colonialism as a rationale for dominance and inequality. In many ways, the concept still serves that purpose, and racial inequality has become a hallmark of modern society and a scathing reminder of the hypocrisy of modernity. Simply put, "Race is a biological fiction with a social function" (Hughey 2017, 27).

We understand media as the means or channels of mass communication through which news, entertainment, education, propaganda, and personal information travel (e.g., broadcasting, publishing, billboards, internet) (Hunt 1997). In this book, we focus on mass media communication, which entails print, press, advertising, cinema, radio and television broadcasting, and digital venues from websites and video games to dark-web illegal economies and social media. Media is a powerful force that not only reflects a view of the world back to us but can shape how our world is engaged and reconstructed. Media is such a part of our everyday world that we are said to live in a media-saturated world, one in which we often do not recognize the extent of our immersion in media because of its banal normality. Especially in the era of industrial capitalism and consumer-driven societies, media is a, if not the, primary vehicle for information, goods, services, and how we understand vital connections between political, economic, cultural, and social life.

Perhaps this is why entire cottage industries exist that proclaim—with either absolute cynicism or optimism—the role of media today. For instance, Malcolm X repeatedly critiqued newspaper coverage for its racial biases, stating in 1964, "The press is so powerful in its image-making role, it can make the criminal look like he's the victim and make the victim look like he's the criminal" ([1964] 1965, 93). Half a century later, in the age of the internet, Jimmy Wales, the founder of Wikipedia, came to maintain more optimism on the power of media: "Imagine a world in which every single person on the planet is given free access to the sum of all human knowledge" (Miller 2004). And the author and cultural critic Roxane Gay (2013) has stated, "Social media is something of a double-edged sword. At its best, social media offers unprecedented opportunities for marginalized people to speak and bring much needed attention to the issues they face. At its worst, social media also offers 'everyone' an unprecedented opportunity to share in collective outrage without reflection." These quotes represent perspectives on both the potential and pitfalls of media in an increasingly media-connected society. The control, access, and uses of media today are vastly unequal and are marshaled toward different ends. The flow of information and what counts as information to be produced, disseminated, and consumed are not ethically neutral topics. Rather, the place of media in society is a polysemous and often contested subject due precisely to its central role in our lives. Racialized media—or media that creates and perpetuates ideas about race—directly implicates, and is intimately connected by, the central social system of racial inequality.

Media and Racial Literacy

Both "media literacy" and "race literacy" are commonly bandied-about terms. In the mid-1950s, the American Council for Better Broadcasts used the phrase "media literacy" (1955, 4) in its newsletter. In 1992, the "National Leadership Conference on Media Literacy" attempted to define media literacy as "the ability to access, analyze, evaluate and communicate messages in a variety of forms" (Aufderheide 1993, 1); and in 1998, the National Communication Association concluded that a media-literate person is one who "understands how words, images, and sounds influence the way meanings are created and shared in contemporary society in ways that are both subtle and profound. A media literate person is equipped to assign value, worth and meaning to media use and media messages."

Researchers still debate the precise definition of "media literacy" (cf. Potter 2010, 670), largely because the term reflects enduring tensions among media practitioners, consumers, policy makers, and critical scholars. In recent years, "media literacy" has become a shorthand term for an array of policies and initiatives that bridge the gap between *what people know* about the changing media environment and *what they need to know* to meet certain pragmatic, policy, and ethical goals (Livingstone and van der Graaf 2010). Moreover, scholars now agree that four resources underpin media literary, in which one must have the ability to (1) access, (2) analyze, (3) evaluate, and (4) create media across a variety of contexts (cf. Koltay 2011).

Racial literacy—a term coined by the legal scholar Lani Guinier—is an approach that directly confronts the belief that race itself and, by extension, racial antagonism and conflict are natural, extant categories, qualities, or behaviors. Simultaneously, the notion of racial literacy means that one does not abide by an optimistic faith that racial inequality, prejudice, discrimination, and racism will simply erode or decline owing to the rise of "modernity" and the assumptions of a more educated, rational, or liberal populace. Aside from what racial literacy opposes, Guinier (2004, 114–15) specifies three tenets of racial literacy:

> First, racial literacy is contextual rather than universal. . . . Racial literacy depends upon the engagement between action and thought, between experimentation and feedback, between bottom-up and top-down initiatives. . . . Second, racial literacy emphasizes the relationship between race and power. . . . It acknowledges the importance of individual agency but refuses to lose sight of institutional and environmental forces that both shape and reflect that agency. It sees little to celebrate when formal equality is claimed within a racialized hierarchy. . . . Third, while racial literacy never loses sight of race, it does not focus exclusively on race. It constantly interrogates the dynamic relationship among race, class, geography, gender, and other explanatory variables.

Given the centrality of racialized media in our everyday lives, and how the varied diffusion of racialized messages across a multitude of mass media platforms serves as both social bond and solvent, we are reminded of the media scholar Marshall McLuhan's twofold prediction that media would create a "global village" while simultaneously engendering tendencies to "retribalize" ([1964] 1994, 34, 24). Thus, it would seem an essential yet Sisyphean task to become literate, if not fluent, in the encyclopedic content of race and media. At the least, we hope this book assists in understanding the form, function, antecedents, and effects of racialized media in our contemporary moment.

The Nexus of Race and Media

Importantly, such understandings necessitate sensitivity toward how the meanings and influences of "race" and "media" inform and alter one another. As Robert Entman and Andrew Rojecki (2001, 2–3) argue, mass media "is both a barometer of race relations and a potential accelerator either to racial cohesion or to cultural separation and political conflict. . . . Media productions offer a revealing indicator of the new forms of racial differentiation. Beyond providing a diagnostic tool, a measuring device for the state of race relations, the media also act as a causal agent: they help to shape and reshape the culture." The sociologist Norman Denzin (2001, 244) states that "the media and the cinematic racial order are basic to the understanding of race relations in any society." And the media scholars Lisa Nakamura and Peter Chow-White (2012, 1–2) remark, "As the shift from analog to digital media formats and ways of knowing continues apace, continued social pressure is brought to bear on the idea of race as a key aspect of identity and an organizing principle for society. Yet no matter how 'digital' we become, the continuing problem of social inequality along racial lines persists. . . . Equally important but often less discussed is this: the digital is altering our understandings of what race is as well as nurturing new types of inequality along racial lines." Along similar lines, Dana Mastro (2015, 4) posits that "it is socially significant to systematically document racial/ethnic representations in the media as these portrayals contribute meaningfully to both real-world intergroup dynamics as well as beliefs about oneself and one's own group in society." Our particular sociohistorical moment has strategically used racialized media in service of upholding and justifying new forms of racism, as well as toward antiracist and resistive praxis (P. Collins 2004; Littlefield 2008, 677). Because of the salience of the mutually constitutive relationship of race and media, it is increasingly difficulty to navigate our social worlds without some understanding of race, media, and their intersection. Toward that end, this book aims to help both veterans of and newcomers to the field of race and media.

Encoding and Decoding

To organize the vast array of theoretical, empirical, and methodological diversity brought to bear in this book, we organize these studies via the media studies framework known as the "circuit of culture." Before this framework was advanced, Stuart Hall created the "encoding/decoding" model of communication in 1973. Hall wished to explain how media messages are always in a process of transmission that is directly related to power and domination. That is, rather than apply the traditional model of *sender-message-receiver*, in which the three elements are distinct from one another, Hall emphasized a new approach. The production, distribution, and consumption of the media product are equally determinate moments of the media product—thereby elevating distribution and consumption to the same creative import as the formal "productive" step. Hall (1980, 128–29) wrote that it is useful to

> think of this process in terms of a structure produced and sustained through the articulation of linked but distinctive moments—production, circulation, distribution/consumption, reproduction. This would be to think of the process as a "complex structure in dominance." . . . The "object" of these practices is meanings and messages in the form of sign-vehicles of a specific kind organized, like any form of communication or language, through the operation of codes within the syntagmatic chain of a discourse. . . . But it is in the *discursive* form that the circulation of the product takes place, as well as its distribution to different audiences. Once accomplished, the discourse must then be translated—transformed, again—into social practices if the circuit is to be both completed and effective. If no "meaning" is taken, there can be no "consumption."

Simply put, the encoding, circulation, and decoding of the message are equally important and creative steps in the meaning of the message. There is no media message that exists asocially. Media is constantly in process: from creating, sharing, and shaping to revising, pushing back, and merging the varied messages. After Hall, many scholars came to focus on the polysemic nature of media. However, there was a lopsided and predominant focus on media representations that either excluded or marginalized empirical examinations of the actual social uses of media or made only theoretical nods to the varied process of media making.

Media "Labor" and the Circuit of Culture

Nearly a quarter century after Hall's encoding/decoding approach, Paul du Gay, Stuart Hall, Linda Janes, Anders Koed Madsen, Hugh Mackay, and Keith Negus introduced the "circuit of culture" (1997). Their approach specifies that any cultural object should be examined from multiple vantage points. In particular, this "radical contextualization" gestures toward the conclusion that to understand how media works, one should examine its signification, identity, production, regulation, and consumption (fig. I.1).[1]

Stuart Hall is perhaps best known for applying the circuit of culture to racial media representations. Hall's 1997 work *Representation: Cultural Representations and Signifying Practices* remains a landmark text for its presentation of a systematic approach to meaning and power, especially in relation to questions of social difference and inequality (seen especially in the chapter titled "The Spectacle of the 'Other'"). Importantly, the book's title is deceiving; Hall does not exclusively concentrate on the "signification" and "identity" (together, the "representations") of racial depictions in mass media but recognizes the equal importance of how the production, distribution, and reception (the three elements of media "labor") of racialized media representations take place in the lived social world. Five years earlier, Hall (1992, 255) wrote that it is not enough to study "how things are represented" but that scholars must also analyze how "the 'machineries' and regimes of representation in a culture do play a constitutive, and not merely a reflexive, after-the-event, role . . . in the constitution of social and political life."

Research on the "labor" at the nexus of race and the media has proceeded unevenly in comparison to the study of racial "representations." Some recent representational studies have led to increased attention to the global circulation of violently racist imagery and discourse, as well as both their effects on vulnerable populations and their ability to rationalize and legitimate unequal social relations among the racially

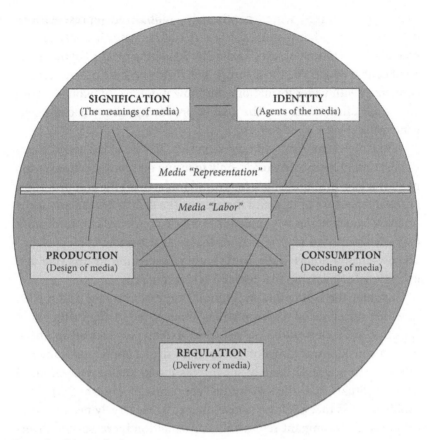

Figure I.1. Circuit of culture.

privileged and media literate (e.g., Bancel, David, and Thomas 2014; Leavitt et al. 2015; Takezawa 2011; Tukachinsky, Mastro, and Yarchi 2015). Concurrently, some have argued that contemporary scholarship has become overpopulated with studies focusing on popular culture representations absent the mechanisms involved in the production of those representations (e.g., Chuang and Roemer 2015; Coleman [1998] 2014; Krijnen and Van Bauwel 2015). Moreover, much of this scholarship has become theory for theory's sake. That is, one does not know the meaning of a mass-mediated racial representation until one discovers how people are actually involved in its production, distribution, and consumption (Bérubé 2009; Peeters and Sterkenburg 2017). Perhaps such one-sidedness, which continually emphasized representations detached from other factors, led Stuart Hall to state, "I really cannot read another cultural-studies analysis of Madonna or *The Sopranos*. . . . So of course we studied those things, but always because of how it interconnected with wider formations. But now it doesn't interconnect with any wider formations. . . . The goal of producing theory became self-generating" (MacCabe 2008, 29).

While the extant focus on representations has provided useful material for critiquing media worlds, only focusing on representations is too narrow a lens through which to see and understand the complex roots of the intersection of race and the media. The dearth of scholarly focus on these "machineries"—coupled with a well-nourished corpus of work on varied racialized representations that regularly traffic in media landscapes—makes Stuart Hall's work both an exception to this rule and exceptional scholarship that remains relevant today.

Consider the still common "clinical" approach to race and media, in which varied racial representations are declared to align with either "positive" characterizations or "negative" stereotypes. Such an approach fails to consider questions of production, distribution, and audience interpretation and ultimately substitutes moral analogy for mindful analysis. Stuart Hall thus wrote in *Representation* (1997b, 274), "The problem . . . is that adding positive images to the largely negative repertoire of the dominant regime of representation increases the diversity of ways that 'being black' is represented, but does not necessarily displace the negative. Since the binaries remain in place, meaning continues to be framed by them. The strategy challenges the binaries—but it does not undermine them. The peace-loving, child-caring, Rastafarian can still appear, in the following day's newspapers, as an exotic and violent black stereotype." Discussions of whether images are essentially "good" or "bad" are generally informed by whether an image or discourse breaks from a racist stereotype or historical trope or perpetuates existing assumptions and expectations regarding race. The complexity of context, form, audience, mode of delivery, legal constraints, experience, and so on (all of which inform the production, distribution, and consumption of racialized media) are all but utterly submerged when evaluations are made on the basis of a binary construction of the "goodness" of representations.

Designed, Delivered, and Decoded

This book brings together an array of both established and emerging scholars from a variety of disciplinary backgrounds to examine the labor of racialized media with regard to how it is *designed, delivered,* and *decoded*. Given that our work here is meant to offer a corrective to the predominance of textual analyses of racial representations, we divide the book into three parts, which focus primarily on either the design, circulation, or reception of media texts about race to present thorough case studies on each. Together, they encompass the breadth of the relationship among design, delivery, and decoding, while individually they afford depth and nuance. Within these three parts, the authors cover how media industries, organizations, and institutions, as well as everyday audiences alongside specific social groups, make, interpret, regulate, and consume racialized media.

Design—or "production"—constitutes the encoded messages via the dominant narratives, plot structure, characters, and drama of the stories. Rather than focusing on representations, analysis of design takes a broader "macro" approach to understanding the dominant forces at play in the construction of representational forms. Furthermore, while the production side of media narratives denotes the beginning of "labor" within the circuit of culture's "circuit," it certainly does not exist in a vacuum. Analysis of production draws topics, treatments, agendas, events, images, and other sources of meaning from the wide social, cultural, and political milieu in which it is embedded. In other words, studying the design of racialized media does not take representations at face value as they appear on screen, paper, or otherwise but situates such representations in the larger media and social scenes from which they emerged. In this sense, this book illuminates the dominant narrative structure and context of varied media forms.

The moment of *delivery*—or "regulation"—is characterized by the ways in which media is marketed and critically reviewed so as to influence mainstream audience engagement. The patterns revealed in reviewers' and gatekeepers' interpretations and practices are indicative of social forces that construct and present a particular actor's persona, how specific targets are chosen as "worthwhile" from an increasing plethora of media forms, selection of technique (from content and stylistic parameters), and the making of value judgments regarding the individuals, interests, and interactions in distributing that media form. Reviewers and gatekeepers, like all social actors, are not free from race-based biases, assumptions, and interpretations. Their valuations do not merely reflect individual opinions but, like all elements of the media "circuit," both reflect and inform a racialized society. If sociological studies of the intersection of media and race are to transcend the now well-rehearsed examination of "racial representations," they should turn toward how these cultural intermediaries play formal and informal roles in shaping meaning between its production and consumption stages.

Finally, the stage of *decoding*—or "consumption"—represents the moments in which the content of the media is received, interpreted, and debated by public audiences. That is, representations do not land on a monolithic audience, and variations in consumption can be just as varied as the people doing the consuming. Here it is important to highlight how different interpretations can align with different subject positions of race, class, ethnicity, gender, age, sexuality, and region. Moreover, the various structures of interpretation, or the devices that people use to make sense of racialized media, can be illuminated and questioned for their usage and effect.

Despite pronouncements that we have reached a "postracial" or "colorblind" society or that racial and racist meanings are only the domain of extremist activism and political rhetoric, this collection demonstrates how dominant racial representations are deployed, negotiated, and contested, inclusive of productive activity, distributive processes, and audience reactions.

An Overview of the Chapters

In part 1, "How Racialized Media Is Designed," we include chapters on Hollywood filmmaking, money-as-media, television, online comics, and news formats. First, Minjeong Kim and Rachelle J. Brunn-Bevel apply a political-economy lens to image production. They suggest that decisions made in the production and marketing processes aim to minimize financial risks but often limit the participation of racial-ethnic-minority filmmakers and actors. At the same time, Hollywood incorporates foreign-born directors and actors to entice international audiences.

Catherine R. Squires and Aisha Upton then take on the debates about the 2016 announcement that the US Department of the Treasury would redesign the twenty-dollar bill to feature Harriet Tubman. While there was jubilation from activists to build a "monument in your pocket," the redesign also brought sharp rebukes from White conservatives. Rather than try to resolve contentious debates over which figures best represent (or deserve to represent) American history, the authors examine how these conflicts elicited by the redesign engender new transracial imaginations of inclusion.

Taking on issues of race, gender, and sexuality emerging from Shonda Rhimes's production company Shondaland, Maretta McDonald examines whether a "Shondaland effect" can be observed in television programming. Examining how stereotypical thinking and microaggressions have been used in television by female content creators who are not Black, and by closely analyzing episodes of Grey's Anatomy from 2015 to 2016, McDonald interrogates the possible effects that a Black female content creator has on the way issues of race, class, gender, and sexuality are developed in the television content that Rhimes produces.

Turning to online comics, Rachel Kuo considers how the form and aesthetics of virtual comics locate ways that racial justice can be visually represented and communicated in digital environments. Kuo shows how the circulation of activist media within visual economies creates different possibilities and limitations for radical politics.

Martin Gilens and Niamh Costello examine "why Americans hate welfare" by puncturing the myths and misconceptions about welfare policy, public opinion, and the role of the media. They show how the production of news media shapes a complex array of views on welfare—a complex mixture of cynicism and compassion, both misinformed and racially charged—which reflect both a distrust of welfare recipients and a desire to help the "deserving" poor.

And concluding the exploration of design, Justin de Leon examines how Native American communities engage in filmmaking not as straightforward acts of cultural production but as "acts of flourishing" toward anticolonial and antiracist praxis. In this sense, filmmaking is revealed as an act of ontological, racial, and spiritual sovereignty.

In part 2, "How Racialized Media Is Delivered," we consider broadcast radio, the demographics of newsrooms, Netflix and NBC documentaries, social media, and film reviews. First, Christopher Chávez explores how National Public Radio (NPR) imagines, institutionalizes, and targets the Latinx listener. On the basis of interviews with public radio practitioners and a review of strategic documents of NPR and the Corporation for Public Broadcasting (CPB), Chávez contends that NPR has defined its ideal Latinx listener in ways that are congruent with its current target-audience profile of liberal Whites.

Next, Carlos Alamo-Pastrana and William Hoynes delve into the persistent racialization of professional journalism, describing the processes that define "mainstream" news as "White media." The Whiteness of US news emanates from cultural practices of professional journalism and institutional forces shaping the journalistic field rather than simple demographic characteristics of the workforce.

In examining unique case studies of two recent Korean-adoptee-created media—the Netflix documentary *Twinsters* (2015) and NBC Asian America's docuseries *aka SEOUL* (2016)—SunAh M. Laybourn examines how adoptee-centered media converges with and diverges from traditional renderings of transnational adoption. Korean-adoptee cultural production shifts portrayals of Korean adoptees from objects in need of rescue to subjects asserting selfhood by exploring previously excluded or unimagined themes.

Leslie Kay Jones delivers a chapter on #BlackLivesMatter and how social media like Twitter plays the role of a movement and public space where outside observers negotiate their own meaning-making surrounding the movement's claims and strategies. Conceptualizing movement mechanics in this way provides a clearer understanding of the importance of digital media in the contemporary Black freedom movement without relying on technological determinism. Jones neither reduces social media to a structural component of the movement nor undermines the importance of physicality for protest.

Nadia Y. Flores-Yeffal and David Elkins offer a unique examination of how cyberspace delivers erroneous media messages to the public, engendering racialized "moral panics" about Latinx populations. Their chapter pushes us to think critically about the role of "moral entrepreneurs" as media gatekeepers and shapers of media content in postproduction, which has the capacity to influence the outcomes of political campaigns or to ease the passage of anti-immigrant legislation.

In part 3, "How Racialized Media Is Decoded," the assembled authors take on newspaper interpretations of scientific debates over race, migrant audience interpretations of film, digital newspaper comment fields as discursive sites of meaning-making, how people make sense of race and violence in video games, and how the film *Dear White People* (2014) is used in collegiate class spaces. First, Sonita R. Moss and Dorothy E. Roberts take on the media spectacle in which "Black" women give birth to "White" children. In conducting a critical discourse analysis of media coverage and online comments, Moss and Roberts found the patterned use of several racialized and gendered logics by the public, which they argue is a kind of seductive "racial voyeurism" that allows people to digest and interpret media narratives that violate deeply held beliefs about racial identity and the reproduction of race.

Next, David J. Leonard takes us on a trip through the video game *Mafia III*—a game that transports players back to 1968 New Orleans— to show how the game provides an outlet for antiracist hope. Through violence directed at White supremacists and a narrative of antiracism, *Mafia III* provides both respite and a truly alternative reality, enabling gamers to enact power in our contemporary moment of rising hopelessness and nihilism.

Michael L. Rosino explicitly draws on Stuart Hall's theory of encoding/decoding to point out that audience interpretations of digital media do not straightforwardly reflect the messages encoded by media producers. Instead, they are the product of an active set of interpretive practices that result in different ways of decoding digital media messages. Through an analysis of online comments on news articles about the "War on Drugs," Rosino demonstrates important aspects of the racial politics of digital audience reception.

In part 3's final chapter, Tina M. Harris, Anna M. Dudney Deeb, and Alysen Wade take on the popular film *Dear White People* and show how it can be used in the collegiate classroom. Their chapter involves a critique of student reaction papers to the film and their efforts to promote awareness and understanding of race in the context of higher education.

As the coeditors of this book, we offer a concluding chapter. Although we have assembled an interdisciplinary collection of scholarship here, we present our conclusion from the perspective of our disciplinary training: sociology. Rather than attempt a holistic and overarching chapter intended to capture all major trends and dilemmas for the future of media and race from all the disciplines that study these phenomena, we limit our discussion to some of the key sociological issues on the study of race and media, namely, where the scholarship has been and where it is going.

***

The range of media covered in this book speaks to the increasing complexity of our media-saturated world. The authors here demonstrate the racialized character of long-standing media forms, from television, newspapers, and money to newer formats like social media, digital comics, and video games. Alongside this plethora of media types, our focus on extending beyond the representational analyses that are so common in both extant scholarship and popular discourse demonstrates that the media scene is far more multifaceted than most people assume. In this book, design analyses situate representational forms in the macro context rather than treating them as stand-alone images and tropes. Examinations of delivery alert readers to the influence of media intermediaries' racializing biases and valuations, which structure the behind-the-scenes processes leading up to the representations that audiences receive. Considerations of the decoding of representations offer new ways for understanding the relevance of social positionality to variegated interpretations across heterogeneous audiences.

Our purpose is not to dismiss the relevance of representational analyses of media forms. Extant literature on racialized media representations has provided a crucial foundation from which the scholarship in this book has emerged, and indeed many of the authors include discussions of representation within their chapters. We believe that representational analyses will continue to be useful in highlighting racial tropes that persist or shift form in an unceasingly racialized social landscape. However, we also firmly maintain that representational examinations can only provide a partial understanding of the media world.

This book can thus encourage future research that examines media elements outside of representation, as well as help situate research on representation within a larger system of media labor. That is, future scholarship that does highlight the images and tropes present in various media forms should no longer contend with these representations as autonomous or neutrally occurring phenomena but should have an obligation to consider the interrelated structural forces occurring in the multiple realms of media as a system.

Note

1. The term "radical contextualization" is often used to describe the work of Stuart Hall in particular and the Centre for Contemporary Cultural Studies in general. As Lawrence Grossberg (2006, 27) states, "Although I am primarily drawing on the work and words of Stuart Hall, I believe this commitment is visible generally in the work of the Centre for Contemporary Cultural Studies. . . . The commitment may have been more or less strong (and more or less conscious) in different practices and practitioners. But as Stuart Hall recently told me (personal conversation 10 April 2005), 'Never trust the teller, trust the tale.'"

PART I

How Racialized Media Is Designed

How do all the media representations we engage with land on our screens, papers, and sound waves? As discussed in the introduction, this book tackles three major phases of the circuit of media labor: the design, decoding, and delivery of racialized media. Although a circuit by definition is interconnected and not unidirectional (the link back to design will become clearer in the part overviews and the chapters of the following two parts), the design of media content can be thought of as the first phase and is the focus of this first part of the book.

Analyzing the production of media content draws the focus not to media representations at face value but to the macro perspective on how certain media contents are constructed. In other words, representations in the media do not exist by some incidental occurrence but result from careful calculation and curation by media creators. In the context of racialized media, dominant racial ideologies inform the multitude of choices made in the production process that result in the representational content that audiences receive. Part 1 explores these ideologies and choices that are often unseen by media audiences.

In chapter 1, Minjeong Kim and Rachelle J. Brunn-Bevel challenge how casting choices for Hollywood films with diverse casts favor international people of color over actors born in the United States. Catherine R. Squires and Aisha Upton fill chapter 2 with an examination of the debate and historical distortions surrounding the possible redesign of the twenty-dollar bill to depict the face of Harriet Tubman. Maretta McDonald's chapter 3 focuses on Shonda Rhimes, a Black woman who is also one of the most successful television showrunners today. McDonald examines how Rhimes used her positionality to construct media representations that challenge assumptions of Black womanhood in her series *Grey's Anatomy*. In chapter 4, Rachel Kuo considers the choices made to design abbreviated visual and narrative indications of race in online comics. Chapter 5, by Martin Gilens and Niamh Costello, examines how news media produced higher rates of news articles on Black poverty in the 1960s, despite the racial makeup of poor populations at the time, thus racializing poverty and contributing to anti-Black stereotypes. In the part's final chapter, Justin de Leon encourages intentionality and emphasis on process in the design of film, highlighting indigenous Lakota Sioux storytelling as a blueprint for enacting the filmmaking process.

1

Political Economy and the
Global-Local Nexus of Hollywood

MINJEONG KIM AND RACHELLE J. BRUNN-BEVEL

After the announcement that *12 Years a Slave* (2013) was nominated for Oscars in nine categories, including Best Picture and Best Director, the popular African American actor Samuel L. Jackson argued that the film was made because its director, Steve McQueen, was of the British nationality. Jackson said, "I would think that if an African-American director went into a studio and pitched that particular film, they would be like: 'No, no, no'" (Akinyemi 2014). Jackson and other members of the African American film community have contended that American producers would not finance African American directors to make films about slavery and that McQueen was a "safer" choice than an African American director, given the assumption that McQueen would pursue a "softer" portrayal of slavery (Akinyemi 2014). Such an approach would be appealing to executives who deem African American perspectives too provocative, but it was problematic for Jackson, who saw McQueen's take as inauthentic.

In an op-ed on Hollywood's hiring of White filmmakers to tell Black stories, the African American director John Singleton (2013) mentions *Get On Up* (2014), a James Brown biopic made with two White British writers, the Butterworth brothers, and questions how one can make "a movie about the icon who laid down the foundation of funk, hip-hop and black economic self-reliance with no African-American involvement behind the scenes." In the film industry, national boundaries are permeable, as evinced by international film festivals, multinational coinvestments, foreign location shooting, overseas production, and global circulation of Hollywood films (Miller et al. 2001). However, when Hollywood produces films about African American stories without considering "cultural nuances and deep-seated emotions that help define the black American experience" (Singleton 2013), it contributes to perpetuating racial divides both in cultural representations and in institutional structures.

Moviemaking is an artistic endeavor, but the film business is fundamentally an economic enterprise. Adherents of political economy theories of image production argue that a small number of "political and economic elites" control media images that audiences see; and the US film industry, namely, Hollywood, prioritizes financial considerations over racial justice or political correctness (Croteau and Hoynes 2014; Gamson et al. 1992). We extend this framework to understand how Hollywood's "going global" impacts local politics of racial-ethnic representation in the US film business. By "going global," we focus on two aspects: the incorporation of foreign-born talent and Hollywood's pursuit of international box-office domination. These two aspects are not mutually exclusive, as the former is a strategy for the latter. But each also presents distinct challenges for underrepresented filmmakers of color in the United States.

As part of a larger study examining the one hundred top-grossing films in the United States since 1995, this chapter focuses on two central research questions. First, how does the involvement of foreign-born directors and actors influence cinematic narratives of people of color in the United States? Second, how does emphasis on the global film market affect representations of people of color in Hollywood?

Political Economy of Hollywood

The film industry consists of three processes: production to make films, distribution to market and bring films to exhibitors, and exhibition to show films (Rhines 1996). Movie theater companies for exhibition are mostly independent from production and distribution processes. The main players of Hollywood are those involved in production and distribution. The so-called Big Six companies that dominate the field include Paramount, Warner Bros., 20th Century Fox, Universal, Columbia, and Walt Disney Studios. In 2017, movies released by the Big Six accounted for 80.4 percent of all earnings at the box office in North America (Statista, n.d.).

This institutional approach hypothesizes that media ownership patterns shape media products, including the stories films tell. David Croteau and William Hoynes (2014, 50) assert, "One possible political consequence of the concentration of media ownership is that, in some ways, it becomes more difficult for alternative media voices to emerge." Independent films, including the genre of Black films, produced outside the major studio system with more creative autonomy for filmmakers, provide one source of divergent media voices that center on the stories and experiences of marginalized groups in a nuanced way and often reject the stereotypes that are widely promoted in mainstream films (Yearwood 2000).

Ultimately, film producers follow a "logic of safety that revolves around minimizing the risk of losing money," seeking projects that are likely to draw a mass audience (Croteau and Hoynes 2014, 55). Consequently, the profit-driven logic of safety encourages producers to replicate successful films, avoid so-called risky or controversial film topics, and use movie stars, if possible, to maximize profits (Croteau and Hoynes 2014; Lewis 2003). For example, spectacular action films and universally appealing comedies starring actors with a track record of successful films are the safest bets.

This logic of safety creates a challenging context for filmmakers of color. Conventionally, Hollywood gatekeepers have envisioned "large, general audiences for 'white films' that often go racially unmarked" (Erigha 2019, 55). Executives believed that films with lead actors of color or with a focus on non-White characters would not appeal to the broader audience, thus labeling such films economically risky. This trend persists despite recent industry reports that point to the importance of diversity. For example, the 2016 Motion Picture Association of America (MPAA) report shows that even though Whites make up the majority of the US population (62 percent) and frequent moviegoers (59 percent), they represent a smaller share of ticket sales (51 percent). Latinos' share of frequent moviegoers (23 percent) is much larger than their share in the general population (18 percent); Asians' per capita annual movie attendance (tickets sold per person) is highest, with an average of 6.1 times in the year, almost double Whites' 3.2 times (MPAA 2016). The UCLA Hollywood Diversity Reports find that "diversity sells" (Hunt, Ramón, and Tran 2019, 50); the films with casts that were from 21 percent to 40 percent minority excel at the box office and in return on investment. First, note how these critics also use the language of economics, such as ticket sales and box-office returns. Second, while acknowledging these positive moves, we still need to push for more. Yes, the films with more diverse casts perform better, and we see an increase in the number of films with diverse casts. But what kinds of roles do minority actors get? What kinds of stories do the films with minority leads tell?

For Hollywood studio executives, racially unmarked, normative films led by Whites and the imagined normative mainstream audience go together. This is attributed to the history of global domination of Hollywood films. Moviegoers outside the United States have been familiar with classic Hollywood films and movie stars, who are mostly White. White audiences, who still make up more than half of ticket sales, show little interest in buying tickets to watch films led by non-White actors (Weaver 2011). Therefore, even in films with non-Whites as the majority of the cast, White actors take or share the lead roles so that the films can attract mainstream audiences who are drawn to familiar faces and names of Hollywood stars.

Racial Politics in Hollywood

When no people of color were nominated for major acting categories at the Academy Awards for two years in a row (2015–16), the twitter hashtag #OscarsSoWhite became a critical sound bite. In 2017 and 2018, there were more nominees of color and a couple of wins—Mahershala Ali for *Moonlight* and Viola Davis for *Fences*—but #OscarsStillSoWhite continued to call for more nominees of color, not only African Americans but also Latinos and Asians, who received only 0.94 percent and 1.11 percent of all Oscar acting nominations since 1929, respectively (Hughey 2018). In *Reel Inequality*, Nancy Wang Yuen (2017, 5) called #OscarsSoWhite "a symptom of Hollywood's larger race problem." White inventors, actors, and capitalists have dominated the film industry from its inception. Actors and filmmakers of color struggle to carve their places in the relentlessly competitive industry, but they still face the issues of segregation, marginalization, and devaluation.

For African Americans, filmmaking has been not only an artistic and commercial enterprise but also a social and political endeavor, from entertaining the Black audience locked out of White theaters in the Jim Crow era to portraying Black representations and aesthetics omitted in mainstream films to bringing the stories of racial conflict and tension from African American perspectives (Cripps 1977). Thus, it is not surprising that the National Association for the Advancement of Colored People (NAACP) recognizes outstanding works of people of color in film and television at the Image Awards.

Although several African American actors, such as Will Smith, Denzel Washington, and Samuel L. Jackson, are major stars with sustaining box-office power, Black films are primarily targeted to "urban markets" because of their perceived "limited appeal," and African American filmmakers of Black films are confined to the segregated market and unable to reach the mainstream audience without the support of big Hollywood studios (G. Alexander 2000). Successful "crossovers"—that is, Black films or Black actors achieving name recognition and box-office success with the mainstream audience—are not readily assumed, so African American actors who are active in Black independent films are usually undervalued in the mainstream film industry (Erigha 2019); an example is Tyler Perry, whose success in Black film and television has placed him professionally and ideologically out of the mainstream.

Mainstream Hollywood, which is mostly controlled by White producers and directors, mainly makes White-centered movies. Even when the representations of people of color appear to be positive or the stories deal with racial inequality or discrimination, most films privilege White characters' transformation in their views and attitudes on racial relations, reinforcing White normativity or superiority (Bogle 2001; Hughey 2009).

To create diverse representations, pundits and scholars contend that we need more diverse filmmakers. However, as John Singleton asked, can this much-needed diversity be fulfilled by foreign-born directors of color? Can they deliver the representational needs of racial-ethnic minorities in the United States? At the risk of appearing to engage in a self-serving nationalist discourse, our examination aims to fill a gap in understanding global Hollywood's impact on racial politics in the United States.

Foreign-Born Talent and Racial-Ethnic Representation in Hollywood

In addition to the film's director, Steve McQueen, 12 Years a Slave stars several foreign-born actors, notably Chiwetel Ejiofor, an English actor who plays the protagonist, Solomon Northup, and Michael Fassbender, an Irish actor who plays the main antagonist. Selma (2014), a historical drama about a voting-rights campaign in Alabama with Martin Luther King Jr. as the central character, also features an English actor, David Oyelowo, as one of the most significant African American figures in US history. This casting reflects international collaboration in the world of moviemaking, which often sparks uneasy controversies over who is selected to direct or star. In Hollywood, the social distance between foreign-born talent and local communities of color can lead to the former group failing to recognize discriminatory practices and unwittingly replicating the same strategies.

One example is foreign-born talent's unfamiliarity with the cultural, historical, and political endeavors and experiences of US minorities. Regarding 12 Years a Slave, the well-circulated narrative has been that McQueen's partner introduced him to Northup's book, which eventually led McQueen to make the award-winning film (D. Lee 2013). As indicated by the title of an article for NPR's Fresh Air, "'12 Years a Slave' Was a Film That 'No One Was Making'" (Fresh Air 2013), the media repeated how Northup's story, which had largely been forgotten, was now brought into the light. Unfortunately, McQueen failed to recognize that the African American director Gordon Parks had adapted the book for a 1984 television movie, Solomon Northup's Odyssey. This oversight of an important African American artist's work did not go unnoticed. Writing for Vulture, Bilge Ebiri (2013) compares the two films, including an excerpt from Parks's memoir about making the film in Atlanta in the early 1980s, when racial tensions were high after the contentious decision to establish Martin Luther King Jr. Day. It was a rather different era from 2013, when McQueen's film was backed by the international star Brad Pitt's production company, Plan B.

This section interrogates how hiring and casting foreign-born directors and stars affect films' content in two ways: first, an association between a director's racial-ethnic identity and cinematic narratives of African American experiences; and second, foreign-born directors' roles in White-dominated Hollywood representations.

Who Is in the Director's Chair?

Steve McQueen, the director of *12 Years a Slave*, became the third Black director nominated for the Best Director category in the eighty-plus-year history of the Academy Awards. In addition to McQueen, only three other Black directors were nominated for directing Best Picture nominees: the African American producer and director Lee Daniels for *Precious: Based on the Novel "Push" by Sapphire* (2009), Barry Jenkins for *Moonlight* (2016), and Jordan Peele for *Get Out* (2017). Although Daniels's next film, *The Butler* (2013), was an award hopeful, it was edged out of the award competition, failing to snag a Best Picture nomination at the Oscars. In the next year, when #OscarsSoWhite started, *Selma* (2014) was nominated for Best Picture, but Ava DuVernay, who many hoped would be the first Black woman director nominated for the Oscars, was snubbed. On the other hand, since 1995, six high-profile Black films made by White directors earned Oscar nominations for Best Director and Best Picture: *Beloved* (1998), *The Hurricane* (2000), *Ali* (2001), *Ray* (2004), *Dreamgirls* (2006), and *Django Unchained* (2012).

Although all these high-profile films are deserving, their award nominations and wins are attributed to their studios' and stakeholders' rigorous advertising campaigns, as well as to deliberate production plans to increase their odds of winning the Academy members' votes (Levy 2003). These coveted award nominations also positively affect films' commercial value (Terry, Butler, and De'Armond 2005). Oscar visibility is an effective marketing tool to increase ticket sales around the globe, especially important for films with relatively small budgets. Moreover, it brings cumulative advantages for the films' DVD and Blu-ray sales, sales for broadcasting rights, and stars' and directors' name values. Given that older White men dominate the Academy membership, which is 94 percent White, 77 percent men, with a median age of sixty-two, studios appear reluctant to hire African American directors for high-profile films that have the potential for awards and financial returns because the studios feel that White directors are more likely to receive the broad support of Academy voters (Horn, Sperling, and Smith 2012).

Scholars and pundits have criticized Black films directed by White filmmakers for exploiting African American suffering, "taming" them, or highlighting self-serving narratives of Whites overcoming racism (Hughey 2009). This is especially evident in the "White savior" film, a subgenre "in which a white messianic character saves a lower- or working-class, usually urban or isolated, nonwhite character from a sad fate" (Hughey 2014, 1). White savior films, such as *Freedom Writers* (2007) and *The Blind Side* (2009), often feature inspirational teachers, mentors, and guardians who transform dysfunctional non-White characters into assets in the (White-dominated) meritocratic world by teaching them to assimilate into mainstream America (Hughey 2014). For example, the film *42* (2013) is a biopic of a notable African American figure, Jackie Robinson, and was directed by a White writer-director, Brian Helgeland. Although the protagonist is Jackie Robinson, played by Chadwick Boseman, the top-billed cast had more White actors than Black actors, including Harrison Ford, a much bigger star in his own right, in the role of Branch Rickey, the general manager of the Brooklyn Dodgers. Indeed, Branch Rickey is highlighted as the White savior who is depicted as the champion of Robinson by dismantling the color lines in baseball. Before Helgeland's film, the African American director Spike Lee had long been attached to a Jackie Robinson project, but what Lee envisioned was critically different from *42*. Instead of focusing on how Robinson learned to "peacefully" endure racist reactions as he entered the Major League, Lee reportedly planned to highlight Robinson's complex political career in post–Major League life, drawing attention to Robinson's involvement in the civil rights movement (Singleton 2013; Zirin 2013).

It is difficult to generalize individual filmmakers' artistic and narrative choices or to comment on their qualities. Many Black films directed by White filmmakers have been effective in portraying African American stories with dramatic and nuanced effects, but films like *Amistad* (1997), *The Help* (2011), *Green Book* (2018), and the like have also been charged with dramatizing Whites triumphantly championing antiracist efforts or overcoming racial inequality to stress racial reconciliation. In doing so, these films downplay deep-seated, prevalent racism in the past or ongoing racial conflicts and tension to appease White audiences as well as (White) film critics and Academy voters. Simultaneously, African American filmmakers, especially those with critical perspectives on racial relations in the United States, struggle to secure financing to make films. Like Lee's unrealized vision of a Jackie Robinson film, one can argue that African American filmmakers could present critical perspectives and cultural aesthetics that are uniquely grounded in Black American experiences as they construct cinematic (counter)narratives that are satisfying to, and empowering of, African American audiences (Hall 1993b). Then, Hollywood's inclination to work with foreign-born talent like McQueen, other Black British actors, and even White British filmmakers contributes to further marginalizing African American filmmakers and actors and missing opportunities to bring Black Americans' innovative storytelling to the screen, which ultimately limits audiences' exposure to multifaceted and nuanced depictions of Black lives.

Foreign-Born Directors Making "Universal Stories"

McQueen, along with four producers, won Best Picture for *12 Years a Slave*, but he lost the Best Director award to Alfonso Cuarón, a Mexican director. In fact, all but one directing award between 2012 and 2017 went to foreign-born, Asian, or Latino directors: Ang Lee for *Life of Pi* (2012), Cuarón for *Gravity* (2013), Alejandro G. Iñarritu for *Birdman* (2014) and *The Revenant* (2015), and Guillermo del Toro for *The Shape of Water* (2017). *Life of Pi* was Lee's second Oscar after his first win for *Brokeback Mountain* (2003). Iñarritu became the third director in the Oscars' history to win Best Director two years in a row. Notably, except for *Life of Pi*, all these films have White lead actors.

Asian and Latino directors making White-led films is not unusual. Between 1995 and 2014, we identified twenty-fix films directed by directors of color and featuring White actors as the majority of the cast. Of the twenty-six films, five were directed by four American directors, such as Antoine Fuqua's *King Arthur* (2004) and M. Night Shyamalan's *The Sixth Sense* (1999). The other twenty-one films were directed by sixteen foreign-born directors. For example, Ang Lee, who was born and raised in Taiwan and received postsecondary education in the United States, initially made his name through Taiwanese films such as *The Wedding Banquet* (1993) and *Eat Drink Man Woman* (1994). From 1995 to 2014, Lee's five films made the list of one hundred top-grossing films, and three films, *Sense and Sensibility* (1996), *Hulk* (2003), and *Brokeback Mountain* (2006), featured White actors as the majority of the cast. Alfonso Cuarón, a Mexican director famous for *Y Tu Mamá También* (2001), directed four films with White actors as leads or as the majority of the cast: *Great Expectations* (1998), *Harry Potter and the Prisoner of Azkaban* (2004), *Children of Men* (2006), and *Gravity* (2013).

When foreign-born Asian or Latino directors make White-led films in Hollywood, it is fair to assume that they understand White-led films as the norm. For example, many Hollywood remakes of foreign-language films entail replacing the characters with Americans, usually White actors as the leads. *The Ring* (2002), a remake of a popular Japanese horror film, *Ringu* (1998), stars the White actor Naomi Watts as the protagonist. For a sequel to the remake, *The Ring Two* (2005), the producers hired Hideo Nakata, the director of the original Japanese film, to direct it, again with Naomi Watts. Similarly, for *The Grudge* (2004), a remake of another popular Japanese horror film, *Ju-on: The Grudge* (2002), the American producers hired Takashi Shimizu, the director of the original *Ju-on* series. Though the remake's story line is even set in Japan, the White actor Sarah Michelle Gellar stars as the protagonist. Hiring foreign-born directors signifies diversity in Hollywood and arouses great pride in the people of their countries of origin. Yet one must question what it means for local filmmaking communities of color and if or how the directors reify insidious patterns of racial hierarchy in casting and filming.

Missing Stories

When it was announced that Scarlett Johansson was going to star in *Ghost in the Shell* (2017), the internet erupted, protesting that the casting decision was another example of whitewashing in Hollywood (Child 2015). The film is based on a Japanese manga series, and Johansson's character was a cyborg originally named Motoko Kusanagi, so many fans complained that an Asian actor should have been cast in the role.

The controversy shows a schism between Japanese producers and the Asian American actors who were publicly speaking out about discriminatory practices in Hollywood (Hess 2016).

Slightly different from racist black-, brown-, or yellow-face practices of White actors, whitewashing is hiring White actors to play characters that were people of color in source materials, another trend that keeps racial-ethnic minorities out of the film industry. For example, in *21* (2008), the White actor Jim Sturgess plays the lead role, based on a Chinese MIT student in real life; in *Doctor Strange* (2015), the White actor Tilda Swinton plays the Ancient One, originally a Tibetan man; and in *Aloha* (2015), the White actor Emma Stone plays Allison Ng, an Asian-White biracial character. Amid a series of whitewashing controversies in these recent movies, #StarringJohnCho went viral. This high-profile social media project posts modified movie posters, with John Cho (a Korean American actor featured in the *Harold & Kumar* series, *Star Trek into Darkness*, and *American Pie*) as a male lead on the posters. It specifically calls out the lack of Asian representations in traditional lead roles or, more specifically, the lack of Asian Americans. The project also sought to interrupt the Black-White framing of #OscarsSoWhite (Rogers 2016).

We identified twenty-nine films released between 1995 and 2014 with Asians or Latinos as the majority of the cast, including eight imported films. Of twenty-one US-produced films, thirteen were made by White directors, five by Latino American directors, and three by two Asian directors, Ang Lee and M. Night Shyamalan. Fifteen films are set in other countries, such as Japan in *Memoirs of a Geisha* (2005), China in *Crouching Tiger, Hidden Dragon* (2000), and Mexico in *Desperado* (1995). Only four films set in the United States feature Latino Americans, and the other two starring Asian protagonists are set in Europe. While two films, the UK-produced *Bend It like Beckham* (2003) and the US-produced *Hundred-Foot Journey* (2014), tell the stories of Indian immigrants in England and France, respectively, what is conspicuously missing are stories centering on Asian American families or communities.

Compared to these films, fifty-nine films with Asian or Latino leads are mostly set in the United States. Again the majority (66.1 percent) of them are helmed by White directors. Notably, over 90 percent of the films in this category are action/crime/thriller films ($n = 43$, or 72.9 percent) or comedy ($n = 13$, or 22 percent) without what could be categorized as traditional dramas. Twelve films directed by Latino or Asian filmmakers include four in the *Spy Kids* series (all directed by the Mexican American Robert Rodriguez) and two in the *Fast and Furious* series (both by the Taiwanese American Justin Lin). Except two films—the Spanish director Jorge Blanco's animated film *Planet 51* (2009) and the Mexican director Luis Mandoki's *Angel Eyes* (2001)—all filmmakers of color are US-born or US-trained directors, yet they rarely incorporate characters of color or their racial or ethnic identities into the central story lines, except as a cultural backdrop associated with martial arts skills.

Regardless of the director's race, somewhat-diverse representations are found in the films with non-Black lead characters of color. Two multiracial actors, Dwayne Johnson and Vin Diesel, are dominant figures, leading eleven and seven films, respectively. While these actors identify themselves as people of color, they often portray "raceless" characters for "colorblind" action films. The Spanish actor Antonio Banderas led five films, and Jennifer Lopez, who identifies as Latina American, starred in six films, but Michael Peña, a co-lead in *End of Watch* (2012), is the sole Latino American actor. While John Cho and Kal Penn of the *Harold & Kumar* series are notable Asian American actors, Jackie Chan and Jet Li are much more prominent, leading eight and five films, respectively. One obvious fact is that, except for John Cho and Kal Penn, most actors just mentioned are frequent stars of action films, which Hollywood views as moneymakers.

Numerous independent filmmakers of color struggle to put Asian American dramas on the silver screen; the issue is whether the mainstream industry is willing to open its doors to them. Wayne Wang, who was born in Hong Kong and educated in the United States, directed *Chan Is Missing* (1982), widely recognized as the first Asian American independent theatrical feature employing an all-Asian cast and crew (Xing 1998). Wang is best known for *The Joy Luck Club* (1993), a rare mainstream film about Asian American families. Since then, he has worked with Susan Sarandon and Natalie Portman for *Anywhere but Here* (1999), Jennifer Lopez for *Maid in Manhattan* (2002), and Queen Latifah for *Last Holiday* (2006). However, Wang's two features about

Asian immigrants, *A Thousand Years of Good Prayers* and *The Princess of Nebraska* (2007), did not have a wide release. Justin Lin also debuted with a critically acclaimed independent film, *Better Luck Tomorrow* (2002), a coming-of-age story of Asian American youth. He then built his career in the action genre with *Fast and Furious* movies and *Star Trek Beyond*. Though his films feature diverse casts, Lin has yet to make mainstream films that tell Asian American stories. These two directors' career trajectories indicate that Asian American filmmakers have to choose between accessing Hollywood's fame and financial resources and telling Asian American stories; they seemingly cannot do both.

Racial-ethnic categories such as "Asian" or "Latino" can lump together people who are born abroad and in the United States. However, the social distance between local US filmmakers and foreign-born talent can create a disjuncture between the two. When Hollywood executives prefer British Black actors because they are "more classically trained" but British Black actors do not appear in Black independent films, the Black American filmmaking community can be further segregated and devalued. When Japanese writers and actors support Hollywood's decisions to cast White actors for the main roles of original Japanese manga series, they can compromise Asian Americans' efforts to challenge the persistent issues, from yellow face to whitewashing, in the film industry.

The Significance of International Markets

Hollywood producers have backed films with Asian or Latino actors as the majority of the cast and set in other countries or films with Asian or Latino leads because they can attract an audience outside the United States and boost the films' international gross. For example, foreign-born actors like Jackie Chan and Jet Li, who had been popular across East and Southeast Asia, were safe bets who could dazzle American audiences with their martial arts skills as well as guarantee box-office returns in Asia. As in the *Rush Hour* series, *Shanghai Knights* (2003), and *War* (2007), these actors were often paired with White or Black American actors, which could further increase the films' appeal to both domestic and international audiences. Unfortunately, the imagery of these films perpetuated Asian stereotypes that have affected, and were critiqued by, Asian Americans without a channel of constructive communication with Asian filmmakers. Ultimately the films did little to provide an opportunity to show meaningful representations of Asian Americans, which #StarringJohnCho calls for. Fundamentally we argue that this is in large part attributed to Hollywood's relentless quest for bigger box-office outcomes in international markets, stemming from assumptions about the inability of mainstream audiences to relate to reasonable representations of people of color on the screen.

The Power of International Markets

Chart-topping films are usually blockbusters with budgets of over $100 million, which are expected to yield an extraordinary amount of box-office income. Often these films make more money internationally than domestically, raising their total gross to more than double the domestic gross. This demonstrates why the international market is so important for Hollywood studios. In 2014, the film that earned the highest international gross was *Transformers: Age of Extinction*, or *Transformers 4*. Its domestic gross ranking was seventh, with $245.44 million, which managed to recover its expensive production budget though was not enough to recoup an additional $100 million in marketing costs (McClintock 2014). However, the international gross elevated its total gross to over $1 billion.

Transformers 4 made $320 million in China alone, becoming the highest-grossing film ever in China. This was not a coincidence. A part of the film was set and filmed in Hong Kong, and its world premiere was held in the city as well. The film stars Chinese actors and is sprinkled with Chinese product placements (B. Lee 2016). That is, the film's producers strategically marketed the film to attract the country that was transforming itself from a source of online-piracy concern to the soon-to-be second-largest box-office market after the United States, and their strategy paid off (Garrahan and Sender 2016).

The Erasure and Marginalization of Black Films in Global Markets

Before the 2009 film *Couples Retreat* was released in the United Kingdom, a controversy erupted over the movie posters. Unlike the original

US poster, which featured eight actors who play four couples, the UK version showed only three couples—all White actors, minus the African American couple played by Faizon Love and Kali Hawk, an omission that understandably offended many people. A Universal Studios spokesperson said that the erasure was "to simplify the poster to actors who are most recognizable in international markets," but many people questioned if excluding Black actors and characters was productive to marketing the film (Goslett 2009).

In relation to this issue of the exclusion of Black actors and characters in international marketing, we return to *12 Years a Slave*. For the film's posters, the Italian distributor, BIM Distribuzione, placed White actors—Brad Pitt (the film's coproducer, who made a so-called White savior appearance) and Michael Fassbender (the film's antagonist)—as the focus of the posters. The actors' photos were also considerably larger than that of the film's star, Chiwetel Ejiofor. The incident sparked another international controversy. By questioning Michael Fassbender's "star" status in Italy, some people argued that the choice was about the film's marketing treatment of Black actors (Child 2013). Later, the Italian distributor issued an apology, and the posters were replaced with the original US posters; but the incident once again raised a question: is it justifiable to exclude Black actors from global marketing, which in turn stifles the promotion of their name value on the global stage?

In Hollywood, a film's budget is determined based on the estimated amount of return, and Black films and Black filmmakers receive lower budgets than their White counterparts do, based on an assumption of "limited appeal" in both domestic and international markets (G. Alexander 2000; Rhines 1996) or are labeled "unbankable" (Erigha 2019). In *The Hollywood Jim Crow*, Maryann Erigha (2019) finds that when Black directors lead films with a predominantly Black cast, their film budgets are most often below $40 million; when Black directors helm films with multiracial or White casts, the film budgets are usually between $20 and $60 million and over $100 million, respectively. She also notes that White directors garner bigger budgets when directing Black casts than do Black directors. This is exactly what we found as well. Our analysis shows that when making Black films, 63 percent of Black directors made films with *less than* $20 million budgets, while 86 percent of White directors did so with *more than* $20 million budgets.

Only two Black directors worked with more than $50 million budgets, for *Little Man* (2006) and *Red Tails* (2012), but fifteen White directors did so for many high-profile dramas such as *Dreamgirls* (2006) and *Django Unchained* (2012) and big-budget comedies like *The Nutty Professor* series and *Dr. Dolittle* series.

Even with low budgets and limited marketing, Black films have proven to generate higher profits than other mainstream films do (McKenzie 2010). When we examined the total gross-to-budget ratio for Black films, the top twenty films included eighteen directed by Black directors—this although many of these films have extremely low international gross. Hollywood executives argue that the weak performance in the international market is why they cannot set higher production budgets for Black films, whereas Black filmmakers and their supporters contend that Black films, which generally make more money with low budgets, have more potential and deserve more financial support from Hollywood.

In South Africa, *Think like a Man* (2013) made $1.2 million, slightly more than the Tom Cruise–starring *Jack Reacher*, which made $1.1 million (Obenson 2013). This suggests that with the right amount of marketing, Black films can do better internationally, which is proven by the recent extraordinary global success of *Black Panther* (2018). Currently distributors spend up to $40 million for marketing medium-sized films made with about $20 million production budgets (McClintock 2014). *Transformers 4* spent $100 million domestically and an additional $100 million internationally to advertise the movie, which makes the enormous total gross appear far from the net profit. If Hollywood could show this kind of confidence in US racial-ethnic minority films and filmmakers, allowing them to build their name values, audiences would have a higher likelihood of watching a variety of cinematic representations. (See also the UCLA Hollywood Diversity Report.)

Discussion and Conclusion

This chapter has examined from a critical perspective how Hollywood's global economic interests make it difficult for US actors and filmmakers of color to star in and helm mainstream films. We argue that Hollywood's formula for maximizing profits sometimes conflicts directly with the interests of people of color in the United States. To appeal to broader audiences, Hollywood executives avoid films centering on a specific group of color, fearing that such films will exclude a White audience. Industry gatekeepers instead prefer people of color to lead action-crime films and comedies. Also, producers and directors hire foreign-born talent to lead action films and comedies to attract international audiences. Unfortunately, this strategy is also the very formula that creates stereotypes associated with Asians and Latinos (e.g., gang members, prone to violence, sexualized women, forever foreigner).

Hollywood oftentimes recruits foreign-born talent—both directors and actors. However, when foreign-born directors make films, they may not understand the representational needs of US people of color. It is a counterintuitive reality that Asian and Latino directors usually make films led by White actors, while White directors make films focusing on people of color. As a result, Asian and Latino directors contribute to reproducing White dominance on-screen, while White directors perpetuate stereotypical images of people of color. We are by no means placing the onus of blame on individual filmmakers' professional or artistic choices. Of course, there is nothing wrong with making movies with foreign-born actors or about stories set in Asia or elsewhere. Rather, we attempt to demonstrate how Hollywood's structural context has failed to present balanced and meaningful representations of Latino and Asian American experiences, not just as token characters but with familial and communal stories. This pattern suggests that Hollywood is not moving toward becoming truly inclusive. It is not just an individual director's or actor's job to change. The situation is shaped by multiple agents, including studio executives, producers, directors, and actors, as well as audiences and diverse collectives in civil society who respond to what Hollywood creates. These agents and their different and competing interests influence the moviemaking business and its processes of production, distribution, exhibition, and consumption.

Since 2014, American moviegoers have seen several exciting developments. Many high-profile Black films have been released and have received award recognition. Black women actors led *Hidden Figures* (2016) and *A Wrinkle in Time* (2018, dir. Ava DuVernay). *Get Out* (2017) was released as a critics' and fan favorite, and its writer-director, Jordan Peele, became the first Black winner of the Best Original Screenplay

Oscar. *Moonlight* (2016), directed by the African American Barry Jenkins, received the highest honor of Best Picture. *Black Panther* (2018, dir. Ryan Coogler) became a global sensation, grossing over $1.3 billion worldwide and becoming the highest-grossing film by a Black director.

Black Panther's blockbuster success is a stunning achievement in its own right but is even more remarkable given that the film has an almost all-Black cast. The film has been an unprecedented cultural phenomenon, as watching *Black Panther* became a social movement. Many celebrities responded to the #BlackPantherChallenge by buying tickets and organizing viewings in cities such as Detroit, Los Angeles, Chicago, and Atlanta (Wurzburger 2018; Lamarre 2018). Racial-ethnic-minority affinity groups in corporations and Black Greek-letter organizations bought out theaters and arranged for private screenings of the film in Black communities. Many Black moviegoers saw *Black Panther* multiple times in theaters, dressed in dashikis, posed doing the "Wakanda Forever" gesture in front of the movie poster, and posted their pictures widely on social media.

Nevertheless, we want to be cautious before deciding that the tide has turned for Black films. First, our findings show that the number of Black films that made the list of one hundred top-grossing films did not increase significantly in the period of twenty years. In fact, the number of Black films declined in the 2000s after peaking from 2000 to 2002 (with seven films each year). So the question remains: How many Black films will make the list of one hundred top-grossing films in the next ten years? Will that number hold steady or increase? We can ask the same questions about films centered on the lives of Asian and Latino American characters. Second, public interest and political consciousness in recent years with the #OscarsSoWhite movement, the *La La Land* and *Moonlight* debacle, and continued calls for diversity and inclusion in Hollywood paved the way for the enormous success of *Black Panther*.[1] Without those critical voices, watching *Black Panther* would not have been a social movement. Yet *Black Panther* was produced by Marvel Studios and is the eighteenth film in Marvel's cinematic universe. This means that a solid fan base exists for Marvel movies, which made the movie a safe bet. Here one should ask, Why the eighteenth? Why in 2018? Why not ten Marvel movies ago? One can assume that with the recent social and political agitation, Marvel saw an opportunity to reap financial profits from a moviegoing public that was hungry for empowering Black representations.

One silver lining in this view is that Marvel hired Ryan Coogler, whose filmography includes *Fruitvale Station* (2013) and *Creed* (2015), films that were praised for realizing Black perspectives in creative ways. With a perspective not typical of superhero films, Coogler manages to interlace the disenfranchisement of African Americans, resistance against colonialism, and Afrofuturistic imagery into *Black Panther*. But then, one has to wonder, Can this level of quality filmmaking be sustained by Marvel Studios? Can we expect this from other Hollywood studios?

Crazy Rich Asians (2018), a romantic dramedy directed by Jon M. Chu, was celebrated for being the first major studio film featuring Asians and Asian Americans as a majority of the cast in twenty-five years since *The Joy Luck Club* (1993). *Crazy Rich Asians* was made possible because, as we argue, it met conditions of Hollywood's political economy for being a safe investment. The film was distributed by Warner Bros., but one of its main funders was a US-based Asian company. The protagonist is Chinese American, but the film is set in Singapore and often glamorously shows the city's skyline. The film features a heterogeneous global cast including the Malaysian Michelle Yeoh, the Asian American Awkwafina, the Korean American Ken Jeong, the Filipino American Nico Santos, the Chinese American Lisa Lu, the Asian British Gemma Chan, the Japanese British Sonoya Mizuno, the Taiwanese Australian Chris Pang, the Malaysian Australian Ronny Chieng, and others. Kevin Kwan, the author of the original novel, insisted that the film would be true to the source, with an all-Asian cast and the perspective of the protagonist, who is a second-generation immigrant, firmly at the center of the film. Yet the end product was a global Asian film that could pull an international gross that surpassed its domestic gross, rather than an Asian American film. Without this potential, one has to wonder if this film would have seen the light of the day.

Compared to twenty years ago, more filmmakers of color are actively working in Hollywood, and they exert more control and influence over their work and the industry. These younger directors' cinematic and aesthetic calibers exhibit exciting potential. Nonetheless, if and how the stories of racial-ethnic minorities in the United States can be brought to the screen and to the global stage remains an unanswered question.

Note

1. At the 2017 Academy Awards, *La La Land* and *Moonlight* were two strong contenders for the Best Picture Oscar. An envelope mix-up led the presenters of the Best Picture award to announce that *La La Land* was the winner instead of *Moonlight*. The blunder was fixed right away in the middle of the acceptance speech, but the debacle was criticized for tainting one of the most significant moments for Black filmmakers, let alone for *Moonlight* and Barry Jenkins.

2

Redesigning a Pocket Monument

A Reparative Reading of the 2016 Twenty-Dollar-Bill Controversy

CATHERINE R. SQUIRES AND AISHA UPTON

In 2016, the United States Department of the Treasury announced its planned redesign of the twenty-dollar bill. The new bill would feature the famous abolitionist and political activist Harriet Tubman. The announcement sparked jubilation from activists who had campaigned for female representation on paper currency, as well as from those who advocated for a person of color to grace US greenbacks. But the redesign also brought sharp rebukes from White conservatives, including Republican presidential candidates, who accused the Treasury of capitulating to "political correctness" at the expense of the honor and memory of President Andrew Jackson. Indeed, then-candidate Donald Trump declared during a *Today Show* town hall that putting Tubman on the twenty-dollar bill was "pure political correctness" (Wright 2016). This essay draws from a larger content analysis of news and editorial coverage (Squires and Upton 2018) of the twenty-dollar bill's redesign to advance a Black feminist reparative reading of the way news media producers and contributors shape and reshape public memories of Tubman and Jackson.

Drawing on interdisciplinary scholarship, we advance two questions: First, how do news media narratives about historical figures contribute to or contest "epistemologies of white ignorance" (Charles Mills 2007)? Second, do we need to renarrate stories of iconic figures such as Jackson and Tubman to generate "usable pasts" that provide frameworks for understanding the range and reach of contemporary problems? After answering these questions and building on critical memories generated by Black journalists and commentators, we engender a reparative reading of the debate over the twenty-dollar bill's redesign.

Harriet Tubman and Andrew Jackson in Public Memory

Harriet Tubman and Andrew Jackson are icons who occupy very different places in the dominant US national story. The stories of these icons were shaped by White scholars and political actors who privileged a fantasy of antebellum southern gentility that (1) erased the violence of slavery, (2) removed traces of the nation's economic and imperial interests in plantation slavery, and (3) delinked American expansion into indigenous territories from the growth of slavery in new territories (Horton and Horton 2006; W. Johnson 2013; Kaufman 2006). At the end of the nineteenth century, Andrew Jackson was transformed from a divisive, scandalous figure into "Old Hickory," the folksy, populist general who saved New Orleans and welcomed the masses into the White House. In contrast, Harriet Tubman became not much more than a historical footnote; the institution of slavery was cast as a troubling artifact of the early republic, and the plight of the enslaved was erased in sentimental renderings of happy Sambos, Mammies, and Uncles. Even later in the twentieth century, when Tubman became one of the most written-about Black women in publishing, her image fit squarely within dominant understandings of reforging the Union at all costs, deemphasizing both her radicalism and the horrors of slavery. These widespread public memories of Tubman and Jackson fit within and reinforce larger patterns identified by the scholar Charles Mills as the "epistemology of white ignorance."

White Ignorance and Public Memory

White ignorance is a *sociostructural* phenomenon that involves "both false belief and the absence of true belief," beliefs that are supported by the premise that racism was an *exceptional* aspect of early America and was erased with the end of slavery and the legal reforms of the civil rights movement (Charles Mills 2007, 16–17). White ignorance is a historical phenomenon that emerged in the colonial period, developing in tandem with Whiteness and White supremacy (20). This phenomenon is not uniform across the White population, and one need not be White or racist to be affected by White ignorance. White ignorance covers dynamics that "include both straightforward racist motivation and more impersonal socio-structural causation" (21). For example, someone who believes "blacks generally had opportunities equal to whites" believes this and feels it is true "because of the social suppression of pertinent knowledge" (21).

White ignorance is structured by and operates in "perception, conception, memory, testimony, and motivational group interest," overlapping components of social cognition and interaction that are impacted by race (Charles Mills 2007, 23). Media are implicated in all these domains, particularly news-media coverage of historical figures. We quote Charles Mills at length:

> Inference from perception involves the overt or tacit appeal to memory, which will be not merely individual but social. As such, it will be founded on testimony and ultimately on the perceptions and conceptions of others. . . . *Testimony will have been recorded*, requiring again perception, conception, and memory; it will have been integrated into a framework and narrative and from the start will have involved the selection of certain voices against others . . . (*if these others have been allowed to speak in the first place*). At all levels, interests may shape cognition, influencing . . . whose testimony is solicited and whose is not. (2007, 24; emphasis added)

This passage suggests how news media contribute to a popular culture, and popular histories, shaped by White ignorance. For the majority of our nation's life span, the testimonies of indigenous peoples and the enslaved were not considered important enough to preserve for posterity; the words, images, and deeds of empowered White settlers like Jackson were enshrined for future generations. These material differences—an abundance of institutional support to preserve and disseminate White Americans' stories versus institutional neglect of indigenous and Black Americans' stories—structure White ignorance. This is not unlike the process whereby Hollywood privileges the perspectives of White figures even when portraying critical events in the struggle for Black civil rights (e.g., Madison 1999). When counternarratives are not in circulation to challenge dominant versions of events, then "a conviction of exceptionalism and superiority . . . seems vindicated by the facts, and thenceforth, circularly, shaping perception of the facts. [Whites] rule the world because we are superior; we are superior because we rule the world" (Charles Mills 2007, 25). When Black or indigenous testimonies challenge that circular logic, they expose the distortions generated and sustained by White ignorance.

Recurrent controversies over including indigenous and African American perspectives in K–12 history textbooks[1] and viral hashtag campaigns such as #OscarsSoWhite[2] and #WeNeedDiverseBooks[3] demonstrate how this perceptual distortion is encouraged by "white refusal to recognize the long history of structural discrimination that has left whites with the differential resources they have today and all of its consequent advantages in negotiating opportunity structures" (Charles Mills 2007, 27–28), including media production and publishing. Part of this refusal is resisting knowledge of how slavery and colonial expansion were twin socioeconomic phenomena that laid the groundwork for White wealth, land distribution and use, and legal frameworks for citizenship (e.g., C. Harris 1993). Dominant histories systematically excluded perspectives of the enslaved and the colonized.[4] Thus, Mills's theory of White ignorance contextualizes the function of historical narratives in maintaining asymmetrical relations of power.

White ignorance is a sociocultural force that limits the scope of change in shared understandings of history and rituals of commemoration. Wanda S. Pillow (2012) interrogates White ignorance in her analysis of the ways Sacajawea was mythologized in the late twentieth century. Sacajawea was a Shoshone girl who was in the custody of a French fur trader. He "offered" her translation and navigation services to the explorers Lewis and Clark when President Jefferson commissioned the pair to chart the lands west of the Mississippi. However, it is only recently that she has been incorporated into the story as a kind of American heroine. Rather, popular histories referred to her as a "squaw" or servant and failed to mention that she bore a child during the journey (Pillow 2012). These narratives also suggested that she was a willing agent of White colonization of the West, the "Manifest Destiny" of European settlers.[5]

Mills explains how "multicultural" narratives of the late twentieth century and the early twenty-first have incorporated Sacajawea as an icon who, looking backward, both validates the Manifest Destiny narrative and provides multicultural cover for those who continue to overlook the contemporary, ongoing struggles of indigenous peoples to reclaim their lands. Pillow provides a sobering example of this from the one hundredth anniversary of the Lewis and Clark expedition, where the "Indian guide" Sacajawea and Clark's slave York were included in dominant media coverage of the anniversary. "What becomes thematically clear in past and current retellings of the [Lewis and Clark] expedition is not so much a reclaiming of Sacajawea, but a reclaiming of Lewis & Clark as modern and progressive men through Sacajawea. . . . The expedition is reasserted as clearly 'our' history, and the presence of one Indian woman and one black man, . . . despite their status as indentured servant and slave, is used to validate a multicultural retelling of a colonizing event" (Pillow 2012, 50).

Similarly, when Tubman has been "included" as an American heroine, it is usually in ways that erase the violence of racism that continued after the end of slavery and suggest her main goal was to save the Union so that individuals could live out personal freedoms. Mainstream historical renderings of Tubman—from children's books to documentaries—portray her as a figure of salvation, a "mother" who will save the nation from the sin of slavery through her personal sacrifices. The patriarchal vision of the sacrificial mother obfuscates both the radical, aggressive acts she took to help slaves escape and her stirring rhetoric at public events to rally public opinion for a war on slavery. Resonating with other pieces in this volume, she becomes the ultimate "Magical Negro" in this story. These narratives also emphasize that she worked *for* the Union army during the Civil War and suggest that her primary desire was to see the United States remain whole rather than to end abuse and capitalist exploitation of Black people. These narratives erase her longer career of radical resistance against White supremacy. As the scholar Vivian M. May summarizes, "Tubman's historical 'makeover' transforms her radical vision and resistant (and at times illegal) actions into benign symbols of progress and family values: this interpretive shift aligns her organized resistance to fit with narratives of the nation's deliverance from its past sins and to render a tender family portrait of the United States. The salvific also reinforces problematic ideas about the state as an otherwise perfect system . . . healed, thanks to Tubman" (2014, 39).

Most dominant renderings of Tubman also end with her Civil War service, obscuring her continued struggles against racism, disfranchisement, and poverty. Distorted public memories that individualize Harriet Tubman, isolating her from collective institutions and struggles, resonate with and reinforce neoliberal postracial discourses that suggest we venerate civil rights icons for their individual merit and exemplary choice making rather than their capacity to craft coalitions within and across communities. The question that emerges from such a narrative then becomes, If Tubman could rise above her circumstances, why can't contemporary Black people do the same? This is a common ideological takeaway from Hollywood storytelling, particularly among White audiences.[6] Isolating Tubman from other African Americans and their antiracist institutions undermines arguments for continued communal struggle. As with conservative co-optations of Martin Luther King Jr., which focus almost exclusively on the singular phrase "content of their character, not the color of their skin" to justify dismantling civil rights laws and race-aware policies like affirmative action (e.g., Younge 2013), Tubman is offered up as a heroine of individual effort and the eventual triumph of democracy rather than antiracism.

Public memories of Jackson similarly play up his "bootstrapping" character and underplay his violent acts against the enslaved and indigenous peoples. These dominant narratives of Jackson are more interested in the continuity of dominant traditions than in confronting the difficult knowledge of historical traumas (Simon 2000). Jackson's reputation has been redeemed through the lens of populist democracy. White American historians who shaped the country's story in the wake of the Civil War reframed him as a man whose "folksy" wisdom and ways served to "expand" democratic practices and inclusivity. His war record was burnished to downplay his scorched-earth tactics, and his (bigamist) elopement with Rachel Donelson was transformed into a passionate, all-American love story by Hollywood (e.g., Brady 2011; Cheathem 2011).

Thus, generations of textbooks, documentaries, and children's literature have presented Harriet Tubman as a "tough old lady" who freed
slaves, and Andrew Jackson as a hotheaded but true patriot who sided
with the common man. Repeating these simplistic renderings of their
lives and legacies does not produce any "creative friction" (Carby 2009)
in the historical imagination. Rather, stories like these neatly dovetail
into postracial neoliberal fantasies of American individualism and
inevitable democratic progress. "There is the risk in such practices of
remembrance that what is of memorial importance serves and confirms
current versions of self and community," which reinforce "conservatism
and potentially reductive violence" (Simon 2000, 12). This is the potential pitfall of the twenty-dollar bill's redesign: including Tubman will
merely reinscribe dominant narratives.

We take up the challenge of engaging difficult histories by resituating
Jackson and Tubman neither as simple opposites (enslaver/liberator)
nor as icons of bootstrapping ingenuity but rather as two compelling
figures in the long narrative of the "trauma of colonialism and slavery"
(Pillow 2012, 53). We draw on results from a previous content analysis (Squires and Upton, forthcoming) to engage in a reparative reading
to uplift "stories that will take responsibility to bear the weight of witnessing" historical racial traumas and their continuing impact on the
present (Pillow 2012, 55). It is notable that the organizers of Women On
20s referred to the bills as "pocket monuments."[7] We contend that these
"pocket monuments," like statues and museums, circulate historical
information as well as economic exchange value. Jackson and Tubman
co-occupying the twenty-dollar bill has the potential to spark different
discussions of slavery and its connection to the founding and growth
of the United States. For such a spark to catch flame, however, sup-
pressed knowledge must come to the fore to challenge a history built on
White ignorance.

News Coverage of the Twenty-Dollar-Bill Debate

To examine how news contributors shaped and reshaped public memories of Tubman and Jackson, we compiled a data set of news and editorial coverage of the redesign. We examined both mainstream and

people-of-color-oriented news sources to see the ways that Tubman, Jackson, and the twenty-dollar bill were discussed. We hypothesized that the discussion of Jackson and Tubman in media oriented toward African Americans would draw on different cultural knowledge and take into account Black audiences' understandings of racism, generating different frames from dominant media, which usually imagines a White audience.

We gathered our data from the LexisNexis, Ethnic News Watch, and ProQuest databases, searching for articles that referred to both Tubman and Jackson in discussion of the decision to redesign the twenty-dollar bill, from December 2014 through March 2017. We used this set of articles (n = 133) for a computer-aided analysis, coding for the specific ways that Tubman, Jackson, and their historical legacies were described. We gathered articles from publications such as the *Washington Post* and the *New Amsterdam News*. We used NVivo qualitative software to track whether and how news media drew on dominate narratives or brought into view facts and events not commonly associated with these figures.

Our content analysis found that writers were slightly more likely to mention President Jackson's failings (slaveholding, Trail of Tears) than his accomplishments (heroism in War of 1812) (table 2.1). Overall, we collected 102 articles mentioning Andrew Jackson in the news. Many of the publications featured multiple themes, such as referring both to Jackson as slave owner and to his role in the Trail of Tears.

TABLE 2.1. Descriptions of Andrew Jackson in News

Descriptor	Mainstream media	POC media	Total
Populist president	2	1	3
Violent	2	0	2
Genocide	4	6	10
Hermitage estate	1	0	1
Hero in War of 1812	4	3	7
Nickname "Old Hickory"	5	2	5
Opposition to banking	6	1	7
Slave owning of	7	24	31
Trail of Tears	12	23	35
Wars against Native Americans	1	0	1

TABLE 2.2. Descriptions of Harriet Tubman in News

Descriptor	Mainstream media	POC media	Total
Abolitionist	19	58	77
Nurse	3	13	16
Spy	6	25	31
Suffrage advocate	5	11	16
Antipoverty / New York home	0	0	0

News contributors were more likely to mention Harriet Tubman's contributions to the antislavery struggle than her work on behalf of the Union army and of women's suffrage. Significantly, none of the articles in either press mentioned Tubman's postwar work to support impoverished and orphaned African Americans, and only a few mainstream articles referenced her work as a spy and nurse or her suffragism (table 2.2). "Abolitionist" was the most popular term used with her name.

The content analysis shows that news-media coverage of the twenty-dollar bill's redesign largely reflected the way dominant historical narratives frame Tubman and Jackson, with a slightly more visible discussion of Jackson's acts against indigenous peoples. We found a higher number of articles about the redesign in POC media than in mainstream media, suggesting that this "first" was deemed more newsworthy and something to celebrate with audiences for those outlets. However, none of the articles in either type of media connected the economics of plantation slavery to the wars Jackson prosecuted against the indigenous peoples and his forced dispossession of the Cherokee. If the United States had not taken those lands, White planters would not have had room to establish their properties and purchase slaves to work the land.

Instead, both critics and defenders of Jackson separated slave owning and dispossession of indigenous peoples. Importantly, his defenders excused his involvement in these phenomena as just part of the historical time and culture. The Democratic senator Jim Webb's op-ed for the *Washington Post* exemplifies this approach. For example, to explain the Trail of Tears, Webb excused Jackson's infamous defiance of the Supreme Court as follows: "As president, Jackson ordered the removal of Indian tribes east of the Mississippi to lands west of the river. This approach, *supported by a string of presidents, including Jefferson and John Quincy*

Adams, was a disaster, resulting in the Trail of Tears where thousands died. But was its motivation genocidal? Robert Remini, Jackson's most prominent biographer, wrote that his intent was to end the increasingly bloody Indian Wars and to protect the Indians from certain annihilation at the hands of an ever-expanding frontier population" (2016).

Though Webb conceded that the Trail of Tears "was a disaster," he simultaneously reaffirmed Manifest Destiny. The "ever-expanding frontier population" is invoked as a fait accompli, the treaties easily swept aside to facilitate White settlerism as a self-evident, inevitable historical formation. This conservative narrative demands that diversity be in the service of reinforcing the already-existing story of the founding and expansion of the United States. Webb crafts a public memory of Jackson in relation to racialized others that includes slaves and indigenous peoples only under the condition that "their incorporation [occurs] within the memorial boundaries that circumscribe one's [own] identifications" (Simon 2000, 12). Whether supporting or opposing the redesign, commentators in mainstream news did not grapple with the violence of slavery or its relation to Jackson's campaigns against indigenous peoples.

Similarly, many mainstream articles looked at Tubman through a conservative lens, framing her as an exceptional individual deserving of a "first" for African American representation on US currency. Descriptions like this were common across articles: "Harriet Tubman was a dedicated abolitionist and women's suffrage advocate" (Carter 2016). But even these descriptions isolated her from the communities of Black activists she worked with and inspired. When writers mentioned other abolitionists or women's suffrage activists, they listed White women and men almost exclusively, erasing a generation of Black women activists.

In addition to isolating Tubman from her Black peers, mainstream news articles affirmed the dominant narrative that individual merit and hard work will always be rewarded within US capitalist democracy, a democracy that will inevitably "correct" its "flaws" given time and contributions from exceptional people. For example, the *Baltimore Sun* reprinted the following segment of Secretary of the Treasury Jacob Lew's speech to contextualize why Tubman deserved to appear on US currency: "Harriet Tubman is one of the great American stories that speaks to the ability of *one individual with vision and an entrepreneurial spirit* to make a difference in democracy and to leave a mark on the

world" (Mary McCauley 2016, emphasis added). This framing of Tubman's value to American history portrays her as a rugged individual,
like Jackson, who used "entrepreneurial" vision to make change within
the system of capitalist democracy.

In contrast, Black commentators, while they did not explicitly mention Tubman's work with orphaned and aged African Americans, drew
on critiques of racial capitalism fomented by scholars such as W. E. B.
Du Bois, Angela Davis, and Cedric Robinson, bringing "endarkened knowledge" (Dillard 2000) to their memories of Tubman and
her relationship to urgent, recurrent problems of race-, gender-, and
class-based oppression. These authors provided fuel for our reparative
reading of the twenty-dollar bill's redesign. For example, in a piece in
the mainstream press, the Black columnist Brent Staples challenged the
dominant framing of Tubman. Hinting that Tubman's fight against slavery was not waged within the boundaries of American exceptionalism,
Staples stated, "Harriet Tubman is more than worthy of a place on the
national currency. In granting it, the country would be *acknowledging
the role that slavery played in the building of the republic* and celebrating
a woman who lived out democracy's highest ideals at a time when it
was worth one's life to do so" (2015, emphasis added).

Reparative Readings of the Twenty-Dollar Bill's Redesign

Commemorations are one mode of "transmi[tting] values, reinvig-
orat[ing] our civic associations, and engag[ing] in public advocacy"
(Wuthnow 2005, 346). When there is controversy, there is opportunity
to shift cultural assumptions and bring to light previously submerged
histories. In short, the redesign of the twenty-dollar bill presents an
opportunity to dismantle narratives structured by White ignorance.
Black feminist reparative reading is one strategy through which we can
suggest directions for such cultural shifts, particularly a shift that calls
out the ways White ignorance has shaped public memory.

We draw inspiration from Esther Oganda Ohito's (2016) deployment
of Eve Sedgwick's notion of *reparative reading*. Ohito notes the resonance between reparative reading and Black feminist critical traditions:
"Among the goals of reparative reading is the elucidation of 'the many
ways in which selves and communities succeed in exacting sustenance

from the objects of a culture—even of a culture whose avowed desire has often been not to sustain them' (Sedgwick 1997, 35). Reparative reading is the methodological equivalent of 'flipping the script'—deviating from the norm—in search of hope" (Ohito 2016, 8). Reparative reading allows for the discovery of something new or hidden rather than just revisiting "well-worn tracks" of critical readings that do not offer ways of theorizing hope. Producing theory in the service of hope is a hallmark of Black feminist thought (James 1999), but many critiques of dominant discourses "regurgitate normative . . . configurations [and] may reinforce understandings" (Ohito 2016, 15) based in White ignorance even when they aim to be critical of racism, sexism, and xenophobia. We showcase how Black writers called attention to Tubman's resistance to *racial capitalism* built on slave labor and White supremacy. We then build on that critical memorialization to read her legacy beyond the Civil War.

Harriet Tubman and Critical Memory

A few Black writers and commentators flipped the dominant script to cast Tubman as an anticapitalist fugitive heroine. These writers used the newsworthiness of the redesign announcement and resulting controversy to describe Tubman as a woman who "stole" herself as well as other enslaved people. For example, Feminista Jones argued that "putting [Tubman's] face on America's currency would undermine her legacy." To Jones, the violence of racial capitalism and slavery are the relevant lenses for considering the Treasury's design decision: "Harriet Tubman did not fight for capitalism, free trade, or competitive markets. . . . She risked her life to ensure that enslaved Black people would know they were worth more than the blood money that exchanged hands to buy and sell them. I do not believe Tubman, who died impoverished in 1913, would accept the 'honor,' were it actually upon her, of having her face on America's money. And until the economic injustice against women in America ends, no woman should" (2015). Jones represents Tubman as an anticapitalist outlaw who would not be flattered by the Treasury's attention. Similarly, Steven Thrasher argued that Tubman was anticapitalist and should not be featured on the twenty-dollar bill: "Why cheapen her by putting her on the face on the 20 dollar bill—the very symbol of the racialized capitalism she was fleeing? . . . I don't want to see Tubman commodified with a price, as she once was a slave. I don't need to see hers as the face of the US treasury, being passed in transactions to underpaid retail workers and appearing in print ads for transnational banks. . . . This is the shit Tubman was escaping: the enslaved exploitation of black bodies for white profit" (2015b).

In this revision of the debate over the twenty-dollar bill, the honor is suspect and requires attention to the past and present operations of racial capitalism. Jones discusses the economic injustice against women in America, while Thrasher ties the use of Tubman on the bill to recurrent and ongoing exploitation of Black labor: "Putting Tubman's face on the $20 would only obfuscate how much exploitation there is still left to fight in America, among those in prison, nail salons—and those exchanging twenties daily who don't even know it. We should not let her be used to distract black and brown people from our present economic bondage every time we pay for something" (2015b). Both Jones and Thrasher create a countermemory of Tubman that rejects the neoliberal, postracial narratives found in the majority of news coverage.

We further add to these critical readings by extending the time line of Tubman's struggles against capitalist exploitation and racist degradation of Black people. To review, most dominant narratives do not engage with her antiracist advocacy after the Civil War, pivoting to her work for women's suffrage (e.g., Hobson 2014). This implies that once the Civil War ended slavery, Tubman turned to her "last" battlefield: women's rights. But Tubman both was victimized by continuing racism and fought against it to make the North a habitable place for African Americans. Her life's work after the war centered on providing dignified living conditions for the elderly, infirm, and orphaned (e.g., Clinton 2004). She championed an ethic of care, resonant with Black feminist and womanist ethics articulated by Alice Walker, Audre Lorde, and others. She wanted to build a society where the most vulnerable people were protected, and she demanded they be treated with respect and care and not ravaged by market exploitation. We agree with May: "Examining Tubman's efforts against institutionalized poverty as a persistent legacy of slavery underscores that poverty agendas and capitalist exploitation should be central" to critical memories of her and understanding of her legacy (2014, 45).

Moreover, the embrace of Tubman's image by the government in monetary design resonates strangely with the actual ways the United States refused to pay her for her labor for the Union. Tubman fought a thirty-year battle to get her war pension. While she waged this battle for her due, Tubman struggled to keep her own family out of poverty and had to rely on charity (Clinton 2004, 192–96). These seldom-told tales of Tubman's life after the war remind us of how many Black people who served in the army were unlikely to have their service recognized in either accolades or pensions because of racist biases of Pension Bureau reviewers (Logue and Blanck 2008). The unequal treatment shown to Black Civil War veterans continued, for example, with racist exclusions of Black veterans from home and education loan programs after World War II, exclusions that contributed to the racial wealth gap that continues to this day.

Interrogating the debate of the twenty-dollar bill through reparative reading facilitates endarkened ways to reframe what it means to place the image of a fugitive slave near that of a slave owner on US currency. Reparative readings of the debate unsettle our sense of national history, freedom and capitalism, race and citizenship. The currency's colocation of Jackson and Tubman "makes the present waver, makes it not quite what we thought it was" (Gordon 2011, 5), thus requiring attention, action. Reparative reading suggests alternative ways to engage the difficult knowledge of traumatic histories and rejects neoliberal tokenization of Tubman and erasure of Black resistance.

Notes

1. Most recently, we note the fight to reverse Arizona's ban on Mexican American Studies, passed by the state legislature in 2010 and overturned in 2017. See Kaleem 2017.
2. The hashtag was launched by the writer, editor, and lawyer April Reign in 2015. Workneh 2016.
3. The campaign draws attention to the fact not only that there is gross underrepresentation of people of color and indigenous people in children's books but also that POCI writers are excluded from the ranks of published authors due to implicit biases and predominantly White networks of agents, publishers, and editors. See We Need Diverse Books, n.d.
4. Mills draws on historians like Kirk Savage who interrogated how "the misrepresentations of national textbooks have their counterpart in monuments and statuary."

This is why even northern states have monuments to or have named parks and streets after icons of the Confederacy: this is part of "a national white reconciliation that required the repudiation of an alternative black memory" of slavery and its impacts (Charles Mills 2007, 30). Denying historical violence against Blacks and indigenous people reinforces the "airbrushed white narrative of discovery, settlement, and building" a democratic republic where all men are created equal. This skewed lens "enables a self-representation in which differential white privilege, and the need to correct for it, does not exist. . . . The erasure of the history of Jim Crow makes it possible to represent the playing field as historically level, so that current black poverty just proves blacks' unwillingness to work. As individual memory is assisted through larger social memory, so individual amnesia is then assisted by a larger collective amnesia" (31).

5. See also Kent A. Ono and Derek T. Buescher's (2001) analysis of Disney's interpretation of Pocahontas as a romantic figure of multiculturalism, erasing the violence of English settlerism.

6. Sadly, this theme that "if Harriet could do it, why can't you" reared its ugly head in rants by Kanye West in the spring of 2018. West recited a widely discredited quotation attributed to Tubman that she would have freed more slaves had they wanted to be free. See also studies of the *The Cosby Show* (e.g., Jhally and Lewis, 1992) *Roots* (e.g., Courbold 2017), and other television shows (e.g., Coleman [1998] 2014) for research and overviews of how White audiences often interpret "successful" Black characters as a legitimation of bootstrapping ideology. See also the growing number of "postracial" media studies that suggest narratives of Blackness and/or biracial Blacks continue to reinforce neoliberal frameworks about racial diversity (e.g., Joseph 2013; Squires 2014).

7. "Our paper bills are like pocket monuments to great figures in our history," wrote Women On 20s executive director, Susan Ades Stone. Quoted in Ohlheiser 2015.

3

Go 'Head Girl, Way to Represent!

Dealing with Issues of Race and Gender in Shondaland

MARETTA MCDONALD

Shonda Rhimes is a superstar in a world where few people know the names of the creators, writers, or executive producers of the television shows they regularly watch. Rhimes is the first Black woman to helm a top-ten prime-time network series, *Grey's Anatomy*. After the success of this medical drama, she created a host of similarly successful televisions shows, including *Private Practice* and *Scandal*. In 2014, prime-time dramas created or executive produced by Rhimes held all three time slots on Thursday night, and critics dubbed her the queen of Thursday nights.

One can assume that, as the queen, Rhimes has attained the power to rule her kingdom, Shondaland, as she pleases while sitting happily on her throne, embraced by her contemporaries. However, one can also assume that financial success and critical acclaim are not enough to shield Black women from negative occupational experiences. Queen Rhimes is likely to have experienced marginalization within an industry historically run by White men, despite her success (Hunt 2017; Hunt, Ramón, and Tran 2019). Previous research argues that Black executives are not protected from discrimination because of their high-level positions, and they often feel more alienated the higher they ascend on the corporate ladder (S. Collins 1989; Fernandez 1981; Holder and Vaux 1998; McDonald 2011). Despite barriers Rhimes may have experienced, she continues to excel, as do Black women in other occupational spaces. Although Rhimes's experiences with discrimination may be similar to those of other Black women, her power to develop mass-media television content provides her with a unique opportunity to illuminate these experiences, while other Black women might suffer in silence.

Shonda Rhimes's position as the queen has a broad impact within the world of television. The showrunner is responsible for hiring the writing staff and modeling the content, which sets the tone of the show going forward. The diversity of the content-creation team is important to the types of characters that are created and the stories that are told (Hunt 2017). Darnell Hunt (2017) found that shows with multiple Black writers create content that facilitates "thoughtful and subtle exploration of the very real role that race plays both in their lives and in society" (74). Most of these inclusive writing teams are led by Black showrunners (Hunt 2017). Research by Hunt shows how having people of color as showrunners and writers can affect the images and stories that illuminate our television screens. What we do not know is, How do the lived experiences of people of color shape the content that is presented? This chapter seeks to answer this question by examining how diversity in leadership roles within prime-time television affects the production of media featuring marginalized groups. Drawing on Black feminist theory, I argue that Rhimes's outsider-within standpoint influences her production of images of cultural stereotypes, negative intergroup interactions, and coping strategies on prime-time television.

Representation in Television Media

There have long been calls for more diversity in mass media, especially television, because of its power to influence how consumers understand race, ethnicity, and gender and to provide models for cross-group interactions (Hunt 2017; Hunt, Ramón, and Tran 2019; Mastro 2015; Tukachinsky, Mastro, and Yarchi 2015). One way media, particularly television, has been found to influence how people understand difference is through the use of cultural stereotypes. A stereotype may be defined as the fixed mental picture one holds about members of a group (Schneider 2004). Individuals are more likely to call on this fixed mental image (or cognitive frame) when interacting with groups in which there are visual biological characteristics. The interaction triggers the instant recall of these images to script our interactions (Schneider 2004). Negative stereotypes maintain dominance of powerful groups within multicultural hierarchical societies by structuring how people see and understand members of groups with which they might not have regular interactions (Schneider 2004; Sidanius and Pratto 1999).

Many popular cognitive frames about race, ethnicity, and gender are based on images presented by the media. Scholars assert that media presentations of marginalized groups misrepresent and confirm already-held misconceptions about them (Entman 1994; Mastro 2009). For example, Dana Mastro and Bradley Greenberg (2000) found that Black characters were more likely to be perceived as lazy, less worthy of respect, inappropriately sexy, and unkempt. These characterizations align with historical tropes of Black women within American society: the welfare queen, the Jezebel, and the Mammy (P. Collins [1990] 2000; Schneider 2004). When images support negative cultural narratives, media consumers use these images as evidence to support stereotypical thinking (Schneider 2004). On the other hand, research also shows that images of racial minorities on television that contradict negative stereotypes affect how Whites view them and influence White support for social policies benefiting them (Fujioka 1999; Mastro 2017; Mastro and Kopacz 2006).

In addition to creating cognitive frames, media portrayals influence consumers' self-perception and self-identity; however, the impact of this influence is different across groups. White consumers have a greater ability to select programming that reinforces their identity needs (Mastro 2015). Meanwhile, negative portrayals of minorities boost White viewers' self-esteem while reducing self-esteem and beliefs about community cohesion among minorities (Mastro 2015). Regardless of this dynamic, people of color have been found to be the heaviest consumers of television (Bales 1986; Blosser 1988; Greenberg 1972; Ward 2004). Research into these higher levels of viewership suggests that Black people watch television as a means to escape the stress of their daily lives or for mental stimulation (Bales 1986) and as a function of interpersonal behavior associated with culture (Blosser 1988). Black adolescents use television to stay informed and tend to enjoy watching television more than their White counterparts do (Greenberg 1972). What they watch is important. Consuming programming with predominantly White casts can lower Black viewers' self-esteem, and more positive self-perceptions can emerge when young people view Black-oriented programming (Ward 2004; Graves 1999; G. Powell 1982).

Media also provides models of interactions between different gender and racial groups. Known as social scripts, these models provide a template for people who have little interaction with persons unlike themselves (Schneider 2004). Sherryl Graves (1999) asserts that most depictions of intergroup encounters in television are framed in a positive light, establishing social scripts for politically correct cross-cultural interaction. The absence of negative intergroup interactions or openly racist acts, however, arguably represents missed opportunities to model how these situations may be managed (Graves 1999). For example, the lack of interactions containing microaggressions is a missed chance to present positive means of cross-group understanding and conflict resolution. A microaggression is a subtle insult that people unknowingly use against people of color, women, and gender-nonconforming individuals (Sue 2010). These negative intergroup relations are part of the reality for many people and, if displayed to the public, could influence these relations in the future (Graves 1999).

Coping with racism and discrimination involves physical and mental labor performed to manage the stress caused by such life events (Taylor and Stanton 2007). Forms of coping are bound by culture. Low-income Black individuals, for example, are more likely to use their religious faith or to detach themselves from the situation to cope with stress that is often related to prejudice (Brantley et al. 2002). Black women also use spirituality, in addition to bonds with other women, to cope with the stress of discrimination (Blackmon et al. 2016; cf. Joseph and Kuo 2009). Black women creatives have used their art and creativity, like poetry, music, and play writing, to address racism and cope with stress associated with their marginalized position (P. Collins [1990] 2000).

Conversations surrounding media influence on perceptions of outgroup members and minority self-perception call for more "positive" images of people of color, particularly Black people, on television. However, W. E. B. Du Bois (1926) argued that Black art should reflect the diverse experiences of Black people as fully human, which includes representations of complex positive and negative attributes. Therefore, diversity on the production side of the camera should strive to create *well-rounded, human* portrayals of characters exemplifying fully human experiences, providing realistic examples of intergroup contact, positively affecting minority self-perception, and modeling various coping strategies. An examination of Shonda Rhimes's work provides a unique opportunity to examine how a Black person in a leadership role, specifically a Black woman, influences representations of Black humanity and racialized and gendered interactions in television content.

The "Outsider Within"

W. E. B. Du Bois conceptualized the state of being socially aware as a Black person as developing a "double-consciousness":

> It is a peculiar sensation, this double-consciousness, this sense of always looking at one's self through the eyes of others, of measuring one's soul by the tape of a world that looks on in amused contempt and pity. One ever feels his two-ness,—an American, a Negro; two souls, two thoughts, two unreconciled strivings; two warring ideals in one dark body, whose dogged strength alone keeps it from being torn asunder. The history of the American Negro is the history of this strife—this longing to attain self-conscious manhood, to merge his double self into a better and truer self. In this merging he wishes neither of the older selves to be lost. ([1903] 1994, 2)

Double-consciousness exists when an individual can see oneself through the eyes of the oppressor while juxtaposing this image of self against one's self-identity.

The eyes of the dominant culture in the United States view people of color through a lens of difference. Audre Lorde, who identified herself as an outsider in many accounts ([1981] 1984a, 114), argues that the archetype of an American is White, male, heterosexual, and financially secure. Any deviation from the list of valued traits brands one as an outsider. It is from an outsider's social position that the marginalized become "watchers" who learn to recognize prejudice in the language and behaviors of dominant group members (Lorde 1984a). Similar to Du Bois's ([1903] 1994) concept of double-consciousness, Lorde's (1984a) argument suggests that the ability to spot discrimination is the result of living through oppressive conditions that are linked to Black women's embodiment—the polar opposite of the White male ideal.

Patricia Hill Collins (1986, [1990] 2000) builds on Lorde's and Du Bois's work in her conceptualization of the "outsider within." The outsider within is specific to Black women and developed as they worked as slaves and low-paid domestics within White households. As they navigated White spaces, often rendered invisible by their subordinate status, Black women learned about the workings of the White world hidden from public view. Through these interactions, they learned how Whites viewed Black people and developed an intimate understanding of White supremacy. This knowledge is handed down across generations, creating an outsider-within context through which Black women view the world when inhabiting spaces created and maintained for the benefit of White men. Because Black women have an extreme and specific form of double-consciousness, they often use their Black feminist praxis (leveraging the knowledge born from lived experience) to transform White-dominated spaces through covert acts of resistance while overtly conforming to the norms of their positions (P. Collins [1990] 2000).

For this analysis, I focus on outsider-within themes of self-definition and self-valuation. Collins (1986) defines self-definition as "challenging the political knowledge-validation process that has resulted in externally defined, stereotypical images of [Black] womanhood" (516). She explains how negative stereotypes of Black women are used to control their behavior and labor. For example, assertive Black women are stigmatized because their use of agency threatens White supremacy (P. Collins 1986). Black women's self-definition calls into question the legitimacy of those who have the power to categorize and affix labels to different groups.

Self-valuation pushes past self-definition's question of who defines Black womanhood to choosing the attributes that actually define what it means to be a Black woman. Collins asserts that many of the negative stereotypes projected onto Black women are distortions of attributes that are valuable when embodied in Whites. Using the attribute of assertiveness again, in Black women this attribute is recast as aggressive, part of the Sapphire trope (women who emasculate men and drive them from the home). However, when Black women "embrace their assertiveness, . . . value their sassiness, and . . . continue to use these qualities" (P. Collins 1986, 518), they use the self-valuation process to turn these negative stereotypes on their heads. By inhabiting a position as an outsider within, Black women in leadership or high-prestige positions can transform the institutions in which they work. In this chapter, I use the outsider-within framework to ground my qualitative content analysis of Shonda Rhimes's social position. Because of her position, Rhimes has the power to produce specific media perceptions of race and gender that push back against the spate of racist and sexist primetime television content, allowing her to display her perception and valuation of Black womanhood.

Data and Methods

Data for this study come from season 12 of the medical drama *Grey's Anatomy*, which aired from September 2015 to May 2016. Three reasons influenced my decision to examine this show: (1) it was the first primetime show Rhimes created; (2) it consists of a multicultural regular cast of men and women, as well as a diverse influx of guest cast members who steer the show to cover different subject matter involving the central characters; and (3) the show is the oldest of the three prime-time series Rhimes created, writes, or executive produces on the American Broadcast Network (ABC). I specifically chose to examine season 12 because it was the first season after her third executive-produced primetime show, *How to Get Away with Murder*, premiered and received high ratings and was critically acclaimed. With the premiere of *How to Get Away with Murder*, Rhimes's produced dramas held all three Thursday prime-time time slots. Based on the longevity of *Grey's Anatomy* and Rhimes having three successful prime-time shows, this season inhabits an important space within Rhimes's career. Her success could have allowed her space to share her lived experience of race and gender relations through her characters and story lines. Therefore, data collected from this season of *Grey's Anatomy* are best suited for this analysis.

I watched all twenty-four episodes for content relevant to issues of race, racism, and sexism. Using an inductive approach, I purposively selected ten episodes because their plotlines about intergroup interactions involved race and gender. I reviewed them closely to examine the

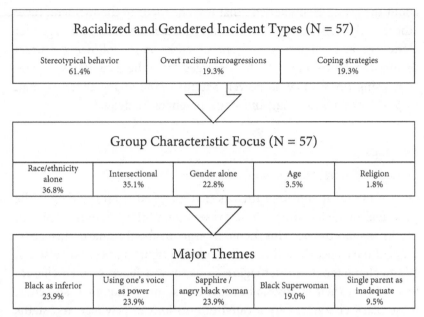

Figure 3.1. Summary of *Grey's Anatomy* code structure.

incidences of racial stereotypes and microaggressions, as well as result-ing responses to these racialized and gendered interactions (Hughey and Muradi 2009; M. Patton 2002). The resulting data provide the best evidence for understanding how Rhimes, as a Black woman, uses the show's cast, dialogue, set, and props to reflect her understanding of race and gender.

I used a constructivist grounded-theory methodological approach to analyze the data (Charmaz 2014). I watched each episode multiple times and transcribed all dialogue (Hesse-Biber 2017; Hughey and Muradi 2009). I generated memos analyzing incident contexts, includ-ing spatial positioning, wardrobe, and physical environment. After ana-lyzing the transcripts and memos, I identified and coded the presence of racialized and gendered interactions between characters. During ini-tial coding, I made tallies of the types of occurrences, which included stereotypical behavior, the experience of overt racism or microaggres-sions, and response to overt racism or microaggressions (coping strate-gies) (fig. 3.1). These initial codes were used to guide deeper and more focused coding. Also seen in figure 3.1, focused codes provided detail about the group characteristic that was the focus of the incident: race/ethnicity alone, intersectional (race and gender simultaneously), gender alone, age, and religion. This chapter focuses on the following abstract themes (analytical memos) that emerged from the data: Black as inferior, using one's voice as power, Sapphire / the angry Black woman trope, Black Superwoman, and single parent as inadequate.

Findings

Black as Inferior: Putting You Back in Your Place

One of the most common themes that emerged from the data is the portrayal of racial interactions presenting Whites as dominant and Blacks as subordinate. This theme emerges in about a quarter (23.8 percent) of the categorized data, as reflected in figure 3.1. Across episodes, White characters use microaggressions toward Black women characters to imply their relative subordinate position, although as surgeons, these Black characters are located in positions of privilege and status within hospitals and broader society. For example, in "Sledgehammer" (September 24, 2015), an upper-class White woman arrives at the hospital looking for her daughter, who has been involved in an accident. Dr. Margaret Pierce (played by Kelly McDreary), the chief cardiothoracic surgeon and the attending doctor for the woman's daughter, is a young Black woman. The mother approaches, using an aggressive tone, demanding that Dr. Pierce go find her daughter's doctor. This example of a racial microaggression reveals that although Dr. Pierce is dressed in surgical scrubs, the patient's mother does not consider the possibility that she is a doctor. The depiction of this interaction is a reflection of the expectations of who should populate certain positions (as outlined by Rosch's prototype theory); anyone who deviates from these requirements is othered or questioned (Schneider 2004).

Similarly, in "Something against You" (November 12, 2015), a White female patient directs her medical questions to Dr. Nathan Riggs (played by Martin Henderson), a middle-aged White man, although Dr. Pierce clearly states that she is the doctor and Dr. Riggs's supervisor. The patient assumes that Dr. Riggs is the leader in this interaction. This reaction to Dr. Pierce is another example of not fitting the cultural ideal of a surgeon. Dr. Riggs is the prototype of a surgeon: White, male, and age appropriate. Dr. Pierce is younger, female, and Black—part of the outgroup in this interaction.

Later, in "Sledgehammer" (September 24, 2015), the same White female character verbally abuses Dr. Pierce and accuses her of interfering in the family's decision to send their lesbian teenage daughter to a conversion camp. The White woman passes two doctors who appear White—including the doctor who has actually called Child Protective Services to report the mother—and continues to berate Dr. Pierce: "Stay away from my little girl. And stop filling her head with your faithless, inappropriate nonsense. You repulse me, you're disgusting." Because Dr. Pierce is a member of the outgroup, the woman feels entitled to speak to her in this manner (Wells-Barnett 1991). The mother, a White, upper-middle-class woman, is surrounded by other White people and reacts in a way that reflects that Dr. Pierce, as a Black woman, is out of place in this social setting (Ahmed 2017). The White character's reaction toward the Black woman character was written to reflect the belief that a White upper-class woman inhabits a superior social location, even in the face of Dr. Pierce's occupational prestige.

The presentation of these interracial interactions reflects Rhimes's practical application of her outsider-within status. As she navigates the world as a Black woman, in spaces where she is a racial and gender outsider, she recognizes how people see her, and that is reflected in the content she produces. Sara Ahmed (2017) discusses how women of color are often considered "space invaders" as they inhabit professional positions that were not designed for them. Rhimes uses her power as showrunner to produce re-creations of experiences of Black women as "misfits" within their professions (Ahmed 2017). Rhimes frequently exemplifies mechanisms that are often used (or fantasized about) to cope with racism and sexism, including the following.

Using One's Voice as Power

Another theme that emerged in this analysis is the use of the coping strategy of "using one's voice as power." Jioni Lewis et al. (2013) define using one's voice as power as the practice of actively speaking up and directly confronting microaggressions. This theme emerges equally as often as "Black as inferior," at 23.9 percent of the incidents (see fig. 3.1), and is a way for the victim to regain power in a situation that is meant to marginalize. In the "Guess Who's Coming to Dinner" episode (October 22, 2015), Dr. Stephanie Edwards (played by Jerrika Hinton), a Black woman surgical resident, is a victim of a series of microaggressions by a White female colleague, Dr. Jo Wilson (played by Camilla Luddington). The goal of the microaggression is to put Dr. Edwards back in her social position of racial subordinance by diminishing her accomplishments. Dr. Wilson's character says, in a relieved tone, that she now understands Dr. Edwards's drive as the by-product of her harrowing childhood illness and then states that they both are survivors of childhood trauma. Dr. Edwards speaks directly to the underlying message hidden beneath the statements:

> You can't even wrap your mind around it, can you, that I just might be better at this than you are, that I might just be stronger or smarter or more savvy? You need a reason for me to have an edge up on you. You need some deep, dark secret motivating me operating circles around you. You need an even playing field just so you can even be good with me. Wow! Stop trying to make us even, Jo. 'Cause we're not even. Deal with your jealousy. Deal with your shortcomings. Those are on you. Don't put your crap on me.

On the basis of this monologue, Dr. Edwards interprets Dr. Wilson's statements as microaggressions that need to be directly addressed. As part of society, Black women often encounter racism through microaggressions and have to make deliberate decisions on when, where, and how to respond (Sue 2010).

Similarly, in "Something against You" (November 12, 2015), Dr. Pierce also uses her voice as power. After the aforementioned incident in which the White woman patient dismisses Dr. Pierce as her doctor and directs her questions to Dr. Riggs, the middle-aged White man, Dr. Pierce continues to direct the conversation back to her treatment plan. She also addresses Dr. Riggs outside the patient's presence, reminding him of his subordinate position by assigning him menial tasks. Dr. Pierce, by virtue of her position as the chief of cardiothoracic surgery, holds power within the hospital. However, her position does not protect her from racism displayed through the microaggression. She states her occupational title to reclaim some of her power in the interaction and uses the power behind her position to verbally remind her work subordinate (but racial-hierarchical superior) that in this venue, she is the one with authority. Ahmed (2017) discusses how women of color must decide how they navigate spaces where they are seen as an outsider and what steps they will take to "pass"—or be viewed as legitimate—as a member of their occupational group.

Returning to "Something against You" (November 12, 2015), Dr. Amelia Shepherd (played by Caterina Scorsone), a White woman surgeon, discounts Dr. Pierce's experience with racism during a conversation about sexism, saying that racism is not "still a thing." However, Dr. Shepherd believes in sexism and admonishes Dr. Alex Karev (played by Justin Chambers), a male colleague, for minimizing it. In fact, referring to sexism, Dr. Karev asks, "That's a thing?" Thereafter, Dr. Shepherd also asks, "Is that still a thing?"—referring to racism—and then says, "I don't believe that." Derald Wing Sue (2010) asserts that one way racial microaggressions operate is that Whites—or men, in the case of sexism—do not even acknowledge that their experience may be different and that another person's experiences may be valid. In this instance, both Dr. Shepherd in her response to Dr. Karev's dismissal of sexism and in the subsequent response of Dr. Pierce when Dr. Shepherd does the same thing with racism are examples of using one's voice as power as a coping mechanism. Both these women outline their experiences with sexism; however, Dr. Pierce's experiences with discrimination are different because they compound sexism and racism. Both characters respond to microaggressions by making the perpetrator aware that disbelieving that their experiences with discrimination are because they are not part of the group it affects is problematic. The way this incident was written provides a multilayered dialogue on bias and clearly reflects the intersectional experience of women of color, marginalized by all men and White women. This reflects an outsider-within consciousness of the unique social position of Black women, which would be required to produce such a multidimensional dialogue.

Lastly, in the same episode, Dr. Shepherd introspectively reflects on her participation in the saga involving Dr. Edwards and Dr. Wilson that was partially outlined earlier. Dr. Shepherd believed that Dr. Edwards was lying about her childhood illness, on the basis of Dr. Wilson's word, and now wonders if Dr. Edwards thinks she is racist. Dr. Shepherd asks Dr. Wilson if she thinks she (Shepherd) believed Dr. Edwards over her (Wilson) because of racial bias. Dr. Wilson tells Dr. Shepherd that she did consider the racial dynamic of the situation but concluded that it was not based on racial bias, telling Dr. Shepherd, "I'm OK." However, Dr. Shepherd doubts Dr. Wilson's honesty and consults Dr. Pierce, her Black roommate and colleague, to interpret Dr. Edwards's response. Dr. Shepherd's desire to get the insight of Dr. Pierce reflects a common stereotype: that all Black people think within a single mind frame (Schneider 2004). Because of this assumption, Whites will ask any person of color in their social circle about all things associated with the group. Once again, the writers depict Dr. Pierce's character as utilizing the "using one's voice as power" coping strategy. Dr. Pierce tells Dr. Shepherd that she should not seek her out as the authority on all things Black. She should trust the experience or reaction of the person of color with whom she has interacted. The portrayal of this interaction not only shows the use of this coping mechanism but also attempts to educate the viewer on making assumptions about one person's ability to represent or speak for an entire group. Black leaders, like Rhimes, are often the only Black person in their social sphere. The production of this scene portrays the lived experience of being the "only," which is born out of an other-within epistemology.

Using brilliant monologues, Rhimes displays different manifestations of intergroup relations, in which a victim of covert racism uses an empowering model of coping. This suggests that Rhimes's outsider-within perspective developed through her lived experience in the White male television showrunner and content-creating realm. That perspective influences how she produces content, a practical application of Black feminist thought praxis. Showing coping strategies for racial and gendered discriminatory acts, Rhimes uses self-definition and self-valuation strategies in her work.

Sapphire / Angry Black Woman and Black Superwoman

Comprising nearly another quarter of the data, the Sapphire, or angry Black woman stereotype, is also a common theme that emerged in the data, as shown in figure 3.1. In multiple incidents across episodes,

Black women characters are portrayed in ways that show anger, assertiveness, and even violence. In "Sledgehammer" (September 24, 2015), the White, upper-middle-class woman who verbally assaults Dr. Pierce (mentioned earlier in the "Black as inferior" section) approaches her in a physically threatening manner. Dr. Pierce's character responds to this perceived threat by punching the woman in the face. The depiction of a Black woman's response to threat can be interpreted as a portrayal of the angry Black woman stereotype. Even granting that her anger may be justified, this reaction could reinforce the ideology of Black people as inherently violent, using violence to solve their problems, even though the White woman is the aggressor. However, Rhimes reclaims the use of anger as a response to racialized sexism and as a form of resistance to the silencing of Black women's emotions. Although Dr. Pierce's violent response is extreme, Rhimes allows the character to respond with rage and anger, which is not often highlighted in prime-time television.

By depicting a Black woman in righteous anger, Rhimes exemplifies the practical application of self-valuation and redefines what an angry Black woman looks like. Rhimes also validates Dr. Pierce's reaction by allowing her colleagues to applaud her response to the White woman's threatening behavior. Additionally, Rhimes adds dimension to this externally defined characterization of Black women as angry. Her use of Dr. Pierce's character in this interaction can be understood as a way to push back against the stereotypical angry Black woman. The Dr. Pierce character is portrayed as the Mammy stereotype (P. Collins [1990] 2000); she is the peacemaker, nonthreatening in her behavior, and asexual in her dress. Dr. Pierce brokers peace among her roommates, is shy, and acts respectably. She usually is dressed in scrubs or clothes that are not form-fitting. By strategically using the character that is the least threatening of all the characters, Rhimes attempts to show that Black women are not homogeneous and that racism can push even the meekest Black women beyond their breaking point.

Another example of the Sapphire / angry Black woman theme is the presentation of the character Dr. Bailey. Throughout the episodes analyzed, Dr. Miranda Bailey's character—casted as a short, larger-bodied, dark-skinned Black woman, played by Chandra Wilson—is at the center of many dimensions of the angry Black woman and Sapphire tropes. Dr. Bailey starts her leadership position of resident chief of surgery, the highest position in the hospital, in "Walking Tall" (October 1, 2015). She begins to micromanage her former colleagues as she learns her position. The doctors she supervises complain that she has become overbearing, is taking advantage of her position, and is too aggressive—read as Sapphire. However, Dr. Bailey's character is written to show how her actions are fueled by additional pressure that she feels about performing her job with perfection. Dr. Bailey's micromanaging response is an example of the use of the "Black Superwoman" coping mechanism to combat the pressure that Black women face when they are located in positions of leadership in occupational spaces. Lewis et al. (2013) define "becoming the Black Superwoman" as a way to deal with negative experiences that are intersectionally gendered and racialized. Because Black women are seen as inferior, they often over- and outperform expectations to contradict this negative stereotype. Dr. Bailey's character is presented as an independent Black woman with a lot to prove, which is the way many Black women navigate occupational and academic spaces because people automatically doubt their abilities (Lewis et al. 2013). The Black Superwoman coping strategy represents about a fifth (19.0 percent) of the categorized incidents, as reflected in figure 3.1.

In addition to navigating a new leadership position, Dr. Bailey also becomes the supervisor of her husband, who is a Black surgical resident. In "Something against You" (November 12, 2015), Dr. Bailey barks orders at her husband/employee, Dr. Benjamin Warren (played by Jason George), which presents her as emasculating. In the same episode, Dr. Bailey is angry with her husband for not doing as she asked him to, so she threatens to withhold sex, which presents her as manipulative and controlling. Dr. Bailey's character is written to fully embody the prototype of the Sapphire, which is a trope of Black women that depicts them as overachieving, emasculating, and overbearing and as eventually driving their husbands out of the home. This characterization of Black women is blamed for single-female-headed households (P. Collins [1990] 2000). However, across the episodes of Grey's Anatomy, Rhimes produces Dr. Bailey's character as a multidimensional successful Black woman who is driven and determined but also vulnerable and self-conscious, showing how her actions are products of her experiences.

The complexities of Dr. Bailey's character and her relationships can be seen throughout the data in her self-doubt, in her coping mechanisms, and in aspects of her relationship with her husband—like her desire for his approval and their mutually supportive bond. In using the outsider-within framework, the writing of Dr. Bailey's character reflects how successful Black women are aware that they are viewed negatively by outsiders when they are assertive. Inherent to outsider-within consciousness, Black women within prestigious occupational spaces are sensitive to the complexities of being a Black woman in a position of authority; they may initially be read as a Sapphire or an angry Black woman by society but actually embody the Black Superwoman persona as a way to cope with perceptions of inferiority. Rhimes produces content that reflects the self-definition and self-valuation tenets of the outsider within by challenging these stereotypes and providing counternarratives about the use of anger and assertiveness.

Single Parent as Inadequate

The last theme, represented in about 10 percent (9.5 percent) of the data, is the stereotype of the single parent as inadequate. This trope is addressed in two major plotlines: one involving a widower single father and the other involving a single mother who had her child as a teenager. In "Sledgehammer" (September 24, 2015), the single father's character is written as a widow with a lesbian teenage daughter who attempts suicide. The writers portray him as a distracted man who is raising a daughter without a mother. Because of his distraction, he is unaware of her sexual orientation or the trauma she is experiencing because of it. This representation of the single father is problematic because it fortifies the assumption that fathers, as a group, are not involved nurturers. Additionally, the father was cast and scripted as a person of Middle Eastern descent (inferring from his name, accent, and physical characteristics), which also promotes the stereotype of the hardworking immigrant, who works long hours and is unable to effectively supervise his child. Immigrant status and lack of child supervision have been linked since the 1940s to juvenile delinquency (Shaw and McKay 1942). This plotline reinforces the long-held theory that inattentive parents are solely responsible for their children's "deviant" choices (Schneider 2004).

It is important to know that no coping mechanism or counter-narrative to address this stereotypical depiction was written into the story line. Although portraying the father as a widow is an attempt to solicit empathy for the character, it does not effectively prevent his behavior from being interpreted as neglectful. The limitations of Rhimes's outsider-within consciousness can explain the absence of reflection on this portrayal of the father. Her identities do not include being a father, an immigrant, or poor. More broadly, this portrayal speaks to the way stereotypes exist across and within marginalized groups and can be reflected in media content.

These data reflect that Rhimes might lack insight on issues outside her lived experience. Rhimes is the daughter of two academics, was raised in an affluent neighborhood, and would have limited knowledge on living in impoverished conditions, single-parent homes, or teenage pregnancy. Rhimes's outsider-within perspective appears to be limited in its ability to produce content that thoughtfully portrays characters vastly different from herself. This gap illustrates the need for writers from diverse backgrounds, including different class backgrounds and other non-White groups, in television writing teams.

Discussion and Conclusion

In this chapter, I have set out to examine Rhimes's plot and character development in *Grey's Anatomy* to understand how race and gender messages emerge from the sea of television content when a Black woman is at the helm. Findings show that there is a plausible relationship between Rhimes's outsider-within perspective and the development of characters and story lines in the episodes examined. In areas involving professional Black women, the production of plotlines, character development, and casting are thoughtful, strategic, and nuanced. Answering the call of Du Bois (1926), Rhimes develops multidimensional Black women characters who are humanly imperfect. This analysis also finds that Rhimes produces content highlighting how all intergroup interactions are not positive; in fact, some are traumatizing and violent. By unapologetically displaying these frequently reoccurring forms of discrimination in conjunction with simulations of justified responses and coping strategies, Rhimes provides models for how these situations can be managed (Graves 1999). Although punching a racist in the face may be extreme, the fear and anger that spawned this response are understood by many Black women. The ability to identify with these characters and situations may positively affect their self-perception by validating their experiences of gendered racism (Graves 1999; G. Powell 1982).

These finding also show Rhimes's outsider-within consciousness is not without its limitations. The data show that the ability to produce content to challenge societal perceptions and stereotypes does not span far from Rhimes's Shondaland Production Company office door. Evidence reflects that Rhimes clearly understands the struggle of upper-middle-class Black professionals against discrimination in occupational spaces. However, in her production of characters whose lived experiences are outside her social locations, like immigrants, the working class, and single parents, biased perceptions of these groups are reflected in the data. This finding supports previous literature on intergroup stereotypical thinking about outgroup members (Schneider 2004), even though the person doing the thinking is a member of multiple outgroups herself. As White content creators are expected to be aware of their prejudices and how they may influence the consumers of their content (Mastro 2009, 2015; Ward 2004), so Rhimes must be held to the same standard. Rhimes can create more empathetic content by hiring people of color from different class backgrounds in her writing teams.

The findings of this study suggest that strategically producing television content concerning interracial gendered relations is extremely important. The data also reflect how content creators who are not White men can present issues of race and gender in a way that centers the conversations on the gendered and racialized experiences of people of color. In Rhimes's work, Black characters are not on the periphery, nor are all their interactions with Whites positive. She allows for the characters within *Grey's Anatomy* to show how issues of power, gender, and race exist in occupational spaces. My findings also show evidence of self-definition and self-valuation strategies used in the reframing of historical negative stereotypes into valuable personal attributes.

These findings must also be analyzed critically to further understand the impact of diversity in television media. Although Black characters are carefully portrayed as multidimensional humans with agency, viewers may not receive the intended messages. The stereotypical portrayal of the Black women on *Grey's Anatomy* may be used to bolster assumptions about Black women as aggressive, unwarrantedly angry, or race baiters. For example, an unintended outcome of the depiction of Dr. Bailey is confirmation of the Sapphire stereotype for those who believe it to be typical behavior of Black women, especially Black women who are highly successful in their careers. The depiction of Dr. Bailey's relationship with her husband can also add to the intraracial conflict between Black women and Black men, as Black men could see her character as confirmation that successful women do not make good spouses.

Audience-analysis research may help to develop a deeper understanding of the impact of diversity behind the camera. Future research may conduct this type of analysis to examine who are the main consumers of this type of media and what they are taking away from the content. Black women historically have used knowledge learned through their social position as the outsider within to disseminate knowledge to empower their communities. In *Grey's Anatomy*, Shonda Rhimes shines a light on the experiences of Black women in high-prestige occupational spaces. She does not show a rosy picture of how economic class protects marginalized groups from experiencing gendered racism. Rhimes uses her power as the queen of Thursday-night prime-time television to center Black women's experiences in a realistic manner and redefine what successful Black women look like on-screen.

4

Comic Forms of Racial Justice

Aesthetics of Racialized Affect and Political Critique

RACHEL KUO

In attempts to change politics through shifting culture, what happens when social justice becomes converted into a commodity object that circulates as visual capital? Considering the gains and losses of rendering racial and political critique into minor forms, this chapter examines the role of online long-form comics, including Shing Yin Khor's *What Would Yellow Ranger Do?*, a comic about the question "Where are you from?" and *Just Eat It*, a comic about the commodification of culture, and Kayan Cheung-Miaw's *Dear Brother* and *Two Mothers*, two comics about police brutality and the confrontation of anti-Black racism in Asian American communities.[1] The scales of racial violence in these comics are disparate, from the daily frustrations of constant racialized and gendered objectification at coffee shops and first dates to interrogations of Asian American complicity in apparatuses of state violence that contribute to the systematic murder of Black people. Yet these comics are both similar in form as well as in the creators' reflexive use of shared experiences and histories to interrogate and negotiate Asian American racialization in a broader cultural and political landscape.

As a format, comics can help make political critique more digestible and accessible for audiences by presenting complex information in a more visual and immediate format (Alverson 2017). Popular print examples of this include Art Spiegelman's *Maus*, Marjane Satrapi's *Persepolis*, and Gene Luen Yang's *Boxers & Saints*. More recently, the online advocacy organization 18 Million Rising has used online comics to share stories against public-charge rules in immigration policy.

Further, the historical uses of illustration in protest posters demonstrate the connections between the visual and political. Similar to the use of GIFs, lists, short videos, memes, and social media posts for political education, online comics rely on wider circulation and spread as well as indexical imagery—signs that reference an object in the context in which an image occurs and rely on existing codes of signification and representation to convey meaning. In addition to the capacities afforded by digital distribution across multiple platforms, online comics uniquely afford detailed storytelling through the interplay of image and text to distill complex political visions into a more accessible message.

This chapter takes into account minor forms of racial critique, like online comics, to examine the processes in which racialized anger and social justice become media objects that are circulated and consumed in digital environments. As objects that move emotions between bodies and signs, comics circulate within affective economies, where emotions function as a form of capital; rather than affect residing within the comic itself, affect is produced as an effect of circulation (Ahmed 2004). The comics discussed in this chapter resonate feelings of co-identification that in turn spark desires to further circulate the media object. Further, this chapter examines comics as a form of visual capital in which racial politics can be digitally and visually materialized, building on discussions of digital visual culture such as Lisa Nakamura's (2008) formative work on the creation, consumption, and circulation of racialized bodies as a form of visual capital online.

To circulate in the new media landscape, activist media and racialized content become embedded with the market logics of the digital information and knowledge economy. Even when used as activist media, comics circulate within the creative industries and/or content industries that include the work of media production, as well as media design, circulation, licensing, and marketing. In addition to having working knowledge of movements' political vision and vernaculars, comic artists need to have technical skills for illustration and production, such as proficiency with and access to both software and hardware, as well as social and cultural capital to distribute across networks and/or promote their work. Creators holding historically marginalized positions also reflexively use difference—"the Othered body and voice, along with discourses of the 'self'"—as a means to market and create value for themselves (Christian 2016, 96). In online spaces, creators and artists as consumer-users of social platforms must also navigate page clicks and reads, search-engine optimization through headlines and keywords, self-marketing, and more in a competitive information marketplace.

For example, online products and platforms like Lela Lee's humor comic *Angry Little Girls*, Phil Yu's culture and political blog *Angry Asian Man*, and Esther Fan and Olivia Park's art-activist site *Sad Asian Girls* mediate racialized affects of anger and melancholy into a brand: the angry Asian. These sites also characterize anger (or sadness) and Asianness as an ontological claim and state of being while also circulating the "angry Asian" as an unhappy subject through "happy objects" (Ahmed 2004) like humorous images and text. While the cultural work of drawing comics, writing posts, and designing graphics began to convert racial anger into politicized media forms, all these sites also currently sell merchandise for profit through products such as apparel, print goods, and toys. Content creators like Yu and Lee can monetize their art and writing—as well as their brand as "angry Asians"—and they are socially and economically rewarded by a sustained investment in reproducing racialized affect.

Further, in today's cultural environment, where "authenticity" is mediated through the self-as-brand, people often self-fashion around different political alignments through consumption as a site of political performance, such as purchasing symbolic T-shirts, mugs, and tote bags (Banet-Weiser 2012; M. Joseph 2002). In online spaces, people may indicate political alignments through circulating particular images and texts on social media platforms. Articles shared, hashtags used, and photos posted function as visible and symbolic evidence of political commitments. While content creators navigate a digital economy of knowledge production and information, part of their creative labor also requires creatively using format and genre to translate and circulate political education.

Taking the preceding ideas as a touchstone, and through a closer analysis of form and aesthetics in online comics, this chapter also draws on aesthetic, linguistic, and affect theory to examine the economies in which minor forms of racial critique circulate and the processes of production and circulation of social justice education as a genre entwined with capital. In making social justice and racial critique more accessible, what kinds of politics can be reproduced or represented and through what aesthetics? Examining how social justice can be visually represented and communicated within affective economies challenges us to engage questions around the formats in which racial politics can be rendered more legible across audiences with different political touch points.

Comics as Racialized Media and Political Critique

Shing Yin Khor's and Kayan Cheung-Miaw's comics are key sites for understanding how online comics can be used as a form of political critique, given their exploration of core themes that mediate Asian American experiences of racialization. Both comics aim to create feelings of shared identification as well as function as an educational tool for facilitating awareness and discourse. Again, while being similar in form, these comics operate on different scales of critique. This study of online comics through the examination of Asian American artists draws on Lori Kido Lopez's (2016) study of Asian American media activism. Taking an expansive definition of activism as intentional acts designed to remedy and address a social injustice, Lopez approaches media activism as ways Asian Americans interact with texts to reflect and transform social realities. For example, in Khor's comics, she identifies with Yellow Ranger (Trini Kwan) because the rest of the faces on television are "white, white, white, and Will Smith." By pointing out the lack of Asian media representation, Khor's comics perform and exemplify the desire for "cultural citizenship" (Lopez 2016), seeking belonging and acceptance in the cultural landscape through media representation. Both Khor's and Cheung-Miaw's works are part of a broader landscape and collective endeavor of Asian American cultural production that seeks to make longer-term changes in media and political systems; while their stories are informed by individual experiences, the comics serve to influence a much larger community and network.

Khor's comics address the dominant racialized and gendered narrative of Asians as "perpetual foreigners" and "exotic" through sharing her own experiences. In *Yellow Ranger*, Khor shares that she is sixteen when she moves to the United States, and she navigates how people confuse

Malaysia and China, call her accent "cute," or suggest that she take ESL classes even though she has spoken English her whole life. In the opening panel, Khor poses the question, "Where are you from?"—a persistent question that shows the perpetuity of how "Asianness" indexes "foreignness" (San Juan 1994; Wu 2002; Huynh 2004). Translated, the question is really a statement: "You don't look like you're from around here." This question feels resonant to Asian Americans, whose racialized bodies signify geographic and spatial distance and become marked as "alien." In sharing anecdotes in which men describe Asian women as "tiny and exotic" or in which White friends ask to find "authentic" food, Khor critiques the exotification of Asianness through highlighting how racialized bodies and cultures become commodified and fetishized.[2]

Cheung-Miaw's piece *Two Mothers* reminds readers that perceptions of Asians as foreign can fall on a broader scale of racial violence when Asians are attacked for perceptions of their foreignness as dangerous and threatening; at the end of her comic, she invokes Asian American victims of police violence, such as Yong Xing Huang, a sixteen-year-old boy who was shot by police while he was playing with a pellet gun, and Cau Bich Tran, who suffered from mental illness and was shot while holding a vegetable peeler, alongside Black victims of police violence, including Aiyana Stanley Jones and Eric Garner.

Both of Cheung-Miaw's pieces respond to the shooting of Akai Gurley by the Chinese American New York Police Department (NYPD) officer Peter Liang; although Liang was the first NYPD officer to be convicted of shooting in the line of duty, he was later sentenced to eight hundred hours of community service. This contentious case itself pushed forward discussions about anti-Blackness within Asian American communities, as some protests mobilized under "Asians4BlackLives" to demand justice against all cases of police violence, while other protests emerged in defense of Liang as a scapegoat and innocent victim. Cheung-Miaw's comics ask for Asian American solidarity with Black communities by emphasizing shared connections to family. In her storytelling, she includes narratives of parents working long shifts for under minimum wage, children growing up in a small apartment, and parents' aspirational dreams for their children—connecting with potential readers' shared experiences of immigrant parents' sacrifice and struggle. She tells the parallel stories of Liang's mother and Gurley's mother and also of a sister whose younger brother goes on to become a police officer who kills a Black transgender teen reaching for her ID. Cheung-Miaw uses intimacy as a way to convey that while individual people cannot be easily be defined as "good" or "bad," they can be actors in systems of violence and enact harm.

Both Gurley's murder and Liang's conviction are situated within the broader historical context of US racial formations, where Asian Americans can be agents in organized, state-sanctioned violence that structures anti-Blackness (Sexton 2010). Further, ideologies around citizenship, including the popular myth of Asian Americans as self-enterprising and exceptional "model minorities," pathologizes Black communities while also serving as a means for Asian Americans to gain proximity to and power from Whiteness through conscious and unconscious participation in anti-Black racism (Yang-Stevens and Quan-Pham 2016). Cheung-Miaw's question at the end of her two comics, "Which side of history will you choose?" is also a call to turn away from Whiteness as an object of desire. She calls for the possibility of locating belonging in ways that divest from Whiteness.

Bringing together Khor's and Cheung-Miaw's comics offers a reading of how Asian Americans constitute complex sites and experiences of power in the United States. As visual objects used as activist media, these online comics visualize racialized bodies, and it is in this visualization and digital representation that readers recognize, identify, and affectively connect with these works to potentially circulate them.

Comics as Form: Digital Reproductions of Racial Aesthetics

Online comics also produce and reproduce digital images of the body, relying on visual articulations of racial difference, such as skin color or hair type. The turn to a more graphical and visual internet beginning in the 1990s contradicts the myth of the internet as a bodiless, thus raceless, space while simultaneously relying on visible determinants to interpret racial identity (Nakamura 2008). The aesthetic reproduction of race emphasizes the primacy of the visual in understandings of race, which tend to rely on physical markers of difference; race is seen and understood through bodily signs. The digital environment also tends to favor visual and textual simplicity, including tidy, clean aesthetics; in order for digital objects to circulate quickly online, information and data must be compressed into smaller file sizes and/or shorter lengths. Hiroki Azuma (2009) describes the semiotic world of the web as governing an aesthetics of "hyperflatness" for works circulated online. The unit of "a work" is defined by both visible surface and invisible code, as the aesthetic design of a webpage depends on the source-code language to load seamlessly and consistently in many different screen environments.

Both the comic as form and website as medium (where comics tend to be hosted) favor visual perception. When the comic is loaded and displayed, panels are either grouped into one JPEG image or chained together as multiple JPEG images with illustrated panels containing both text and image, where narrative text is also part of the graphic. In the case of Khor's and Cheung-Miaw's comics, their works are akin to illustrated short essays; they are laid out as a chain of panels and intended to be read by scrolling downward on the webpage.[3] Readers interact with these pieces by revealing subsequent images and texts via a smooth, vertical scrolling motion, producing a "haptic visuality of the text" (Nabizadeh 2016, 354) that remains smooth and flat. Navigating the work via the physical act of scrolling takes on material and digital dimensions, as textual and graphic meaning are shaped by both content and form (Nabizadeh 2016, 349). For example, while both comics are text heavy, readers can still interact with the works across varying levels of engagement, either by carefully reading, pausing, and lingering or by quickly skimming. Scrolling, as reading practice, demands visuals that can clearly communicate ideas and enable general understanding of content.

As racialized media, comics use abbreviated visual cues to communicate racial identity, expression, and experience. Lisa Nakamura (2001) takes up Lev Manovich's (2001) concept of "transcoding" to think about "cybertyping," the collaborative process of translating racial experience and expressions in online environments. Machine-enabled interactions produce images that signify race, stemming from a common cultural layer. As "blasts" of image and text, online forms often appear to operate in "singularity"—present without past of future—yet are reused over and over (Jameson 2015). Popular images, videos, and articles—content that is most widely shared—encapsulate an essence intended to endure multiple operations (Ngai 2017, 485). Nakamura describes the etymology of "stereotype" as an example of machine language, a "mechanical device that could reproduce images relatively cheaply, quickly, and in mass quantities" (Nakamura 2001, 4). Stereotypes, also ideas about people, "shape figures as recognizable social personae that circulate along identifiable trajectories across space and time" (Reyes 2016, 313). A stereotype instructs the interpretation of signs, creating infinite realities that allow a reader to hear nonpresent signs, translate visual signs into audible ones and vice versa, or erase signs that do not align with the stereotype's logic.

In the comic form, specific formal qualities stand for specific personality and character traits, like darker skin and hair type for characters of color or a red shirt for anger. Khor's comic *Yellow Ranger* opens with a large illustration of the yellow Power Ranger, Trini Kwan (fig. 4.1). It is not until later into the comic that the reader sees Khor's drawing of herself: short black hair, black dots as eyes, glasses, and a yellow T-shirt. In the repeated use of the color yellow, yellowness comes to signify Khor's depiction of her subjectivity and also indexes "yellow" alongside "Asianness."[4]

Comics rely on widely understood signs to represent subjects and situations. The racialized faces in comics, such as in work by Khor, seem equalized into a generic form—they all "look" the same with slight variations on hair and skin that "totalize" racialized aesthetics through simplification. As simple, representative racial "afterimages" (Nakamura 2001) with aesthetics that rely on the deindividuation of identity, these faces also produce a generic affect that condenses an emotional state. Stuart Hall (2013) defines "transcoding" as the reappropriation of existing meaning toward something new; Khor's comics can be read as strategies of racial representations that make stereotypes work against themselves to leverage racial critique.

In the opening panel of *Yellow Ranger*, under the question "Where are you from?" there are five disembodied heads floating along an indeterminate space, each with speech bubbles (fig. 4.2). For example, the first head has wavy brown hair, brown eyes, light-yellow skin with freckles and says, "My mom's Filipino and my dad's Canadian"; another

Figure 4.1. Opening panel with Yellow Ranger, also known as Trini Kwan, from the US television series *Mighty Morphin' Power Rangers* and played by the Vietnamese American actress Thuy Trang (Khor 2014b).

has wavy red hair, blue eyes, and skin with almost no color, saying, "We're British, I guess. My family's been here FOREVER."

Placed over a white background, the lack of color on the "British" head signals the color white—and, of note, this character proclaims a nativist relationship with a European country. Hair color and style and skin color become signals for race and also nationality.[5] These racialized faces are actually faceless, expressing the face of no particular individual—"stripped of all determinate qualities and reduced to its simplest form," "dedifferentiated," and "generic," relating individual

Figure 4.2. The "Where are you from?" panel in Khor's comic semiotically links together visual signifiers with race and nationality (Khor 2014b).

faces to a "totality" of faces and thus producing an implicit act of equalization, with regard to racialized aesthetic (Ngai 2015, 35). Readers attribute the racialization of Khor's figures through the aesthetic production of the tones of their skin, hair, and eyes. In a digital environment, online comics must use codes to signify recognizable types to convey racial meaning. Made up of "collectively achieved abstractions," race also becomes digitally "transcoded" (Manovich 2001) into "types" optimized for further reproduction and circulation across different online media platforms.

Animating Chains of Meaning

Beyond the representational drawing of a racialized subject in simple shapes, colors, and lines, comics rely on speech. The characters in online comics are staged figures, fictive characters that approximately mimic live, flesh-and-blood bodies (Goffman 1986, 456–60). Comics include informal, conversational speech, internal monologues, and also text that uses replaying as a narrative strategy. "Replaying" is a reporting of a temporally located event that is couched in a personal perspective (Goffman 1986). In comics, images of staged figures are "voiced," or given recognizable qualities—when a character becomes voiced, speech mechanisms that construct that figure must be organized in a way to invite a particular interpretation; speech must be relayed for the reader to take up meaning (Reyes 2016). Both medium and register affect ways that characters are voiced, which may also reveal the affective meaning of a work. Like stereotyped images, character positions and interactions enable comics as a form to be a site of ideological reproduction and circulation.

Khor and Cheung-Miaw as artists and creators voice, inhabit, and perform multiple roles in the creation of different characters; in a way, comics function as a remediation of puppet theater (Silvio 2010). Through the presence of performing objects, animation focuses on a range of technologies and practices (*techne*) that create the illusion of life and lived reality. When the comic form is used as a mode of activist media that attempts to resist controlling racial images and experiences, depicted characters animate and voice their responses to racial injury.

Khor writes to "you," producing multiple possibilities of "you," plural, as figures. The recognizable qualities of the staged figures are those associated with the adjective "authentic" and those who seek authenticity. "You" could evoke a subject for a reader who identifies more with Khor, or "you" could be the person who "means well," who "loudly proclaims the authenticity of our foil wrapped food," who points out that "the restaurant is filled with Mexicans, which means it's good" (Khor 2014a). In Cheung-Miaw's comics, she primarily writes from the perspective of the sister to the brother, in *Dear Brother*, and of Gurley's mother, in *Two Mothers*. However, she performatively affects and effects an unnamed interlocuter subject: "you." She writes to "you," thus invoking "you" as figure: "How would you feel if a police officer has his gun out in a place where families live, where your children play? . . . If Akai Gurley had been your son, father or family member, how would you have felt after his death?" (2016b); and, repeated in both comics, she asks the reader, "*Which side of history will you choose to be on?*" (2016a, 2016b). In voicing, Cheung-Miaw appeals to readers to make a choice—ideologically and politically—in how they view and take action with regard to the issue of police brutality.

Khor's and Cheung-Miaw's comics stylistically use repetition as a narrative tactic. Repetitive scripts index the process of racialization and also function as glossing to explain the formation of racial metalanguages that conceptualize representations of Asianness in the United States. Glossing, or speech events that define language or make equivalent one stretch of language to another, is a referential speech event that takes language as the referent, or object of description (Silverstein 1976). These "scripts" rely on indexical order to create micro and macro social frames (Silverstein 2003). Through chains of analogies, individual experiences are connected to institutional and ideological frameworks. This repetitive looping produces an affect of anger and frustration.

Rather than having dialogue and action cues between characters, the four comics rely heavily on narrative text as the primary context for supplementary drawings. As supplements, the images reinforce the text. The layout of a comic also condenses and compartmentalizes space, where sign systems are organized within a particular media format. For example, in Cheung-Miaw's *Dear Brother*, the last panel depicts an Asian woman cradling the head of a Black man whose chest is covered in bullets, with the caption, "February 21, 1965, Audubon Ballroom, NYC," and the text, "Our liberation and freedom are tied to those of black folks and other oppressed people" (fig. 4.3). The graphic image paraphrases the famous photo in *Life* magazine, in which Yuri Kochiyama cradles Malcolm X's head when he was assassinated,[6] and draws on the uses of Kochiyama's support of Black liberation movements to signify possibilities of Black and Asian solidarity. This widely circulated scene of Black death and dying is both a stark reminder of racialized state violence and an urgent demand for reflection and resistance from

Figure 4.3. Which side of history will you be on? Cheung-Miaw's final panel in *Dear Brother* brings together Asian American history with futures of Black liberation (Cheung-Miaw 2014a).

Asian American participants; the *Life* photo becomes further mediated and given different contextual meaning: from reality to photography to illustration.

Saving Time: Digital Translations of Political Critique

In the introduction to *Just Eat It*, Khor (2014a) writes the following: "I'm writing from the viewpoint of a cranky immigrant, but also as someone who considers bell hooks' essay 'Eating the Other' and Edward Said's book *Orientalism* as major touchstones that have informed a lot of my work (and viewpoint). How does this comic read to someone that doesn't share that same viewpoint? Or background?" Khor acknowledges the limitations of both shared access to the viewpoint and background of "cranky immigrant" (or "angry Asian") and also to the academic scholarship like hooks and Said. In this way, she hails multiple readerships—other "cranky immigrants" like herself, those who induce crankiness, and those who may be outside such experiences. Her online comics have multiple layers of translation: the translation of personal experience into academic theory and vice versa, the translation of both theory and experience into a short essay, and the translation of an essay into comic form and digital image.

In *Just Eat It*, Khor describes her frustration—her cranky feelings—toward her personhood becoming abstracted into "authentic ethnic food advice" (2014a). In the accompanying images, she shows three characters introducing themselves as Pho Nguyen, Palak Paneer Gupta, and Albondigas Martinez. These figures show how fantasies of authenticity abstract personhood into food (for example, "pho" represents "authentic Vietnameseness"). Another accompanying image features an imagined object of a "cultural diversity bingo" card with boxes that say things like, "black friend!," "cabeza burrito," "k-town karaoke," "Chinese only menu," "native friend," "yellow friend," and "visit Thailand" (see fig. 4.4). Here, Khor shows how "cultural diversity" becomes accessed through commodities and/or the commodification of identities.

Khor's work critiques the quest for racial, national, and ethnic authenticity as one that reduces race, nationality, and ethnicity into a singular symbolic device, yet, as mentioned earlier, the racio-visual logic of the internet operationalizes these same devices. As much as

Figure 4.4. Racialized characters with food items as first names and "cultural diversity bingo" (Khor 2014a).

"Asianness" becomes represented through shades of yellow, cultural identities become represented through food. In navigating the boundaries of media and format, Khor must aesthetically reproduce these very logics of simplicity and reduction. As race and affect become embedded within capitalist logics of efficient reproduction—as racial gimmicks—they can still be useful as a means of critique. For example, Khor's tongue-in-cheek observation of diversity as a bingo game of eating burritos, going on destination vacations, and singing karaoke not only highlights how racialized politics have become reduced to cultural diversity but also exposes diversity as a gimmick, what Sianne Ngai (2017) describes as a "capitalist aesthetic phenomenon" (468). Khor's examples demonstrate how diversity as a "labor-saving device"—both a "trick" and "dodge" (Ngai 2017, 468–70, citing North 2008)—has been abbreviated into acts of cultural tourism and consumption.

Simultaneously, the narratives of comics themselves also rely on gimmicks. Khor's critique of the quest for authenticity as stand-in for cultural understanding is made possible because of the iterative nature of this experience. The exotification of people through the fetishization of food cultures as commodity object, in the device of "seeking authentic food," offers a readily accessible means to make sense of entangled convergences of colonialism and migration in cultural production. In the production of racialized aesthetics and subsequent online circulation, comics can function as a form of abstract labor. Online comics must also circulate for their value to be realized. As the commodity is made of a duality of abstract and concrete dimensions, abstract labor is thus dialectically related to concrete labor, which represents the racial, gendered, and qualitatively distinct form of actual labor rendered abstract as a value expression—"the law of value obscures the racial and gendered character of labor power" (Day 2016, 9). In referring to Karl Marx's *Grundisse* ([1939] 1993), Ngai (2015) writes, "It is crucial to emphasize that abstract labor is not an abstraction by thought, but rather achieved by the collective practice of actors who do not know they are achieving it. . . . The '*connection of the individual with all,* but at the same time also *the independence of this connection from the individual*'" (37–39). Gimmicks also abbreviate work and time by producing a frame that repeatedly flashes a particular logic. In this way, readers can read a comic and believe they easily understand racialized anger. For example, Khor's anger and her "cranky immigrant" subjectivity become legible through the frame of her being angry about ways that other people consume and categorize ethnic food. What Khor wants is for readers to understand how the legacies and logics of colonialism and racial capitalism produce the myth of "authenticity"; to do this, the complexities of these legacies and logics must become simplified.

(Un)Happy Circulations

The organization of information and communications also organizes shared experiences, meanings, and *feelings* that form and inform different communities. In the essay "The Uses of Anger," Audre Lorde ([1981] 1984b) writes that "anger is loaded with information and energy" (127). Anger becomes an arsenal that is useful against the forces that brought that anger into being. If articulated with precision, anger can produce insights into power to recognize differences and generate change toward racial justice. Anger demands self-reflexivity. Racial anger as shared information translates anger into gestures, speech, and writing. As a medium, online comics organize visuals spatially through the careful arrangement of objects within panels, as well as the organization of panels themselves. Information flows throughout the story to move racial anger in ways that produce feelings of collectivity and sometimes disruptive breaks.

In responding to racism, online comics can express, translate, and modulate anger. Sometimes, anger gets switched on and then off. It can be held in and later displaced. Anger can isolate. Anger breaks and bursts. Throughout both of Khor's comics, her character models patience and politeness in interactions with other characters, although "something simmers underneath the surface, something angry and rebellious" (Khor 2014b). In *Yellow Ranger*, Khor repeatedly outlines moments when people ask her where she is from or where her parents are from. She translates the question and feeling of frustration and being "sick of being expected to tell nosey white men" where she is from for the reader through various anecdotes such as an incident with a barista misspelling her name to be "more exotic" or a first date who tells her that he "loves Asian girls": "you're all so tiny." She juxtaposes these anecdotes with her internal monologue that interprets the racial meaning of these moments and that embraces the function and state of anger through the proliferative production of snarky, humorous images and text. Notably, near the end of *Yellow Ranger*, after multiple iterations of Khor's character being told she is "exotic," she exclaims, "I am going to shove my tiny exotic Asian fist so far up your ass that you're going to have the most exotic rectal prolapse in the Western world, DICKBUCKET" (2014b). Sara Ahmed (2017) calls this a moment of "snap"—when racial anger breaks apart the comfort, preservation, and protection of Whiteness—-a moment when one realizes what one does not have to be, such as rethinking fixed attachments or declining normative impulses of connection.

While Khor's comic functions as racialized anger that tells an unhappy narrative and exposes the fractures, costs, and erasures of the perceived happy sociality of everyday space, the form of the comic translates this anger into a "happy object" (Ahmed 2004). Khor's writing and drawings, like the cultural bingo card, tiny exotic fist, and Yellow Ranger, are punchily humorous. Although she is cranky and angry, her comics take on a lighthearted, teasing tone, poking fun while taking on more serious topics. Bad feelings get converted into a happy commodity-object. *Yellow Ranger* was originally published on the popular online feminist humor site *The Toast*[7] and was tagged as "literally perfect things we are happy to publish" (Khor 2014b). To date, the comic has over 190 comments, many of which say things like, "I love this so much!"; "This is perfect"; and "This encompassed my feelings about everything" (comments by shirleymacp, tiffany, and rauzi, Khor 2014b). On the other hand, *Colorlines* described Cheung-Miaw's comic *Dear Brother* as "heartbreaking" in its capacity to demonstrate the importance and necessity of Asian and Black solidarity against police brutality (Rao 2016); in circulating the comic on Twitter, users have also described it as "powerful." In reflections on teaching *Dear Brother* in the classroom, Caroline Kyungah Hong (2017) describes the letter frame and hand-drawn aesthetic as "making the piece feel really intimate and personal."

Comics are aligned with affective communities. Within affective economies, the intensity of attachment of subject and object mediates a relationships between psychic and social and between individual and collective; emotions align people with communities and align bodily space in digital space (Ahmed 2004). Objects, through their circulation, accumulate affective value—as subjects, we can align ourselves with affective communities by investing in similar objects as causes of happiness, sadness, anger, and so on. By relaying Khor's own experiences, her comics create individual moments of identification when readers feel uniquely understood. The critique of power in Khor's comics lies within interpersonal dynamics that cause racial injury through the everyday interrogation of "otherness." The possible change in these comics gestures toward individual behavior—one can stop asking "Where are you from?" or saying "just eat it" without turning sustenance into an "adventure story." Cheung-Miaw's comics use the familial and the personal to challenge readers who may feel unaffected by police violence to make connections toward broader struggles for liberation—like a sister writing a letter to her younger brother who becomes a police officer and shoots an unarmed Black trans youth.[8]

Cheung-Miaw's comic *Dear Brother* was originally published in the comic book anthology *APB: Artists against Police Brutality*, a benefit project that donated proceeds to the organization the Innocence Project. The comic was later posted on *Colorlines*, the daily news site published by Race Forward. *Two Mothers* was originally posted anonymously on the *Asians4Peace* Tumblr site, a primarily Chinese-language blog emphasizing justice for Akai Gurley, and then later on the Asian American Writers' Workshop site. These websites are explicitly focused on racial justice, using different media and literary forms to address issues such as policing and mass incarceration. The networked spread of Cheung-Miaw's comics is much more targeted, circulating primarily among digital spaces that are already committed to engaging the difficulty of addressing anti-Blackness among non-Black Asian American communities. The pedagogical aim of her comics pushes readers to understand intimate registers of racialized state violence beyond individual experiences.

While both Khor's and Cheung-Miaw's comics demonstrate the ways certain behaviors perpetuate social structures within White supremacy, they do so at different scales and registers. The circulation of these objects within affective economies also demonstrates how different types of political and racial critique get valued across digital spaces—more difficult forms of critique circulate less widely and less readily into mainstream spaces. Khor's comics circulate in more "mainstream" networks, where readers may fall along a broad range of political engagement, including not at all. Cheung-Miaw's comics circulate within networks of progressive Asian American online publics and people connected to racial justice. Where readers might more readily identify with personal experiences of racism, self-reflection on participation within larger systems of racism can be trickier. However, Khor's comics can be seen as entry points for readers to recognize racism as not just individual but part of larger systems and histories and to be moved to locate broader scales of racial violence beyond personal injury.

Conclusion

As a way to intervene in politics via cultural work, artists engage in a specific type of time-saving labor that reproduces racialized anger and racial injury as visual objects that can be more readily understood by various audiences that may or may not already be attending to questions and issues of social justice. Through the aesthetic and publicly accessible form of the comic, artists can make racial and political critique more legible. By mediating how racial identity functions as a political argument, online comics play a role in how racial anger can mobilize political subjectivities by producing spaces of political encounter, bodily experiences of politics, and affective frames that shape politics. Rather than discuss the political efficacy of online activism and networks of circulation, I have focused primarily on the ways aesthetics and narrative mobilize racial affect to engage comics as a form within a larger genre of social justice education and also have discussed the process of producing aesthetics and affects of racial critique in minor forms. This analysis also gestures toward a future discussion around the labor of other online cultural workers whose production focuses on translating social justice and racial injury into something that can be readily understood (and perhaps later presumed to be "knowable"). What kind of work does the cultural production of defining, naming, and describing racial injuries in ways that make such injuries legible actually do? What forms of redress are then made (im)possible?

Notes

1. With regard to the artists' background, Khor self-identifies as a sculptor, cartoonist, and installation artist, and Cheung-Miaw self-identifies as an educator and

cartoonist and has previously worked as a community organizer for labor rights in the restaurant industry.

2. In Edward Said's (1978) *Orientalism*, he describes Orientalism as a system of knowledge as well as an imperial project and practice in which the "Orient" was identified against the "West." Further, Ella Shohat's (2001) introduction to *Talking Visions: Multicultural Feminism in a Transnational Age* discusses the "eroticizing of geography." As seemingly faraway cultures and places begin being defined by objects, so-called exotic aesthetics also end up getting imposed onto people and their physical appearance.

3. To read the version of Cheung-Miaw's comic *Two Mothers* hosted on her site, one clicks, holds, and swipes away the top image to view the next image set.

4. In a historical connotation, "yellow" also signifies "Yellow Peril," a period when East Asians were feared as immoral, economic threats to the US nation-state.

5. Comparatively, readers may also be interested in Lela Lee's character cast for her comic series *Angry Little Girls* (angrylittlegirls.com), which also uses simple visual cues around hair and skin color as ways to signify race.

6. This photograph of Kochiyama and Malcolm X is often described as one of her most "iconic" images with regard to her public recognition of her activism, even though she is unidentified in the original *Life* publication. While more formal historical records of Kochiyama remain sparse, many artists and organizers have created multiple media artifacts recognizing her work. For more, see the Smithsonian Asian Pacific American Center's *Folk Hero: Remembering Yuri Kochiyama through Grassroots Art* exhibit.

7. When *The Toast* closed in 2016, many media outlets such as NPR and Slate lamented the loss; Vox describes it as one of the "weirdest and most beautiful places on the Internet." As a site, *The Toast* does not have broad, mainstream appeal, yet it was incredibly popular across different online communities, given the site's relatable quality, in which readers feel as if pieces were written specifically for them. See Quinn 2016; Grady 2018.

8. The structure of Cheung-Miaw's comic *Dear Brother* is a letter from a sister to her brother, using a mode of intimate address to make a broader statement about Asian-Black relations and racial positioning in the United States. A similar project is the crowdsourced initiative Letters for Black Lives, which culturally and linguistically translates letters by children of immigrants about anti-Black racism to their parents.

5

The News Media and the Racialization of American Poverty

MARTIN GILENS AND NIAMH COSTELLO

Given the dominant role that race has long played in American social life, it is no surprise that news coverage of social issues often has a decidedly racial character. But racial realities and racial portrayals of social issues in the mass media can diverge dramatically. And portrayals can shift radically even when the underlying reality remains relatively constant. In popular discourse, poverty is now strongly associated with racial minorities, especially African Americans. But for decades, discussions of American poverty neglected Blacks altogether. Although African Americans have always been disproportionately poor,[1] Black poverty was ignored by White society throughout most of our history.

In this chapter, we explore the coverage of poverty in four American newspapers in the 1960s. Expanding on the analyses of national newsmagazine content in Martin Gilens's *Why Americans Hate Welfare* (1999), we address three key questions: First, did attention to poverty in local newspapers expand in the 1960s in parallel alongside the increased attention to poverty in the national newsmagazines? Second, did newspaper coverage of poverty become "racialized" in the mid-1960s, paralleling trends in the national newsmagazines? And third, did the racialization of poverty coverage reflect the different contexts of American cities that had smaller or larger African American communities?

Our analyses of newspaper content adds to our understanding of the racialization of poverty coverage in the American news media in two ways. First, we add considerable new data to Gilens's (1999) analyses of newsmagazine content from the 1960s. Second, by leveraging variation in the racial context of American cities, we can assess Gilens's claim that the most important factor explaining the racialization of poverty in the news in the 1960s was a turn toward a more negative discourse about poverty, not the increased visibility of poor Blacks resulting from decades of migration from the rural South to nonsouthern cities, the changing composition of welfare recipients, or the riots in American cities that took place in those years.

Previous Research on Race and Poverty in the American News Media

The most extensive previous research on racial portrayals of poverty in the United States is Martin Gilens's *Why Americans Hate Welfare: Race, Media, and the Politics of Antipoverty Policy* (1999) and associated publications (Gilens 1996, 2000, 2004). Gilens analyzed the coverage of poverty in the three most widely read weekly newsmagazines—*Time*, *Newsweek*, and *U.S. News and World Report*—between 1950 and 1992. He chose these magazines, he explained, because they were widely read, were national in scope and distribution, and had been published continuously for many decades. During the 1950–92 period, Gilens found 1,256 stories on poverty and related topics.[2]

To determine the racial content of newsmagazine coverage of poverty, each poor person pictured in each of these stories was identified as Black, non-Black, or undeterminable. In all, Gilens found 6,117 pictures of individual poor people among the 1,256 poverty stories, and of these race could be determined for 4,388, or 72 percent. Gilens focused on African Americans rather than other racial or ethnic minorities because Blacks constituted by far the largest minority group among America's poor in earlier decades.[3]

Over the forty-three years of newsmagazine content that Gilens analyzed, African Americans made up over half (53.4 percent) of all pictures of poor people, with only minor variation across magazines.[4] In reality, the average percentage of African Americans among the poor during this period was 29.3 percent.[5] This strong overrepresentation of Blacks among the poor in newsmagazines is consistent with the highly racialized nature of poverty in public discourse and consistent with surveys that show the American public to strongly associate poverty with African Americans.[6] But Gilens also found dramatic differences over time in both the amount of attention the newsmagazines devoted to poverty and the extent to which they featured Black faces in their portrayals of the poor.

Newsmagazine coverage of poverty was virtually absent in the 1950s, spiked briefly in 1961 in response to new Kennedy-administration antipoverty initiatives, and then jumped dramatically starting in 1964, peaking in 1968 and 1969 before tapering off. The racial portrayal of poverty also changed dramatically in the mid-1960s, Gilens found. Few Blacks were featured in poverty stories during the 1950s and early 1960s. But the racial composition of the poor in newsmagazines jumped dramatically from 27 percent in 1964 to 49 percent in 1965, peaking at 72 percent in 1967. Although the true racial composition of the American poor remained stable, the face of poverty in these newsmagazines increasingly became that of Black Americans between 1964 and 1967.

The portrayal of the poor never returned to its previous, overwhelmingly White, orientation in the following decades. Although there were important declines and fluctuations in the extent to which Blacks were overrepresented in pictures of poverty, African Americans have dominated news-media images of the poor since the late 1960s. Between 1967 and 1992, Blacks averaged 57 percent of the poor people pictured in these three magazines.

The most obvious explanations for the news media's changing racial portrayal of the poor—the civil rights movement and the urban riots of the mid-1960s—played a role but cannot account for the nature or timing of these shifts in media images. Instead, Gilens argued, the changing racial images of the poor in the newsmagazines is best understood as reflecting two very different processes that converged in the mid-1960s.

First, the stage was set by a series of historical changes and events that made Black poverty a less remote concern for White Americans. These included the migration of African Americans from the rural South to the urban North, the increasing representation of Blacks among Aid to Families with Dependent Children (AFDC) beneficiaries, the civil rights movement, and the riots of the mid-1960s. But these changes only created the environment in which racial portrayals of poverty were transformed. The proximate cause of that transformation, Gilens argued, was the shift in the moral tone of poverty coverage in the news. As news stories about the poor became less sympathetic, the images of poor Blacks in the newsmagazines swelled.

Newsmagazine stories on poverty in 1964 were strongly focused on President Johnson's War on Poverty (announced in January of that year). These stories, like earlier poverty coverage in the 1960s, portrayed America's poor as predominantly White. A good example of this overall tendency is the most substantial poverty story of the year, a twelve-page cover story called "Poverty, U.S.A." that *Newsweek* ran on February 17. The cover of the magazine showed a White girl, about eight or ten years old, looking out from a rustic shack, her hair disheveled and her face covered with dirt. As this picture suggests, the story had a strong focus on Appalachia, but it profiled a variety of poor people from around the country. Reflecting a more accurate representation than would be seen later in the era, only fourteen of the fifty-four poor people pictured in this story (26 percent) were Black.

This story was typical of War on Poverty coverage during 1964 in its substantial focus on rural poverty, its emphasis on images of poor Whites, and its generally neutral tone toward the War on Poverty. Like this story, most of the early coverage of the War on Poverty consisted of descriptions of antipoverty programs, profiles of Johnson's "poverty warriors," and accounts of poverty in America, most often illustrated with examples of individual poor people. Clearly, the expansion of news coverage that accompanied the War on Poverty did not coincide with the racialization of poverty images. At its inception at least, the War on Poverty was not portrayed by the news media as a program for Blacks.

The clear turning point in the racialization of poverty in these news-magazines came in 1965, when the percentage of Blacks among pictures of the poor jumped to 49 percent from only from 27 percent the year before. One factor that clearly does *not* explain the racialization of poverty in the news during this period is true change in the proportion of Blacks among the poor, which increased only marginally between the early and late 1960s (from 27 percent to 30 percent). Nor can the dramatic change in the racial portrayal of poverty be attributed to a broader increase in the representation of African Americans in these newsmagazines. In fact, the overall proportion of African Americans actually declined slightly between 1964 and 1965.[7]

What did change dramatically between 1964 and 1965 was the evaluative tone of stories covering welfare and the War on Poverty. Whereas coverage in 1964 focused on the initiation of the War on Poverty and general descriptions of the American poor, stories in 1965 were much more critical examinations of the government's antipoverty efforts. First, many stories questioned Sargent Shriver's leadership of the antipoverty effort, focusing on mismanagement, confusion, and waste in the Office of Economic Opportunity. Second, considerable attention was devoted to local disputes between city government and community groups over control of War on Poverty resources. Finally, substantial coverage focused on difficulties within the Job Corps program, one of the first War on Poverty programs to get off the ground.

As coverage of the War on Poverty became more critical, portrayals of the poor became "more Black." This association of African Americans with negative stories on poverty is clearest in coverage of the Job Corps. The most visible of the War on Poverty's numerous job-training programs, the Job Corps consisted of dozens of residential centers in both urban and rural locations at which young men (and less often young women) were to learn discipline along with basic job skills.

Newsmagazine coverage of the Job Corps program focused on problems such as poor screening of participants, inadequate facilities, and high dropout rates. But the most sensational objections concerned the behavior of Job Corps members and the aversion to Job Corps centers by nearby towns. For example, a long story in *U.S. News and World Report* published in July 1965 (and illustrated with about equal numbers of Blacks and non-Blacks) reported charges of "rowdyism" at Job Corps centers, including a dormitory riot in Tongue Point, Oregon, "in which lead pipes were hurled" and the expulsion of eight girls from a center in St. Petersburg, Florida, for drinking. "Another worry," the story indicated, was the "antagonism between Corpsmen and nearby townsmen." People in Astoria, Oregon, for example, "complain about hearing obscene language at the movie theater," while residents of Marion, Illinois, were upset about a disturbance at a roller-skating rink that occurred when some Job Corps members showed up with liquor. Although these incidents were not explicitly linked to Black Job Corps participants, the pictures of Blacks in Job Corps stories (comprising 55 percent of all Job Corps members pictured) was much higher than the proportion of African Americans pictured in the more neutral stories about the War on Poverty from the previous year.

One alternative explanation for the upsurge in Black faces in news-magazine poverty stories in 1965 is the Watts riots in Los Angeles, which began on August 11 of that year. The large number of "race riots" during the summers of the 1965 through 1967 did draw increased national attention to Black poverty (as did a shift in emphasis among civil rights leaders from legal to economic inequality after the passage of the 1964 Civil Rights Act and the 1965 Voting Rights Act). But the shift in the racial representation of the poor occurred before the first large-scale urban riots. The proportion of African Americans in newsmagazine poverty stories was just as great in the first half of 1965 (before the Watts riots) as it was in the second half. In addition, poverty stories in the second half of 1965 continued to focus on the War on Poverty, with only one-quarter of such stories even mentioning the uprisings in Black neighborhoods.

Our focus in this chapter is on this fundamental shift in news coverage of poverty that took place in the mid-1960s. Gilens showed that in the following decades, African Americans continued to be found in large numbers in negative stories on poverty but were comparatively absent when poverty stories took a more sympathetic tone. For example, the early 1980s saw high levels of unemployment and increasing hardships for less-well-off Americans during the "Reagan recession." Newsmagazine coverage of poverty focused on the suffering caused by President Reagan's efforts to "trim the safety net" and on formerly middle-class Americans who had fallen into poverty.

A good example is *Newsweek*'s prominent story titled "The Hard-Luck Christmas of '82," which proclaimed, "With 12 million unemployed and 2 million homeless, private charity cannot make up for federal cutbacks." The story went on to describe the desperate condition of poor families living in camp tents or in automobiles, portraying them as the noble victims "who are paying the price of America's failure of nerve in the war on poverty" (*Newsweek* 1982, 12). Reflecting the general lack of Black faces in these sympathetic poverty stories, "The Hard-Luck Christmas of '82" included only three African Americans among the eighteen poor people pictured.[8] Overall, Blacks made up only 30 percent of the poor people pictured in general stories on poverty and antipoverty programs from 1982 to 1983.

These sympathetic stories from the early 1980s contrasted sharply with negative stories about welfare that dominated newsmagazine coverage in the early 1970s. Coverage of poverty in these years focused largely on perceived problems with welfare and efforts at welfare reform. The percentage of all Americans receiving welfare increased dramatically from about 2 percent in the mid-1960s to about 6 percent in the mid-1970s. By the early 1970s, the expansion of welfare came to be viewed as an urgent national problem that demanded action. Newsmagazine stories during 1972 and 1973 almost invariably referred to this situation as the "welfare mess" and published story after story focused on mismanagement in state welfare bureaucracies and abuse of welfare by people who could be supporting themselves.

Poor people and welfare recipients were no more likely to be Black during 1972–73 than they were a few years earlier. Nevertheless, this period of sustained negative coverage of welfare portrayed poor people and welfare recipients as Black to the greatest extent of any point in the forty-three years of coverage that Gilens examined. Three-quarters of all poor people pictured in newsmagazine poverty stories during 1972 and 1973 were Black. The racialized vilification of antipoverty programs during this period has had long-term consequences for American politics. This racial demonization has contributed to the current appeal of candidates who promise to cut welfare and reduce the size of government, even among poor Whites who benefit from a range of government social programs (Mettler 2018; Sides, Tesler, and Vavreck 2018).

In addition to analyzing change over time, Gilens examined the racial representations of different subgroups of the poor. Since the true proportion of African Americans differs across different poverty subgroups, some of the differences in racial portrayals over time may be accounted for by the shifts in focus on different subgroups. For example, in the mid-1960s, Blacks accounted for about 30 percent of all poor people but about 40 percent of welfare recipients. Nevertheless, Gilens (1999, 127–29) showed that actual variation in the racial composition of poverty subgroups could only account for a small portion of the variation in newsmagazine portrayals, which differed dramatically (and far more than an accurate portrayal would warrant).

It is not surprising, of course, that poverty is portrayed in a more sympathetic light during economic hard times or that welfare recipients are treated less sympathetically than struggling low-wage workers are. What is noteworthy, however, is that along with shifts in the tone of news reporting on the poor come shifts in the racial mix of the poor people featured in news stories. The true proportion of Blacks among America's poor hardly changed at all during the entire latter half of the twentieth century. But the racial portrayals of the poor in newsmagazines shifted dramatically as media attention became more and less sympathetic in response to the changing political and economic contexts over those years.

The Limitations of Earlier Research

Gilens's analyses of newsmagazines has been extended to more recent years by Rosalee Clawson and Rakyua Trice (2000) and Bas van Doorn (2015). But to date, we know of no other analyses of the racialization of poverty coverage during the 1960s. Although Gilens augmented his study of newsmagazines with similar content analysis of television news, TV news archives do not extend before 1968. Consequently, our understanding of the most critical period of changing media portrayals of poverty currently rest on just three national news magazines.

As Gilens argued, the three newsmagazines he examined were influential not only in their wide readership but also as sources that other journalists turned to. Yet the combined newsmagazine circulation of about nine million in the mid-1960s paled in comparison to daily newspapers, which had a combined circulation of about sixty million at the time. In addition, Gilens's focus on national news may have obscured important variation in the way poverty was covered in the widely varying racial contexts of different American cities.

By turning our attention to daily newspapers from four cities, we can assess whether the patterns that Gilens documented in newsmagazines during the 1960s held true for other news media as well, thus confirming or complicating some of Gilens's core findings. In addition, we can leverage the variation in local racial context to assess Gilens's account of the factors that gave rise to the racialization of poverty in the American news media. As noted earlier, Gilens attributed the timing of racialized poverty news in the mid-1960s to the emergence of a more negative discourse on poverty. He argued that the greater visibility of the Black poor (as a result of migration out of the rural South and the opening up of welfare programs to previously excluded African American poor) was a "background condition" that did not explain the abrupt shift in racialized media images of poverty. We can assess this account by contrasting news coverage of poverty in cities with large and small African American populations. If increasing visibility, rather than negative discourse, played a central role in explaining the racialization of poverty in the American news media, then we would expect to find significantly greater attention to Black poverty in cities with higher proportions of African Americans and the timing of racialized coverage to be largely independent of the negative turn in national news media in response to the growing criticism of War on Poverty programs in 1965.

Coverage of Poverty in Four Local Newspapers, 1960–70

To examine newspaper coverage of poverty during the 1960s, we analyzed the largest-circulation daily paper in four cities, two with larger proportions of African Americans (Atlanta and Baltimore) and two with smaller proportions (Boston and Hartford). We chose these cities because their largest-circulation papers are available in the Pro-Quest Historical Newspaper archive for the relevant years with both abstract and full text searching availability, and they are all major population centers.[9]

To identify articles on poverty in these four newspapers, we developed a keyword search that contained thirteen referents to poverty or antipoverty programs. After examining the articles retrieved, we identified twenty-nine exclusion criteria designed to filter out stories that

TABLE 5.1. Newspapers Analyzed

City	Newspaper	Percentage African American, 1960	Number of poverty stories, 1960–1970	Percentage poverty stories among all stories, 1960–1970
Boston	Boston Globe	3.0	2,637	0.46
Hartford	Hartford Courant	5.2	3,503	0.50
Atlanta	Atlanta Constitution	22.8	2,324	0.38
Baltimore	Baltimore Sun	21.4	4,250	0.29

Sources: Percentage African American: US Bureau of the Census 1971.

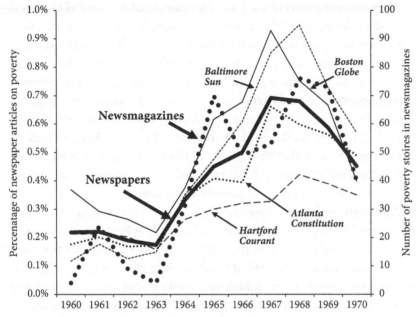

Figure 5.1. Attention to poverty in newspapers and newsmagazines.

were not relevant (e.g., stories about poverty in other countries or stories about health care or education that referred to the Department of Health, Education, and Welfare).[10] Across the eleven years from 1960 through 1970, our search retrieved 12,714 articles on poverty in the United States (table 5.1).

Did Attention to Poverty in Local News Expand in the 1960s in Parallel to Attention to Poverty in National Newsmagazines?

We first examine changes over time in newspaper attention to poverty, to determine whether patterns in these four newspapers parallel the patterns that Gilens found in his study of national newsmagazines. Figure 5.1 shows that this was in fact the case. The solid thick line in the figure shows the average percentage of poverty stories out of all stories published in these four newspapers in each year and can be compared with the dotted thick line, which shows the number of newsmagazine poverty stories.[11]

Attention to poverty in the four cities examined did parallel the trend that Gilens found for national newsmagazines. In both media, attention to poverty was quite sparse in the early 1960s, rose dramatically starting in 1964, and peaked in 1968. Poverty coverage in the newspapers did increase somewhat more gradually than was the case in the national newsmagazines, but the overall pattern and timing of both the increase in attention to poverty and the (less dramatic) decline in attention in the late 1960s are similar in the two different media. This provides an initial confirmation that the content of the newsmagazines that Gilens studied was not idiosyncratic but reflected broader trends in the American news media's coverage of poverty at the time.

Although the four newspapers all showed similar patterns over time, they varied by degree. The *Baltimore Sun* and the *Boston Globe* showed the most dramatic increases in attention to poverty between the early and late 1960s, and the *Hartford Courant* showed the least. In addition, we see a somewhat larger number of poverty stories around 1960 in the *Sun* compared to the other three papers. (This deviation is explained by the *Sun*'s coverage of a high-profile local effort to combat welfare fraud, which accounted for about two-thirds of the *Sun*'s poverty-related stories in 1960, an observation we return to shortly.)

Did Local News Coverage of Poverty Become "Racialized" in the Mid-1960s, Paralleling Trends in National Newsmagazines?

Gilens's analysis of the racialization of poverty in newsmagazines relied on the pictures of poor people in poverty-related stories. Gilens argued that even when the race of the poor was not explicitly discussed in the text of these articles (as it seldom was), the pictures gave readers impactful information about the racial composition of America's poor.

Compared to the weekly newsmagazines that Gilens examined, newspapers contain far more stories per year and far fewer pictures per story (in fact, few of the poverty-related newspaper stories from these years contained any pictures of poor people at all). Accordingly, our analysis of these newspaper stories focuses not on pictures but on textual references to African Americans.[12] Consequently, we cannot directly compare the extent to which poverty coverage in the two media was racialized. But we can compare the patterns of change over time

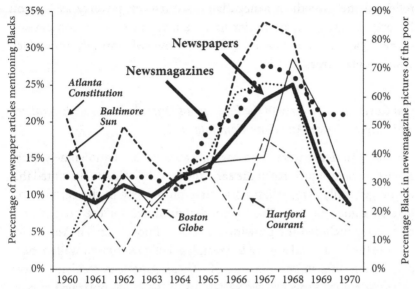

Figure 5.2. The racialization of poverty coverage in newspapers and newsmagazines.

to assess whether the trends in racialized portrayals of the poor were parallel. Following Gilens's earlier analyses, we focus on African Americans to the exclusion of other racial and ethnic minorities. (As noted earlier, Blacks composed the overwhelming majority of poor non-White Americans during the 1960s.)

Figure 5.2 shows similar trends in the racialization of poverty in local newspapers and national newsmagazines. Recognizing that one cannot directly compare pictorial content and textual references, it is nevertheless clear that attention to African Americans in poverty coverage in both media increased substantially in the mid-1960s. The pictorial representations in newsmagazines changed more suddenly between 1964 and 1967, while the newspaper mentions of African Americans in stories on poverty increased more gradually and peaked one year later (in 1968 rather than 1967). In both media, attention to Blacks in poverty coverage waned toward the end of the 1960s.

These broadly parallel trajectories does not mean that the factors shaping the racialization of poverty coverage were necessarily the same in the national newsmagazines and the local newspapers. To assess Gilens's argument that the racialization of poverty in newsmagazines reflected the growth of a negative discourse on poverty as War on Poverty programs came under fire, we next turn to the comparison of newspapers from heavily Black and overwhelmingly non-Black cosmopolitan areas.

Did Coverage of Poverty in the Early 1960s Differ in Places with Smaller and Larger African American Communities?

African Americans were almost wholly absent from national newsmagazine coverage of poverty in the early 1960s. While Gilens attributed this to the generally sympathetic discourse on poverty in the early 1960s, he also argued that the "background conditions" for the racialization of poverty included the growing numbers of poor African Americans outside the South and among the recipients of government welfare benefits. Given differing proportions of African American residents across cities, we might expect to see variations in the racial portrayal of poverty in cities with larger and smaller African American populations. In other words, we can shed some light on the relative importance of visibility versus political context (i.e., an unsympathetic orientation toward the poor) in explaining the racialization of poverty in the news.

The thick solid line in figure 5.3 shows the percentage of poverty stories that referenced African Americans in the two cities with higher proportions of Blacks (Baltimore and Atlanta), while the thick dashed line shows the same thing for the two cities with lower proportions of Blacks (Boston and Hartford). In most years, the newspapers in Baltimore and Atlanta did reference Black poverty at a higher rate than those in Boston and Hartford did. At the same time, it is clear that in both sets of cities, attention to Blacks in newspaper coverage of poverty traced a similar trajectory, compatible with the trends Gilens observed in national newsmagazines: poverty stories in the early 1960s rarely mentioned Blacks; attention to Black poverty grew in the mid-1960s and then waned in the latter years of the decade. This bolsters one of Gilens's key findings from his analysis of newsmagazines and suggests that shifts in the national discourse on poverty exerted a broad influence on the racial portrayal of the poor across a variety of news media.

The one year that diverges the most from this general pattern is 1960, when African Americans were essentially absent from newspaper

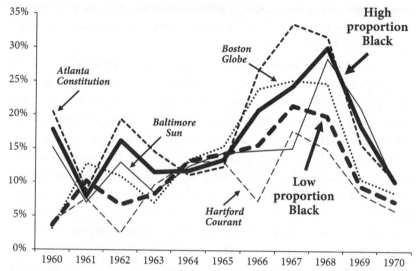

Figure 5.3. Percentage of newspaper poverty stories featuring Blacks in cities with low and high Black populations.

coverage of poverty in the two low-Black-population cities of Boston and Hartford (as they were in the national newsmagazines) but were mentioned in almost one out of five poverty stories in Atlanta and Baltimore. In Baltimore, these stories largely focused on welfare fraud and a local effort to pare the welfare rolls, as noted earlier. In Atlanta, in contrast, stories referencing Black poverty in 1960 frequently described new or proposed urban redevelopment programs and efforts to expand public housing and "clean up" blighted Black neighborhoods. These stories were more sympathetic to poor Blacks than were the stories on welfare fraud in the *Baltimore Sun*.

One possible explanation for the unexpectedly positive portrayal of the Black poor in Atlanta in 1960 is as follows: Discourse on poverty in the American news media occasionally takes on a positive valence (specifically, when new antipoverty efforts are first being discussed, when economic downturns generate sympathy for the less well-off, and when stories focus on sympathetic subgroups of the poor, like the elderly or infirm). Local news coverage will sometimes reflect these more positive discourses, as the *Atlanta Constitution*'s coverage of new urban-renewal programs in 1960 did. In places with large African American populations, these sympathetic stories—especially if they reference local events or conditions—will tend to connect their positive portrayals with poor Blacks.

Assessing this hypothesis would require a much broader analysis of the thousands of poverty stories collected from these four newspapers—a project that is beyond the scope of this chapter. But even if positive stories on poverty were more likely to feature African Americans in heavily Black cities than in cities with smaller Black populations, two countervailing factors might nevertheless result in overwhelmingly negative portrayals of the Black poor overall, even in these more heavily Black places. First, newspapers in cities with large Black populations might be even more likely to reference poor Blacks in negative poverty stories than in positive poverty stories. And second, compared with cities with small proportions of African Americans, newspapers in cities with large Black populations might publish more negative and fewer positive poverty stories. This latter pattern is consistent with poverty coverage in Atlanta and Baltimore in 1960: the *Baltimore Sun*'s largely negative stories about Black poverty outnumbered the *Atlanta Constitution*'s largely positive stories thirty-two to twenty, and poverty coverage in Baltimore in the same year was about twice as prominent as poverty coverage in Atlanta (0.37 percent of all news stories compared with 0.18 percent).

Of course, one set of positive news stories about Black poverty in one city in one year hardly indicates a solid break from the broader pattern of negative characterizations of the Black poor. Moreover, the *Baltimore Sun*'s negative and more numerous coverage of Black poverty in that same year stands as a clear counterexample. Nevertheless, the possibility of at least a partial deviation from the consistent pattern of negative portrayals of the Black poor in the American news media suggests that future analyses of newspaper poverty coverage across different cities and years might shed more light on exceptions to the socially destructive portrayals of poor Blacks.

Conclusion

Beliefs about racial minorities now dominate Americans' understating of poverty, shape their views of the poor, and inform their support or opposition to antipoverty programs. But this was not always the case. The evidence in this chapter reinforces earlier findings that poverty became racialized in the American news media in the 1960s. The increased attention to the poor across this decade in both local and national news outlets was accompanied by increased attention to Black poverty—not simply as a function of the greater attention to all subgroups of the poor but as a proportion of all news coverage of poverty.

The greater visibility of poverty in general and Black poverty in particular during these years did not reflect a worsening of the underlying realities. Poverty rates were declining in America during the 1960s, and the percentage of African Americans among the poor held steady (Gilens 1999, 113–14). None of the cities whose newspapers we analyzed experienced substantial change in the proportion of Black residents during these years, meaning that the greater attention to Black poverty was not driven by changes in local racial demography.

In Gilens's analyses of national newsmagazines, he explained the racialization of the poor as a consequence of the changed discourse toward poverty that occurred as a result of attacks on War on Poverty programs in the mid-1960s. He went on to show that newsmagazine stories sympathetic to poverty over the following decades tended to be illustrated with poor Whites and unsympathetic stories with poor Blacks. This held true whether the sympathetic stories reflected concern for the less well-off expressed during economic downturns or concern for the more "deserving" subgroups of the poor, such as children, the elderly, or the infirm.

Our analyses of newspaper stories largely parallel Gilens's findings in the newsmagazines (and TV news) he studied. But we did find one hint of a potential divergence: while sympathetic newsmagazine stories about proposed or newly adopted antipoverty programs tended to focus on White poverty, similar stories in the *Atlanta Constitution* in 1960 did reference Black poverty at a higher rate than might be expected. This suggests that sympathetic stories in cities with larger African American populations might offer a more positive view of the Black poor than was found in national newsmagazines or might be found in cities with smaller Black populations. Yet any hopes for a more equitable portrayal of the Black poor must be tempered by the more numerous negative stories about the Black poor that appeared in the *Baltimore Sun* in that same year.

The broader takeaway from this chapter, as well as from earlier work on the racialization of poverty in the news, is that media portrayals and social realities can diverge strongly. Journalists are professional observers and chroniclers of our social world. But they are also residents of that world and are exposed to the same stereotypes and misperceptions that characterize society at large. The racialization of poverty in the mid-1960s reflects both the previously ignored reality of Black poverty in America and the emergence of a racially exaggerated and stereotyped image of America's poor. In the decades since, this image has served to undercut support for antipoverty programs and reinforce the cynicism toward recipients of government assistance that is seen in America today. Race is one of the most important and powerful lenses through which Americans make sense of their society. When news coverage distorts racial realities, citizens' understandings are distorted, and democracy suffers.

Notes

1. Currently, about 21 percent of African Americans fall below the official poverty line, compared with 18 percent of Hispanics and 9 percent of non-Hispanic Whites (US Bureau of the Census 2018c).

2. In Gilens's analyses, he excluded stories that had a primary focus on race relations, civil rights, urban riots, or other racial topics even if those stories also included discussions of poverty. In those contexts, readers would expect to find coverage of Black poverty in particular and might not draw conclusions about the nature of American poverty in general. By excluding race-related stories, however, Gilens's analysis provides a conservative estimate of the extent to which African Americans populated media images of the poor.

3. In 1972, for example, the US Bureau of the Census (2018b) counted 3.2 poor African Americans for every 1 poor Hispanic (figures for the much smaller numbers of poor Asian Americans and Native Americans were not reported).

4. The percentage who were Black in pictures of the poor ranged from 52 percent in *U.S. News and World Report* to 57 percent in *Time*. See Gilens 1999 for details on the coding of race in newsmagazine and television news stories.

5. The figure for the average percentage of Blacks among the poor includes only the years 1960 through 1992, since poverty data broken down by race are not available before 1960.

6. For example, majorities of both Blacks and Whites believe that there are more poor Blacks than poor Whites in the United States, and the average guess when Blacks and Whites are asked what proportion of poor Americans are Black is over 50 percent (Gilens 1999, 137–38).

7. Examining every fifth issue of *Time* and *Newsweek* between January 1963 and December 1965, Gilens (1999) found that the proportion of African Americans (excluding advertisements) in newsmagazine photographs increased from 6.4 percent in 1963 to 8.7 percent in 1964 and then decreased to 5.5 percent in 1965. (The total number of individuals coded in the three years was 2,668, 2,744, and 3,115 for 1963, 1964, and 1965, respectively.)

8. These figures for the "Hard-Luck Christmas" story reflect the adjusted counts of poor people using a maximum of twelve poor people per picture. The raw counts from this story are seventy-three non-Black and seventeen Black poor. In this case, the adjusted percentage Black (3/18 = 17 percent) and the raw percentage Black (17/90 = 19 percent) are quite similar.

9. All four cities were among the fifty most populous metropolitan areas in 1970 (US Bureau of the Census 1971).

10. The full search string applied to each newspaper for each year was "Dtype(Article) AND AB((welfare OR poverty OR ghett* OR "food vouche*" OR homeles* OR "low-income" OR "public housing" OR slum OR AFDC OR ADC OR "job corps" OR indigent OR impoverished) NOT (Israel* OR Siberia OR Japan OR Ecuador OR Chinese OR Peru OR theatre OR Russia* OR "health and welfare" OR Britain OR Nazi OR Europe OR Germany OR France OR Liverpool OR Brazil OR Rome OR "United Nations" OR Tokyo OR China OR India OR Cuba OR Soviet OR animal OR Africa OR Philippin* OR international OR Haiti OR "health, education and welfare")).

11. The ProQuest database content for the *Hartford Courant* appears to contain more nonarticles (e.g., editorials, puzzles, etc.) that are nonetheless labeled as articles than the other three papers. To make the comparisons across papers more comparable, the total number of articles for the *Hartford Courant* is reduced by 31 percent, to match the average proportion of documents identified as articles in the other three papers examined.

12. The search string we added to the poverty keyword search reported in note 10 was ""Blacks" OR "African American" OR "African-American" OR "Negro*" OR "people of color" OR colored." Note that the poverty-related terms had to appear in the news articles' abstract, ensuring that poverty was a central focus of the article. The search for African American–related terms was conducted on the full text of the articles.

6

Process as Product

Native American Filmmaking and Storytelling

JUSTIN DE LEON

Much can be learned from the original stewards of the land we currently call the United States. The Lakota Sioux of the Great Plains, in particular, hold a disproportionately large location in the American imaginary. Quintessential, and often romanticized, images of Native Americans are headdress-wearing, horseback-riding warriors who live in tipis in the Great Plains. These are the *Oceti Sakowin*, or the Seven Council Fires that includes the Lakota, the Nakota, and the Dakota Sioux of the Great Plains.[1]

This chapter asks the questions, What lessons can filmmakers learn from the Lakota approach to constructing a tipi? How can lessons of constructing a tipi transform approaches to filmmaking and the training of filmmakers? How can attentiveness to process transform the purpose, meanings, and outcomes of filmmaking and training? As a critical scholar and film practitioner who is interested in implications of racialized media, I offer probing questions and cursory connections to open new possibilities for filmmaking praxis.[2] It is not an attempt to craft a definitive take on Indigenous storytelling or Indigenous approaches to filmmaking. This chapter proceeds by examining (1) lessons to be learned from the Lakota tipi, (2) how films are popularly evaluated, (3) Indigenous approaches to storytelling and process, and (4) potentialities of foregrounding process through an example of the Native Film and Storytelling Institute (NFSI), a nascent Native American film-training program that held a pilot program at the University of California, San Diego, in the spring of 2018. The third section, "Indigenous

Approaches to Storytelling and Process," is further divided into five sub-sections: "Power, Peace, and Decolonization"; "Creative Acts as Resistance"; "Cyclical, Not Linear"; "Creative Acts and the Spirit World"; and "Importance of Journey." The chapter concludes with a discussion on learnings and outcomes of NFSI's efforts to reorient approaches to process in filmmaking and training and how attentiveness to process could provide a critical, holistic, and profound space for decolonizing interventions for Native communities and communities of color.

Learning from the Lakota Tipi

There is a unique remoteness about the Great Plains that simultaneously embodies expansive isolation and bustling life.[3] Located at the geographic center of the country, the Great Plains are remote enough that purchasing a plane ticket from one of the coasts is nearly the same cost as flying to Europe. The weather is extreme and unpredictable. It is normal to have long stretches of below-zero temperatures, and when it does get warmer, torrential downpours and tornados batter the Plains. Hail the size of golf balls, windstorms that rip roofs off buildings, grasshopper migrations in which thousands descend on farms, and dry seasons of brush fires are all day-to-day challenges of living in the Great Plains. Even with today's modern amenities, living in this environment is challenging. The original people of this area, the Lakota, have lived in this unforgiving environment for centuries.

The first time I visited South Dakota was in early spring. Just a week prior, in late March, there had been a blizzard. As I pulled off a dirt road onto a smaller muddy path, only one house was visible. But as I got closer, I saw that there were four tipis, a trailer, and multiple tents arranged with a grassy center opening. After I spent some time visiting and observing preparations, a Lakota elder began to speak, and the group of twenty men, women, and children gathered and listened attentively. He began to talk about the Lakota way of life, explaining significant aspects of Lakota culture and prayer. "These young women set up the tipis themselves," he said as he motioned to the tipis now at our back. "We start off [the process] with three poles." A central aspect to the knowledge shared at that gathering was through the construction of the tipis.

Over the past five years I spent a handful of summers on the Lakota reservation in South Dakota. I come into this space from a unique perspective: I am not Native American, but I am a racialized, colonially produced body that is both a product of colonialism and a producer of colonial violence. This is to say that central to my learning from the Lakota is a personal journey of unraveling the complexity of colonial forces that are enacted on myself and my family. Exploring indigeneity in the United States, where my family relocated, is an attempt not to appropriate Indigenous knowledges but, rather, to understand the intersections and productive logics of experience, realities, and teachings and to incorporate them into a larger analytic framework and knowledge.[4] This is the space from which I observe and, ultimately, from which I write.

I found it striking that many of the traditional community gatherings included conversations on the importance of the tipi. As an outsider, I did not know much about tipis other than the obvious, that it was the dwelling structure of the Great Plains tribes. Being on a reservation, I found that tipis are much more than just dwelling structures. The Lakota's very presence was dependent on this ingenious technology of survival. The Lakota construct every pole of the tipi with intention. The first three poles align with particular stars and provide the foundation of the Lakota understanding of the world. The Lakota Tribal University scholar Ronald Goodman (1992) asserts, "[Setting up a tipi] is nothing less than re-creating or replicating a world" (17). This re-creating of the Lakota world requires great attention to process in crafting and erection. The process is equally important as, if not more important than, the outcome of the physical structure. Every detail of the structure is practically, cosmologically, and spiritually calculated. Practically, orienting the door eastward makes the entrance the most protected side of the tipi in the face of harsh winds, also allowing for the first rays of the sun to bring warmth into the structure and symbolizing the meeting of a new day (Marshall 2001). The circular design of the poles makes the tipi structure extremely robust and sturdy, able to withstand tornados, winds, and snowstorms. Retractable top flaps give the ability to use fire even in the most hazardous conditions.

Cosmologically, the first three poles created a star (Goodman 1992). The next seven poles represented the seven sacred directions (north, east, south, west, above, below, and inside), allowing for orientation and stabilization. These first ten poles represent the laws of the world, connecting the celestial and terrestrial, as well as representing morality and ethics. The last two poles act as storm flaps that allow for ventilation and also represent the ability for breath of the spirit to enter and exit, symbolizing the ability to communicate with higher powers. Twelve poles of the tipi symbolize the cyclical nature of life. The internal structure of the tipi and the circular design of the traditional encampment, which consisted of twenty to forty families, acted as a "constant reminder for the inhabitants that life flowed in a circle and that they were unalterably connected to everything that was a part of it" (Marshall 2001, 224). Spiritually, the tipi represents a relationship between the celestial and terrestrial, or divine and earthly. Likewise, for every event, action, or undertaking, there are spiritual and divine principles present and at play. The Sioux historian Vine Deloria Jr. (1995) suggests, "American Indians look at events to determine the spiritual activity supporting or undergirding them" (55). Every aspect of traditional Lakota life is carried out in a sacred manner. Not only was and is the tipi sacred in itself, but so too is the process of constructing the tipi.

How Films Are Evaluated

A film that I worked on was recently nominated for best documentary at one of the longest running Native American film festivals in the country.[5] The night before the showing, there was an awards banquet where prizes were being awarded for the typical categories of best actor, short, documentary, feature, and so on. It was great to see how many Native filmmakers are producing meaningful and professional content. As the night progressed, I noticed an interesting pattern about the winners who took the stage and spoke directly to the audience of a few hundred. They tended to talk about their family, the people who inspired them, the crew they worked with, or those individuals who supported them. They were onstage because of their films, yet instead of speaking directly about the finished product of their works, they spoke almost entirely about the process of making their films. Their most meaningful moments were not about the finalized, sound- and color-mastered film but how they were able to see their creative vision transform into material form and the relationships that made that possible. Even in the process of evaluating the quality of a particular film, one often thinks of elements such as cinematography, storytelling, production, and acting. Rarely considered is the impact of the process of making the film on the empowerment of the community or its impact on those who were part of the filmmaking process.[6]

For a filmmaker, the prizes your films have won, official selections to prestigious film festivals, or winning audience awards are so highly valued. How many screenings, what types of reviews, or even how many views you received through social media are used to measure the success and impact of a film. Academic distribution agreements make arrangements in which initial investments would be made up through DVD sales to universities, libraries, and private individuals. Noticeable in distributors' evaluative metrics is the lack of attention to outcomes related to process, the very same outcomes that so many of the film-makers spoke about while receiving awards.

Moreover, in searching for courses offered by top US film and television programs, you would be hard-pressed to find any course that covers the importance of process-oriented approaches to filmmaking, let alone find a course entirely committed to exploring the importance of process (of training filmmakers and making films). Courses that foreground process, particularly within marginalized communities and Native communities, simply do not exist in the spaces where film is being taught.[7] I have never attended any of these top programs, though I have received film training. One such opportunity was to train with renowned Iranian filmmaker Mohsen Makhmalbaf. Facing censure, exile, and imprisonment, Makhmalbaf used his films to challenge, comment on, and shape Iranian society. He also used his more than twenty feature films to contribute to the communities he worked in, building schools, constructing community centers, and even using film resources to build homes for his amateur homeless actors. While this approach is laudable and worth emulating, even in this setting little attention was given to the importance of process.[8]

Indigenous Approaches to Storytelling and Process

Stories connect Indigenous people to place and purpose, not only acting as vehicles for culture but also allowing for the transfer of knowledge across time, distance, and generation (Kovach 2010). Storytelling acts as an important mechanism that has allowed individuals and groups to create coherent narratives of personhood, identity, and purpose. Though storytelling has been "essential in the creation of all human realities," it has been particularly important for Indigenous peoples, including the Lakota, whose cultures are oral history based (M. Powell 2002, 429).[9] Indigenous stories are wide ranging in theme, from origin stories, stories on worldviews, histories, prayers, traditions, and life lessons to more humorous ones for entertainment or personal expression (Weber-Pillwax 2001). Stories provide lessons of reciprocity, transferring important aspects of culture between peoples and families, as well as providing documentation for lived realities (R. Thomas 2005). Stories honor; they "connect us to how we come to know our place and purpose in the world" (Carlson et al. 2017, 24).

The following is a brief exploration of the role and potentialities of Indigenous storytelling, as well as the spirit-world origins of creativity and process. This includes how stories can be used as power, for peace, and as a tool for decolonization; that creative acts of storytelling can act as resistance; how time, processes, and stories are not linear but cyclical; that creative acts are an important connection to the spirit world; and how there is importance in the journey.

Power, Peace, and Decolonization

There are important roles for stories and storytelling within many Indigenous cultures. They provide a way for Indigenous peoples to awaken possibilities and power. Kim Anderson (2000) explains, "The respect accorded to Native women in many traditional stories provides the foundation for strong Native female identity and helps us retain an understanding of our power" (132). Origin stories and mythology provide the foundations and archetypes to understand and explore cultural values. They are a source of power and revitalization. They can also serve a peacemaking function. Often, when difficult community discussions take place, it is the story by an elder that provides guidance and persuasion. The Anishinaabe political scientist Sheryl Lightfoot (2016) explains the importance of elders' stories: "Contained in that story is a metaphor or central message that convinces the group of the best course of action" (79).

Storytelling can act as a decolonizing methodology, playing a central role in reclaiming humanity and authoring a community's own experience (L. Smith 2012). Colonization, as a structure (Wolfe 2006), is built on dehumanizing attitudes and thoughts. Suzan Joy Harjo explains, "If you have an attitude about something, about a people, that they're less than human, you don't attach rights to them" (Little and Little 2017). Storytelling can act as a tool that not only passes down values to new generations but also crafts larger humanizing collective stories, providing a means to destabilize hegemonic social configurations.[10] It does so by foregrounding individual or community experience over that of an outside researcher. The Indigenous scholar Linda T. Smith (2012) states, "Story telling is a useful and culturally appropriate way of representing the 'diversities of truth' within which the story teller rather than the researcher retains control" (242–43). Stories convey meaning on many levels, not only being closely tied to knowledge and knowing but also speaking to the heart, mind, and spirit (L. Smith 2012). As such, they offer a holistic corrective to limited and narrow studies of culture.

Creative Acts as Resistance

As a form of creative power, stories hold great potentialities for Indigenous resistance and resurgence. They recenter and reassert Native presence and agency and can undermine stereotypes constructed and reinforced by popular (mis)representations. "Creative act[s] of self-representation" are attempts to persevere and affirm (Raheja 2007, 1162). Creative acts are intimately related to sovereignty, or what Michelle Raheja (2015) calls "visual sovereignty." Scott Lyons asserts, "Our claims to sovereignty entail much more than arguments for tax exempt status or the right to build and operate casinos; they are nothing less than our attempt to survive and flourish as a people" (Grande 2015, 49). As such, creative acts of reclaiming and asserting personhood through stories allow Native peoples to engage popular discourses about Native personhood, presence, and agency. Sovereignty is about not only being but also doing.

Traditional approaches to storytelling act as a means of resistance, as well as cultural resurgence. The Cree-Metis scholar Kim Anderson (2000) explains, "Indigenous stories are significant because they are anchors of resistance. They are also ways of preserving the language and the power and meaningfulness of the spoken word. Our stories are unadulterated versions of our history and creation" (131). Stories allow not only for preservation but also for the expression of a distinct and coherent culture and people. This so-called peoplehood model holds significant promise for the resurgence of Indigenous communities. It allows for what the Osage scholar Robert Warrior (1992) refers to as "intellectual sovereignty," or the ability to craft statements of self-determination and intellectual autonomy. Intellectual sovereignty refers to the notion that Native scholars must engage in both intellectual creation and criticism, thus avoiding confinement to limited intellectual spaces. Warrior (1992) explains, "Though we have been good at proclaiming our inclusion among the oppressed of the world, we have remained by and large still caught in the death dance of dependence between abandoning ourselves to the intellectual strategies and categories of White, European thought or declaring that we need nothing outside of ourselves and our cultures in order to understand the world and our place in it" (18). Indigenous peoples have long conceived of themselves as autonomous and independent nations and peoples, though it has not always been described in those terms (Alfred and Corntassel 2005). Having defined themselves around land and place, cultural practice and worldview, and language, Indigenous people outwardly express these values through creative expressions of storytelling and providing a means of individual and communal resistance and resurgence.

Cyclical, Not Linear

Central to Lakota understandings of resistance is the belief in the cyclical nature of life. A cyclical understanding of time challenges the favoring of outcomes and the decentering of process, or the notion that ends justify means. Indigenous societies have viewed time and life in a cyclical manner, most easily seen in the seasonal cycles of nature. The Lakota symbol of the hoop is a sacred symbol that represents continuity—no beginning and no end. "For all peoples on the planet, that shape represents unity, harmony, beauty, balance, perfection," the Lakota artist Kevin Locke states. "There are no corners, there is no dark place, there is no back row, there is no third or second row. It's all front row" (interview, July 5, 2015). No one part of the circle is favored over the other, no one phase greater than the next. Instead, each season folds into the next, and each is dependent on the previous; all seasons and phases of life are connected. This is reflected and reinforced by the Lakota principle of *Mitakuye Oyasin*, translating to "all are related" or "all my relation."[11] It refers not only to all human beings but also to all animals and trees, all earth and water. Interconnectedness and unity permeate all reality. This is the foundation of the hoop, the spiritual understanding of the circle. It is also reflected in how the Lakota view the soul. The fourth aspect *Nagila* is the "embodiment of the cosmic energy, or *Taku Sakan Skan*, which infuses the entire universe" (Brown and Cousins 2001, 90).[12] It connects all people and things and points to the importance of all things. Again, no one element is greater than the next, all stages are connected to one truth (Goodman 1992).

Creative Acts and the Spirit World

The guiding principles of interconnectedness and unity are sacred principles that connect all reality and inform the significance of creative acts. Traditionally, the Lakota viewed creativity as something sacred that everyone could engage. Creative acts of storytelling are a way to connect to other worlds, both providing a link to ancestors and acting as expressions of the Creator (Marshall 2007). Lakota connection to their ancestors is very important. Their belief that who we are depends on the experiences, values, traditions, and customs of family members who came before us makes the stories of ancestors even more powerful. Bringing our ancestors' experiences to life through stories carries on their memories and allows for various aspects of that person to be passed on to those who are still living (Marshall 2007, xiv). Simply, stories are a way for the Lakota to connect to the spirits of their ancestors. Joseph Marshall III (2007) explains, "Stories do have a way of connecting us. We may not have photographs of all of our ancestors, but we do have stories. Sometimes those stories can reveal things a two-dimensional image cannot. They can reveal a person's character, for example, because they look behind the image into the heart and soul" (xv).

Stories also bring the divine into every day. Creativity and artistic forms of expression are windows into other cultures' worldview and inner world; as such, they "constitute precious documents no less important than the sacred written texts of antiquity" (Brown and Cousins 2001, 61). Traditionally there was no Lakota word for art; all life was imbued with beauty and inner meaning. All individuals had the ability to express themselves creatively, not merely as an act of self-expression but rather as a way to reflect the beauty and spiritual powers around them. Through various ceremonies and traditions, Lakota would receive visions, typically in the form of an animal messenger, that would reveal important community information, provide healing, or imbue spiritual powers. Creative forms derived from those visions would act as physical materializations of those powers and visions, thereby bringing the powers of other worlds into this world. The purpose of creative expression was not the end expression itself but what it meant to bring what it stood for in the spirit world into this world. James Archibald Houston, a Canadian artist who spent most of his life in the Arctic and who was instrumental in the Canadian recognition of Inuit art, states, "Like most other hunting societies, they have thought of the whole act of living in harmony with nature as their art. The small objects that they carve or decorate are to them insignificant reflections of their total art of living" (Brown and Cousins 2001, 61). Value is found in the process of creation, not the preservation of the final product.

Importance of Journey

The process of creation is directly connected to the lessons drawn from the importance of the journey, a principle emphasized in many traditional Lakota stories. One such story is the Lakota Seven Generations Vision. The Vision goes that years ago, when White men first arrived on Turtle Island (the United States), the spirits of the land told the Lakota of their arrival and that they needed to prepare. The Lakota were told that for seven generations the Lakota people will walk away from what they have now, and after some time, a generation is going to be born that has the curiosity to know who and what they are and where they come from. This will be the seventh generation, which will turn around and start the journey back. Everything that is passed on the way there needs to be remembered and addressed on the way back. As each new generation comes, new tools are needed to understand the things embedded in today's modern culture. It is through reviewing history, or the journey, that the problems needed to be addressed will be resolved.

The Vision suggests that attentiveness to the journey is the only way to bring back and renew the cultural beauty of the past. "We need to start sharing this [Vision] and getting it out there so people will look at us and know that we're not just sitting here burdened with diabetes, cancer, and alcoholism," Lucas, a Lakota man in his fifties who is working to revitalize the traditional Lakota ways of life, told me. "There is a subtle movement going on here, but we need help in defining what happened between then and now, by people that were born and raised in it and understand the terminology and how to use that terminology to readdress all of these wrongs, so that we can continue that process of decolonization" (interview, August 14, 2014).[13]

There is a subtle movement happening within Native communities, a movement based on attentiveness to journey, patient rebuilding, and revitalizing Indigenous culture through modern tools. As this section illustrates, storytelling and the making of films provide a way to engage power and decolonization, creative acts of resistance, cyclical expressions of time, a connection to the spirit world, and a way to emphasize the importance of the journey.

Potentialities of Process? Native Filmmaking and Storytelling

Insights developed through the experience at NFSI act as an example of intentional approaches to training filmmakers. The same attention to process was also reflected throughout the training content and programming, as well as in the ongoing production-based trainings and learnings being developed.

The NFSI pilot program was the culmination of years of collaborative relationships among Native filmmakers, storytellers, and communities. Five years ago, I had the opportunity to serve as media director for an indigenous oral-history project with Native media makers from around North America. The program was composed of young artists and scholars who were collecting oral histories of Indigenous participants of the first-ever UN-level conference in 1977, the International NGO Conference on Discrimination Against Indigenous Peoples in America. I was introduced to the opportunity through one of the original 1977 participants whom I had befriended. The oral-history group worked together over the span of two years, documenting important histories and gaining a basic film training. I developed deeper relationships with a handful of those participants, which has led to multiple film collaborations, social media projects, grants applications, and cowriting.

In the midst of these collaboration, the 2016 Dakota Access Pipeline events took place at the Standing Rock Sioux Reservation in North and South Dakota. The Lakota and their allies from around the world were standing up against the construction of a dangerous oil pipeline through Lakota treaty territory, an area that included sacred burial sites and the Missouri River, an important watershed for multiple Native reservations and communities downstream. The experiences that took place at Standing Rock galvanized Indigenous youth around the world and inspired many to learn more about Indigenous experiences. Beautiful stories began to emerge from those experiences at Standing Rock, and through conversation with my collaborators, we noticed that there was little, if any, content created by Lakota people themselves or even Native people more broadly. From this realization came the desire to create a training program that would bring together Native youth to learn and explore the potentials of media making. Through relationships with Native students and communities at the University of California, San Diego (UCSD), support for NFSI developed.[14] The Program consisted of multiple phases, starting with a five-day on-campus residency in which participants were exposed to an overview of film production, as well as a deep study of feminist and indigenous theory on representation. These ten-hour days were split between in-class theory and experiential field practice and included a field outing to Los Angeles to visit with an Emmy Award–winning cinematographer and a roundtable discussion with professional actors. The second phase was a remote three-month accompaniment period during which participants were paired with dramaturgs to work to develop

scripts. After this accompaniment period, in which dramaturg graduate students were able to receive academic credit, NFSI moved into the
production and film development phase. This has included additional
participant-led and community-based film trainings, multiple developed screenplays including one adapted for the stage and premiered at
a local festival, and a participant-facilitator collaboration feature film
that is currently in preproduction.

There were six facilitators and four administrators involved in programming. Of the six facilitators, four were Native, while the other two
were Canadian filmmakers (from Colombia and Jamaica) who had
been working with marginalized communities and First Nations filmmakers in Canada. The four administrators included the director of the
InterTribal Resource Center (ITRC), a professor from the Department
of Theatre and Dance, myself, and my partner as the program's project manager. In total, the facilitators and administrators involved six
women, four men, and five Natives and represented seven nations and
four countries. Participants were drawn from local Southern California communities and UCSD's student body, as well as from throughout
the country. It included fourteen participants, seven women and seven
men, seven of whom were Native and represented eight nations, three
Latinx (some with Indigenous origins), two African Americans, and
two Filipino Americans. Ages ranged from eighteen to the early forties,
with varied previous film experiences.

Planning started a year in advance and increased in intensity six
months before the intensive training. Throughout the months leading
to the program, we held weekly meetings with facilitators and administrators. The curriculum included lessons on representation, picture and
composition, storytelling, scriptwriting, production, editing and style,
and distribution. The importance of process was emphasized throughout each session and also modeled throughout the collaborative facilitator orientation.

Intentional Process

Central to NFSI's planning and nascent successes was an intentional
approach to pedagogy and collaboration, not just in the process of making films but also through the training of budding filmmakers. This was

codified through a document of principles crafted by facilitators and administrators. Meeting weekly for months before the residency, we discussed all these principles in great detail, added to and edited them multiple times, and reviewed them throughout the program. The principles acted as a living document to be revisited and to remain open to further revision throughout our next iterations of NFSI. The following are the twelve developed principles:

- *Foregrounding pedagogy.* We strive to be open and clear about our process and our convictions that animate our process. This includes being open about our principles and being attentive to various modes of learning and knowing.
- *Importance of traditional languages.* Language contains unique symbolic orders that carry with them knowledges, ways of being, and possibilities. We must be aware of the power of reclaiming language.
- *Centering Indigenous experience.* Participants will have differing experiences and encounters, as well as differences in how those experiences relate to their work. We will be attentive to lived experience.
- *Process oriented.* This emphasis elevates process to the level of product. It allows us to encourage participants to acknowledge that even the process of creation is a pregnant and brave moment. The means in which we operate must be coherent with the ends we seek, requiring consistent reflection and consultation.
- *Spiritual endeavor.* We recognize that our involvements deal with more than just material experiences and understandings. This refers to intentional approaches to how we interact with participants and each other, how we create films with spiritual content, and how we portray our subjects and our communities. We recognize that we are motivated by larger principles.
- *Service orientation.* Our work should be done in service to our communities.
- *Consultative framework.* Dialogue should be marked by frankness, universal participation, and a recognition of the need for underlying unity. It aims at group coherence through forgoing excessive emotional attachment, avoidance of backbiting or name-calling, and a recognition that agreement of the whole is preferable to any particular "right" answer.
- *Praxis.* We recognize that the combination of action and critical reflection is needed to transform our communities and society (Freire [1970] 2005).

- *Action, reflection, and consultation.* This cycle of knowledge generation emphasizes a learning-in-action approach, a hands-on learning environment, and a valuing of the input of all participants involved.[15]
- *Usefulness for communities.* We must continually ask how we can make our learnings useful to our communities.
- *Collaboration.* Building relationships of trust will lead to advancement of our personal, community, and shared goals. To be most effective, our efforts must be collaborative and need to be built on trust and relationships.
- *Honor people, challenge structures.* Awareness of the structures that make possible a person's behavior allows for a deeper understanding. Excessive focus on an individual's character, without structural considerations, makes behavior easy to be dismissed as anomalous. A structural focus pushes us to change dominant narratives and foreground positive depictions of Native communities.[16]

Putting these convictions into action was, in many ways, more challenging than merely describing them, especially since this language and attention to motivation and process are not typically found in academic and filmmaking spaces. Additionally, our efforts emphasized a learning-in-action orientation that relies on an iterative process of thinking and doing—we know as we continue acting and garnering insights that we will refine implementation practices. As a result, experiences gathered from NFSI at this stage involve the process of training of filmmakers, rather than experience-based insights of production, the latter of which are still being developed through additional stages of NFSI.

Operationalizing these twelve principles meant incorporating best practices of inclusion, facilitation, and pedagogy (of which our facilitators were already familiar) and then discussing the extent that our principles were reflected in such practices. This translated to taking pedagogical practices and linking them directly to our deep-seated motivating values, giving them more significance and potency. Take, for example, participation, a common goal for all youth programming. When we reframed participation as our collective need to (re)center complex Indigenous experiences, value the importance of Indigenous languages and traditions, and honor people and challenge structures, participation took on deeper significance. It was more than just dealing with individual levels of shyness or outgoingness but rather about the historical and systematic context of settler-colonial marginalization.[17]

The principle of recognizing filmmaking and training as a spiritual endeavor was modeled through creating practices of prayer and spiritual reflection. Every morning, we started with a prayer circle, inviting each person to share a blessing, a prayer, or a moment of gratitude from previous days. Burning sage and other medicines was prohibited within university buildings, so we stood outside in a circle and centered ourselves before daily activities. The circle was voluntary, and our group consisted of various tribal backgrounds, as well as Indigenous peoples from outside the United States; so many participants explained the significance of their shared prayers and traditional practices. We decided when we were defining this principle to make participation in the daily prayer circles voluntary to avoid any semblance of objectification or performativity, as it is sometimes seen within academic settings with opening prayer or land recognitions.[18] It developed naturally into an open and accepting spiritual space of reflection and set the tone for the residency and how we want to approach filmmaking.

Centering Indigenous experiences was achieved through the way we invited participants to craft their own screenplays. We started with studying the history of misrepresentation of Indigenous peoples, tracing its beginnings through the academic project of anthropology and then through the technological advances of photography and film.[19] After that, we guided participants in developing screenplays about stories they want to see about themselves and their communities. Having been widely underrepresented in popular media, as well as within the vast majority of academic texts, participants were flush with meaningful stories. It was clear that there were certain stories that needed to be told. One participant described it as having big stories stuck in one's throat, stories swallowed for so long that they need to get out. Once these emotional stories were allowed out, even if merely through acts of writing and verbalization, then other, less emotional stories depicting the complexities of human life could be told. As a result, some participants developed stories of great seriousness, dealing with oppression and hardship, while others were much more lighthearted and dealt with the complexities and paradoxes of Indigenous (human) life. We modeled a storytelling practice that was not premised solely on damage-based research but that allowed for stories about complex Indigenous personhood and centered Indigenous experiences.

Feedback received from facilitators and participants pointed both to the significance of storytelling for Indigenous communities and the potentialities of focusing on process in filmmaking spaces. A few emergent themes from the NFSI feedback included storytelling as a means of resistance and resilience, a recognition of the significance and responsibility of storytelling, a recognition of connections between the spirit world and creativity, and an honoring of one's humanity.

Storytelling as Resistance and Resilience

There was a recognition of the power of potentialities of storytelling. One female facilitator stated, "Our stories are unique, and the more we tell different versions of what people believe of what it means to be Indigenous in America, the more we build an idea of who we are— which is urban, rural, mixed, queer, feminine, masculine. There are so many different areas where we don't get to represent who we are."[20] Another facilitator, a male, suggested, "Our communities make us who we are, whether it's through storytelling or through struggle. I am excited to see what participants will do because they'll take a lot of what they're doing here and take it back to their communes."[21] This was also reflected in the participants' sense of the importance of what we were doing. One male participant said, "This program is revolutionary, in the sense we heal and we're reclaiming and we're proud of [the stories we have to tell]."[22]

Responsibilities of Storytelling

Along with the recognition of the important role of storytelling, there was also the recognition of the potentials of engaging filmmaking. One male participant shared, "Learning how to be proud of ourselves as Native people . . . and networking with other people who aren't Native, and they say that you deserve this space. This is your land, and you deserve to be here. This your vessel; we're in your vessel, and when is your creativity going to flow? It's exciting because that's never been done before, and I am excited to see what change it's going to do for our communities and society on a systematic level."[23] Another female participant suggested, "I've been really comforted to know that there are other people who are interested in Native storytelling that is really empowering. . . . [We saw] the ways we as marginalized peoples can still produce meaningful work in film while being accountable to our communities and affirming of peer/emerging filmmakers."[24]

Spirit World and Creativity

One male participant explained how the spirits of his ancestors compelled him to write in particular ways: "I choked up today when I mentioned how my great-grandmother would ask my young father in Ajachemen, Hoot Kazun? or 'What is Your Heart Thinking?' This will be the title of my story. . . . [NFSI] is teaching me to be brave and bold, to get my story out. It needs to come out. It is all bottled up inside me."[25] Another male participant stated, "This experience completely gave me the confidence, enthusiasm, and spirit needed to pursue my storytelling project. There is so much knowledge gained from today about the art(s) of storytelling that, honestly, I will forever use beyond NFSI."[26]

Honoring One's Humanity

The twelve principles allowed us to create a safe space where the complexities and uniquenesses of each individual could come forth. One male participant stated,

I think what stood out most from today was the discussions around the connections and relationships that exist within productions and, ultimately, are required to maintain a creative and safe space. Being thoughtful about the working atmosphere we establish in creative and collaborative spaces will no doubt benefit me when it comes to forming a professional environment grounded in humanity. Ultimately, storytelling is about humanity. By ensuring we keep that humanity in our work and in our collaborations, we ensure our own humanity in the journey of storytelling. It really provides a fresh outlook on the power of our work and the realities of being an artist.[27]

Two other male participants suggested that "just having a safe space and the encouragement to dive right in" was so important for him. Another said, "I really enjoyed how comfortable I felt about my heritage," whereas in other spaces, he did not. One female participant captured this sentiment, saying, "The conversations we've had—I've spoken to other people who said, 'There is no other space I feel comfortable discussing this. There is no other space I feel safe discussing these things.' And here there is this acknowledgment of our humanity. That is something that does not happen everywhere. A lot of the times, we are just seen as objects or just sources of specific resource. But here, we are humans, complex and recognized as such."[28]

Just as each of the twelve poles of the tipi represent unique aspects of the Lakota world and worldview, the twelve principles of NFSI represent distinct foundational aspects of the world we want to live in and collaborate within. Though these principles were never shared directly with the participants, our attention to process shaped the space in a way that was noticeable for all who were involved. By foregrounding the motivating principles that shaped our process, we were able to create a space where participants' humanity and complexities were honored.

Conclusion

The Lakota construction of the tipi holds important lessons about valuing the significance and potentialities of an attentiveness to process. In the tipi, the entire Lakota world is carefully (re)created, representing and bringing forth celestial principles to the terrestrial. Lakota cultural values are represented through every aspect of this otherwise seemingly simple structure. This attention to process and journey, combined with the potentialities of storytelling for Indigenous communities, makes the act of making films and training filmmakers a unique decolonial space, a pregnant space that falls at the convergence of sacred approaches to creativity, modes of resistance, nonlinear conceptualizations of time and life, and, ultimately, representation and cultural rejuvenation and reclamation.

NFSI offers an early contribution to thinking through the significance of filmmaking processes, illustrating how intentional approaches to principles and convictions can affect a filmmaking space. It is an attempt to foreground lessons of the hoop by emphasizing process as a product on its own, the approach to creativity as a sacred act, and the creation of foundations for the world in which we want to create and live. This approach can reorient filmmaking processes in ways that provide critical, holistic, and humanizing interventions for Native communities and communities of color.

This chapter has asked, What lessons can filmmakers learn from the Lakota approach to construct a tipi? How can the lessons of constructing a tipi transform approaches to filmmaking? How can attentiveness to process transform the purpose, meanings, and outcomes of filmmaking and filmmaker training? To answer these questions, the chapter has examined the construction of the Lakota tipi, how films are popularly evaluated, Indigenous approaches to storytelling and process, and the example of NFSI as a Native-based effort to foreground process in filmmaking and the training of Native filmmakers. It has explored the cultural role of storytelling, decolonial potentialities of storytelling, the significance of cyclical time, sacred approaches to creativity, and the importance of focusing on journey or process.

This chapter leaves a few questions for scholars and practitioners to explore further: How does attentiveness to filmmaking processes affect youth and community empowerment? What does an iterative learning cycle between process and the resulting film look like? How can an attentiveness to process further our understanding of the purpose of filmmaking? What does a systematic approach to Native filmmaking look like, and how can it provide a potential avenue for community claims to sovereignty and revitalization?

Notes

1. There is great diversity among Native peoples. Within the Lakota there are seven subtribes, including Sichangu, Oglala, Itazipcho, Hunkpapha, Mnikhowozu, Sihasapa, and Oohenunpa. Of the 567 federally recognized and over 550 nonrecognized tribes (these numbers fluctuate), each has a unique governing configuration (Schilling 2015). This chapter does not motion to a single Indigenous approach; rather, it represents a singular experience of an ethnographer on one tribe's reservation. I use the term "Native" as a noun, to refer to the original inhabitants of the Americas. I am aware that this term has pejorative connotations (see Beier 2005, 9), though it is how the Natives I work with refer to themselves.

2. This is one attempt of an Asian settler to incorporate Indigenous knowledge into new spaces (see Fujikane and Okamura 2008). Focusing on the Native Film and Storytelling Institute (NFSI) is not to suggest that it will be successful or is being carried out in the right way; rather, it is a site of ongoing learning. Undoubtedly, modifications will be made as NFSI efforts continue.

3. The chapter stems from larger research that is a multisite, political ethnography premised on feminist methodology and abductive research (Enloe 2004; Tickner 2005; Schwartz-Shea and Yanow 2012). J. Ann Tickner (2005) outlines four key aspects to this feminist methodology: asking feminist questions, research being useful to communities, a commitment to reflexivity, and an approach to knowledge as emancipatory.

4. Robert Allen Warrior (1992) refers to this as "intellectual sovereignty": Native thought should not be relegated to merely Indigenous-related issues.

5. *More Than a Word* (Media Education Foundation, 2017), directed by the brothers Kenn and John Little (Dakota Sioux), was nominated for best documentary at 2018 San Francisco American Indian Film Festival. I served as contributing editor and cinematographer for the film.

6. There are notable exceptions, including moviemaking as critical conscientization (Walker 2018), participatory video (Lunch and Lunch 2006), community communication through filmmaking (Quarry 1994), shared-goal documentary film (Silvey 2010), oppositional film practice (Waldman and Walker 1999), collaborative film practice (Silvey 2010), and radical documentary (Gaines 1999).

7. Of hundreds of undergraduate courses at top universities in the United States, not one has a course dedicated to filmmaking processes, including New York University, the American Film Institute, the University of California, Los Angeles, and the University of Southern California.

8. This is not meant as a critique but merely as an observation. I owe much of my knowledge to Makhmalbaf and his family. The program was sponsored by the Bahá'í World Centre and the Institute for Studies in Global Prosperity.

9. This is not a comprehensive account of Lakota storytelling but, rather, a cursory account for readers' understanding.

10. Storytelling is a tool that can be used in various ways—it holds decolonial potential but can reinforce settler configurations (see Regan 2010 on "settler storytelling").

11. There are differing accounts of *Mitakuye Oyasin*: Francis White Bird (2008) suggests a narrower definition of "everything is related to the existence of all MY Lakota relatives."

12. Along with *Niya*, *Nagi*, and *Sicum*, these various dimensions of the soul inform how Lakota constitute relations.

13. Pseudonyms are used throughout unless otherwise stated.

14. This support was through the InterTribal Resource Center, Dr. Julie Burelle, and the Department of Theatre and Dance.

15. Inspired by the Bahá'í faith's framework of community learning and social action (see Bahá'í Office of Social and Economic Development 2012).
16. Developed by Makhmalbaf and his approach to filmmaking.
17. Settler colonialism—as distinct from franchise colonialism, requiring human resources to produce wealth—foregrounds land to produce wealth. In the United States, the American project needed land to expand, having already secured human labor through slavery, and Indigenous peoples were on that land and, therefore, needed to be removed. Settler colonialism is an ongoing process of dispossession (see Wolfe 2006).
18. Opening prayers and land recognitions can be good, but when seen as the solution or practiced superficially rather than as a part of a decolonial process, they can become performative and problematic (see H. King 2019).
19. This included studying Eve Tuck's "Suspending Damage: A Letter to Communities" (2009) and Linda T. Smith's *Decolonizing Methodologies: Research and Indigenous Peoples* (2012).
20. Halley, exit interview, March 28, 2018.
21. Miguel, exit interview, March 28, 2018.
22. Michael, exit interview, March 28, 2018.
23. Michael, exit interview, March 28, 2018.
24. Daniela, exit interview, March 28, 2018.
25. Luis, written reflection, March 24, 2018.
26. Michael, exit interview, March 28, 2018.
27. Junior, written reflection, March 26–27, 2018.
28. Aliya, exit interview, March 28, 2018.

PART II

How Racialized Media Is Delivered

Once media content has been designed, there are still additional processes of the media labor circuit that determine audience engagement. This is the phase of delivery, and it occurs through the marketing and reviewing of media, in which gatekeepers' assumptions and interpretations can drastically influence audience consumption. While all individuals who interact with media make their own interpretations, the interpretations of those in gatekeeping positions are given structural power over the extent to which, and how, audiences receive media.

Media gatekeepers operate like a swinging pendulum between the construction and consumption of media. For example, reviews indicate to both current audiences and future media designers which media content (media forms, plots, casting, imagery) is worthwhile. Operating as key decision-makers in the media circuit, these gatekeepers pass judgement on media content from this position of power, and they are just as influenced by race-based ideologies as any other social actor. It is through gatekeepers that racialized opinions regarding media worthiness are fomented in the general social consciousness. Just as favorable reviews of romantic comedies lead to the continual churning out of new rom-coms, certain racialized plots are regularly repeated in the media, such as "racial buddy films," emphasizing interracial friendships and distorting realities of racism. Furthermore, reviewers tell audiences how to perceive racialized media by hailing certain content as racially "progressive," even when they actually reproduce existing racist tropes. The influence that gatekeepers have on audience reception is the central theme in the next five chapters of this text.

Chapter 7, written by Christopher Chávez, examines how NPR (National Public Radio) constructs its radio content on the basis of racialized assumptions regarding who Latino audiences are and what they want to hear in radio broadcasting. Carlos Alamo-Pastrana and William Hoynes, in chapter 8, demonstrate how gatekeeping within news media functions not by media reviewers but through processes of hiring and promoting journalists that favor Whites and ideological frameworks of the profession that emphasize objectivity and neutral perspectives. In chapter 9, SunAh M. Laybourn examines another side of gatekeeping, in which Korean adoptee adults have begun to take the reins in the gatekeeping of media portrayals surrounding their experience, creating their own content by and for Korean adoptees. Similarly exploring how social actors divert typical gatekeeping processes of mainstream media, Leslie Kay Jones analyzes the Twitter-based movement of #BlackLivesMatter in chapter 10, taking on questions of agency, resistance, and the performance of activism. In chapter 11, Nadia Y. Flores-Yeffal and David Elkins uncover the more malicious side of taking the reins of the media. In their timely chapter, Flores-Yeffal and Elkins discuss the construction of societal panic regarding Latino immigrants from Mexico and Central America.

7

Rethinking the American Public

NPR and the Pursuit of the Ideal Latinx Listener

CHRISTOPHER CHÁVEZ

On August 25, 2015, Donald Trump, then the frontrunner for the Republican Party's presidential nomination, made a campaign stop in the state of Iowa. Trump had gained momentum largely by stoking nativist sentiments, proposing to build an expansive wall on the border between the United States and Mexico and a ban on all Muslim immigration to the United States. During his Iowa stop, Trump had planned to discuss a policy that would forcibly deport eleven million undocumented immigrants residing in the United States, the scale of which would have been unprecedented in the country's history.

During the event, Jorge Ramos, a journalist representing the Spanish-language television network Univision, began to question Mr. Trump regarding the details of his policy. At first, Trump dismissed him, but when Ramos pursued his line of questioning, Trump ordered him to "go back to Univision," which some observers interpreted as a coded way of saying "go back to Mexico" (Mai-Duc 2015). When Ramos persisted, he was physically removed from the room.

Reaction to the incident within the journalism community was bifurcated. Some saw the incident as an affront to a free press, while others criticized Ramos for blurring the line between advocacy and journalism. In the reporting on the incident by National Public Radio (NPR), the country's flagship public radio network seemed uncertain as to whether to frame Ramos, who is a US citizen, as an authentic member of the US press corps or as a de facto member of the foreign press. During a segment on *All Things Considered*, the NPR media correspondent David Folkenflik described Ramos as a "man of two countries, both Mexico and the US," while the host, Audie Cornish, questioned Ramos's influence beyond "Spanish-speaking Americans" (Folkenflik 2015).

NPR's focus on Ramos's citizenship reflects ongoing discourses surrounding the Latinx community itself, whose members are frequently not considered to be fully American, regardless of their citizenship status and residential tenure. In this chapter, I engage the question of how US Latinxs figure into NPR's imagination of the American public. Since its creation, NPR was designed with two clear mandates: to engage listeners in civic discourses and to represent the diversity of the nation. However, the country has experienced profound demographic change in recent years, raising new questions regarding how media organizations create programming for the audiences they purport to serve. US Latinxs have figured prominently in this change. At 18 percent of the country's population (US Bureau of the Census 2018a), US Latinxs are becoming increasingly important to the American electorate that NPR is tasked with serving.

Based on interviews with public-radio practitioners and a review of NPR and Corporation for Public Broadcasting (CPB) strategic documents, I argue that NPR employs a number of industry practices that secure its position as a White public space, while relegating Latinx listeners to the periphery. I further argue that these practices are themselves tied to a larger cultural logic, in which Latinx identity is differentiated from national identity (Dávila 2008). Finally, I argue that such practices have important implications for Latinx participation in civic discourses. After all, identifying whom to include in one's target audience necessarily involves a process of whom to exclude.

The Bifurcation of the Media Landscape

Institutional discourses, which distinguish Latinx media from national media, reflect the overall logic by which the media marketplace has historically organized itself. As early as 1922, the sociologist Robert E. Park described a media landscape that included a thriving "immigrant press," composed of a multitude of small publications with modest circulations. In his book *The Immigrant Press and Its Control* (1922), however, Park began the long-standing practice of conflating three distinct concepts: citizenship, language, and ethnicity.

Employing the terms "immigrant press" and "foreign-language press" interchangeably, Park set up the dichotomy between an ideal, American reader (an English monolingual of western European descent) who is contrasted with a foreign-speaking Other. In doing so, Park made the implicit case that language serves as a barrier to inclusion and belonging. In Park's words, the readers of these publications belong to "the groups most separate from the American life or, the exotics. It is the press of a people who live in cities, but more or less in isolation from the American community" (1922, 150).

The distinction between national and ethnic audiences became further entrenched with the advent of radio. While early newspapers were primarily regional efforts, radio stations had the capacity to cross county, state, and national borders. This enabled listeners to more easily see themselves as part of the imagined community of the nation (Anderson [1983] 2006). This is not to say, however, that radio was particularly democratic. At the onset of broadcasting, the stories, music, and voices of ethnic communities were largely absent from national radio. Thus, it appears that such decisions about the specific nature of the audience were based on economic as well as racial considerations. The Radio Act of 1927 set the stage for a broadcasting system that was intended to operate in the public interest but that heavily favored commercial interests. Almost immediately after radio's advent, companies like Westinghouse, General Electric, and RCA established radio stations across the country in an effort to cultivate national markets for their products. Given the broad scope of the reach of radio broadcasters, they abandoned the practice of pursuing smaller, regional subscribers, opting instead to cultivate a larger, more lucrative mass audience.

Scholars working within the Frankfurt School tradition were quick to critique the uneasy relationship between radio content and the marketplace. In an effort to reach the largest possible audiences, critics argued, media companies had appropriated the logic and processes of mass production, including standardization and repetition. As a result, listening itself had taken on exchange values, what Theodor Adorno (1945) called "commodity listening." From this perspective, listeners were not conceived of by radio stations as a public, or "the people," but rather as "consumers," viewed primarily in terms of their economic value.

But economic considerations are not independent from racial considerations. Initially, radio stations targeted a normative audience of White, middle-class listeners, presuming them to be the most profitable. By contrast, scholars including Jason Chambers (2008), Arlene Dávila (2008), and Katherine Sender (2004) have argued that racialized communities historically have not been seen as viable consumers and, therefore, were left out of early programming strategies. However, Latinxs faced unique barriers to inclusion because of suspicions about their citizenship and national loyalties. For example, Delores-Ines Casillas (2014) found in her research on early Latinx radio that the Federal Communications Commission (FCC) was originally reluctant to issue licenses to "foreign-language" stations out of fear they would undermine national unity during the war effort.

Public Radio as Alternative Media

In a critique of commercial media, Jürgen Habermas (1970) was skeptical that radio could promote his notion of a public sphere, in which citizens come together to collectively discuss matters of public concern. To ensure that all members of the public could be heard on equal terms, Habermas called for an "ideal speech situation" (367), in which speakers would evaluate one another's arguments on the basis of reason and evidence and free of any physical and psychological coercion.

Because commercial media are driven primarily by economic interests, Habermas was doubtful that public discourse could occur outside the influence of the marketplace. However, Michael McCauley (2005) has argued that NPR was born out of the desire to achieve a more democratic version of Habermas's public sphere, which critics saw as an idealized portrait of a bourgeois public sphere that favored propertied, educated males. Rather than seeing radio's broad reach as a defect, proponents of public radio saw its potential for achieving greater civic participation. It was precisely because of its ability to reach a wide audience that communities that had traditionally been left out of civic discourses could now be included. Information of civic, cultural, and social importance could now extend beyond the town hall and the classroom and be delivered directly to the masses.

NPR's organizational structure was designed to ensure that this happened. NPR's national overlay was seen as a way to serve the full range of US society, while stations rooted in diverse regions could affirm the nation's cultural diversity. Furthermore, the network's organizational structure was meant to ensure that NPR could deliver civic information to the most disenfranchised communities that had been traditionally left out of civic discourses, not just focusing on the most elite.

NPR's nonprofit status was meant to address concerns about the coercive influence of the marketplace. According to Ralph Engelman (1996), the Public Broadcasting Act, the legislation that established the Corporation for Public Broadcasting (CPB), gave the CPB responsibility to provide federal funds and political insulation for public broadcasting's two arms: NPR (radio) and PBS (television). By separating NPR's funding from both the government and corporate America, NPR would be able to pursue stories that better serve the interests of the public. "We are unbought and unbossed" is how NPR's Michel Martin put it, borrowing a quote from Shirley Chisholm. "Our listeners own us" (Holmes 2017).

Within NPR discourses, however, there appears to be significant slippage between the terms "listeners," "the public," and "the audience." Furthermore, the exact nature of NPR's "listeners" has been the subject of ongoing critique. Critics of the network have argued that NPR has created programming primarily for an educated audience of middle-class, White listeners. During an interview about NPR's aging audience, Jeff Hansen, the program director at KUOW, argued that NPR's targeting strategy was short-sighted, stating, "What they didn't realize at the time was that what they were inventing was programming for people like themselves—baby boomers with college degrees" (Farhi 2015).

In 1977, the CPB took up the issue of diversity, by commissioning a task force to examine public media's success at addressing the needs of minority publics. The product of this task force was a report titled *A Formula for Change: The Report on Minorities in Public Broadcasting*, which cited a number of shortcomings. According to Sonia De La Cruz (2017), the establishment of the Task Force on Minorities resulted in the channeling of support and financing to minority and community radio stations. De La Cruz argues that this led to a flourishing Spanish-language public-radio system, including Radio Bilingüe, a community-based radio network founded in 1976. Established by Hugo Morales along with Latinx activists, farmworkers, and community members, Radio Bilingüe became the first full-power FM radio station to provide relevant news to the country's growing Spanish-speaking community.

The emergence of a thriving Spanish-language public-radio system led to a separate Latinx public sphere on public radio, where matters of Latinx public interest could be discussed outside White public space. In the book *Sounds of Belonging* (2014), Casillas argues that these stations affirmed the ethnic identity of its listeners and promoted direct civic participation, which included organizing protests, informing listeners about policy, and promoting voter drives. Thus, Radio Bilingüe more closely delivers on public radio's original mandate of engaging its listeners civically.

Meanwhile, NPR, which purports to represent the American public writ large, has continued to target its programs to an almost exclusively upscale audience of White, educated baby boomers (McChesney 2008). Consequently, the conception of public radio as a shared space that represents a broad swath of the American public remains allusive. In its place, public radio remains bifurcated into separate systems: one that serves a Spanish-speaking Latinx listener through Spanish-language programming and one that purports to serve a "national audience" but that is narrowly focused in its scope.

Rethinking the American Public

Industry discourses that disconnect Latinxs from the national audience are themselves tied to larger discourses about national identity. As Michel Foucault (1984) argues, the representation of space is not arbitrary. Rather, how somebody categorizes, imagines, and institutionalizes space is based on power relations, and where one lies in the social space determines one's position in the power structure and, therefore, one's perspective.

Dávila (2008) has argued that US Latinxs continue to be perceived as outsiders and "immigrants," regardless of their residential tenure or legal status. According to Dávila, such perceptions are based in the regulation and maintenance of a particular national identity, which privileges Whiteness and English monolingualism. But this model that distinguishes Latinx from American is increasingly at odds with an America that is becoming more demographically diverse. According to the Pew Research Center (2016a), the size of the Latinx electorate is expected to number 27.3 million eligible voters in 2016, accounting for 12 percent of all eligible voters. Furthermore, since 2000, the primary source of Latinx population growth has swung from immigration to native births, which undermines popular perceptions of Latinxs as an immigrant community that is unable to participate civically.

NPR is not unaware of its problem addressing Latinxs. In articulating its strategic vision for the future, NPR acknowledged that it needs "to create or showcase talent that appeals to people of varied ages, ideologies, ethnic backgrounds (with an emphasis on Latino audiences as one of the fastest growing demographic segments), and geographic affiliations, using relevant platforms and venues" (NPR 2014). However, NPR's reckoning with diversity seems less like a social mission and more like an economic imperative. The baby boomers whom NPR has long pursued are now reaching sixty-five and older, which means that NPR is finding itself in a position where its audience is becoming older and Whiter while the population at large skews younger and more ethnically diverse. NPR projects that by 2020, its stations' audience of forty-four-year-olds and younger will be around 30 percent of its total audience, half of what that audience accounted for in 1985 (Falk 2015). In 1995, the median age of the NPR listener was forty-five years old. Today, he or she is fifty-four (Farhi 2015).

Meanwhile, the US Latinx population is expected to grow exponentially in the next few years. By 2060, Latinxs are expected to account for 28 percent of the total US population (US Bureau of the Census 2018a). Furthermore, the Latinx population is defined by its youth. About one-third of US Latinxs are under the age of eighteen, which means that they figure prominently in NPR's audience of the future (Pew Research Center 2016b). Given the growing importance of Latinxs to NPR's future well-being, I examine how NPR has altered it broadcasting practices to ensure the integration of Latinxs into its overall vision. In this chapter, I focus on three primary areas: target segmentation, programming strategy, and talent acquisition. Specifically, I examine the ways in which NPR imagines its ideal Latinx audience. Second, I am interested in the kinds of programming changes that NPR has made to accommodate its Latinx listeners. Finally, I explore the ways in which NPR recruits and retains Latinx talent.

Courting the Ideal Latinx Listener

While NPR was designed to be a civic-oriented institution, Alan Stavitsky (1995) argues that NPR has shifted from conceiving of its listeners as a public to thinking of them as an audience that can be measured for underwriting purposes. According to Stavitsky, this move began during the 1980s, when network executives began to rely more on audience research for market considerations. On the basis of audience data, NPR and its member stations could identify not only the most likely listeners but also the most lucrative.

Certainly, audience research suggests that Latinxs are becoming more important to NPR's economic well-being. According to Nielsen (2016), Latinxs are prolific users of radio: 97 percent of Latino adults tune in to radio each week. Since 2011, the weekly national Latinx radio audience has grown from 36.5 million to 40.4 million. Furthermore, Latinxs are becoming a dominant social, cultural, and economic force in the country's large metropolitan areas as well as smaller cities. Given their significant presence in these cities, it no longer seems appropriate to think of Latinxs as a numerical minority.

During an interview with Bill Davis, the station president of KPCC in Los Angeles, we discussed the unique challenges of creating programming in a city that is 47 percent Latinx. Davis acknowledged that framing Latinx issues as minority issues in a market like Los Angeles is misguided, stating, "Everything in Los Angeles is a Latino issue." But Davis was also keenly aware that while his station serves an important civic function, it is also a commodity in the media marketplace.

According to Davis, the "Spanish-speaking audience is overserved" in Los Angeles, given the number of Spanish-language radio stations competing in the market. In an effort for the station to find its niche among listeners, therefore, it had to narrowly define the Latinx audience it wanted to pursue. In doing so, the station engaged the logic of market segmentation, or the practice of dividing a given population into distinct subgroups, which are presupposed to have similar attitudes, behaviors, and lifestyle characteristics. This practice allows the organization to efficiently channel resources to the group that will be most responsive to its efforts.

According to a report issued by the Latino Public Radio Consortium (Berson 2014), the CPB and KPCC invested heavily in research that would help them determine the specific segment of the Latinx community on which to focus. The research broke up the Los Angeles Latinx population into three segments: recently arrived immigrants, first-generation Latinxs, and second- and third-generation Latinxs (Stuart 2012b). On the basis of this research, the station concluded that immigrant Latinxs have little interest in the news and feel well served by commercial Spanish-language radio, a finding that is problematic because it frames the issue as a deficiency with the listener rather than the network. In other words, rather than considering how NPR could overcome the linguistic and associational barriers faced by immigrant Latinxs, the network simply moved on to an audience that would receive its existing product more favorably.

The research also found that first-generation Latinxs were active consumers of news and music but had almost no awareness of or interest in public radio. Ultimately, it was decided that the station would best be served by creating programming for second- and third-generation Latinxs, whom the research indicated are English dominant and already civically engaged. According to Bruce Theriault, then vice president of radio at the CPB, this listener is "well informed and has a strong desire for news programming that presents multiple perspectives of an issue" (quoted in Stuart 2012b). Focus groups helped determine that late-second-generation and early-third-generation Latinxs are most likely to prefer English-language news and information services, rather than Spanish or bilingual programming.

NPR's *Audience '88* report (Thomas and Clifford 1988) was among the first to substantiate the notion that public radio listeners tended to be well educated, well-off, and civically engaged. However, NPR's practice of targeting society's most privileged citizens continues to this day. In documents that are designed to encourage potential sponsors to invest in public media, NPR touts the elite status of its current listeners, including the "Affluent Business Leader," one of its primary segments.

The Affluent Business Leader is a C-level employee, has an investment portfolio of $150,000 or more, and holds a leadership position in a club or organization. NPR also touts the "Cultural Connoisseur," who has a postgraduate degree, drinks four glasses of wine, and spends over $1,000 on foreign travel. Then there is the "Power Mom," who enjoys outdoor activities and spends significant time online searching for information on museums and music concerts (National Public Media 2017).

My interviews suggest that NPR is motivated to define its ideal Latinx listener in a way that is congruent with its current audience. In doing so, the network hopes to diversify its listening audience without significantly altering its programming strategy, thereby maintaining organizational efficiencies. The decision to pursue a Latinx audience that is already "well informed" and already consuming news makes sense from a market perspective but comes at the cost of NPR's social and civic imperatives. In the following section, I address the ways in which economic imperatives shape the specific nature of Latinx programming.

NPR's Programming Strategy

In 1988, NPR announced its decision to cancel *Enfoque Nacional*, a thirty-minute Spanish-language newscast. At the time, NPR cited a decline in listeners as the reason for the show's demise, but the decision prompted some debate regarding NPR's responsibility for producing content for Spanish speakers. NPR's then president, Douglas J. Bennet, defended this move by arguing that *Enfoque Nacional* was better suited for commercial radio. Because, in his words, "the point is to reach the Spanish-speaking audiences," Bennet seemed to suggest that NPR was neither motivated to reach nor capable of reaching Latinx listeners. Critics of the move, however, argued that NPR, by relegating responsibility for Spanish-language programming to commercial outlets, was abdicating its responsibility to create minority programming (Harper 1988).

In 2017, NPR revisited its decision to cancel *Enfoque Nacional*. In an essay titled "NPR in Spanish: Approaching Content for a Bilingual Audience" (2017), the ombudsperson Holly Pretsky made the case that, because over forty million US Latinxs speak Spanish at home, NPR had an obligation to create Spanish-language programming. To help meet this demand, Pretsky touted the promise of podcasting and pointed to NPR's support of *Radio Ambulante*, which the network began to distribute and promote in 2016. *Radio Ambulante* is a Spanish-language narrative podcast that tells stories of Spanish speakers across the Americas. The podcast is produced in Spanish, with transcripts made available in English. NPR supports the podcast by promoting it on the NPR website and distributing it on the NPR One app and iTunes.

But while NPR would support *Radio Ambulante* as a podcast, network executives were explicitly clear that they would not integrate Spanish-language programming into its on-air broadcasts. "We're basically an English-language American broadcaster trying to bring in all perspectives," stated Anya Grundmann, NPR's vice president for programming and audience development. "For that reason, it's unlikely NPR listeners will again hear news content entirely in Spanish on the radio as in *Enfoque Nacional* days" (Pretsky 2017).

By conflating "English-language" with "American," NPR is continuing the ongoing practice of conflating citizenship, language, and ethnicity. NPR's past experimentation with different linguistic formats suggests that the network had historically defined the American public in more inclusive ways, but Pretsky's statement suggests gravitational pull toward sameness.

NPR's commitment to English monolingualism is mirrored at the member-station level and was most directly evident in stations operating in markets with emerging Latinx populations. During an interview with the president of a station in a midsize market with a growing Latinx population, I asked about the possibility of using Spanish-language programming. According to one participant, "We have a lot more of the population here that is native Spanish speaking, but if we were like, 'Let's throw an hour of Spanish-language news on there,' I don't think it would work."

When I asked the station president why he believed that an hour of Spanish-language news would not work, he argued that it would be disruptive for the station's core listeners. I received similar responses from other programming managers and news directors, who were adamant that slight disruptions to the storytelling process could lose listeners. This was not limited to the inclusion of Spanish but also included accented English, which is minimized at NPR. As one producer responded to my question about why there is not more linguistic range, "People would be thrown off by that."

It appears that these broadcast practices around language are rooted in economic concerns. Specifically, there is a general concern that any steps taken to diversify must be taken without isolating NPR's core audience of older, wealthy listeners, what one participant referred to as its "legacy audience." Here, one participant with whom I spoke described the issue: "We have an older cohort who is going to continue media the way they always did. And we've got to continue to be there for them. . . . We have to be very cognizant of not destabilizing our older donor base." Here, the participant was candid about the economic concerns that drive programming. From this perspective, online programming provides a convenient "solution" to this dilemma by allowing NPR to claim that it is meeting its diversity mandate while maintaining its "legacy audience."

While NPR has gravitated toward English monolingualism, there is little to suggest that the network has meaningfully integrated Latinxs and Latinx issues into its overall programming strategy. NPR's flagship programs *All Things Considered* and *Morning Edition* remain primarily White spaces. Meanwhile, the network has opted to invest minimally in separate Latinx-oriented programs, including *Latino USA* and *Alt. Latino*. These programs are available to stations at the discretion of programming managers as well as online.

Where Are the Latinxs in Public Radio?

My final question centered on the hiring and retention of Latinx talent. Overall, I found there to be a lack of Latinxs in public radio relative to the overall population. In a report on NPR's staffing (NPR 2018), NPR's ombudsman reported that only 8.08 percent of employees in the news division were Latinx, which is far below the national average of 17 percent.

There are a variety of grants that are intended to diversify newsrooms across the country; these grants are made available through the CPB, as well as from organizations within the public and private sectors, such as the Raul Ramirez Diversity Fund, the One Nation Project, and the Next Generation Radio program. Despite the opportunity for funding, however, the practitioners whom I interviewed cited a number of barriers to diversification. For example, one news director with whom I spoke reported, "This is an interesting challenge. Low turnover equals less diversity. In public media, you have a lot of long-timers who stay for the state benefits or because of the mission. This impedes the entry of a lot of younger, more diverse folks." Other participants with whom I spoke agreed that the overall workforce in public radio is smaller relative to commercial radio, which means that there are fewer opportunities to enter the field. Contributing to the lack of opportunity is the lack of turnover in public radio. According to my interviews, those who work in public radio tend to stay at the stations for much longer, thereby creating a logjam of talent. I found that this concern was particularly pronounced at stations located in smaller markets, which have relatively smaller budgets and a smaller number of employees.

For the limited number of Latinxs who do find their way into featured on-air positions, their integration into the community can be uneasy. For example, a number of Latinx practitioners with whom I spoke reported that they had received some resistance, not only internally but also from the listening community. Consider the case of A. Martinez, host of *Take Two*, a morning news and culture show featured on 89.3 KPCC in Los Angeles. In 2012, Martinez was originally recruited to serve as cohost for the popular *Madeleine Brand Show*, which was later renamed *Brand and Martinez*.

According to Martinez, his hiring was met with some resistance by some listeners and the local media; some of this resistance had racial undertones. "Do you know what 'swarthy' means?" Martinez asked me during our interview in Los Angeles. "Because I didn't. I had to look it up. It means dark-skinned." Martinez was referring to an article written in *LA Weekly*, which stated that Madeleine Brand would be "bantering with a swarthy new co-host" (Stuart 2012a). According to Martinez, the scrutiny he received upon his arrival at NPR caught him by surprise: "I didn't realize this would make news. Someone gets hired at a radio station. Why is that news? It turned out to be huge news because of the directive of the grant, what they were looking for. [People believed] 'Well, we found a brown dude. Let's just stuff him in there.' That made news." Martinez is referring to the One Nation Media Project, which provided the grant that made his hire possible. The goal of the organization is to provide coverage to multiethnic communities in Southern California. KPCC had applied for the grant to diversify its newsroom, but Martinez said that he suspects that some members of the community may have perceived this as "forced affirmative action." According to Martinez, his education and his legitimacy as an NPR host were immediately suspect.

Unlike Martinez's counterpart, Madeleine Brand, who was professionally groomed in public radio, Martinez began his career in sports radio. Ultimately, the collaboration was too difficult, and after four weeks, Brand abruptly left KPCC, citing incompatibility with Martinez. Fans of the show, however, were critical of the station's Latinx outreach efforts. In 2012, *LA Weekly* ran an article titled "How KPCC's Quest for Latino Listeners Doomed the Madeleine Brand Show," in which the author, Tessa Stuart, laments the loss of her show: "Gone was Brand's theme song by indie band Fool's Gold; in its place was the trilling pan flute of 'Oye Mi Amore' by Maná, a Mexican rock group whose popularity peaked in the 1990s. Suddenly, instead of the usual segments about *Downton Abbey* and disputes at a Brooklyn co-op, there was a segment about the death of a tortilla magnate, followed by one on Hatch chile season" (Stuart 2012b). In her assessment of KPCC, Stuart frames the station's pursuit of Latinx listeners as economic opportunism rather than civic responsibility. According to Stuart, the station's diversification strategies were driven by the desire to increase ratings and pursue grant dollars, which she believes are misguided. The product of such a strategy, she argues, will be programming that appeals neither to Latinxs nor to NPR's current audience.

In Stuart's critique of KPCC, she articulates a question faced by many station managers operating in markets where there is a significant Latinx population: How do you integrate Latinx listeners without isolating your core audience of listeners? In Los Angeles, KPCC made a concerted effort to invest significant resources to alter its programming, but this was an exceptional case. During my interviews at stations across the country, I found that station managers and news directors are fearful of isolating their core listeners, a fear that has led to an overall conservative approach to programming.

Conclusion

In this chapter, I have argued that NPR was originally designed to be autonomous, outside the control of both the state and the marketplace so that it could deliver civic information to publics that were underserved in the media landscape. In reality, NPR has never achieved this kind of autonomy and has, over time, increasingly functioned like other commercial news outlets. Over the course of its history, funding for the network has been politicized, based on the perception that NPR serves as a vehicle for liberal ideals. In response to its constant state of funding crisis, NPR has embraced the concepts of privatization, flexibility, and efficiency, which has resulted in an impressive rise in audience, market share, membership donations, and corporate underwriting.

Because NPR has increasingly appropriated the logic of the marketplace, listeners are no longer conceived of as a public but rather seen as a set of market segments that can be evaluated according to their economic potential. This, in turn, has informed how NPR assesses its commitment to the US Latinx community. I found that NPR has targeted an ideal Latinx listener that possesses significant economic and cultural capital. In short, NPR has pursued a Latinx audience that is most congruent with its current audience profile, resulting in a programming strategy that maintains, rather than subverts, the status quo. NPR's lack of investment in Latinx talent and new programming supports this finding. Consequently, the network has continued to create programming for a normative audience of White, middle-class listeners while continuing to relegate Spanish-dominant Latinxs to the periphery.

However, this strategy runs counter to NPR's original mission of engaging those who were left out of civic discourses. After all, these are not the disenfranchised listeners that NPR's architects imagined the network would serve. In a moment of introspection, NPR invited a number of national leaders to publicly reflect on NPR's diversity efforts (NPR 2012). In the piece, Janet Murguía, president and CEO of the National Council of La Raza, argues that "focusing on just serving college graduates underestimates the appeal and value of NPR's programming to the Latino community." Murguía goes on to argue that NPR could grow its Latinx audience if it simply had the will to hire more Latinxs as journalists and producers and to invest in new programming. According to Murguía, this practice is much needed and too long overdue. The findings of this research suggest that although NPR and its member stations are fully aware that Latinxs are becoming an important part of their future audiences, they frequently pursue strategies that are conservative, rather than transformative, in nature. While these practices certainly make sense from the perspective of an organization that wants to remain economically viable, they also ensure that NPR underdelivers on its original mandate to represent the diversity of the nation.

8

Journalistic Whiteout

Whiteness and the Racialization of News

CARLOS ALAMO-PASTRANA AND WILLIAM HOYNES

News media in the United States are in crisis. With audiences for once-dominant print and broadcast news in steady decline, especially among younger audiences, media organizations continue to search for a viable economic model to support serious journalism. The crisis facing the news extends beyond economic uncertainty. Public trust in national news organizations has declined sharply over the past three decades. By 2017, the Pew Research Center (Barthel and Mitchell 2017) reported that only 20 percent of American adults have a high degree of trust in national news media. National news organizations are facing increasingly aggressive criticism, led by President Trump, who regularly lambasts national news as "fake news" and has described journalists as the "enemy of the American people" (Grynbaum 2017).

In all of this, a widespread assumption across the political spectrum is that what is wrong with news is a problem of "media bias." From this perspective, journalists are one-sided, unfair, doing advocacy work, or just plain dishonest—all of which are violations of the expectations of objective reporting. Charges of bias are, in essence, claims that news organizations are systematically distorting reality through newsroom decisions about the stories they cover, perspectives they highlight, and information they include. Conservative media critics have long claimed that the primary source of such bias is a widely shared liberal political perspective among elite journalists (Goldberg 2002; Lichter, Rothman, and Lichter 1986). Critics from the left generally identify the roots of media bias within the news-making process, emphasizing reporters' reliance on public officials as sources and the influence of corporate media owners (Alterman 2003; Herman and Chomsky 1988; Lee and Solomon 1992).

While media research has long examined how media frame events (Ferree et al. 2002; Reese, Gandy, and Grant 2003), recognizing the political consequences of patterns in media framing (Entman 2004; Haynes, Merolla, and Ramakrishnan 2016; Ryan 1991), media scholarship has raised questions about how we define and measure media bias. For example, Tawnya Adkins Covert and Philo Wasburn (2007) found little evidence in their study of twenty-five years of US newsmagazine coverage to support claims of consistent ideological bias in reporting of domestic political issues, instead finding an overall "centrist" nature to the coverage. Such centrist coverage may not align with bias claims, but it does help us to understand the role of professional journalism in upholding core social arrangements, including the legitimacy of the contemporary distribution of economic, political, and cultural resources. Questions about media bias, then, may offer little insight into how media intersect with central sociological questions about power and inequality.

The limits of the media-bias framework extend beyond uneven empirical support and disagreements about what, precisely, bias requires us to evaluate (Entman 2007). Charges of media bias are also limited by an epistemological framework rooted in an assumption that journalists are capable of producing news reports that can ever capture the full complexity of events or issues, without the limitations of author and source perspective (Croteau and Hoynes 1994). An unspoken assumption in typical claims of media bias, within both public and academic circles, is rooted in an untenable truth standard for the journalistic enterprise. If we take news seriously, we should recognize that journalists report stories—always partial and limited by contextual factors—such that news is always already articulated to contestation about the nature of truth.

While media scholarship has long recognized the complex dynamics shaping journalistic invocations of objectivity as a response to criticism (Mindich 2000; Tuchman 1972), critics claiming media bias typically invoke some version of objectivity as a central part of any remedy to ostensible bias. Even as journalists, media critics, and scholars sort through the complex web of contestation about the politics of news, the persistent racialization of news remains undertheorized. African American media critics, both inside and outside the academy, have long recognized the limitations of national news media, highlighting the Black press as a much-needed arena for the articulation of perspectives that are underrepresented or simply ignored by the national news (Washburn 2006; Jordan 2001). The earliest traces of an emergent Black press that was focused on presenting alternative perspectives that were underreported in the national media are found in the antebellum period. During this time, Northern abolitionist papers including *Freedom's Journal* and the *Mystery* reframed debates about slavery and Black humanity against proslavery periodicals while also attempting to unify and educate the broader Black community (Jordan 2001). Still, largely unacknowledged within journalism circles is an understanding of how professional journalism itself is (and has historically been) a cultural practice that defines and reproduces normative Whiteness. That is, understanding the racialization of news requires us to look beyond the political economic dynamics of the news industry, recognizing the limits of explanations that focus on the production processes within capitalist culture industries (Golding and Murdock 1991), such as the impact of profit pressures, advertiser preferences, or shrinking newsroom employment. A more robust analysis of the racialization of news must include analysis of the culture of professional journalism, the norms governing journalistic work and how media become salient enough to warrant delivering to the public, and the assumptions about audience identities and preferences (Alamo-Pastrana and Hoynes 2018).

Professional journalism in the United States has always been a largely White profession (Chideya 2018; Wilson, Gutierrez, and Chao 2013). News organizations have long recognized the narrow demographics of newsroom personnel. Facing criticism in the wake of the civil rights movement, many national news organizations publicly pledged to hire more journalists of color (Sylvie 2011). In 1978, the American Society of News Editors (ASNE), made a commitment to a more racially diverse newsroom; "Goal 2000" identified the year 2000 as the target date for when each member news organization's staff should match the demographic profile of its local community. ASNE's commitment to newsroom diversity emerged as a long-delayed response to the urban riots of the 1960s, which caught the virtually all-White news staffs at the major daily newspapers and broadcast networks by surprise (Frissell et al. 2017). The report of the National Advisory Commission on Civil Disorders (1968), widely known as the Kerner Commission, highlighted the almost exclusively White news profession as a serious problem—"the journalistic profession has been shockingly backward in seeking out, hiring, training, and promoting" African Americans (211)—calling on news organizations to move beyond a White perspective and "make a reality of integration—in both their product and personnel" (213). In the face of pressure from civil rights activists, ASNE initiated its Newsroom Employment Census (now called the annual Newsroom Employment Diversity Survey), which produced an annual report of the demographic makeup of journalists working at daily newspapers. The initial census collected data on "minority" journalists; in 1998, ASNE began collecting data on women in newsrooms. The ASNE census aimed to give news-industry leaders data to track progress toward the goal of racial parity in the newsroom (Mellinger 2013).

By 1998, with the target year of 2000 approaching, journalists of color constituted 11.5 percent of daily newspaper reporters, up from only 4 percent in 1978. However, this was still far below the goal of 26 percent of newsroom staff, then the percentage of the US population who identified as African American, Hispanic/Latinx, Asian American, or Native American (ASNE 1998). Recognizing the failure to achieve its diversity target, ASNE set a new target date of 2025 for achieving a newsroom workforce that reflects national racial diversity. By 2017 newsroom diversity was still an elusive goal; the annual ASNE Diversity Survey reported that journalists of color comprised 16.6 percent of newspaper employees (ASNE 2017), far below the US population goal of 39 percent. Amid ASNE's public commitment to racial and gender diversity in the newsroom, the US population was diversifying more quickly than newsroom employees were, so journalists of color actually lost ground relative to their White counterparts in the years between 1978 and 2017. Notably, the Pew Research Center reported in 2018 that US newsrooms are disproportionately White to a greater degree than other occupations: 77 percent of all newsroom employees are non-Hispanic White, while White non-Hispanic workers constitute 65 percent of the adult civilian labor force in the United States. This disparity

JOURNALISTIC WHITEOUT | 159

is largest among the youngest workers; newsroom workers ages eighteen to twenty-nine are 74 percent White, in contrast to an overall young labor force that is 59 percent White (Grieco 2018).

Simply put, the corps of professional journalists remains disproportionately White, even forty years after national news organizations announced their commitment to a diverse newsroom. In a study of ASNE's diversity efforts, Gwyneth Mellinger (2013) highlights the historical structures of exclusion within journalism—including widely shared ideas about journalistic "exceptionalism," a long-standing ban on ASNE membership for editors of weekly newspapers, and racial inequality in university-based journalism education—that helped reproduce such a White profession. Importantly, Mellinger reminds us that the process of creating more racially diverse newsrooms is more than a question of hiring practices. In seeking to explain the failure of Goal 2000, Mellinger explains, "Opening the doors of daily newspaper newsrooms to non-Whites and others entailed a reconceptualization of *who could be a journalist*" (2013, 15, emphasis in original).

Understanding how journalism has remained such a White profession, even after nearly half a century of public proclamations about enhancing newsroom diversity, requires us to consider two major factors regarding the foundational Whiteness of news media. First, we are concerned with the specific ways news has been racialized in the United States, that is, defined as a White field staffed largely by White professionals, which ultimately reaffirms its own legitimacy. Second, the Whiteness of the newsroom invites us to better understand the practices that allow narratives to be distributed and received as normative and "commonsensed" media products.

This chapter analyzes the relationship between professional journalism and the distribution of new forms of White-nationalist media, exploring how their interactional dynamics reinforce White supremacy even as they render it invisible. First, we clarify the slippery usage of terms including "White nationalism," "White privilege," and "White supremacy." Understanding White privilege and White nationalism helps to show how they can, at times, be antithetical to each other during our new era of liberal multiculturalism, even as both ultimately reinforce White supremacy. We consider how professional journalism and White-nationalist media navigate a media terrain characterized by both expressions of overt racial hostility and silence. These dynamics demonstrate how these particular strands of media ultimately depend on each other to shield themselves from serious critique and interrogation of their investment in White supremacy.

Conceptualizing White Supremacy

To theorize the racialization of news in a way that adequately accounts for both long-standing patterns and contemporary developments, we need to recognize the complexity of journalism's relationship to Whiteness. To begin, we consider the ways professional journalism should be understood as an example of what the literary scholar Jodi Melamed (2011b) terms "official antiracisms." Melamed contends that cultural products and, specifically, literary texts are key forms of racial epistemologies that manifested themselves following World War II and evolved into our contemporary era of neoliberal multiculturalism. Most important, official antiracisms seek to detach and minimize material understandings about race that shape structural outcomes. This was accomplished most prominently by shifting the demands made by social movements and moving them inside universities, where they were transformed into conversations about aesthetics and how an emergent managerial class could learn about racial groups through inclusive reading lists (Melamed 2011b, 91). New forms of media strongly interface with traditional cultural texts such as the novel as literary forms that promote and strengthen official antiracisms.

For purposes of clarity, we distinguish between the terms "White nationalism," "White privilege," and "White supremacy." "White supremacy" is an umbrella term that houses both White nationalism and White privilege. According to the Indigenous studies scholar Andrea Smith (2012), White supremacy encapsulates three defining features: slavery, genocide, and Orientalism. Within Smith's framework, the anti-Blackness prevalent in slavery helps to anchor the materialist roots of capitalism, while genocide and Orientalism help to explain colonialism and permanent war as constituent features of White supremacy. Though not mentioned directly by Smith, we consider White privilege and White nationalism as important, yet distinct, strands that also undergird and permeate the overarching system of White supremacy.

The geographer Laura Pulido (2015) notes that White privilege details the benefits in housing, education, and wealth afforded to Whites that require little, if any, direct and/or conscious forms of racial animus by Whites toward other groups. White privilege exists as a defining feature of White supremacy in the United States after World War II, what the sociologist Howard Winant (2001) refers to as the racial break, when overt and institutionalized forms of racism were outlawed and considered socially unacceptable, even as de facto forms of racism and inequality persisted. One important feature of this shift is that racism is identified as an individual trait or behavior rather than a structural arrangement that was legally codified before World War II and in which a different form of White privilege flourished. Specifically, before the racial break, racism could only be considered legitimate inasmuch as it is present in the conscious and direct actions of individuals rather than as a structural relationship highlighting "the production and exploitation of group differentiated vulnerabilities to premature death" (Gilmore 2007, 28). The post–World War II moment is historically significant because "white supremacy entered a phase of permanent crisis, spurred initially by the fight against racism and fascism and by the numerous and overlapping postwar anticolonial and antiracism movements." More simply, the United States needed to grapple with the claims being made by anticolonial and antiracist social movements at the precise moment that the Soviet Union, its Cold War rival, sought to portray the United States as innately undemocratic and defined by White supremacy (Melamed 2011a, 84).

The "dematerialization" of racism, argues Melamed (2011b), explains the rise and use of cultural forms such as race novels as key epistemological tools of official antiracist regimes between the mid-1930s and the early 2000s. While official antiracisms did not begin until after the post–World War II racial break, Melamed locates their earliest manifestation among alliances between southern liberals and northern philanthropists and (Black) intellectuals encapsulated in Gunnar Myrdal's *An American Dilemma: The Negro Problem and American Democracy*, published in 1944 (Melamed 2011b, 20). Unlike academic texts, novels promoted an emergent multicultural and cultural pluralist impulse, which enabled dominant groups to learn about marginalized racial and ethnic groups through inclusive reading lists. Such multicultural reading lists provided in institutional spaces such as the university enabled Whites, especially those being prepared as a managerial class, to see themselves as an informed public and, perhaps most importantly, as morally "good white people" (Sullivan 2014). The shift away from overt practices of racism, argues Melamed, rationalizes our current neoliberal multicultural era of wealth concentration, elimination of the social safety net, and continued extraction of low-wage labor from certain groups. For neoliberalism to maintain its legitimacy, it must therefore reject and conceal structural forms of racism, all while reducing racism to an individualized phenomena.

In contrast to the discreet manifestations of White privilege, we use the term "White nationalism" in this chapter to identify the conscious and intentional ways in which groups of Whites across the globe seek to create an exclusive, normative, and heteropatriarchal racial state (see also Hughey 2012b, 197). White nationalism opposes neoliberal social and economic priorities on the grounds that they lead to the disenfranchisement and disempowerment of White male majorities. In response, White nationalists resort to varying strategies such as physical violence as well as discursive strategies that include the use of terms like "White genocide," "invasion," and "terrorism" that establish themselves as victims who are under attack and who must simply defend themselves and the essentialist features of a White racial state.

These and other terms are meant to highlight shifting population demographics and, most importantly, the resulting perceived loss of political power of White men. In other words, there is a conflation between increasing demographic shifts and political power that ignores the ways in which White men maintain social privileges afforded them based on their racial and gendered identities (Kimmel 2015). The adoption of strict voting laws by state legislatures, most especially felony disenfranchisement, and the gerrymandering of voting districts under the pretense of maintaining the integrity of elections have also served to shore up the voting power of White majorities throughout the country (Rhodes 2017). Accordingly, the narratives that frame Whites as victims traffic in the use of explicitly racist, homophobic, sexist, and anti-Semitic imagery and language that is often paired with unfounded conspiracy theories.

Although White privilege and White nationalism are both products of White supremacy, they may at times be antithetical and hostile to each other. White-nationalist media's pronounced racism and use of "alternative facts" are a direct threat to the seemingly objective and multicultural antiracism of White professional media. Even so, professional journalism's desire to defend and police itself against White-nationalist newspapers helps to reinforce White professional media's investment in colorblind rhetoric *and its dependency* on White nationalism as a means of affirming its own value. In the end, White supremacy in the news media, and in society more broadly, escapes critique as White privilege and White nationalism attempt to maneuver against each other.

The Emergence of Professional Journalism

Journalism was not always regarded as a profession, and the eighteenth- and nineteenth-century press was not rooted in now-familiar ideas about objectivity. In fact, the emergence of professional journalism is precisely when objective reporting became the defining idea within US journalism. The sociologist Michael Schudson (1978) explains in his classic study of the origins of objectivity in journalism that the idea of objective journalism is a twentieth-century concept. Only in the years after World War I did objectivity become the dominant value in US journalism.

Before World War I, reporters did not subscribe to a belief in what we now term "objectivity." In the late eighteenth and the early nineteenth centuries, most newspapers were run by political parties, offering a partisan account of events aimed at engaging and mobilizing sympathetic voters. By the middle of the nineteenth century, a new fact-based journalism replaced the partisan press; the media historian Gerald Baldasty (1992) argues that economic forces drove the growth of this new kind of journalism. For example, the Associated Press—one of the first wire services—sought to present news in a way that would be acceptable to the many different newspapers that printed its reports, and the *New York Times* introduced an "information" model of reporting aimed at attracting an upscale audience.

Still, journalists did not aim for objective reporting; they were not concerned with the separation of facts and values, nor did they believe that facts themselves were messy (Schudson 1978). To the contrary; for journalists before the emergence of professional journalism, the facts spoke for themselves. The goal of fact-based reporting was simply to uncover these facts, and that task was straightforward: find and report the truth. As late as the early twentieth century, journalists were confident in their ability to identify the relevant facts and to report them accurately.

This faith in facts held by American journalists was thrown into doubt in the years during and after World War I. Many American journalists participated in wartime propaganda efforts during World War I, working with the Committee on Public Information (CPI), led by the journalist George Creel (Ewen 1996). The success of the CPI in using news to mobilize public support for the war made journalists uncomfortable with any simple understanding of "facts." Having seen how effectively facts could be manipulated, journalists began to question the very foundation of the news (Schudson 1978).

The recognition that information could be manipulated and the rise of a new public-relations profession that was dedicated to the shaping of public opinion left journalists with a crisis of confidence about their ability to report facts in any straightforward way. In Schudson's (1978) account, objectivity emerged as a solution to this crisis; rooted in a belief in science and professional expertise, objectivity offered journalists "a method designed for a world in which even facts could not be trusted" (122). By training reporters in the method of objectivity, journalists transformed their naive fact-based craft into a profession with a distinctive method (Glasser 1984). This method could be taught to aspiring journalists, who would be credentialed and professionalized through formal higher education at the growing number of journalism schools at colleges and universities.

By the 1930s, professional journalism had become institutionalized within the news industry. Over the next several decades, this new journalism became an increasingly high-status (and influential) profession. The foundation of professional journalism—the source of self-confidence among reporters and the roots of public trust in the news—was the commitment to the practice of objective reporting.

Whiteness and Objectivity

For many journalists, objectivity stands as an unattainable goal, an ideal, of what professional journalists should strive for. At the same time, objectivity is codified in routine reporting methods that are taught in journalism schools and reinforced in newsrooms. Objectivity is both norm and practice. The normative dimensions of objectivity define expectations for an appropriate journalistic approach (Santos 2009). Objective reporters aim to inhabit a mind-set that values neutrality, even disinterestedness; they are expected to express no opinion and to produce accounts that do not reflect any specific perspective. In fact, professional journalists remove themselves from their reporting—a commitment to objective reporting leaves little room for subjectivity—and this discourages reflection about the relevance of journalists' background and identity (Jenkins and Padgett 2012). Objectivity as norm, then, positions journalists as having no standpoint or, more precisely, renders invisible the standpoint(s) from which journalistic knowledge is produced.

Objectivity as practice, similarly, affirms professional journalism as knowledge with an invisible standpoint. The practice of professional journalism emphasizes a two-sided version of balance, separating facts from opinion, attributing opinions to (preferably named) sources, an emphasis on description over interpretation, and an avoidance of highly charged language. These practices ensure that news is not one-sided (by definition, since reporters include two sides) and contains expressions of opinion limited to the perspectives of news sources rather than journalists themselves. Following standard practices of objective reporting relieves journalists of the responsibility to account for the forces that structure their professional standpoint.

Professional journalists see objectivity as the foundation of their profession's legitimacy (Schudson and Anderson 2009). In defining journalistic knowledge as objective and highlighting the limitations of subjective accounts, objectivity, like other claims to expertise, attempts to erase the traces of the humans that produce journalistic knowledge. This is consistent with Gaye Tuchman's (1972) argument that objectivity is, fundamentally, a "strategic ritual" designed to protect reporters and news organizations from claims of bias or potential lawsuits. But the dimensions of strategy inherent in objectivity are far deeper than simply professional or organizational protection. Indeed, the assumptions embedded in the *practice* of objective journalism—the work of erasing journalistic subjectivity, elevating political detachment, and fetishizing a both-sides version of balance as a journalistic ideal—serve to conceal the social and cultural forces that reproduce the profession's own long-standing Whiteness. It is no wonder that four decades of public statements endorsing a more diverse newsroom have failed.

For professional journalists, objectivity is what elevates standard-format news reports over other forms of knowledge. If journalistic accounts are still "stories," objectivity defines the stories produced by professional journalists as more reliable and accurate—if, perhaps, less engaging or accessible—than other modes of storytelling. In this regard, news organizations promote objectivity as the most consequential difference between journalistic stories and other narrative accounts. Since objectivity and the professionalization of journalism emerged in response to journalists' own anxiety about the status of "facts" and "truth" (Schudson 1978), it may be no surprise that professional journalists hold tightly to the ideal of objective journalism.

Scholars of Whiteness and media (Jessie Daniels 2009; Dyer 1997; Feagin 2013) offer a valuable perspective on the limitations of a professional journalism defined by objectivity. In removing subjectivity from professional journalism, while simultaneously ignoring the persistently narrow demographic makeup of newsroom staff, objective journalism has long managed to both marginalize journalists of color and reify the perspectives and experiences of White reporters as a form of disembodied, neutral knowledge.

Just as there has long been silence among White people about their own racial identity, with questions about "race" being reserved for people of color, so too does professional journalism define objective reporting for major news organizations as an unraced form of knowledge, while racializing the reporting of journalists of color and publications and programs aimed specifically at audiences of color. For example, many journalists of color, including those who work for major national news organizations, are defined by their racial identity through their membership in organizations such as the National Association of Black Journalists, the National Association of Hispanic Journalists, and the

Asian American Journalists Association. White journalists are not similarly racialized; the associations they belong to (and to which many journalists of color also belong) are identified by their commitment to journalistic practice, such as the Society for Professional Journalists; by non-race-based identities, such as the Association of LGBTQ Journalists; or by areas of professional expertise, such as the Society of Environmental Journalists.

Similarly, news organizations that cover stories focused on the experiences of and perspectives within communities of color are labeled with a specific racial identity. For example, African American media, most prominently the long-standing Black press during its heyday in the mid-twentieth century, has long offered reporting of events, issues, and perspectives that receive little attention in the national news. Media labeled as "Hispanic" media, including Spanish-language newspapers and television, cover Latinx communities with a regularity and depth that is not available from the major national news outlets.

In short, news that is produced primarily by White journalists, focused primarily on White communities, and targeted primarily at White audiences claims the label of professional journalism. In refusing a racial identity, professional journalism claims a universal perspective, and this stands in sharp contrast to the racially specific identities of news by and for communities of color. This invisibility of professional journalism's Whiteness is what requires critical attention.

In the current climate of political polarization, however, the project of professional journalism and the idea of objective reporting are becoming increasingly unstable. Charges of bias and "fake news" and the emergence of popular and aggressively conservative forms of news are helping to shift the news landscape (McNair 2017). Amid such change, the invisible Whiteness of professional journalism may be becoming far more legible and, as it is recognized and discussed, may be simultaneously opening space to challenge the norms and practices of professional journalism and facilitate the emergence of new, explicitly White-nationalist forms of news.

White-Nationalist News as a Challenge to
Professional Journalism

The growth of explicitly White-nationalist media, a genre that announces its White identity with pride and anger, highlights the changing
racial dynamics of the journalistic field in the late 2010s. As professional
journalism remains largely unable to confront its own invisible Whiteness, emphasizing the importance of objectivity and a reliance on verifiable facts in the face of a changing political culture that seems to render
such values old-fashioned, the newly emboldened White-nationalist
media confront professional journalism from a new direction.

To explore the challenge of White-nationalist media, we focus here
on the most prominent White-nationalist online publication: the *Daily
Stormer*. The *Daily Stormer*, launched by the neo-Nazi Andrew Anglin
in 2013 (O'Brien 2017), is full of content about racial politics. In the
wake of the August 2017 White-supremacist rally in Charlottesville,
Virginia, when the *Daily Stormer* mocked a peaceful counterprotester
who was killed by a White supremacist at the rally, the *Daily Stormer's*
web host, GoDaddy, dropped the *Daily Stormer*, taking it offline tempo-
rarily. In scrambling to get back online, the *Daily Stormer* briefly found
a web host in Iceland, then Anguilla, then Hong Kong (Lavin 2018),
before returning to a US-based web host in November 2017. The *Daily
Stormer* (n.d.) calls itself "the most censored publication in history" and
features a disclaimer on the front page of the site that reads, "we here at
the *Daily Stormer* are opposed to violence."

One look at the content of the site, however, demonstrates that the
disclaimer, a strategic statement to support the *Daily Stormer's* effort to
find and maintain an online host, rings hollow. While the editors assert
their opposition to violence, the site is full of violent rhetoric that promotes dehumanization and hate. This strategic disavowal of violence
suggests a very limited, or perhaps disingenuous, understanding of the
meanings and forms of violence. While claiming to oppose violence,
the *Daily Stormer* is certainly not opposed to racism. In Anglin's *A
Normie's Guide to the Alt-Right* (2016), central principles of the ideology
of the movement include anti-Semitism, scientific racism, opposition
to gender equality, a celebration of "White history," and a commitment
to the establishment of "pure White racial states in all formerly White

countries," which would require mass deportation of all non-Whites from the United States.

The *Daily Stormer*, especially with its newly refreshed 2018 design, is stylistically similar to many popular news websites: the front page announces featured stories, includes links to video stories, shows a Twitter feed, and highlights US and World news sections. Visually, the *Daily Stormer* might seem like just another partisan news site. While the site's editors and authors are not journalists, the site employs an aesthetic and organization of "stories" that suggests a journalistic approach. This pretense to journalism is a contemporary version of what Jessie Daniels (2009) labels "cloaked websites," which serve as powerful spaces for the distribution of cyber racism. Daniels emphasizes the political significance of such cloaked websites: "White supremacists have customized Internet technologies in ways that are innovative, sophisticated, and cunning. And the Internet is an increasingly important front on the political struggle to contest the meanings of race, racism, and civil rights" (3). The *Daily Stormer* seeks legitimacy by hiding behind a thin veneer of journalistic form; looking like a news website is undoubtedly a key part of its appeal.

The content of the *Daily Stormer*, however, is assertively racist. One of the tabs at the top of each the *Daily Stormer* page is titled "Race War"—and the *Daily Stormer* stories are full of racially inflammatory claims. Headlines, for example, routinely use boldly racist and anti-Semitic language, the kind of language widely regarded as offensive that is virtually nonexistent in professional journalism. Virtually all of the stories in the "Race War" section are sensationalistic accounts of crimes committed by people of color and immigrants. The perpetrators of crime and violence in these stories are marked as racial/ethnic others—African American, Latino, Muslim—and the victims are depicted as White.

The story-selection process offers little journalistic coherence; rather, the "Race War" section is simply a collection of crime stories, curated to emphasize White suffering as a result of Black and Brown violence. The not-so-subtle message is that a race war is under way, and Whites are losing. In this narrative, stories of Black and Brown crime and violence are typically framed as a result of biological or cultural inferiorities, for which there is no remedy. This curated set of stories serves to reify race as an essential marker of difference, implying that the only "solution" is racial separation through the creation of a White ethnostate, reaffirming a core tenet of White-nationalist ideology.

While the *Daily Stormer* does not contribute any original journalism to these stories, the editors attach their own headlines and a brief, snarky tagline, appearing with a provocative or mocking image that links to the actual news story. These headlines and taglines work to aggressively frame the stories that follow. For example, all of the stories explicitly invoke race (of the victim, perpetrator, or both) in the headline or tagline. Most of this race-marking uses openly racist language: explicit racial epithets in the the *Daily Stormer*-inserted headline or tagline, most commonly some version of the N-word. Such derogatory labels are not present in the news reports that are linked to by the racist headlines but are used by the *Daily Stormer* to transform crime news into inflammatory race (and racist) news. The *Daily Stormer* offers a version of "news" from a White-nationalist perspective. The site embraces, even shouts, its commitment to telling stories about current events from a decidedly White standpoint, a racialized lens rooted in a belief in White superiority and committed to support for the practices of White supremacy.

Our case study of the *Daily Stormer*, a salient voice of a broad network of White nationalism that has become more visible in the Trump era, illustrates how contemporary White-nationalist media make no pretense to objective reporting, nor do these media follow standards associated with professional journalism. In fact, much of what appears on White-nationalist sites is a form of commentary on journalism itself; the White-nationalist news sites do not do original reporting, follow journalistic methods, or rely on traditional norms of fact-checking. Rather, White-nationalist media typically provide a lens for interpreting the news, for making sense of selected current events. This lens is unapologetically defined as a White way of seeing the world, one that presents itself as a stark contrast to a multicultural, neoliberal worldview. In asserting this contrast, White-nationalist media implicitly represent this lens as preferable to the perspective of professional journalism, which White nationalists, even as they selectively repost and assertively reframe content from mainstream news outlets, mock as elitist, dishonest, and out of touch with the interests of White Americans.

The *Daily Stormer* employs a heavy dose of in-your-face racial slurs, invokes a White culture under attack, and highlights violence by people it defines as non-White, key components of how White-nationalist media assert a White racial subjectivity. This explicitly subjective approach to the news is part of what makes White-nationalist media stand out from professional journalism. In repurposing a highly curated set of news articles and framing the news with inflammatory headlines and often-snarky commentary, White-nationalist media are a critique of both the form and content of professional journalism.

Conclusion

The current visibility of White-nationalist media highlights the complexity of the contemporary racial politics of professional journalism. The invisible Whiteness of professional journalism, hidden, as we have seen, by the norms and practices of objectivity, is decidedly different from the openly racist embrace of White identity by White-nationalist media. And these differences are meaningful. White-nationalist media normalize racist stereotypes and endorse the creation of a White society, while professional journalism promotes a colorblind approach that strengthens the invisibility of Whiteness.

In professional journalists' defense of their own craft in the face of the challenge posed by White-nationalist media, they have, perhaps ironically, made it more difficult to recognize the structural sources of racial inequality in the United States. Shannon Sullivan's (2014) analysis of the problem of "good White people," who define their own virtue in opposition to their openly racist neighbors, is helpful here. White nationalists offer professional journalists an easy foil that highlights the goodness of professional journalism's commitment to fairness, balance, and diversity. However, comparing themselves favorably to White-nationalist media may, ultimately, let professional journalists off the hook. Just as Sullivan's good White people avoid confronting the structures that support White privilege, professional journalism's implicit critique of White-nationalist media pushes the invisibility of journalism's Whiteness further into hiding. As a result, we are left with a well-meaning professional journalism that is unable to engage its own role in the reproduction of White privilege.

The resurgent visibility of White-nationalist media may open new possibilities for conversation about the racialization of news. But this will require journalists to look squarely at how professional journalism fails to explain historical forms of racial exclusion and, in its inability to confront its own enduring Whiteness, helps to reproduce, even in its liberal critique of White nationalism, unremitting forms of White privilege.

9

Reframing Adoptee Narratives

Korean-Adoptee Identity and Culture in
Twinsters *and* aka SEOUL

SUNAH M. LAYBOURN

"Yours is from Vietnam, right?" Simon asks Cam and
Mitchell.
Then, with an air of superiority, Simon continues, "*We*
were able to adopt one from Korea."
Cam whispers to Mitchell, "Are Koreans really better?"
Mitchell answers, "I don't know."
—*Modern Family*, season 6, episode 17

In the 1950s, in the aftermath of the Korean War, adoption from Korea
began. So too started the first *sustained* intercountry adoption program
to the United States. Since its inception, over 150,000 Korean children
have been adopted to the United States, primarily to White families
(Kim 2008; Tuan and Shiao 2011). To date, Korean adoptees make up 25
percent of transnational adoptions to the United States and are the largest group of transracial adoptees currently in adulthood (R. Lee 2003;
Park Nelson 2009). Though intercountry adoption from Korea may
seem unlikely given the exclusionary Asian immigration policies and
anti-Asian sentiment that characterized the United States at the time, a
coordinated public-relations effort by media and the government promoted the inclusion of these Asian children into White American families. This framing not only shaped popular sentiment about Korean
adoptees but also facilitated decades of transnational, transracial adoption that followed, continuing into the present day (Park Nelson 2009;
Pate 2004).

This chapter's opening excerpt from ABC's prime-time sitcom *Modern Family* jokingly alludes to the established framing of Korean adoption and the racialized adoption marketplace and continues the portrayal of international adoption from the parents' perspective (Brian 2012; Park Nelson 2016; Raleigh 2018). However, now that a critical mass of this longest-standing group of transnational, transracial adoptees is in adulthood, they are creating their own media, raising the questions, How do adoptee-created media shape the distribution of Korean adoptee images? and How do these media intervene in Asian American portrayals more broadly?

While the late 1990s and early 2000s saw Korean adoptees authoring their own stories through blogs and anthologies (Bishoff and Rankin 1997; Trenka, Oparah, and Shin 2006), currently Korean adoptees are leveraging social media technologies to create full-length films. This chapter examines how adoptee-centered media converge with and diverge from traditional renderings of transnational adoption and how these media reshape understanding of transnational, transracial adoptees, specifically, and conceptions of Asian and Korean American racial, ethnic, and familial identities, generally.

The chapter begins with a review of mainstream-media portrayals of Korean adoptees in the early decades of Korean adoption before turning to two recent, mainstream Korean-adoptee-created media—*Twinsters* (Futerman and Miyamoto 2015) and *aka SEOUL* (Maxwell 2016). Through an examination of these two documentaries, this chapter examines the implications of these media in shaping the distribution of Korean-adoptee and Asian American images. Audiences are provided with a new lens to understand adoptee experiences through these Korean-adoptee cultural productions' exploration of previously excluded or unimagined themes, such as birth-family search, the falsification of adoption paperwork, "unhappy" adoptees, the formation of a communal adoptee identity, and the establishment of a sense of "place" for a group that often feels in between places, spaces, and identities. The avenues of distribution—Netflix for *Twinsters* and NBC Asian America for *aka SEOUL*—also situate adoptee experiences in the universal experience of belonging while reasserting Asian adoptees as part of the broader Asian American immigration story and contemporary Asian America.

Children in Need of Rescue:
Historical Representations of Korean Adoptees

In the immediate post–Korean War period, Korean orphans were depicted in the media as "Korean waifs," "waifs of war," and military "mascots" (Kim 2008; Park Nelson 2009). Newspapers highlighted stories of military personnel's humanitarian efforts caring for Korean children. Accompanying the features were pictures of GIs giving food to Korean children in tattered clothing, playing with smiling Korean children, and even engaging in fatherly behavior, such as disciplining or teaching life skills, to Korean boy orphans, whom platoons had unofficially adopted as their "mascots" (Oh 2015). Ultimately, many US GIs returned to the United States with their military "mascots." Media covered the journey of these Korean children from Korea to the United States and their seamless integration into US society (Oh 2015).

In addition to the military's efforts in Korea, US soldiers and chaplains wrote home to their families and churches asking for supplies for orphanages they had established (Ceniza Choy 2013. Through donations, people at home were able to contribute to the humanitarian effort while simultaneously showing support for the military. Emphasizing this link between the military, humanitarian aid, and Christian duty were American Christian missionaries. Missionaries were some of the only American civilians in Korea immediately before and after the Korean War. As missionaries returned to the United States, they shared stories with their home congregations about the material and spiritual needs of Korean children (Oh 2015). Missionaries' reports mirrored broader messaging about the dangers of Communism and the inherent need for US intervention to combat the spread of not only an inferior political ideology but also an inferior spiritual practice. Through missionaries' reports and solicitations, Korean adoption became linked to ideas of Christian duty (Kim 2008).

Early depictions of Korean orphans in newspapers spurred many US families to adopt from Korea and even inquire about specific Korean children shown in photographs (Oh 2015). Due to prevailing anti-Asian immigration policies, special adoption policies were created to allow the immigration of these Asian children, including individual visas in some cases (Park Nelson 2016). These special policies highlighted the exceptional status of this wave of Asian immigrants. After Harry and Bertha Holt's very public adoption of eight Korean children in 1955, the demand for Korean children soared (Kim 2010). The Holts not only publicized Korean adoption but also created the first formalized inter-country adoption agency, Holt Adoption Agency.[1] The Holts framed their adoptions from Korea and facilitating adoption for other couples as a direct mission from God (Pate 2014). Through adoption, US families were able to fulfill their supposedly Christ-directed duty to help the fatherless.

As Korean children traveled to the United States to join their adoptive families, local newspapers and television stations were on site to capture the initial unification of children and adoptive parents. Newspapers included pictures of adoptive families meeting their Korean children for the first time at the airport. Stories even followed up on these Korean children as they entered adolescence, reporting on their smooth adjustment to American life. Photo editorials and the accompanying news stories depicted Korean adoptees living "all-American" lives—playing baseball, eating hotdogs, and joining Boy and Girl Scout troops (Oh 2015; Park Nelson 2016). The underlying message was that loving American households were enough to overcome any potential racial, ethnic, or cultural differences, even in the face of open, nationwide anti-Asian sentiment. These portrayals were in line with social-work practices at the time that dictated that no special attention be given to adoptees' heritage culture (Scroggs and Heitfield 2001).

Taken together, these media portrayals served dual purposes: they framed White adoptive parents as "saviors" to these presumed orphaned non-White children while emphasizing adopted Korean children's assimilation within their new country, culture, and family. The latter point merged with the emergent model-minority myth, effectively elevating Asian Americans to a "good" minority status in comparison to less desirable racial-minority-group members. In short, Korean adoption was a success. Korean children, like their Asian American counterparts, were assimilating seamlessly into US society.

Adoptees Asserting Selfhood:
Contemporary Korean-Adoptee-Created Media

Early depictions of adoptable Korean children encouraged prospec-
tive adoptive parents and assuaged any doubts around the assimilability of these non-White children. However, they did not encompass
the realities of Korean adoptees' lived experiences. Two documentaries
created by and centering Korean adoptees, *Twinsters* (Futerman and
Miyamoto 2015) and *aka SEOUL* (Maxwell 2016), present an image of
Korean adoptees that was formerly missing from mainstream media:
Korean-adoptee adults on their own terms.[2] Through these mainstream Korean-adoptee cultural productions, audiences and Korean
adoptees specifically are offered a narrative that normalizes Korean-
adoptee experiences while providing a glimpse of a cross-national
Korean-adoptee community, one that is intricately linked to the Asian
American experience. Importantly, these productions incorporate
themes central to the adoptee experience but ignored within adoptive-
parent-centered media (e.g., race, identity, and belonging in the United
States and Korea, birth-family search, falsification of adoption paperwork, and "unhappy" experiences).

Twinsters is an independently made documentary that follows the
initial reunification of twin Korean adoptees, who were adopted to
separate families in different countries. It was released on Netflix after
successful debuts at SXSW, winning special jury recognition for editing, and the Los Angeles Asian Pacific Film Festival, winning the Grand
Jury Prize for best documentary. It was also viewed at international
Korean-adoptee conferences.

In the film, Samantha Futerman, a US Korean adoptee and aspiring actress, and Anaïs Bordier, a French Korean adoptee and art student, find each other, facilitated by social media (YouTube and then
Facebook). The documentary tracks their initial communication via
Facebook Messenger, WhatsApp, text, and Skype to their face-to-face
meeting in London, where Anaïs lives, and then to California, where
Samantha lives. The documentary closes with the twins' return to Korea,
Anaïs for the first time, for the 2013 International Korean Adoptee Associations' Gathering. During their Korea trip, they also attempt a birth-
family search and visit their adoption agencies and foster mothers.

Throughout *Twinsters*, the audience learns more about the twins' upbringing and how they came to understand their adoptive status. Samantha and Anaïs, though adopted to separate countries, were both raised in homogeneous communities where they were the only Asians. This is a common experience reported by adoptees (Park Nelson 2016). Even for those who are adopted to areas with some Asian or Korean community presence, adoptive parents typically do not facilitate interactions between their adopted Korean children and heritage-culture communities (Park Nelson 2016).

Whereas Samantha does not feel that she was treated differently because of her race, Anaïs was teased and feels very alienated. These divergent experiences shaped their views on adoption. Samantha feels as though adoption has been a positive component of her life, whereas Anaïs feels that it is something terrible that had happened to her. Anaïs reflects on her view of herself, sharing,

> Before I used to say that I wasn't born on the nineteenth of November. I was born on the fifth of March, when I arrived in France. For me, there was no life before, to me, because I was nothing without my parents. [*cries*] Yeah. Yeah. Yeah, now I see, I see that I existed before as well. It felt like, you know, you're adopted. And so I started living with my parents. For me, being born—not born at the airport but when your parents stop wanting you—and I just realized here coming to Korea, I realized that people loved me like the whole time before.

Within this quote, Anaïs describes how her adoption story contributed to a narrative of belonging that, unbeknownst to her adoptive parents, instilled the belief that she was unwanted by her birth parents. These feelings of being unwanted and unloved led her to completely discard her early years from her existence. Ultimately, this narrative shaped how she views herself.

Anaïs's adoption story mirrors the broader framing in traditional media representations of transnational adoption—that adoptive children are a blank slate, whose lives begin once they enter their adoptive families. This narrative of their belonging as predicated on a complete separation from their birth family and birth culture has detrimental consequences for adoptees' understanding of their belonging within their adoptive family as well as their racial and ethnic identity development (Laybourn 2017). This framing also shaped how adoptive parents approached race with their adopted children and how Korean adoptees thought about themselves. Korean adoptees generally report that their parents took a colorblind approach to their racial socialization, and with little to no racial representation or counters to mainstream adoptee portrayals, most Korean adoptees report identifying as White during childhood and adolescence, some even through adulthood (Laybourn 2018; Park Nelson 2016). Through Anaïs's meeting her twin sister and embarking on their shared journey of discovery, she learns an alternate way of understanding her story and her place in the world.

In addition to the role that Anaïs's connecting with her twin plays in this new vision of herself is their attendance at the International Korean Adoptee Associations' Gathering. Another Korean-adoptee creative in California, Dan Matthews, the creator behind *aka SEOUL*, tells Samantha about the gathering. Founded in 2004 in Europe and the United States, the International Korean Adoptee Associations (IKAA) serve as a centralized hub for the Korean-adoptee diaspora. Beginning in 2004, every three years IKAA hosts a multiday international gathering of Korean adoptees in Seoul, South Korea. The gathering itself is often referred to as "IKAA" by attendees.

In the years in between the Korea gatherings, gatherings are held in Europe and the United States, though the Korea gatherings typically attract a larger attendance, as it provides first-time attendees and first-time travelers to Korea a more structured way to visit their homeland. The gatherings include a flexible schedule, so participants can attend as many of the preplanned activities, or not, as they wish. Most of the activities are more social in nature, such as scavenger hunts, tourist attractions, karaoke, and family-oriented activities. There is one day of panel sessions and a half day of research presentations. The panel sessions include topics such as identity and race, LGBTQ experiences, birth-family search, and, at the 2016 gathering, adoptees and citizenship. One of the most significant offerings is the breakout sessions by age cohort, where participants are able to meet adoptees around the same age and discuss issues relevant to their age group. In 2007, IKAA hosted the inaugural international symposium on Korean-adoption studies. Here the world's foremost Korean-adoption scholars present their research on Korean adoptees and Korean adoption. The symposium continues to be held every three years at the Seoul gatherings.

Although the intricacies of IKAA may not have been apparent in the documentary, the effect of being in Korea with hundreds of Korean adoptees from across the globe is clear. Anaïs describes her experience at IKAA, stating, "You feel like you're a part of something. . . . You know you're going to have a lot of fun for a whole week with people that understand you completely. And you know that you're in Korea and that your birth country cares about you as well. It's really moving." Through her attendance at IKAA, Anaïs reframes her conception of Korea, from one of neglect to acceptance, and in doing so reframes her conception of herself as a Korean person. Anaïs and Sam's attendance at IKAA also illustrates the global community of Korean adoptees, as adoptees from the United States and across Europe come together each year to commune with and learn from one another. The portrayal of IKAA and Anaïs's reflection of experiencing a community "with people that understand you completely" resonated with Korean-adoptee viewers. In informal conversations with IKAA 2016 attendees, about half of the first-time attendees mentioned *Twinsters* as the impetus for their attendance (Laybourn 2018).

During *Twinsters*, the audience watches as Anaïs reaches a sense of acceptance around her adoptive status. Whereas Anaïs's adoption experience seems more fraught with feelings of nonbelonging, Sam appears as though her adoptive status has been a nonissue. Toward the end of the documentary, Sam offers this reflection on her reunification with her twin sister:

> It's comforting to know that life unfolds in a way that it's supposed to, I guess. I have my sister now, and I'm happy. It's not looking back to what happened; it's moving on. . . . I have my parents. I have my foster mom. I have Anaïs's mom. I have Sue [guide from her homeland tour]. I have my sister. I have my brothers [two brothers biological to her adoptive parents]. I have like five different types of moms, and that's okay. And I love each and every one of them. And I love my birth mom, too. I don't know her—still love her. . . . Family's what you make of it. There's no definition.

Whereas Anaïs seems constrained within conventional ideas of family and devastated by the idea that she was unwanted by her birth family, Sam offers a broader and more inclusive view of family, one that runs counter to the promises of transnational adoption as offering a clean break from birth family.

Through the reunification of Sam and Anaïs, viewers are offered two extreme responses to adoption while also getting a glimpse of an unfolding Korean-adoptee identity and culture. Sam and Anaïs demonstrate key features of a Korean-adoptee identity that exists across countries—growing up as the only transracial adoptee within their community, navigating racial difference between themselves and their communities, questions around belonging, curiosity around reasons for their relinquishment, and unfamiliarity or even resistance to connecting with other Asians and/or Korean adoptees. Importantly, *Twinsters* gives viewers a glimpse into the global Korean-adoptee community through the twins' attendance at IKAA.

Whereas *Twinsters* focuses primarily on the reunification of Samantha Futerman and Anaïs Bordier, *aka SEOUL* (Maxwell 2016) concentrates on the return of five Korean adoptees from the United States and Sweden to South Korea for the 2016 IKAA. This seven-part docuseries was cocreated by and released through NBC Asian America and viewed at the San Diego and Boston Asian Film Festivals. In contrast to *Twinsters*, with its release through Netflix, *aka SEOUL* primarily targets an Asian American audience. The inclusion of adoptees within the broader Asian American narrative departs from Asian adoptees' historical exclusion from Asian American history and Asian American communities (Ceniza Choy 2016).

aka SEOUL is the follow-up to *aka DAN* (Maxwell 2014), which follows the US Korean adoptee Dan Matthews as he meets his twin brother (not adopted) and biological family in Korea. Like Sam, Dan is part of an Asian American creative community in California. Dan was able to draw on his industry connections to create *aka DAN* and then partner with NBC Asian America to create *aka SEOUL*.

In part 1 of *aka SEOUL*, Dan's adoptive mother and birth mother meet for the first time. Dan describes his nervousness around his two mothers' meeting, a different type of feeling than when he met his biological family. The documentary then shifts to interviewing Dan's adoptive mother, Lynn. Lynn says, "I can't imagine living life without my children. They are everything to me." While Lynn's words convey how central her children are to her life, one is left to wonder how her children's biological mothers may feel as they live life without *their* children. Lynn then reflects on their upcoming trip, stating her apprehension around meeting "the mother," particularly because of the language barrier. However, once they meet, she remarks, "We didn't really have a language barrier because the love that she expressed, it was just palpable." The framing of "love" as breaking down any potential barriers across cultures and language emphasizes the traditional adoption trope of love being enough. As video of Lynn and Dan's meeting with Dan's biological family fills the screen, viewers continue to gain insight into Lynn's and Dan's thoughts and feelings around the meeting. However, the perspective of Dan's birth mother and birth family are silenced. Even as we see the centrality of Dan's birth parents, they remain in the background. Though part 1 reinforces the adoptive parent's perspective, by highlighting this nontraditional family relationship, the film offers viewers an expanded vision of adoptive and biological family that traditional representations (and social-work best practices) would not have previously imagined.

Part 2 opens with Dan and three of the four other Korean adoptees at a bar in Korea. Dan, Siri, Peter, and Chelsea are playing Korean drinking games. In addition to having to drink, the loser has to try a traditional Korean snack. As the adoptees gawk at the unrecognizable foods, the novelty of Korean food and adoptees' unfamiliarity with Korean culture are displayed. Though common Korean foods are exoticized, viewers see how adoptees bond over experiencing these Korean snacks for the first time free from assumptions that they should be familiar with these Korean foods and free from shame that they are not.

The rest of part 2 focuses on Siri Szemenkar, a Sweden adoptee living in Glasgow. Like most Korean adoptees, Siri grew up in a predominantly White town (Park Nelson 2016). Although her parents traveled to Korea to pick her up with the express purpose of experiencing Korea so they could tell her about her birth country, their stories were all negative. According to her parents, Korea was "a weird culture, where nothing was 'right.'" Their stories led to a negative connection in Siri's mind that stopped her from wanting to visit Korea and from developing her Asianness. Siri's parents took a colorblind approach to her upbringing, in which they wanted her to simply feel Swedish while ignoring her racial or adoptive difference. Illustrating Siri's words, childhood pictures flash across the screen with her as the only non-White face. Although Siri knew she was different from the people in her family and community, her parents' approach to her upbringing did not provide an environment where she could talk about these differences.

At the end of part 1, Siri visits her Korean adoption agency to continue her birth-family search. According to her case manager, only 60 percent of adoptees who search find an address for their birth mother, and only 2 percent ultimately meet. Siri has cautious optimism about being able to meet her birth mother on this trip, but she is satisfied with the new information she receives from her file at the Korean agency. Through Siri's vignette, viewers learn about the limited information that adoptees (and adoptive parents) receive from their adoption agencies, the selectivity in records shared across agencies, and the potential for inaccurate information, a theme revisited in a later segment.

Whereas race and adoptive status are two layers of difference that Korean adoptees must navigate, the following three segments of the film examine another layer—sexuality. Part 3 focuses on Peter Boskey, a US adoptee from Boston with two adopted, nonbiological siblings from Korea. Although Peter also grew up in a predominantly White neighborhood, his mom was very proactive about infusing Korean culture, food, and culture camp. His adoptive status set him apart from his peers, but Peter found negotiating his sexuality a more central part of his adolescence due to expanded social understanding and support around homosexuality. Whereas Peter found support from his adoptive family for exploration into both his Korean culture and his sexuality, in part 4, viewers see another possible outcome through the vignette of Chelsea Katsaros, a twenty-eight-year-old US adoptee from Minneapolis.

Like Peter, Chelsea also attended Korean culture camp during elementary and middle school. Korean culture camps are typically weeklong sleepaway camps where attendees learn about Korean history, culture, and food. The majority of attendees are Korean adoptees, and oftentimes the camp counselors are also Korean adoptees. For Chelsea, it was the one time when she "could feel *not* like the outsider." During culture camp, Chelsea had respite from intrusive questions such as, "Why don't you look like your mom or dad? Didn't your parents want you?" She was also free from the expectation of being a spokesperson for anyone Asian. Adoptees share these experiences of intrusive questioning (Docan-Morgan 2010). Some view them as opportunities to educate people, others as repeated evidence of their nonbelonging, and for Chelsea, these questions made her want to be invisible. However, despite growing up in a family supportive of her exploration of Korean culture, Chelsea's family was not supportive of her sexual identity. She is currently not in communication with her adoptive family due to their strong religious beliefs against her sexuality.

Part 5 continues a focus on sexuality as it features Min, a US Korean adoptee from San Francisco. Though traveling to Korea is often a transformative experience for adoptees who have spent most of their lives feeling conspicuous because of their racialized physical features (Park Nelson 2016), Min was not able to find solace in his initial trip back to Korea. The first time he traveled to Korea, he presented as a Korean woman. On this trip, Min confidently experiences Korea as a Korean man and is even able to build community with other LGBTQ Korean adoptees attending IKAA through his participation in a panel about LGBTQ adoptees. Through the inclusion of LGBTQ adoptees, *aka SEOUL* examines the multifaceted experiences not only of adoptees but also of Asian Americans more broadly as they are navigating their identities.

In part 6, viewers rejoin Siri as she describes the emotional roller coaster of her birth-family search. As she is leaving her social-work agency, her social worker rushes out with news that her birth mother would meet with her after all. Whereas Siri is preparing for meeting her birth mother, the remainder of the featured adoptees are at different places in their search. Peter is "not too invested in that right now." Chelsea reviews her Korean agency's file, where she learns that her birth mother has been located. Min's search is complicated by his gender change. Reflecting on the search process, he shares, "I had never really thought about doing a birth search. Honestly, I don't think in 2004 I even knew it was an option until I got here [to Korea for IKAA]. And I had no expectations. I had been told I had been left on a doorstep when I was one day old." A Korea Social Service file fills the screen. Min finds out that the story he had been told about his relinquishment is false. His mother had arranged for him to be relinquished to the agency when he was born; he was not abandoned. His initial search was unsuccessful, and now with his gender change, Min wonders how that complicates search and reunion.

The closing segment of the docuseries opens with Dan and Lynn in Korea walking through the street markets. In a reversal from how adoptive families are often portrayed, Lynn is the only White face in a sea of Asians. Dan voices over the scene, reflecting on changes in family and conceptions of family, asking, "What does 'family' really mean?" While Dan questions how emotionally invested he should be in his birth family and how he should feel about his new familial relations, Siri shares her hope: "that I will maybe come to terms with myself and my Korean heritage a little more," now that she has been reunited with her birth mother. As part of her acceptance of herself, Siri mentions maybe reclaiming her birth name now that she has learned that her mother named her. The process of birth-name reclamation is one way that Korean adoptees assert their Korean heritage (Reynolds et al. 2017). Though Siri wants to build a relationship with her birth mother, who is now married, it may be difficult. Highlighting another common experience among adoptees in reunion, Siri learns that her existence is a secret. For some adoptees, finding their birth family is central to answering questions about their own belonging and past, but for some, even if they find their birth family, they still experience barriers to their belonging when they learn that due to social stigma around unwed mothers, they must remain a secret.

aka SEOUL closes with the featured adoptees reflecting on the role this trip to Korea is playing in their individual journeys. The adoptees share what they have learned through the trip to attend IKAA, including "There's a space where I fit" (Min) and "My biggest takeaway is more acceptance about myself—something I didn't even know I was looking for when I came" (Siri). Overall, whether or not the adoptees conducted a birth-family search and whether or not they were successful, they all ultimately had positive experiences on their return to Korea. This positive feeling and feelings of acceptance in Korea are not always the case, just as the overwhelmingly positive adoptive-family experiences are only one part of the adoptee experience.

Discussion

While we may often think of family's role in socializing people into an understanding of themselves and their belonging (e.g., national values, family values, community membership), mainstream media also play an important role. It was, after all, newspaper and television media that publicized the humanitarian crisis in war-torn Korea and encouraged White American families to adopt transnationally and transracially. It was that same media that crafted the impression of Korean children's assimilability into White American families. Likewise, contemporary Korean-adoptee-created media, such as *Twinsters* and *aka SEOUL*, play a role in reshaping Korean, Asian American, and adoptee identity and belonging. Rather than displaying adoptees' "benign racial difference" and smooth incorporation into White American families (Oh 2015), they demonstrate Korean adoptees' experiences as a "forever foreigner" (Tuan 1998). In these new portrayals, adoptees' immigrant and non-White group membership is foregrounded in stark contrast to traditional promises of inclusion.

The portrayals of Korean adoptees in *Twinsters* and *aka SEOUL* intervene in traditional constructions on two levels. First, in contrast to historical or traditional portrayals of adoptees, which are created through an adoptive parent's point of view, both documentaries center adoptees' experiences. This is seen not only through the subject of the films (adoptees themselves) but also through the production of the films (adoptees as executive producers and creative directors). Furthermore, the production crews of both films are composed primarily of Asian Americans.

Second and relatedly, because of the perspective of the films and the creative teams that produced them, viewers receive a more nuanced view of both transnational, transracial adoptee and Asian American experiences. Through *Twinsters* and *aka SEOUL*, adoptee experiences are reinserted into the Asian American experience more broadly, challenging monolithic portrayals of Asian Americans. As the adoptees in the films demonstrate, they experience the world as Asian Americans regardless of their community involvement or familial relationships. These experiences show the limitation of the misguided, though presumably well-intentioned, belief that love is enough with regard to overcoming racial, ethnic, and assumed nationality differences.

While both films explicitly interrogate themes that have historically been absent from adoptee portrayals, they do so at the exclusion of the full range of adoptee experiences. The majority of the highlighted adoptees have generally positive experiences. As Samantha shares in *Twinsters*, "everything happens for a reason," and that reason culminates in a renewed sense of self, sense of belonging, and connection to a community of similar others. This is certainly not always the case. For some adoptees, this type of connection is viewed as superficial—simply bonding due to family formation rather than shared interests. Furthermore, adoptees have a higher rate of mental health issues and suicide rates compared to the general public (Mohanty and Newhill 2006; Slap, Goodman, and Huang 2001), points that are largely omitted within both documentaries.

Even as the featured adoptees are reframing their belonging and finding a sense of social citizenship within a global Korean-adoptee community and by proxy encouraging other adoptees to do the same, US adoptee deportations are ongoing (M. Jones 2015). In fact, as *aka SEOUL* was filming, a very public Korean-adoptee deportation case was under way (M. Jones 2015), and issues of adoptee citizenship were featured during IKAA 2016. Though both documentaries are implicitly about national belonging or lack of social citizenship, the concrete refusal of Korean adoptees' (and other international adoptees') US citizenship was precluded from these media portrayals.

Finally, *Twinsters* and *aka SEOUL* primarily focus on the redeeming quality of birth-family searches and returns to Korea. While these stories provide a feel-good resolution to prior feelings of nonbelonging and, in doing so, draw on cinematic conventions of happy endings, they are in fact exceptional, as emphasized by the statistics shared by Siri's case worker. For the majority of adoptees who search, reunification is not possible. Even as these birth-family searches expand conceptions of family to incorporate first family as well as adoptive family, they can reify common misconceptions about "real" family.

Conclusion

For adoptees and nonadoptees, family stories play an important role. Through these origin stories, children learn their place within the family, the meaning of their role within the family, and the emotional significance of their inclusion (Kiser, Baumgardner, and Dorado 2010). This initial family story becomes a foundation as children begin to craft their own stories about themselves, including who they think they are and who they think they can become (Habermas and Bluck 2000; Habermas and de Silveira 2008).

Korean adoptees must reconcile competing narratives of identity and belonging. This begins with the family stories about their entrance into their adoptive families, continues through intrusive questions around their "real" family and heritage culture, and is affected by mainstream-media portrayals that infantilize adoptees. Whereas specific sociohistorical contexts facilitated Korean adoption and traditional framing of Korean adoptees, contemporary contexts make Korean-adoptee cultural production possible. Similar to other Asian American and marginalized groups, Korean adoptees are capitalizing on the internet to create alternative programming where they are centered (Considine 2011; Gao 2012). In presenting themselves as the subjects of their own stories, Korean adoptees' cultural production contrasts historical media representations that portrayed adoptees negatively or in stigmatizing frames (Kline, Karel, and Chatterjee 2006) and provides a unique opportunity for Korean-adoptee identity development, one that normalizes the lived experiences of adoptees separate from traditional limiting portrayals but also that reinserts adoptees into the Asian American experience.

Through the reunification of twin adoptees separated at birth and the vignettes of the five Korean adoptees attending IKAA, *Twinsters* and *aka SEOUL* highlight experiences of adversity and personal discovery through the lens of transnational, transracial adoption. In documenting the identity exploration of these Korean adoptees, *Twinsters* and *aka SEOUL* broaden mainstream portrayals of transnational, transracial adoptees while providing a script for identity for Korean adoptees themselves to follow.

Though these documentaries provide one alternative view of adoptees (and Asian Americans), they leave open the question of the effects of these media on J192s. Existing research on the effects of media portrayals on racial attitudes and intergroup relations suggests that positive representations can facilitate favorable attitudes and shared identity and can decrease feelings of social distance (Tukachinsky 2015). Whereas historically mainstream media perpetuated stereotypical portrayals of Asian Americans and whereas Asian Americans were the primary consumers of alternative media created by and centering Asian Americans, such as that found on YouTube (Sun et al. 2015), given the presence of *Twinsters* and *aka SEOUL* on mainstream-media outlets, there is greater likelihood that broader audiences will be exposed to these films. Accordingly, future research should examine if and how these portrayals have reshaped viewers' perceptions of Asian American and/or adoptees and if those effects vary by audience demographics.

Notes

1. The Holt Adoption Agency continues its work in the present day as Holt International and is one of the leading international adoption agencies.
2. This is not to discount previous Korean-adoptee documentaries. For example, Deann Borshay Liem's films *First Person Plural* (2000) and *In the Matter of Cha Jung Hee* (2010), which were both aired on PBS, are foundational to the Korean-adoptee community. Borshay Liem is currently in the postproduction phase of her next Korean-adoptee documentary, *Geographies of Kinship—The Korean Adoption Story* (forthcoming).

10

#BlackLivesMatter and Twitter

Mediation as a Dramaturgical Analysis

LESLIE KAY JONES

Scholars, journalists, and Americans agree that the United States is in the midst of a new Black civil and human rights movement called Black Lives Matter, often written colloquially as #BlackLivesMatter to reflect the hashtag created on Twitter by the Black feminist activists Opal Tometi, Alicia Garza, and Patrisse Cullors (cf. Carney 2016; Taylor 2016; Hitlin and Vogt 2014). Garza explained in a 2014 essay published on *The Feminist Wire* that the hashtag was a "call to action for Black people after 17-year-old Trayvon Martin was post-humously placed on trial for his own murder and the killer, George Zimmerman, was not held accountable for the crime he committed." Garza also named herself and her cocreators as queer Black women and explicitly called for this new movement to affirm "the lives of Black queer and trans folks, disabled folks, Black-undocumented folks, folks with records, women and all Black lives along the gender spectrum." #BlackLivesMatter has since become an international activist movement concerned particularly with state violence against Black people, but activists frequently observe imbalances in movement support and media coverage of violence against Black women (especially trans women) and disabled and queer folks. How do audiences negotiate these competing models for interpreting what the #BlackLivesMatter movement is and for whom it seeks justice?

The internet is pivotal to mediating public understandings of this new movement, attitudes toward its claims, and beliefs about how the movement has been received by the general public (Taylor 2016; Hooker

2016). In particular, the social media platform Twitter is home to "Black Twitter," a thriving digital counterpublic where participants discuss issues that primarily affect Black people, especially African Americans. The protests in Ferguson, Missouri, and in Baltimore, Maryland, dominated national attention through 2014 and 2015, in large part due to citizen journalism and discussion on Twitter. Protesters have thereby successfully gained the attention of elite power brokers, which collective action scholars have identified as a necessary step in the social movement process (cf. Ray et al. 2017). But what narratives can audiences consult when formulating their ideas of a movement, and how are they mediated? The study of, and activities pertaining to, #BlackLivesMatter both hold many insights about mobilization if researchers are willing to take Black discursive power and the mediation of intellectual production more seriously as subjects of analysis.

Research on #BlackLivesMatter tends to fall into three categories of inquiry. One category intervenes in the resource mobilization and network effects literature by examining movement mechanics, especially successes and failures in generating and sustaining public attention for an event or cause (Freelon, McIlwain, and Clark 2018; Carney 2016; Gallagher et al. 2018). Another category of research focuses on the impact of #BlackLivesMatter on the political landscape, using the movement as a lens for examining historical and contemporary racism in the United States (Everbach, Clark, and Nisbett 2017; Freelon, McIlwain, and Clark 2018; Obasogie and Newman 2016; Kelley 2015). Finally, a growing body of work focuses on Black cultural and intellectual spaces as dynamic sources of transgressive social imaginaries. #BlackLivesMatter is one such imaginary, and it exists alongside other contemporary articulations of social justice, like Black cyberfeminism and anticapitalism. This chapter offers collective mobilization scholars a strategy for disarticulating public social media discussions from movement actions by examining how Black Twitter is implicated in mediating the public imaginary of the #BlackLivesMatter movement as a political project.

Critics of #BlackLivesMatter have argued that the movement is disorganized and leaderless (Collins and Mak 2015; Reynolds 2015). However, this critique reflects a fundamental misunderstanding of the extent to which #BlackLivesMatter was intended to be a discursive and ideological intervention. That is, it treats audience interaction with #BlackLivesMatter's ideological claims on social media only as the outcome of movement action, without taking seriously the extent to which movement actors rely on Black counterpublics—discursive spaces where people marginalized in the mainstream public sphere can shape their own discussions of social issues—as a source of movement direction and attention. These counterpublics include social movement actors, but they also include bystanders and antagonists.

In this chapter, I argue that a sociological "dramaturgy" metaphor offers a framework for revealing how social media is implicated in the structure and meaning-making of #BlackLivesMatter. Like theatrical performances, social movements require a complex coordination of many elements (actors, a story, a stage), any one of which might ruin the entire project or propel it far beyond expectations. Additionally, I borrow the concept of a *chorus* from Greek tragedy to the dramaturgy framework to better clarify the role that Twitter plays in the movement as a public space in which outside observers negotiate their own meaning-making surrounding the movement's claims and strategies. The Greek chorus is a character in the performance, represented by one or more performers, whose role is to articulate observations about the action directly to the audience. Conceptualizing movement mechanics in this way provides a clearer understanding of the high importance of digital media in the contemporary Black civil rights movement while avoiding three pitfalls: (1) assuming that technological advances entirely shape social structure and behavior (technological determinism); (2) treating Black social media users as digital activists by default and overlooking their role as a movement audience; and (3) discounting the role of nondigital actions in digitally mediated social movements.

Performance and Social Movements

Sociology has used theatrical metaphors to shed light on a number of collective behavioral processes. Individuals present certain facets of themselves according to their perceptions of the audience. They perform on the "frontstage" in ways that will grant them entry to particular spaces and various material and symbolic resources and will abandon these performances (or adapt other more appropriate behaviors) when they interact in their "backstage" environments (Goffman 1959). These imaginaries of who composes an audience are also at work when individuals work together to construct social movements. Social movements require collective performances, in which success depends on the audience buying into the actors' grievance claims (Alexander 2006; Gamson and Wolfsfeld 1993). Movement actors may disagree on the character of multiple audiences for social movement claims, as well as which audiences they should target or even dismiss. For example, NAACP leaders strategized to employ Rosa Parks as a catalyst for the Montgomery Bus Boycott, in part because of her history of twelve years serving in the organization. Weeks before Parks's action, a fifteen-year-old teenager named Claudette Colvin refused to move to the back of the bus, for which she was jailed. However, Colvin was pregnant and unmarried; and leaders in the NAACP and Women's Political Council (WPC) ultimately decided she would not be part of their local campaign to generate grassroots support (Giddings 1985; Carson 2005). On Twitter, such deliberations are often more visible than ever before and are continuously accessible through the platform itself and digital archiving practices (like screenshots), potentially providing even more nuanced insight into what compromises various actors are making to carry out a collective project.

Audiences interpret performances according to any number of scripts, which are historically and culturally contingent. These scripts serve as a blueprint for movement choreography—that is, the mechanical means by which movement actors mobilize. The civil rights movement—and widespread misapprehensions about it—is commonly evoked as a script to which Black social movements should adhere, both by Black political actors and by critics of contemporary Black social movements like #BlackLivesMatter.

The dramaturgical framework is particularly useful for identifying steps in the collective process of meaning-making in online collective mobilization, which is crucial to making sense of ongoing social movements. Dramaturgy reminds us that each feature is contingent on the other. For example, the movement script must be legible to both the actors and the audience, requiring activists to carefully negotiate the tension between maintaining fidelity to movement goals and recruiting new participants. According to Robert D. Benford and Scott A. Hunt

(1992), "Finally, the analytical scope of dramaturgy is quite broad. It goes beyond the study of rhetorical strategies to consider a plethora of additional processes associated with the social construction and communication of meaning, including formulating roles and characterizations, managing performance regions, controlling information, sustaining dramatic tensions, and orchestrating emotions" (37). Movement actors are charged with *scripting*, *staging*, and *performing* the movement, while the audience is tasked with *interpreting*. At each moment, activists and audiences both are doing the work of encoding and decoding social meaning using a shared cultural language (Hall 1993). This interpretive work is mediated by a complex media ecosystem that is itself a product of competing cultural scripts. Studying #BlackLivesMatter requires attention to sources of discursive mediation, like partisan journalism. The goal of this chapter is to clarify the discursive processes that tether Black digital interlocutors in the Black Twitter counterpublic to public interpretations of #BlackLivesMatter as a performance in this new media ecosystem.

I propose that we should further refine this framework to include an understanding of Twitter, particularly Black Twitter, as a communication mediator between actors and audiences, as a Greek chorus. The Greek chorus refers to an element particular to classical Greek drama that serves to draw attention to particular themes and to model appropriate responses (Weiner 1980). The chorus was often composed of individuals who belonged to the main characters' "backstage" (in the sociological sense), such as maids or other servants. Albert Weiner suggests, "It is perhaps the most efficient and direct method of arousing the emotions and passions of the audience while simultaneously forcing the audience to think" (1980, 211). In other words, the Greek chorus "alienates" the audience by drawing its attention away from the perspective of the main characters toward the often critical or ambivalent gaze of bystander witnesses.

The viral spread of hashtag campaigns across social media accounts and traditional news media reveals the massive collective energy that can be generated through digital protest. Twitter functions similarly in relation to collective mobilization by sustaining dialogue about movement performances long after they have taken place and synthesizing multitudes of public conversations with media coverage and movement publications. What is colloquially called "Black Twitter" is particularly important in extending discourse about #BlackLivesMatter.

André Brock has argued, "Black Twitter *can* be understood as a 'public'; albeit a terribly understudied one. Like other Black online activities, Black Twitter would have been considered 'niche' without the intervention of the hashtag/trending topic. These two features brought the activities of tech literate Blacks to mainstream attention, contravening popular conceptions of Black capitulation to the digital divide" (2012, 545, emphasis in original). Several years since this insight, Black Twitter has transitioned from a tentative space about an emergent social phenomenon to a widely referenced imaginary of the Black social media public. Adding the concept of the Greek chorus to the dramaturgy model is meant to make space for the cultural power of this discursive imaginary in an analysis of movement progression.

Methods

The analysis for this chapter focuses on Twitter as a mediated environment in part of a larger media ecosystem that is rapidly changing due to the use of social media platforms as information-organizing hubs. In particular, it takes the relationship between Black Twitter and #BlackLivesMatter as a case, including reflections on these phenomena, such as the #BlackLivesMatter website and news articles and Google searches pertaining to the hashtag and Black Twitter. I draw on insight from my ethnographic observation of Black discursive activity on Twitter from January 2015 to December 2017, during which time I became intimately familiar with Twitter as a field site and as a node in a broader media context. In the first step of my analysis, I apply the dramaturgical framework for social movements to several social media artifacts that directly reference #BlackLivesMatter. I then consider how Black Twitter as a Black counterpublic in a social media salon has played a role in shaping audience interpretation of #BlackLivesMatter, as well as how the dramaturgical model can be expanded to address these nuances. I also offer discussion of the significant independent intellectual mediation mechanisms that shape Black Twitter as cultural gatekeeping structure for #BlackLivesMatter's claims. After adjusting the dramaturgy model to include the concept of a Greek chorus, I return to a reflection of Black audience mediation as a crucial component of the study of Black social movements.

Specifically, I performed a Google search of "Black Twitter hashtags" in December 2014 and collected all the articles returned by the search. Each of the articles, which were published in online magazines or newspapers, offered a catalog of Black Twitter hashtags, in the style of the popular digital "listicle." Table 10.1 presents the proportion of hashtags in articles from six news outlets that were reactions to instances of racism. *Essence* magazine, a magazine created for Black women in 1970, published an article naming the most memorable Black Twitter hashtags of 2013. Among them were #PaulasBestDishes, #SmartBlack-WomenofTwitter, #JusticeForTrayvon, and #SolidarityIsForWhite-Women. Of the nine hashtags listed in the article, five were responses to instances of racism, and two were responses to misogyny. The targets of hashtagged tweets included celebrities, the US justice system, mainstream media, and entertainment media (Sangweni 2013). Note that although BET is an entertainment publication, it still identified 75 percent of the most important Black Twitter hashtags as being related to social justice. Likewise, although *Essence* is primarily a fashion and lifestyle magazine for Black women, it identified primarily social justice hashtags as the definitive contribution of Black Twitter in 2013.

TABLE 10.1. Journalistic Coverage of "Black Twitter" Hashtags

Name of publication	Proportion of hashtags related to social justice issues	Date of publication
Essence	7 out of 9	December 13, 2013
Black Entertainment Television (BET)	9 out of 12	December 26, 2013
Huffington Post	6 out of 9	December 31, 2013
Washington Post	5 out of 7	January 20, 2014
Associated Press	5 out of 6	March 10, 2014
Articles published after the Ferguson incident		
New York Times	5 out of 5	August 13, 2014
Huffington Post	5 out of 5	August 15, 2014
NOLA.com, *Times-Picayune*	4 out of 4	December 4, 2014
The Root	14 out of 19	December 12, 2014

Social activism seems to play a large role in how the public is coming to understand what Black Twitter is and does.

A Dramaturgical Analysis of #BlackLivesMatter through Digital Artifacts

The #BlackLivesMatter Hashtag as a Movement Script

In the *scripting* stage of the social movement performance, movement actors articulate the power relations that are being contested and identify themselves in opposition to specified power holders (Benford and Hunt 1992). In New Social Movements (NSMs), which are characterized by claims against broad cultural practices or systems, the power imbalances may be identified in institutions or practices that are upheld by the majority (H. Johnston 2014; Van De Donk et al. 2004). In more traditional social movements, movement actors may specify the state and its various representatives or social elites as accountable to movement claims.

The #BlackLivesMatter hashtag was created in 2012 after a jury returned a verdict of "not guilty" for George Zimmerman, who fatally shot Trayvon Martin, a seventeen-year-old African American boy. A brief history of the hashtag can be found on blacklivesmatter.com, which was created on July 17, 2013. The website chronicles the creation of the #BlackLivesMatter hashtag by a group of Black women and is described by its founders as "a call to action for Black people after 17-year-old Trayvon Martin was post-humously placed on trial for his own murder and the killer, George Zimmerman, was not held accountable for the crime he committed. It was a response to the anti-Black racism that permeates our society and also, unfortunately, our movements" (Garza 2014). The three Black women who created the hashtag, Alicia Garza, Opal Tometi, and Patrisse Cullors, decided to expand their project beyond the Twitter hashtag with the help of volunteer labor from the community (Garza 2014). They created "an infrastructure for this movement project—moving the hashtag from social media to the streets" (Garza 2014). In this way, they created a social movement organization (SMO) structured on the national public dialogue that they had initiated with the original hashtag protest.

Because the #BlackLivesMatter Network is an SMO, it is socially recognized as an authoritative source of information about the larger movement, even when movement actions (under the umbrella of the original #BlackLivesMatter call to action) fall outside of its coordination. Movement participants and media outlets both look to #BlackLivesMatter to understand movement goals, anticipate collective action, and clarify the movement's relationship to other social justice agendas and political processes. Recognizing this role, the #BlackLivesMatter Network strategically publicizes press releases on its website.

Staging Complexities on Social Media

The creators of #BlackLivesMatter have produced a comprehensive website and manifesto and have spoken publicly about the movement to mainstream and countercurrent media. Because the American schema for understanding social movements requires a sense of hierarchy and leadership (Freeman 2015), #BlackLivesMatter has been appointed the de facto leader of the movement, despite the reluctance of its founders to espouse that role. When local movement chapters act independently, movement observers perceive it as a leadership failure. In other words, movement staging conflicts with audience expectations of how a civil rights movement should be conducted.

"Staging" refers to all labor required to execute social movement activities in a way that presents the movement script to its target audiences. When organizers publicize current and future actions, craft press releases, and display culturally resonant symbols, they are engaging in a staging process (Benford and Hunt 1992). However, staging can be complicated for large movements with diffuse leaderships and uncertain hierarchies. This can be observed in media reactions to the interruption of 2016 presidential candidate Bernie Sanders at a speech on August 8, 2015. As Sanders took the stage, the cofounders of the Seattle chapter of the #BlackLivesMatter Network claimed the microphone to demand that he provide a policy agenda to address disproportionate police violence against Black citizens. Seattle activists rightly determined that drawing the ire of self-identified progressives and liberals would force Sanders to address racial violence as part of his platform

and draw attention to the ideological boundaries between the #Black-
LivesMatter script and mainstream US liberalism.

When people nationwide observed a Seattle-based group interrupt-
ing a speech targeted at Seattle supporters of Sanders, the protest became
geographically decontextualized. Furthermore, the media's de facto
appointment of the original creators of #BlackLivesMatter to a position
of authoritative leadership meant that audiences were not prepared to
distinguish between local staging and performance and the national
script. Nor were they able to reconcile the specific targeting of Sanders
for protest with the heavy focus on police violence that has characterized the national #BlackLivesMatter movement frame. Black Twitter
provides a space where Black audiences can recontextualize movement
actions, often through explicit interventions by activists themselves or
through the careful analysis of public activist intellectuals, like the artist
and human rights activist Bree Newsome (@BreeNewsome), who have
dedicated their digital platform to educating audiences about collective
mobilization. These voices create a unique environment for Black social
media users in which they can evaluate different movements and ideologies alongside one another and choose which to support, build on,
or refuse.

*Media and Digital Media Influence Audience Interpretation
of #BlackLivesMatter*

Because social movements are a dynamic process, rather than a single
event, audience interpretation is a constant, reiterative process. A movement's multiple audiences will need to decode the scripting, staging,
and performing of movement actors using the symbols and ideas available to them as members of a shared culture (Hall 1993a). Additionally,
they must consider the perspectives of other audience members and
audiences. Finally, they must synthesize all of this information, which
is often in competition, to form their own constantly evolving understanding of movement actors, goals, successes, and failures (Benford
and Hunt 1992).

Audience members are assisted (or foiled) in this process by the
media, which presents framed coverage of movement events (Koop-

mans 2004; Roscigno and Danaher 2001). Media frames, such as protest frames, are narrative structures that signal to audiences what aspects of the story demand their focus and the broad context in which they should be interpreted. Although the public is primed to accept news coverage as an objective presentation of the facts surrounding an event, mainstream-media frames for reporting on protest in the United States have been shown to reflect a pattern of "delegitimization, marginalization, and demonization" (McLeod and Detenber 1999, 5).

Citizenship journalism via digital media is playing an increasing role in complicating the predominant framing of mainstream media (Earl and Kimport 2011; Penney and Dadas 2014). This is clearly observed in the spread of media coverage during the #BlackLivesMatter protests in Ferguson, Missouri, beginning in 2014 with the police killing of Michael Brown. The Pew Research Center found that the Ferguson story broke on Twitter before it surfaced on cable news, although coverage of the incident between the two media converged soon afterward (Hitlin and Vogt 2014). The same report found a massive difference in the number of Tweets generated after Ferguson compared to those generated after the death of the Black teen Trayvon Martin two years earlier. Tweets related to the latter shooting numbered at around 4.7 million aggregated over a month after the incident, whereas Ferguson-related tweets numbered at 10.6 million from the day of the shooting until eight days after. Of these, nearly 80 percent used the #Ferguson hashtag. Although many of the #Ferguson hashtags were used to designate physical protest activity, other users employed the hashtag to call attention to news coverage of the event, to show solidarity with protest activities, or to tag broader discussions about police brutality.

However, to reduce the unique relationship between #BlackLives-Matter and Twitter to an "alternative media" framework would be a mistake. "Black Twitter" has become a shorthand way of referring to a public conversation happening among Twitter users about issues that primarily affect African Americans and the African Diaspora; over time, it has become a thriving counterpublic. Black Twitter is an accountability structure for Black social movements, to the extent that it represents the collectivized voices of many disparate Black audiences with competing views about what "Black Lives Matter" even means. The self-identified Black Twitter participant Feminista Jones (2013) likened Twitter to the "Underground Railroad of activism" and defined it as "a collective of active, primarily African-American Twitter users who have created a virtual community that participates in continuous real-time conversations." By contrast, the journalist Kwame Opam (2013) expressed reservations about the interchangeability of the term "Black Twitter" with "Black culture" in mainstream-media coverage of the phenomenon. Still, he too identified Black Twitter as something of a movement. In each case, the authors provided general contours of Black Twitter that included aspects of collective identity development, networked interaction, public discussion, and social activism.

There have been several analyses of #BlackLivesMatter using hashtags as a source of data about movement narratives. Yarimar Bonilla and Jonathan Rosa (2015) argue that hashtag protests create a "shared temporality" in which users can contest representations of racialized bodies. Hashtag data can reveal important information about movements, such as how movement narratives spread between and within social networks. They are artifacts of the discussion frames that multiple audiences are using to understand movement performances. However, hashtag data capture both protest activity and discursive mediation of protest activity without necessarily distinguishing between them. That can only be done by modeling for Black Twitter, a digital African American public sphere, as a cultural artifact demanding study in its own right. I argue that the dramaturgical framework provides a lens through which sociologists can begin to understand Black Twitter, as well as a tool to theorize its relationship to #BlackLivesMatter.

The Greek Chorus

Analyses of #BlackLivesMatter have correctly identified the many ways in which the movement strategically harnesses Twitter. However, they have oversimplified the role of Twitter in this movement by focusing solely on citizen journalism or on protest coordination by activists. This limits analysis to the logistical, rather than cultural, aspects of the movement. Mainstream-media stories related to the movement suggest that in addition to relaying details and accounts of protests, Black Twitter engages in constant meaning-making surrounding movement claims and events.

As with a Greek chorus in a play, audience members may look to Twitter for cues on how to react to the scripting, staging, and performance of #BlackLivesMatter and indeed of other contemporary racial justice movements. In the long moments between widely covered social actions, audiences are left to interpret what they have seen. Twitter allows this process to happen collectively and publicly. The immense popularity of the platform as an alternative information source means that audiences are tuned in to these conversations. Moreover, the mainstream media's fascination with the high representation of African Americans on Twitter, and their apparent collective power, means that Twitter has become an aggregated voice that outsiders can consult to better understand the United States' racial climate.

Fully illuminating the symbiotic relationship between what is colloquially called Black Twitter and the #BlackLivesMatter movement requires a framework of social movements that explains how the former is contributive to but not constitutive of the latter. Together, Black Twitter and #BlackLivesMatter work to create, interrogate, and reformulate meaning around assaults on Black humanity.

Table 10.1 lists a combination of news and entertainment media outlets, that is, organizations that have been publishing news and entertainment since before the advent and heyday of the internet. Each article refers to several hashtags that have supposedly produced antiracist or antimisogynist outcomes through their viral popularity. #PaulasBestDishes, for example, is credited with divesting the celebrity chef Paula Deen of numerous endorsement contracts after she admitted to having used racial epithets against African Americans. In the wake of the George Zimmerman trial for the killing of the unarmed Black teenager Trayvon Martin, the anonymous figure "B37" secured a book deal to reveal conversations that had taken place behind closed doors during the trial. That contract was publicly canceled, an announcement for which came in the form of a tweet. Several media outlets have attributed the cancellation of the contract to Black Twitter, including CNN and the Associated Press (Kelly 2013; Holland 2014).

Black Twitter users are acutely aware of the ways in which their tweets are used in the aggregate as fodder for mainstream-media coverage of racialized events and as a means of tracking the popularity of ideas and products among the digitally connected Black community.

Because of this, just as the Greek chorus speaks directly to the audience while espousing its own understanding of the narrative, Black Twitter participants engage in public debate with the awareness of their influence on their audience. That is, participants express their honest views with the understanding that those views are nakedly public:

> How many articles have we seen posting tweets from the Wiz last night? But if you walk around posting articles from their site as ur own . . . (@ReaganGomez, 2015)

> Everything our youth creates gets stolen from them. I never really noticed it until social media. (@SuperBasedNique, 2015)

However, Black Twitter participants do have boundaries, often explicitly expressed as instructions about who can and should interact with the content they produce (by retweeting it, for example). They refuse to reify a "frontstage" and "backstage" binary, choosing instead to assert autonomy, authorship, and privacy by placing the onus on the audience to refrain from intervening in conversations about oppressions they do not experience. These boundaries ensure an authentic Black counterpublic that can offer Black political movements like #BlackLiveMatter otherwise-inaccessible insight into how their claims and strategies are received by the Black constituents they aspire to serve. Despite these boundaries, Black Twitter users continue to publicize their intellectual labor, ensuring that African Americans maintain a source of media power outside the White-dominated mainstream-media complex.

On the day of the Bernie Sanders interruption, the @BlkLivesMatter account fielded over three hundred mentions of (public messages to) its account. The popularity of searches about "Black Lives Matter" on Google skyrocketed, as did searches of the activist who spoke. When a search term grows by more than 5,000 percent, Google Trends labels the category a "Breakout" category. Among queries related to #BlackLivesMatter on August 8, 2015, the search phrase "Black Lives Matter Twitter" was a Breakout category, indicating that not only were users posting on Twitter about the topic but Google users were actively searching for social media reactions to the protest. Reddit, where political debates and collective mobilization are also common, was a

Breakout related topic. Another Breakout search phrase was "george soros black lives matter," referencing the conspiracy theory that liberal magnates orchestrated the movement. The narrative is especially popular on social media websites like Reddit and other White-supremacist digital media outlets like Breitbart.com. As these information seekers evaluate the available data, including choral consensus, more dominant narratives receive a growing audience of potential movement actors.

Conclusion

As #BlackLivesMatter continues to solidify itself as an enduring racial justice movement of this generation, social scientists must seriously grapple with how our current models for social movements can be used to understand its particularities. Many strides have been made to understand how digital media influences collective action generally, but #BlackLivesMatter still lacks the robust treatment of its relation to social media that has been granted to the Arab Spring (Howard et al. 2011; Howard and Hussain 2013; Gerbaudo 2012). This may indicate that sociologists are avoiding the technological determinism that characterized the earliest analyses of the series of uprisings in the Middle East. Nevertheless, my analysis indicates that #BlackLivesMatter cannot be fully understood without deliberate and nuanced attention to the cultural production of Black social media users as mediators in a public discourse about racism that includes but is not limited to the movement.

A dramaturgical framework is one way to approach such a multidirectional analysis since it enables the identification and synthesis of many simultaneous processes. Furthermore, it allows for an appreciation of both the agency of social movement actors and the independent work being performed by their audiences. However, where Black-led social movements are concerned, the dramaturgical perspective risks collapsing movement mechanics and broader Black cultural work. By accounting for a Greek chorus—a space of discursive mediation with an impact that requires its own empirical analysis—we can complicate our understanding of #BlackLivesMatter and social movements more generally.

Future research may find it useful to extend this work into a comparative analysis between the dramaturgical structure of #BlackLivesMatter and that of previous Black liberation movements. While the media technology that has paved the way for Twitter to emerge did not exist during the civil rights movement, scholars should consider the extent to which similar dramaturgical processes occurred within the available media contexts of the time. This may help illuminate what roles a public insider audience like Black Twitter plays that may have been employed by other actors or left out altogether.

While #BlackLivesMatter and Black Twitter can be understood performatively and collectively, they are, respectively, a real movement and a real network of agentic individuals. The consideration of the way audiences may incorporate these phenomena into their schema for understanding racial justice should not be synonymous with undermining the real labor and vulnerability that we are consuming as observers and scholars. To that end, scholars seeking to understand #BlackLivesMatter should consider the collection of data artifacts like tweets, Facebook posts, and news articles as preliminary steps, with the ultimate goal of engaging activists and insiders in meaningful dialogue about the roles they play within these spaces.

11

Moral Framing Networks

How Moral Entrepreneurs Create Power through the Media

NADIA Y. FLORES-YEFFAL AND DAVID ELKINS

Moral entrepreneurs create what are known as "moral panics" by distorting and spreading false claims through mass media against a group of people or the "folk devils" (Cohen 1972). Folk devils are a particular group of people who are personified as evil; they are stripped of any positive characteristics and given negative ones (Goode and Ben-Yehuda 1994). Given the false claims placed on the folk devils, individuals within the public sphere begin to see them as threats to their societal values that could also represent a threat to their social, cultural, and economic existence. Moral entrepreneurs then propose solutions for the perceived threat. However, the public needs to have a consensus that matches the ideology of the moral entrepreneur for these perceived threats to be substantiated. The moral panic created by the moral entrepreneurs (such as a supposed threat of immigrants who will "take" jobs) is a distraction for the people from the real ills of society, such as the massive loss of jobs due to bad trading policies (i.e., S. Andreson 2018). Instead, the construction of a wall on the US-Mexico border to defend the nation against the folk devils, in this case immigrants, is given a priority (Root 2018).

Now, with the help of technological advances such as the internet and with social media outlets such as Instagram, Facebook, Twitter, Snapchat, and Reddit, creating moral panics has become more accessible and easier (Cohen 2011). Nadia Y. Flores-Yeffal, Guadalupe Vidales, and April Plemons (2011) refer to "the Latino cyber-moral panic," a type of moral panic that uses cyberspace to target Latino immigrants from Mexico and Central America.

Immigrants have long been used as folk devils by moral entrepreneurs (Foner 2000). Immigrants have often been accused of stealing jobs, being criminals, lowering wages, living off welfare benefits, abusing the system, and drawing down the economic growth, despite these claims being mostly unfounded (see, e.g., Becerra et al. 2012). The concept of "immigrants" has been used to manipulate the public, and so the moral entrepreneurs can reap the benefits from the creation of the immigrant as folk devil.

In this chapter, we use contemporary sociological theory and examples from current events found on the internet (or the Web 2.0, where regular people can create content and interact using easy-to-use computing technology) to explain how power and mass-media messages are used strategically by moral entrepreneurs to deliver and spread erroneous messages to the public against the folk devils. Our findings suggest that moral framing networks are created and used by moral entrepreneurs to increase social, political, and economic power.

Network Power Creation

It is important to understand who the moral entrepreneurs are and how they operate to gain power. The moral entrepreneurs (MEs) are actors who lead within society by holding positions of power; they are bureaucrats (government officials or public servants), politicians, pundits (e.g., media and academic experts), or any other person who holds an important position of power in society (Massey, Pren, and Durand 2016). Their position of power within society provides these individuals with the means and access necessary to fulfill their ME role and to create more power for themselves. There are two types of people who exhibit the power of moral entrepreneurs: rule creators and rule enforcers (Becker 1963). The rule creator, or "crusading reformer," who is interested only in the creation of morally defined social rules, believes that "existing rules do not satisfy the needs of the society and that there is an 'evil' that exist because the current rules allow it to exist" (Becker 1963, 141). The crusading reformer believes that society is not functional until rules are created to solve the problems associated with the designated "other," or folk devil, who is threatening the moral values of society.

The moral entrepreneurs through their reforms are only interested in enforcing their moral framework on others to make them do and believe that they and/or their moral values are in danger. According to Howard Becker (1963), the legitimacy of MEs' claims is driven by the superiority of their position in society. The ME maintains or creates power by creating rules that would delegitimize and destabilize the social position of the "other" in society. For example, not allowing undocumented immigrants to obtain driver licenses places them in an illegitimate position, and they also cannot be full members of society. Asking for a wall to be built between Mexico and the United States and not between the United States and Canada sends out the message to the public that Mexican immigrants are criminals and Canadian immigrants are not. This criminalization of Mexican immigrants is part of Flores-Yeffal et al.'s (2011) "Latino cyber-moral panic," as much of the fear from the public against Mexican immigrants is created through media messages in cyberspace.

Moral Framing Network

There is a power shift resulting from the moral entrepreneur's interference with the public sphere (Flores-Yeffal, Vidales, and Martinez 2017). The public sphere (J. Habermas 1989) is a group of concerned citizens who share and discuss concerns about politics and other issues that have to do with the well-being of society. By manipulating the minds of a particular sector of the public sphere through claims against folk devils (accusing them of being deviant and morally wrong), the ME can induce fear in a particular sector of the public sphere that shares those same moral values being violated—or a moral framing network (MFN). MFNs are the result of the rallying movement or power shift given to MEs through their domination of a sector of the public sphere, from which their followers will be drawn. The whole purpose of the MFN is for its MEs to increase their power (i.e., for politicians to win a campaign and get positions of power to change policy). According to Manuel Castells (2007), "The fundamental battle being fought in society is the battle over the minds of people. The way people think [or the framing] determines the fate of norms and values on which societies are constructed. . . . Torturing bodies is less effective than shaping minds" (238). Castells (2007) argues that most people in society may not agree with the values and norms being imposed by social institutions, which can lead to social change; the social production of meaning is battled through communication in a "multimodal hypertext" (239). Such communication in the new global network society is "global and local, generic and customized in an ever-changing pattern" (239). Power relations are about domination and counterdomination, and so social actors can challenge and transform the norms and values imposed by social institutions and by those in power, such as the ME. Therefore, power relations do not just go in one direction but can be about power and counterpower (regaining power taken from others who are also in power). Therefore, MEs must be strategic about what method they use to manipulate the minds of people (or their moral framing) in order to create power. A conscripted network of individuals forms around the ME and supports the new rule system, creating a fledgling network, or MFN, based on that specific moral "right" ideology imposed by the ME.

According to Castells (2011), networking power is performed by the members of the networks and organizations, which execute power through either inclusion or exclusion of collectives or individuals that are not included currently in the networks:

[Scholars] have advocated a formal analysis that shows that the cost of exclusion from networks increases exponentially at a faster rate than do the benefits of inclusion in those same networks. . . . The value of being in the network increases exponentially with the size of the network. . . . Social actors may establish their power position by constituting a network that accumulates valuable resources and then by exercising their gatekeeping strategies to bar access to those who do not add value to the network or who jeopardize the interests that are dominant in the network's programs. (774)

Therefore, we argue that MEs deliver messages against the threats to their networks by also using gatekeeping strategies through mass media to delegitimize the factual information that could threaten the stability of the MFN. These MFNs become functionally closed networks that are self-regulated by their ideology. Self-regulation can be seen in the mass self-communication methods such as Twitter, using simple messages, visuals, videos, or "memes," which are one-way communications intended to perpetuate an MFN's specific ideology. Moral entrepreneurs and mass media both act as a mouthpiece to protect access to the MFN.

Through these standards or practices by the MFN, new rules are created, and power is exercised, "not by the exclusion from the networks, but by the imposition of the rules of inclusion" (Castells 2011, 775). A recent example of this exclusion is when President Trump took away the journalist Jim Acosta's access to the White House by claiming that he broke the rules (Wang and Farhi 2018). The reporter was asking why the president was calling immigrants "invaders," calling into question the legitimacy of the MFN regarding immigration as a threat to Americans. For the president to maintain his moral authority and protect the stability of his MFN, he ridiculed and delegitimized the reporter on national television by saying he should not be working as a journalist and falsely accusing him of molesting an intern during the incident. By taking away Acosta's press pass to the White House, the rest of the mass-media networks also learned the rules or the gatekeeping standards of the ME.

Castells (2007) argues that politicians shape the minds of people not necessarily by using explicit messages but by "the absence of a given content in the media. What does not exist in the media does not exist in the public mind" (241). Castells argues that the media is the space in which power is decided through the control of message delivery. Castells cites W. Lance Bennett's (1990) indexing theory, focusing on the media expressly reporting only on issues related to its specific political mainstream. If the MEs are the moral gatekeepers, the mass media is the gatekeeper of the flow. Therefore, indexing is a tool used to create images that are easily understood that reflect the ideology of the specific moral framing MEs want to promote. Indexing, then, is mostly built around symbolic or labeled meanings. Castells argues that the most powerful messages are the simple messages attached to an image. He also argues that "the simplest message in politics is a human face" (242). That is, the personalization of the ME is created by sending the message as a leader and by gaining the trust of the people in society through the

ME's character. Castells argues that "effective campaigns must communicate the candidate's values and use issues symbolically, as indicative of their moral values and their trustworthiness" (242). It is for this reason that the destruction of the character of other politicians can become the most important political ammunition in this battle of the manipulation of the minds of people. Political battles are driven by scandal politics, which can lead to a variety of outcomes depending on how the minds of people are manipulated; therefore, "media are the space of power making, not the source of power holding" (244).

An additional source of power for MEs is through discourse. Michel Foucault (1978) argued that discourse is a way of constituting knowledge and imposing social and moral values, social practices, and subjectivity, and it is also an avenue to govern the conscious and unconscious minds of people and ways of life. He claimed that knowledge produced through discourse also means power (knowledge/power). Therefore, we argue that the indexing used by the media through gatekeeping, or the "absence" of information, creates discourse because it constitutes a direct control over the specific impositions to be reinforced within the MFN. Through the use of simple messages or simplifications of entire discourses that carry more profound messages and deeper meanings, the knowledge specific to an MFN can be used to recruit and maintain the membership of that MFN's ideology.

Castells (2007) also introduces the concept of mass self-communication as a new form of socialized communication. Through the use of the tools available on the internet, such as blogs, comment forums, web pages, Twitter accounts, Facebook pages, and so on, individuals can self-generate content that is self-directed and that can be self-selected and then shared within the specific MFNs the individual belongs to. This makes possible the "unlimited diversity, and the largely autonomous origin of most of the communication flows that construct and reconstruct every second the global and local production of meaning in the public mind" (Castells 2007, 248). This power can be exemplified by Donald Trump using his Twitter account and many other MEs who also create content (such as posts or videos) and use the internet through blogs or media sites as a medium to communicate to the public in a matter of seconds. Stanley Cohen (2011) argues that today we have more immediate access to MEs than in the 1960s: "We are closer to them in social class, education, and ideology. Moreover, we are more likely to agree with them about the distinction between moral panic (the problem is taken too seriously) and denial (the problem is not taken seriously enough)" (240). Therefore, moral panics can evolve more rapidly today due to our access to cyberspace.

Discipline is the MFN's means of creating in-network complacency and adherence to a particular moral framing ideology. This disciplinary power is not direct, but the members of the MFN can perceive their social costs from the ME and everyone else within the network as a means of disciplinary action. This power of disciplined action is the driving force of behavior for the MFN, and it is the principal idea of media influence on perceptions of the network members. The mass media acts as the voice or the intercom that communicates between the public sphere and the MEs all of the manipulations and distortions of information against the folk devils within the MFN.

Foucault's theory of the panopticon can be used to explain the intricacies of discourse. The panopticon refers to individuals in a circular structure that is constantly being watched by someone in a tower in the middle and by other individuals in the same circular structure. They modify their behavior according to how they believe the tower and their peers view them (Foucault 2012). This same idea of panopticism can be applied to the interaction between the ME and the MFN because the power structure and functionality of the MFN ensures the internalization of the rules and disciplinary behavior for each member of the public sphere in that particular network. The concept of the panopticon suggests that subconsciously this dynamic is almost an entrapment by social values. People are integrated into social networks of oppression and subordination through false knowledge (Stoddart 2007). However, Antonio Gramsci's (1992) notion of "hegemony" works differently: it is rooted between two mechanisms of social power: coercion and consent (Stoddart 2007, 200). The moral framing network is hegemonic in function and "works to convince individuals and social classes to subscribe to the social values and norms of an inherently exploitative system. It is a form of social power that relies on voluntarism and participation rather the threat of punishment from disobedience" (Stoddart 2007, 201). Flores-Yeffal et al. (2017) found that members of the public sphere also contribute to the creation of moral panics; therefore, through the particular MFN they join, they can also become accomplices in the attacks against the folk devils. Panopticism functions in that MEs need participants within the MFNs, but in this case, the participants are afraid not of being punished but rather of being excluded from the MFN.

Furthermore, Castells (2007) points out that all ME actors are present both in mass media and mass self-communication, and they aim at finding the connecting bridge between the two media systems to maximize their potential influence of public opinion. The mass media is considered a vertical kind of network access, as it is influenced by advertisement via mass-media messages or capitalism. The horizontal access, which is done through mass self-communication, is a one-way type of communication, such as Twitter, that stays within the network (Castells 2007). These modes of communication provide access to what Castells identifies as the most important avenues to information control for the formation of the MFN. Thus, MFNs function through horizontal and vertical means of network communication. Through these diversified forms of communication and simple messages being exchanged, the minds and behavior of the members of the MFN are manipulated and observed by others.

Examples of Moral Framing Networks

A good example of how MFNs function and operate is Joe Feagin's (2013) "White racial frame." When White Europeans gained the advantage of resources such as technology and science, the power dynamics of racial inequality around the world began to take shape. Through colonization and oppression, the ideology of the White race's superiority spread out, building the structural foundation for what is called the "White racial frame." Feagin describes White racial framing as a critical aspect of the social reality of "systemic racism"; the White racial frame is a generic meaning system that has long been propagated and held by most White Americans and even transmitted as a social norm to be accepted by people of color as a subframe. Members who carry the White racial frame tend to ignore the history of inequities of astonishing discriminatory behavior, such as slavery. Among Whites, this framing is deeply held and encompasses many pieces of racialized knowledge and understandings, working in concert to shape human action and behavior in many ways that can be automatic or unconscious. The White racial frame is more than cognitive; it is a deep racial framing that has racial images, interpretations, emotions, and action inclinations that are closely tied to racial cognitions and understandings.

One of the main goals of the White racial framing is to put "the other" down through stereotyping, bigotry, or discrimination (Feagin 2013). The goal of White racial framing is to create power, making it a tangible commodity that gives privilege and resources beyond what could be naturally earned for those who are willing to take it from others. More recently, White racial framing in the United States adopted a more covert approach through the microaggressions of racism and secretive actions and inactions. The thought process of US society has internalized this covert ideology of White racial framing to encompass every aspect of social interaction, decision-making, law, and regulation. White Americans' social interactions are derived from these elements of racial categorization and stereotypes. Because White framing has become so embedded in US culture, any social interaction with racial minorities in the United States is based on the structural framework of White racial framing. Media has become a tool to enforce covert White racial framing. Feagin (2013) argues that this White racial framing, together with White privilege, is heavily embedded, so that most Americans are unaware of it. Therefore, we argue that White racial framing can serve as an example of a type of moral framing that takes place inside a MFN and that it is relevant to the type of MFN that is promoting the Latino cyber-moral panic in the United States.

Flores-Yeffal et al. (2011) describe the increase of fear against immigrants promoted through MEs, which in turn creates the Latino cyber-moral panic. Through the White racial framing ideology, the fear that Mexican immigrants will not be able to assimilate into US society has led to what Leo Chavez (2013) calls the "Latino Threat Narrative" (LTN). Chavez explains, "According to the assumptions and taken-for-granted 'truths' inherent in this narrative, Latinos are unwilling or incapable of integrating, of becoming part of the national community. Rather, they are part of an invading force from south of the border that is bent on reconquering land that was formerly theirs (the U.S. Southwest) and destroying the American way of life" (3).

An example of an academic ME who has contributed to this narrative is Samuel Huntington. In 1996, Huntington published a book titled *The Clash of Civilizations and the Remaking of World Order*, in which he argued that cultural and religious identities were the roots of conflict. He then published "The Hispanic Challenge" in 2004 in the online *Foreign Policy* magazine, which was part of a think tank that he had founded (Huntington 2009). He argued that Mexican immigrants were a threat to the United States because they did not want to assimilate and were dividing the nation into two different worlds. The fear from the White racial frame has developed into a false idea that Mexican immigrants' goals for immigrating to the United States are to dismantle society from within. Years of "constructed 'truths' have created this narrative which in turn has created a response both politically and socially to deal with this perceived fear (Chavez 2013, 71).

These narrative images are then passed on through mass media using newspaper headlines (tied to particular images) or videos, which can then be shared through social media platforms such as Facebook, Twitter, and Instagram. As Flores-Yeffal et al. (2017) point out, the use of hashtags allows the MFN to find all the information associated with a particular hashtag, for example, #migrantcaravan or #illegalaliens. This is how manipulations and distortions are spread through cyberspace, and in a matter of minutes, millions of people can gain access to those headlines, images, or videos associated with the folk devils. The manipulation of information is essential because as the information is distributed faster, social media users are less likely to verify their sources of information (Zubiaga and Ji 2014; Zubiaga et al. 2016) as what they see in the media becomes their own reality (Berger and Luckmann 1991). The problem then becomes not the information that is being spread out but the lack of information (Castells 2007). MEs know that through their position of power within the MFN, the information being spread can inherently be considered legitimate within the MFN. As Peter Berger and Thomas Luckmann (1991) argue, "The reality of everyday life is taken for granted as reality. It does not require additional verification over and beyond its simple presence. It is simply there, as self-evident and compelling facticity" (37). Therefore, the members of the network would believe what others are saying or passing along to each other, and the panopticism of the network structure will prevent individuals from searching for the truth or verifying the information that the MEs are sharing or stating.

Mass media is used to portray Latino immigrants as folk devils, or to reinforce the ideology of Mexican immigrants being a threat to US social order (Flores-Yeffal et al. 2011). We found that this is done through the manipulation and distortion of information or simplified parts of discourses from MEs, who want to create different kinds of MFNs that vary by the type of moral values and behavioral expectations of the ME or the type of moral frame that exists in the network, such as the White racial frame.

Manipulation

There are several ways that these messages are created, controlled, and delivered to create and maintain the power structure necessary for the formation of MFNs. Media acts as a mouthpiece for MEs and creates a space of power making, but it is not the source for power holding (Castells 2007). This is because there is also counterpower in these MFNs. There is not only one kind of a moral framing network functioning in society but several. Societies are diversified, and almost everyone has access to cyberspace via mass self-communication; but media outlets mostly only support those in power, as media outlets are also businesses and they also have capital interests. These economic interests lead to manipulation by creating sensational stories to propagate specific messages to sell more news quickly.

There is a competition over who can get a story for the public to consume that can bring more substantial revenue from viewership and advertisements to the mass-media agency that breaks the story first. Mass-media outlets have resorted to what is called "sensationalism" or "tabloidizing" the news to be the first and to reap these economic benefits. Sensationalism finds its origins from the tabloid culture, in which "news topics displace socially significant stories, and flashy production styles overpower substantive information" (Wang 2012, 712). News stories are made more scandalous or flashier and neglect the intellectual discussions regarding the subjective information in the news. For example, media outlets such as CNN or Fox News have started using a "Breaking News" headline and small news updates in which the extremely brief statements describing the events often seem exaggerations of the real situation. For MEs, this is a platform where they can sell moral panic because ignoring subjective information reduces the chances of individuals within the MFN questioning the delivery of the messages.

Depending on who has more power in a society and who has a more significant (or larger) MFN, that MFN will dominate other sectors of society that belong to other MFNs (for instance, as Republicans and Democrats each have their own MFN). Flores-Yeffal et al. (2017) found evidence that particular sectors of the public sphere create and participate in their MFNs to spread moral panics. For example, Andrew Prokop (2018) argues that legislators of both parties had reasons why they did not want to keep the government shut down in January 2018 (due to the cancellation of DACA [Deferred Action for Childhood Arrivals] protections for undocumented youth who are also called DREAMers) for too long, as they were worried about losing voters (MFN members) in the upcoming elections: "The Democratic worry was that keeping the government shut down on behalf of unauthorized immigrants—even the DREAMers—is a political loser. Furthermore, many Democratic senators are facing tough reelections in red states this year and fear being tagged as extremists. Meanwhile, Republicans worry that since Trump is president and their party controls Congress, they'll be blamed for the shutdown and deemed incompetent." Castells (2007) argues that the members of the public who are most vulnerable to being victims of mind manipulation are undecided voters. In this case, the undecided voters would have been more likely to be recruited by these MEs to either one of the MFNs by using the media's sensationalism.

Sensationalism is described as news stories that make people feel challenged and violate their comfort and psychological distance between their perceptions of an event as audience members and the real physical world. These stories "could be considered sensational news stories (Grabe et al., 2001:637) for their potential to provoke more sensory and emotional reactions than what society generally deems proper to experience" (Wang 2012, 712). These manipulations are done by using camera angles, imagery that is not relevant but invokes a specific emotional response, and dramatic voice-overs that conjure images and labels that are not entirely realistic. These are the type of ways that MEs use the media to influence the minds of the members of the MFN or to recruit members from a different MFN (e.g., when Democrats vote for Republican candidates or vice versa). The negative stories do not contain the whole truth either, and they bypass the subjective information needed to see the entire account of what indeed occurred, which would put into question the moral crusade of the ME to designate who the folk devils are. Therefore, there is the risk that one MFN will lose its members to another MFN if the recruiting strategies of manipulation through the moral panics is not successful. The sensationalist messages have to be delivered effectively so that the MEs can maintain or increase their power through the MFNs.

Manipulation uses imagery and words to create specific reactions through sensationalism. An example of this would be the coverage of the "caravan" at the Guatemalan border. Before the 2018 midterm elections, MEs used the caravan to invoke fear through their messages and to elicit participation in their MFN. Sensationalism was used by the media through imagery and wording to describe the caravan, which had halted at the Guatemalan border. Two mass-media news sites used different types of imagery and wording to describe what was happening at the border. *Time* magazine did a write-up with the title "Caravans Help Migrants Travel Safely. But Recent Attention from Trump Might Change That" (Root 2018). The article has pictures of individuals and the facilities where they are helping one another and creating a social ecology in which they can exist. Compare this to the headline from Fox News, which is more of a conservative indexing news site: "Migrant Caravan Showdown: Crowds Reach Guatemalan Border Town as Mexico Prepares for Potential Mass Crossing" (Norman 2018); the article pictures the immigrants in massive groups crowding in one area, sensationalizing the idea that this is a mob rather than individuals.

Distortion

According to Cohen (1972), distortions occur to create moral panics. Mass media, through indexing (or through a simple message from a discourse), defines the folk devils as dangerous. The major type of distortion lies in grossly exaggerating the seriousness of the events, including the number of people taking part, the number of people involved in violence, and the amount and effects of any damage or violence. Like manipulation, distortions take place primarily regarding the mode and style of the presentation of characteristics, such as sensational headlines, melodramatic vocabulary, and deliberate heightening of those elements. News media outlets sensationalize stories particularly of people of color or immigrants, focusing on stories of crime. The reason for this focus on crime is because as Franklin Gilliam and Shanto Iyengar (2000) argue, "Stories about crime provide several necessary ingredients for the successful marketing of news-concrete events with powerful impact on ordinary people, drama, and emotions, and, above all, attention-getting visuals" (560). This reinforces the idea that sensationalizing stories and more specifically crime stories brings in more viewership. This type of "overreporting," as Cohen (1972) calls it, is not particular to any one specific distortion but is characterized by media representations of such events as political protests, racial disturbances, and criminal activity (27). Thus, a story whose headline includes the word "violence" but reports no violence at all occurring within the reported incident is a distortion. Many cyberspace network viewers will not even open a story link. Instead, they are more likely only to rely on the false message of the headline itself if it matches their MFN ideology.

A good example of distortion is how undocumented or "illegal" immigrants are explicitly targeted in political messages by being symbolically associated with MS-13, a criminal gang. This distortion also reinforces the ideology of MEs when selected instances can be amplified to increase their importance. Focusing only on these specific acts enables MEs to use a concept called a "script," which is "a coherent sequence of events expected by the individual, involving him [or her] either as a participant or as an observer" (Gilliam and Iyengar 2000, 561).

MEs too often have latched onto these symbolisms and, through scripts, have associated Central American immigrants directly to MS-13. Cohen (1972) states that there are three processes in such symbolization of a word (e.g., "MS-13") for it to become symbolic of a certain status (e.g., delinquent or deviant): (1) objects, such as racial stereotypes in this case, symbolizing the word (MS 13); (2) the objects themselves becoming symbolic of the status (in this case, the gang members or Central American immigrants); (3) the emotions attached to the status (in this case, fear of the Central American immigrants). The cumulative effect of these three processes in the case of "MS-13" is that the term acquired wholly negative meaning by association (Cohen 1972). Only through the similarity of coming from Central America or Mexico, together with being undocumented or "illegal," it is enough to create a symbolism in which any attempts at immigration reform are laced with fear, through overreporting or sensationalism by associating criminal activities, through scripts, to Mexican immigrants. According to Otto Santa Ana (2013), this sensationalism shifts the idea of the immigrant from human to animal to criminal because of the term and usage of "illegal" (159). Mass media reflects the ideology of the ME because through the script, it creates a culture of fear in the public—either as an indirect victim, such as a bystander, or as a primary victim, such as the person whom the crime is being committed against. These events cause the viewer to make stereotypical assumptions based on their MFN. Because mass media mainly focuses on crimes committed by minorities, these assumptions become stereotypical, supporting, for example, the anti-other subframe of the White racial frame. The criminality aspect of sensationalism is the focal point for MEs when they want to label a group of people as deviant and to declare a need for separation to prevent the identified deviant group from affecting the MFN.

Simple distortions often are also effective when cyberspace is used. During the campaign races in the 2018 US midterm election, Ann Coulter, a pundit, made comments about an American singer named Taylor Swift, whose celebrity status would also make her a pundit. Swift had just endorsed two Democratic candidates from her home state of Tennessee through her Instagram account by sending a message that she was voting and that others within her MFN should do the same. Coulter tweeted a response through her own Twitter account, stating, "Swift was under vicious attack for being a pretty White girl, so her agent told her to endorse a Democrat" (Wynne 2018). This is a simple distortion because both MEs are delivering a message through one-way mass self-communication to reach their specific MFNs. Swift is legitimizing other MEs by creating accessibility to other political networks where Democratic ideology would be dominant. Coulter counters through word usage by trying to delegitimize the power Swift has within her network. The distortion is simple because facts or information are not being changed. Instead, attacks to the legitimacy of other political networks call into question the credibility of opposing MFNs to destabilize their power dynamics.

Often MEs also use videos as a way of distorting information and use broadcast media to create and deliver messages with imagery that evokes specific thought process related to the MFN. During the 2017 race for governor in Virginia between the Democratic candidate, Ralph Northam, and the Republican candidate, Ed Gillespie, the media broadcast a political commercial endorsed by Gillespie that used MS-13 criminality to attack undocumented immigrants. In this video, the Republican candidate attacks Northam on immigration (*Washington Post* 2017). The thirty-second video shows quick-flashing pictures depicting imagery that is evocative of the criminality of MS-13. While this is occurring, a woman's voice can be heard first stating facts about MS-13's criminality while headlines from news articles are quoted and flashed across the screen. The narrator states that Northam supports sanctuary cities, which "lets illegal immigrants who commit crimes back on the streets."

As per Cohen, the similarity of both MS-13 and Mexican immigrants coming from Latin America is enough to create a symbolism reflecting criminal behavior. Through this symbolism and sensationalism, an association between MS-13 and Mexican immigrants begins to form, and all Mexican immigrants are then perceived as gang members.

Circular Reporting

MEs rely on laws and rules to maintain the power structure and to create fear. By doing so, MEs must draw advice from experts and facts. This is where circular reporting is used as a delivery method, along with distortion, to perpetuate the moral panic by using or creating misconstrued facts that originate from the specific moral framing ideology (i.e., White racial framing). Looking at how circular reporting is established provides context into how the White racial frame is being transmitted to the public sphere. Circular reporting functions when a specific publication (X) publishes misinformation, which is followed by another publication (Y) reprinting the misinformation. Then publication X will cite publication Y as the source lending credibility to the original misinformation (Tavlin, n.d.). Circular reporting can be used to explain many of the occurrences of distortion. It brings legitimacy to MEs' creation of the folk devil and prevents challenges to their power within the MFN by delegitimizing facts that threaten to change the public's mind-set.

Another excellent example of circular reporting is what Flores-Yeffal et al. (2011) call the "recycling factory" in cyberspace. They identify three think thanks (NumbersUSA, FAIR, and the Center for Immigration Studies) whose funders and directors all wanted to promote the White racial frame against immigrants (which is mostly about lowering the numbers of immigrants in the United States). Through these think tanks and via cyberspace, first, these MEs created reports with manipulated information and specific derogatory language used multiple times, such as the word "illegal" against the immigrants, supporting anti-immigrant stereotypes. Then they distributed these false reports through cyberspace via anti-immigrant alarmist websites, newspaper headlines, and media networking sites. The reports look legitimate, as they come from the think thanks, gain credibility through circular reporting citation, and then are backed by MEs who represent the think tanks. The directors also often present their findings on radio shows that are also broadcast via the internet. The findings of these reports are also periodically presented in congressional and Senate hearings, and new anti-immigrant legislation is often developed, as policy makers also believe in the validity of these reports (Flores-Yeffal et al. 2011).

Conclusion

As just described, new legislation can result from the misinformation and moral values spread by MEs, such as the White racial frame ideology. For an act to be viewed as deviant and any class of people to be labeled and treated as outsiders for committing the act, someone must create a rule that defines the act as deviant (Becker 1963). MEs do not automatically create the rules, but rather there is a process in which the harm or deviant act needs to be discovered and objectively pointed out as coming from the folk devils (Becker 1963). This creates a set of emotions and an urgency within the delivery of the message that something must be done against this wrong to correct it or prevent it from recurring. MEs need to make the public sphere an accomplice in this endeavor, as without the public's membership in the MFN, there is no power or position of power to be gained. An example of this process can be seen in President Trump's direct communication with his MFN (or "base") through his daily tweets.

We have found that MEs use vertical and horizontal media networks and social media outlets and mass self-communication to create and increase power through the control of MFNs via the manipulation and distortion of information and the use of circular reporting via mass media. As a result, the minds of the members of the MFNs are manipulated to recruit, monitor, and maintain their membership through the imposition of a set of rules and moral values that share a specific ideology with each specific MFN, such as the White racial frame. The manipulated information provokes a moral panic among the members of the MFN against the folk devils. Through the recruitment of members into the MFN with the aid of mass media, the MEs create and increase power for themselves through the increase of membership in their MFN. If their manipulations are not successful enough, the MEs can experience a decrease in power (e.g., losing political elections, being fired from a position, or being asked to resign from that position). We have also found that the type of moral panic depends on the type of moral framing being imposed by MEs to their followers. Unfortunately, as a result of the Latino cyber-moral panic in the United States, inhumane legislation is being implemented, such as the separation of children at the Mexican-US border, which led to the incarceration of innocent children in cages and permanent separation from their parents (see PBS 2018). Most Americans are unaware that the MEs are manipulating them and that they are accomplices in the attacks and new legislation created against the folk devils and their innocent children. These Americans are unaware that through social media and their use of cyberspace and their voluntary and active participation in a moral framing network, they are adopting a moral frame that helps to increase the social, political, or economic power of the moral entrepreneurs in society.

PART III

How Racialized Media Is Decoded

As mentioned earlier in this text, most of the typical research on media considers representations. But representations are not purposeless ideological manifestations wandering around aimlessly. After media content has been through the processes of design and delivery, the last stage is consumption. It is the process of consuming media that, in fact, gives the media its purpose—and consequence.

Perhaps it is more apt to refer to media's *purposes* and *consequences*, in the plural. As the chapters in this section will demonstrate, media has but many variations in the decoding of its content. Decoding involves all audience interaction with media, including interpretations and public debates surrounding the representations that people receive. These are the moments when media collide with social actors who are responding from their myriad subject positions of race, ethnicity, gender, class, sexuality, and other identity categories. The seemingly infinite possibilities of interpretations reflect both the salience of identity categories and the other media labor processes of design and delivery that enable audiences to receive certain media content. An underlying thread among the chapters of this section asks, Which story lines, characters, images, or headlines resonate with whom, and how do they resonate?

Chapter 12, written by Sonita R. Moss and Dorothy E. Roberts, delves into online comment sections on news articles about White-appearing children born to Black mothers, in which audiences often reproduce biologizing narratives of race to affirm their racial worldviews. In David J. Leonard's chapter 13, he considers the satisfaction that people of color may feel when they are able to confront White racism in the virtual reality of a video game. Chapter 14 also tackles online news-story comment sections. Michael L. Rosino shows that public discussions on news stories about the War on Drugs are highly influenced by racial positionality, such as people of color referencing personal encounters with racism to support their argument that the War on Drugs was indeed racially motivated. In chapter 15, Tina M. Harris, Anna M. Dudney Deeb, and Alysen Wade examine college student audiences and the potential for films about racism—specifically *Dear White People* in this chapter—to spark students' racial consciousness.

12

"It Is Likely a White Gene"

Racial Voyeurism and Consumption of Black Mothers and "White" Babies in Online News Media

SONITA R. MOSS AND DOROTHY E. ROBERTS

Scholars have consistently found that anti-Blackness is a central project of the mass media (Campbell 2016; Mask 2012; Erigha 2019). Racist representations of Black people remain prevalent in television and film (Littlefield 2008; Feagin 2013; Campbell 2016). Still, there is a gap in the literature regarding why racialized stories remain so popular among consumers. Given the past decades' emphatic discourse on inclusion, diversity, and multiracialism, there is now increased attention to both the meaning and practice of families that have crossed the color line (Gardner and Hughey 2017; R. Joseph 2013; Binning et al. 2009). In particular, media consumers vociferously seek coverage of interracial, transracial, and racially mixed families online. For instance, when the reality star Kylie Jenner's baby did not look "brown enough" to be fathered by the Black rapper Travis Scott, online news media launched articles and videos questioning the paternity of the child. Speculation centered on the baby's light skin color and eye shape; there were claims that the biological father was Jenner's Asian bodyguard, because the baby's features were perceived as more "Asian" than conventional notions of what "Black" should look like. As this example illustrates, societal fixation on race and reproduction is localized in biological race and phenotype, and the stories reflecting this fixation are broadly disseminated online. Understudied aspects of racialized media include examining how ideas about racial reproduction are constructed and reified online. While many studies offer examples of racist representation, few consider how race is considered a natural by-product of birth, an inheritance that is evinced through physical features.

This study examines media reports of Black women who gave birth to so-called White babies—children who were racialized as White on the basis of phenotypic features, such as skin shade, hair color and texture, and eye color. Drawing on critical race theory's frame of colorblindness and Black feminism's intersectionality theory, we analyze how both producers and consumers of these stories rely on several core tenets of White supremacy to evaluate Black women and their children. This study asks, What can we learn about popular understandings of race from the public's fascination with media coverage surrounding "White" babies born to Black mothers? Further, what racial discourses guide how such stories are produced and consumed online?

To answer these questions, we conducted a textual and discourse analysis of two cases of Black women giving birth to babies identified as White, as well as the commentary responses from consumers.[1] We found that biological conceptions of race, colorblind discourses, and celebrating Whiteness are the primary frames through which these stories are both produced and consumed. More specifically, we found that three race-based assumptions underlie, and are reinforced by, sensationalized media reports of Black mothers and their so-called White children. First, race is believed to be a biological trait that is "in the blood," or genetic, rather than a constructed sociopolitical category. Thus, a baby's racial identity is presumed to be a natural by-product of the parents. Second, phenotypic features determine race. A baby with fair skin, blue eyes, and blond hair is therefore racialized as White. The third assumption—which contradicts the second assumption in the cases we studied—asserts that Black people cannot produce Whiteness. Long-held anti-Black thinking about racial heritage claims that, because Blackness is opposite and inferior to Whiteness, Black people are incapable of bearing White children.

We argue that media coverage of "miraculous" births of White children to Black mothers generates racial voyeurism among consumers because these births contradict deeply held beliefs about racial classification, identity, and heritage. Such stories entice and disturb consumers because these seemingly mismatched families violate the tenet that race is a natural product of procreation. Thus, our study goes beyond examining racial representation in the media to illuminate how both media and consumers promote fictive, biological concepts of race that support White supremacy.

This study draws on scholarship that articulates a social constructionist approach to race to elucidate White-supremacist logics embedded in racialized media (Rocchio 2018; Behnken and Smithers 2015; Berg 2002). Evelyn Nakano Glenn's (2002) integrated framework of social constructionism is useful here. She asserts that social categories like race and gender are formulated within dynamics of power that are related to one another. Glenn explains, "Race and gender are defined as mutually constituted and systems of relationships—including norms, symbols, and practices—organized around perceived differences. . . . These processes take place at multiple levels, including representation, micro-interaction, social structure" (2002, 12). The key to understand is that race and gender are relational constructs that concern material and repressive relations, and power is constituted within each of them; in race, White has been constructed and deployed as opposite to Black. Further, the category of race has been constructed and deployed as a dimension of power, and sociologists have long argued that it is the most powerful organizing feature of modern society (Omi and Winant 2015; Bonilla-Silva 1997; Brown et al. 2003; Glenn 2002).

Critical race theorists have refuted the long-standing biological concept of race, arguing instead that race is a social category created and used to classify and govern people for the advantage of Whites and at the expense of racialized or non-White groups (Bonilla-Silva 2014; Delgado and Stefancic 2012; Kendi 2016; Omi and Winant 2015). This view contends that the United States operates as a racial caste system that routinely denigrates Black and Brown bodies while privileging White bodies and Whiteness. Further, Whites have responded to the gains of the civil rights movement with a colorblind ideology that claims racism no longer impedes minority progress (Brown et al. 2003; Bonilla-Silva 2014; Obasogie 2013; Taylor 2016).

The New Race Science

Critical race scholars have broken new ground by investigating how the biological understanding of race is being revived in multiple domains of public life (J. Thomas 2014; Byrd et al. 2015; Benjamin 2016; Bliss 2015). Dorothy Roberts demonstrates the emergence of a "new race science" interested in gene-based racial differences, which relies on global DNA databases and statistical analyses to treat race as a genetic grouping. Genomic scientists use "gene frequencies among geographic populations as a more objective, scientific and politically palatable alternative to race, an approach that tends to repackage race as a genetic category rather than replace it" (Roberts 2011, 202). Roberts asserts that this is a part of a larger biopolitical agenda that, by explaining race as *natural, inherited, and fixed*, provides a biological explanation for persistent racial inequality in a supposedly postracial society.

Global White Supremacy

Critical race scholars are also calling for studies of White supremacy to move beyond the borders of the US racial order to show its global implications (Allen 2001; Bashi 2004; Macedo and Gounari 2006). As global empires, the United States and the United Kingdom share many of the same features of White supremacy, particularly in the vulnerability and repressed mobility of their Black populations (Small 2018). Scholars of race in the United Kingdom show that similar White-supremacist structures pervade British media (Andreassen 2017; Gillborn 2006b; Kapoor 2013). Digital discourses in the United Kingdom and the United States reflect shared histories of racism and contemporary "postracial" denials (W. Anderson 2018, 116). This study will examine racial discourses and rhetoric that extend White supremacy from a US-centric White-Black paradigm to a global phenomenon in which European and American racial understandings cooperate.

Racial Voyeurism

The theory of racial voyeurism is ideal to analyze how contradictory postracial logics work to fuel interest in producing and consuming racialized media stories. Theorized by Elizabeth Alexander and coined by Patricia Williams, racial voyeurism refers to the surveillance and display of racialized (usually Black) bodies for the consumption of White spectators (E. Alexander 1994; Williams 2016). In this practice, race is treated as a spectacle, often at the expense of Black agency (J. Y. Daniels 2000). Scholars have traced the practice of racial voyeurism to colonial discourses that produced fictive truths about the essential inferiority of Brown and Black bodies (Hobson 2005; Lindfors 1999). These racial spectacles include the capture and exhibition of Saartjie Baartman's body parts in 1810 (widely known as the "Hottentot Venus"), public lynchings of Black people witnessed by thousands of White onlookers in the twentieth century, and worldwide slave auctions. Scholars have also used racial voyeurism as a global phenomenon to explain White people's motivation for interactions with people of color today. Contemporary examples include White fascination with the highly publicized O. J. Simpson murder trial, consumption of rap, interest in minority pornography, and participation in "ghetto" tours (Appiah 2018; Bossenger 2017; Duffett 2013; Hartnell 2009).

The media play a key role in racial voyeurism by disseminating racial spectacles as objective fact while reinforcing stereotypical images of people of color. J. Yolande Daniels (2000) explains that negative media images of Black life are so rife with "racial spectacle" that individual negative acts are thought to be proof of broad, racial failure. For example, the news media's disproportionate portrayal of crime committed by Black individuals relies on racist discourses about Black people's supposedly inherent criminality in order to attract White viewers' racial voyeurism (Dixon 2017a, 2017b). Daniels writes, "Black space has become the site for the latent spectacle. Categorization and classification are a means by which the private is made public. The black ghetto and the Projects represent the classification and marginalization of physical space; they have been enforced through mediation and are spectacularized as pathological" (J. Y. Daniels 2000, 215). The spectacle itself becomes proof of the pathology of racialized groups, largely reifying preestablished beliefs about them.

bell hooks's (1992) concept of "eating the Other" illuminates how White people's embrace of multicultural diversity does little to displace preexisting White-supremacist relations or ways of thinking. hooks argues that mass consumption of Black culture and bodies represents deeply held White-supremacist fantasies to be in contact with the "Other" along with a simultaneous desire to preserve the racial order (hooks 1992, 22). Within the frame of postracial consciousness is the embrace of cross-cultural celebration or multicultural diversity that ostensibly mollifies claims of White-supremacist domination. However, despite any cross-racial exchange that may occur, "the hope is that . . . such exploitation can occur in a manner that reinscribes and maintains the status quo" (hooks 1992, 22). In other words, while Whites may proclaim their admiration of "exotic" Black bodies, even engaging in intimate interactions with these bodies, they do so in a way that supports rather than subverts racist frameworks.

Intersectionality

Understanding racial voyeurism from an intersectional perspective helps to explain the production and consumption of sensationalized media stories related to Black women and so-called White children. Black feminists developed intersectionality theory to explain how Black women experience racialized *and* gendered discrimination because of their position in a matrix of interlocking systems of domination that differentiates their oppression from that of White women and Black men (P. Collins [1990] 2000; Crenshaw 1991). Black feminist scholars have argued that the surveillance and control of the Black female body constitute a long-standing tradition of racial voyeurism in the United States. From enslavement to modern forms of regulation over Black citizens in the criminal justice, child protective services, welfare, education, and health care systems, surveillance of Black citizens is seen as both normative and necessary for the security of White citizens (Armenta 2017; Hunter 2017; Oeur 2016; Roberts 1997, 2012). Because of the marginal status of Black women, they have been deemed entitled to less privacy and protection against surveillance, increasing their likelihood of maltreatment (Roberts 1997; Perry 2011). In addition, Patricia Hill Collins points out that "controlling images" of Black women in the mainstream media, such as "welfare queen," "jezebel," "matriarch," and "mammy," deny them access to the entitlements of the White "cult of true womanhood" and distinctively treat them as "Other" (P. Collins [1990] 2000, 70; V. Patton 2000, 29–30). Thus, intersectionality provides a framework not only to examine the consumption and production of racialized media but also to explain how Black women as mothers may be targeted for unique forms of disparagement.

We use this intersectional approach to racial voyeurism to analyze how media coverage of White babies born to Black mothers employs oppressive understandings of race and reproduction to attract spectators. In this coverage, race is flattened into a one-dimensional identity that does not leave room for complexities, such as accounting for how phenotypes commonly vary in biologically related families or for race as a socially constructed category. As Roberts (2011) asserts, race is a political category that has real impacts on people's lives. While we are taught to understand race as a fixed, genetic identity with predictable phenotypical features, the existence of multiracial families in which there are various hair textures, skin shades, and facial features works to displace this popular fiction. A basic understanding of how each individual's unique sequence of DNA is inherited from both parents, after being passed down and reshuffled from generation to generation, makes it clear that one can carry genes for lighter skin, hair, and eyes than one's parents or siblings (Zimmer 2018). The expression of these inherited genes is also determined by environmental factors, including factors that can affect fetal development. Thus, the birth of a child who possesses features that are different from those of his or her family members is not miraculous but an expected result of DNA inheritance, recombination, and expression. Moreover, Africa is the most genetically diverse region of the globe, and people with African ancestry can inherit alleles for a wide range of physical features.

Despite these principles of genetic inheritance, binary and reductionist notions of race in all major institutions of modern life equate "Black" with dark skin, hair, and eyes, represented by caricature-like renderings of features—wide noses, full lips, and round faces. At the same time, Whiteness is still constructed as fair skin, light hair and eyes, and narrow features. For instance, the common conception of a phenotypically different child as the "milkman's baby" is a representation of these simplistic notions of race.

As consumers of news stories about White babies born to Black mothers use the comment section to debate the legitimacy of the stories' racial logics, paradoxical results emerge. Some commenters are fixated on the phenotype of the child as proof of racial authenticity, while others point to the incompatibility of Whiteness and Blackness to determine the child's race. Thus, we show that the racial voyeurism at play in the consumption of these sensational news stories does not disrupt but rather reinforces White-supremacist logics about racial reproduction.

Methodology

Critical Discourse Analysis

This study employs critical discourse analysis (CDA) to investigate the framing and language used by journalists and commenters responding to the online news stories. CDA uses a social constructionist approach, which understands that dominant discourses are direct reflections of powerful institutions in society (van Dijk 1993). For this study, we used the approach of textual analysis, identifying ideologies that reinforce and naturalize White-supremacist logics about biological race and cultural stereotypes. We sought specific key words and phrases that aligned with broad assumptions about race and biology, underscoring which race-based assumptions were embedded in the text. For instance, we highlighted any comments that discuss race as "in the blood," stereotypes about Black women's fertility or hypersexuality, beauty associated with lighter skin, and disbelief that babies with light skin can be born to women with darker skin. Broadly, we paid attention to the controlling images that frequently accompany media coverage of Black women.

Racial Internet Literacy

Comment sections are spaces that can contest or support White-supremacist views. As scholars of racial discourse in online forums have discovered, users often privilege views that support colorblind racism and discount oppositional racial views and are more likely to be critical of Black commenters or Black authors (Kettrey and Laster 2014; Sumner, Stanley, and Burrow 2015). Colorblind language often discreetly or politely states what was once considered openly hateful speech (Bonilla-Silva and Forman 2000).

Hughey and Daniels's study of racist online comments lays out a systematic method called "racial internet literacy," or RIL, to identify "coded language" that "increasingly disguises forms of racist discourse

in public and virtual contexts" (2013, 334). Symbols, such as stereotypical African American vernacular, can be coded to connote Black inferiority; "commonsense" racism is cloaked as "matter-of-fact" statements
that are based on stereotypes. As Hughey and Daniels point out, "such
rhetorical strategies evade moderation because they shift focus from
the specifics of racialized content to . . . supposedly scientific or 'obvious' racial differences thought natural or innate" (2013, 340). We found
RIL useful in coding for language that reinforces biological notions of
race that are taken for granted as neutral, rather than political modes
of thought.

Data

We focus on two case studies of so-called White babies born to Black
mothers rather than a random sample of numerous stories because
of the dearth of popular news outlets that permit user commentary.
Although numerous online US news outlets published stories about
one or both of the families in these case studies, comment sections were
limited or nonexistent.[2]

Therefore, to conduct a textual analysis of these cases, we selected
two recent news articles that received more than one hundred comments published on the same media outlet—*Daily Mail*, a popular news
site based in the United Kingdom. We randomly sampled fifty comments total from each article for analysis (N = 100; J. Johnston 2010;
Smith Squire 2017).

The Igheboro Family

The first case involves the Igheboro family in the United Kingdom, a
Black Nigerian immigrant couple who gave birth to a "White" baby girl
with blond hair and blue eyes in 2010 (J. Johnston 2010). The story calls
the birth of the couple's third child "miraculous" because the first two
children have dark hair, skin, and eyes like their parents. It devotes significant attention to explaining the baby's features as possibly resulting
from infidelity or albinism. The article received 212 comments before
the comment section was closed.

The Howarth Family

The second case involves an interracial Black-White couple living in the United Kingdom, the Howarth family (Smith Squire 2017). The mother is Black and hails from Nigeria, while her husband is described as "completely white." The news article, published in 2017, claims that the family hit "a million to one odds" by having not just one but two "white, blue eyed" babies. The mother was featured in similar sensationalized news stories after she gave birth to a "miracle" baby with light skin and light eyes several years earlier. The article received 274 comments before moderators closed the comment section.

While these stories do not focus on US families, we analyzed the rhetoric used in the articles and comments to identify the assumptions about race and procreation that have broadly supported White supremacy in both the United States and Europe. The commenters self-disclose their location. A significant number of commenters cited their location as the United States or the United Kingdom. A 2007 study found that 69 percent of *Daily Mail* readers are outside the United Kingdom, and a 2016 study reported that the site receives over sixty-six thousand unique viewers per month (Comscore 2008, 2016).

Findings

Our analysis of the sample found that the media coverage and comments reinforce three key assumptions about the biological reproduction of race: race is a genetic inheritance, phenotypic characteristics determine race, and Black people are incapable of producing Whiteness. Throughout both the articles and comments, we also found strong colorblind-racist narratives demonizing the discussion of race, as well as controlling images that evoked common stereotypes of Black women. The most prevalent comment was about the miraculous beauty of the children, as evinced by their light skin, blond hair, and blue eyes.

The Articles' Racial Logics

BIOLOGICAL RACE AND ATAVISTIC WHITE GENES

Although the Igheboro parents are both Black Nigerians and the Howarth parents are an interracial couple, the babies born to both Black women are described as "miracles." The articles use language that mystifies the birth of the babies while also conflating race with genetics. In Catherine Howarth's explanation of why her daughter had blond hair and blue eyes, she quotes a geneticist as saying there must be "white ancestry" in the family's background: "The only explanation seems to be there must have been a white gene in my family that has remained dormant for years until now. And now it seems to be very dominant." The geneticist explains further, "it is likely there is a white gene somewhere in the woman's remote ancestry and due to an evolutionary throwback—known as atavism—this trait has suddenly reappeared" (Smith Squire 2017).

The article about Angela Igheboro describes her "White" daughter in the same terms: "Experts say that, in this extreme case, there would have to be history of white ancestry on both sides." It quotes a genetics expert who says, "The hair is extremely unusual; even many blonde children don't have blonde hair like this at birth. This might be a case where there is a lot of genetic mixing, as in Afro-Caribbean populations. But in Nigeria there is little mixing" (J. Johnston 2010). These explanations propagate the belief that race is "in the blood" or "genetic," rather than a sociopolitical construction.

PHENOTYPE DETERMINES RACE, BUT BLACKNESS CANNOT PRODUCE WHITENESS

In addition, the articles reflect the view that phenotypic features determine race. The journalists' description of the babies as "White" is based in their physical features. Thus, a baby with fair skin and blond hair is called White, so a child with darker skin would be deemed mixed or even Black. On the basis of the biological concept of race described earlier, the authors therefore conclude that White family members who passed down "White genes" bear responsibility for the children's features. A third racial logic—that Black people cannot produce Whiteness—reinforces this conclusion. Especially in the explanation of the Black Nigerian family, the geneticists are convinced that fair skin, blond hair, and blue eyes cannot come from a Black woman's genetic makeup because of the belief that being Black means naturally producing dark skin, hair, and eyes, exclusively. In other words, being racially identified as Black precludes one from having genes that carry phenotypic diversity.

The Comment Section's Paradoxical Discourse

"THOSE CHILDREN ARE NOT WHITE"

The comments on both articles significantly push back on the claim that the children born to Black women are White, using narratives that reflect racial voyeurism. The commenters evoke the assumption that Blackness is incompatible with Whiteness. The most frequent comment in both samples is that the children, regardless of how they look, are not White. For the Howarth family, $n = 18$; and for the Igheboros, $n = 14$. This conclusion reflects a core belief in the natural reproduction of race and the one-drop rule, that a child with a Black parent is irrevocably Black and barred from claiming White racial identity, which is predicated on assumptions of purity. The following comments are particularly illustrative:

1. "She is Albino. Accept it and do not try to make money out of her. She is to be loved and praised like all others."

   This comment provides an alternative "commonsense" view that the child has albinism, which removes pigment from the skin. The second part of the commentary evokes Collins's notion of controlling images by intimating that the parents are attempting to make money from their child by appearing in the media. This aligns with stereotypes of pathological parenting in the Black community by "bad black mothers" (Moss 2016).

2. "Did she pick up the wrong baby, is there a white couple somewhere with their baby?"

   Disbelieving that the child could be born to a Black woman, the comment denies the bonds between mother and child because of their differing phenotypes. The statement that she picked up the "wrong" baby and that the true parents of the child are White implies that it is impossible for a woman with brown skin and eyes, racialized as Black, to give birth to a baby with phenotypic traits associated with Whiteness.

3. "This is stupid, whilst they are very fair skinned, they still look mixed race. This is not a story, I don't know why she keeps on appearing in the media, do her or her husband not have a job?"

This comment denies that the children can be White while also insinuating that the parents are trying to take advantage of their children because they do not work. This comment's intentions are twofold: First, it calls the story "stupid," establishing that the child's features do not pass a litmus test for Whiteness. Second, the implication that the children's parents do not work and are merely using the media attention to line their pockets is a common stereotype of Black people as lazy grifters.

4. "I think the milk man may have paid a visit while the husband was away"

5. "Yeah we heard of black babies from white couples . . . its called cheating!!!! Lol"

These two comments reflect disbelief that a Black couple could give birth to a light-skinned child unless the biological father was White. Thus, race is a natural by-product of procreation. The comments also use humor to reinforce stereotypes about Black female hypersexuality by alleging that the mother must have cheated on her spouse.

"BLUE EYED, BLONDE HAIRED GIFT FROM GOD"

Both articles describe the physical differences between the Black mothers and their fair-skinned children, without accompanying scientific explanations for why children are born with a variety of skin hues. Instead, more attention is paid to portraying the children's physical features as positive. Scholars of race remind us that media typically consider physical features that are associated with Whiteness as superior while considering features associated with Blackness less attractive (Phoenix 2014; Wilder 2015). Thus, the lighter the hair, skin, and eye color, the closer one perceives a child's alignment with White-supremacist notions of beauty, innocence, and goodness. Despite the reality that the continent of Africa has the greatest genetic diversity, including alleles for phenotype, the articles underscore the beauty and presumed rareness of the children's fair skin, blond hair, and blue eyes.

1. "Her name means Beauty of God in our language, and we think it suits her so well."
2. "And her hair! She looked like a doll."
3. "Each time doctors and midwives have all commented on our babies' amazing colouring. People often get confused when they meet me with the children for the first time."
4. "At just three weeks she landed her first modelling job."

The same degree of adulation is reflected in the commenters' frequent compliments of the babies' appearance ($n = 11$, $n = 13$). In contrast, commenters pointed to the "African features" as validation that the children could not possibly be White.

5. "I could just eat them. Beautiful."

This comment reflects the most common type of compliment: celebration of the babies' beauty. The writer specifically notes that the child's beauty is her blond, curly hair and her blue eyes, the exact features that supposedly prove the inheritance of White genes.

6. "Mixed race children are stunning."
7. "The kids look mixed race African to me, not white Anglo-Saxon. Beautiful as they are, this shouldn't even be an article."
8. "She actually looks like their other daughter except has white skin (definite black features). Very good looking family though."

Like many of the comments, these view the children as an exotic and beautiful result of interracial pairings. They reflect the notion that children are not White because their features are more "African" than "Caucasian," as well as reflecting racialized standards of beauty. Inherent in these comments is the principle that racial purity exists, and despite proximity to Whiteness, the children are not granted access to Whiteness.

All That Matters Is . . . Colorblindness

Another important aspect of the articles and commentary is a strong commitment to colorblind narratives—primarily that race does not matter and is an inappropriate subject matter. The way the articles were produced and consumed contributes to an acute cognitive dissonance about the importance of race. Although the very reason the articles were published with bombastic language like "the only black woman in the world to give birth to two white children," the comments emphasize the sentiment that race should have little bearing on the children's lives. The racial voyeurism of the consumers, and their eagerness to comment on the personal lives, genetic ancestry, and physical features of the Black women and their babies, is activated by their anxiety about colorblindness ($n = 4$, $n = 6$).

1. "What a lovely story! A beautiful baby with a loving family to welcome her. Skin colour doesn't matter, you baby could be purple with yellow spots but you would still love it. If we all had different colour babies regularly, surely racism would disappear overnight."
2. "Who cares what colour she is. She is absolutely gorgeous, simple!"
3. "Beautiful children, regardless what color their skin is . . . They are a perfect mix of mom and dad, love their hair too"
4. "All that matters is the children are healthy and happy . . . enjoy your babies, they are Beautiful. God bless"

These comments emphasize the importance of ignoring racial difference. The first comment reflects a commonly heard phrase reported by scholars of colorblind racism: proclamations that humans can be any color, even unrealistic colors such as "polka dotted," to further remove oneself from the realities of racism. The commenter's argument that mixed-raced babies will reduce racism is immediately belied by other comments on the very same article.

Comments 2, 3, and 4 reflect different linguistic rhetorics of racial colorblindness and a refusal to acknowledge how race is already playing a significant role in shaping the lives of the children. For instance, both Black women report receiving strange reactions from loved ones about their babies. Mrs. Howarth reports her frustration when strangers stop to ask her if she is the nanny of her baby. Each comment simultaneously dismisses that race should be discussed at all ("who cares," "regardless," "all that matters") and praises the physical features of the children. The commenters' emphasis on the beauty of the blond-haired, blue-eyed babies is contradicted by their racial anxiety that insists on the denial of "seeing" race. The children's beauty, which is inescapably related to their light features, cannot be separated from the fetishization of biracial children and European-associated features. Thus, the commenters' decision to focus on the beauty of the children functions to shield their discomfort with open discussions of race and racism while also engaging in racial voyeurism.

Discussion

The findings of our study are significant for understanding multiple themes about the production and consumption of racialized media online. News stories about White babies born to Black mothers reproduce narratives about race, biology, and spectacle. These narratives are guided by three underlying principles about the meaning of race.

First, the primary claim of the articles and the response of the consumers is that race is a genetic inheritance rather than a sociopolitical construction. Instead of treating these cases as examples of human genetic variation, the media sensationalize the births of light-skinned, blue-eyed, blond-haired babies as if it were an unheard-of phenomenon. Indeed, several of the commenters react strongly to the claim that Howarth is the "only black woman" in the world to give birth to "White" children by sharing a personal anecdote ($n = 9$). One person even states, "This is not rare. Go on Instagram" (Smith Squire 2017). There are an array of websites, Pinterest pages, and Instagram accounts dedicated to multiracial families with pictures of "White" children and Black parents. Therefore, the articles are predicated on a false view of humanity that relies on shoddy science to explain the children as being recipients of "White genes."

The second primary claim undergirding the articles is that phenotype determines race. Therefore, because the babies were born with fair skin, eyes, and hair, they are declared White, even though their mothers identify as Black. However, in one-third of the sampled comments in both articles, the consumers dispute this claim. The commenters often use terms that support scientific notions of race to validate their claims, like "African features" and "black features." From the perspective of the consumers, the children do not look White enough to be considered White ($n = 3$, $n = 15$).

Finally, the most prevalent theme throughout the two stories is the assertion that "Black cannot make White." According to this view, it is impossible for Black women to produce a so-called White child without a "distant White ancestor" or a "White gene." From comments that declare that the babies have "African" features to statements about their lack of "Anglo-Saxon" features, the greatest percentage of comments declare that the children are not White ($n = 14$, $n = 16$). There is a significant paradox in the commentary of the consumers: while the articles propagate the narrative that race is both biologically reproduced and determined by phenotypic features, commenters push back against describing the babies as "White" because of the core logic that the Black race cannot produce the White race. It is this contradiction in stories of White babies born to Black mothers that attracts consumers' racial voyeurism. Finally, commenters apply stereotypical controlling images to the Black mothers, implying that they are lazy, unfaithful, and opportunistic. While the focus of the articles is on the births of babies described as exceptionally beautiful, the mothers are subject to consumers' vilification.

Conclusion: Media, Racial Voyeurism, and the New Race Science

In mainstream discussions of race in the United States and the United Kingdom, the "epistemology of ignorance" is in full effect (Charles Mills 1997; Sullivan and Tuana 2012): despite the rise of overt White nationalism and racial hate crimes, Whites still widely believe that race is a natural inheritance and that racism is not a factor in determining one's life chances (Center for the Study of Hate and Extremism 2017). Further, increasing numbers of Whites in the United States and the United Kingdom believe that Whiteness is a victimized or subjugated racial status. As demographic changes in the United States and the United Kingdom shift to a non-White majority, there is a marked increase in xenophobia and anti-Black racism. Far-right conservative ideologies have gained power in both the United States and the United Kingdom, with political figures echoing centuries-old stereotypes about the dangers of racialized bodies and the innocence of Whiteness. The news media facilitate racial violence by failing to question or challenge inaccurate beliefs about race and racism.

Although sociological analyses of White supremacy have tended to focus on the United States, these UK news articles indicate that White supremacy is a global phenomenon that is nuanced but relies on shared assumptions—namely, biological race concepts, assumptions of White superiority, anti-Black stereotypes, and colorblind ideology that dismisses the persistence of institutionalized racism.

The consumer discourses of the two cases we studied reflect the continued popularity of antiquated beliefs about the category of race as well as stereotypes of Black women. By defining race as a natural grouping associated with differing genetic predispositions, this science casts race as a cause for racial inequalities rather than as a sociopolitical construction that arranges society unequally. It obscures the reality that White supremacy, not innate racial pathologies, is responsible for Black people's disadvantaged status. Our study shows that scholars should pay greater critical attention to media stories—and their reception by consumers—that promote false and dangerous assumptions about the biological procreation of race, assumptions that continue to support White supremacy in a colorblind era.

Notes

1. This study focuses on media coverage of two UK-based families but includes the commentary of consumers worldwide.
2. *Huffington Post, The Daily Beast, Essence,* BBC, Fox News, *New York Post,* and CBS News published online articles without comment sections.

13

Virtual Antiracism

Pleasure, Catharsis, and Hope in Mafia III *and* Watch Dogs 2

DAVID J. LEONARD

Video games do not care about Black people.[1] Black lives, voices, stories, and futures do not matter in virtual reality. Rampant stereotypes and reactionary politics have long defined the world of games. Evident in the ubiquity of racist representations, the types of narratives available, the politics of gaming, the demographics of designers, and the experience of gamers of color, the gaming world remains a place dominated by White heterosexual men. At least that is the case for the majority of gaming during its history. Games reflect and remain an instrument of hegemony (Gray 2012a, 2012b; Higgin 2009; Williams et al. 2009).

Games have also been a site of change. Yet such resistance and opposition has long emanated from independent designers. For example, games like *Depression Quest, Never Alone, Darfur Is Dying,* and *We Are Chicago* each offer narratives and characters that are otherwise marginalized within mainstream video games (Gray and Leonard 2018; Malkowski and Russworm 2017; Gray 2012a; Higgin 2010; Frasca 2006), challenging not only existing virtual representations but the broader political landscapes. These are games we might describe as "video games of the oppressed" (Frasca, quoted in Dyer-Withford and Peuter 2009, 197), those virtual inscriptions that have sought to document, challenge, and give hope to marginalized and dehumanized communities.

For much of the history of gaming, these types of transgressive games, as in other forms of popular culture, sat at the periphery, lacking resources, visibility, and acceptance from hegemonic gaming. Recently, however, we have seen the emergence of "woke games" (Gray and Leonard 2018). These games inscribe and encode the experiences of marginalized communities, offering "freedom dreams" (Kelley 2002) within/from more mainstream virtual spaces. At the same time, the power and potential of the games rest with their embrace (in part because of the technology available) of the aesthetics of mainstream games, their deployment of the grammar of virtual crime dramas and violence, and their ability to provide intact a gaming experience that is commonplace to mainstream games. The social justice message and the links to existing social movements come through a familiar vehicle that defines mainstream games. This shift or potential shift reflects the demands from gamers, particularly those of color, and the broader shifts in popular culture.

The rising tide of politically progressive games should be of little surprise given our current moment. In the face of daily reminders that Black lives do not matter, we are in a golden age of Black popular culture. In an era defined by Charlottesville and Trump, Black popular culture has become a site of protest and dissent. From Colin Kaepernick's kneeling to countless performances from Beyoncé, from *Get Out* to *Black Panther*, from Kendrick Lamar to Janelle Monáe, from Black Twitter to countless other examples, Black popular culture not only has challenged the history of racism within mediated culture but is giving voice to the protests happening throughout the nation. Reflecting on "how #BlackLivesMatter started a musical revolution," Daphne Brooks writes, "But this is a new age of injustice, one with a heightened awareness of state violence and a national reckoning with the state-sanctioned disposability of Black lives, and so this moment clearly demands a new set of jams" (2016). Writing in 2015, Steven Thrasher made clear the importance of popular culture as both a source of hope and a space for the articulation of a politics of freedom, for the language of justice and Black Lives Matter: "Heading into this summer we need black heroes and black superheroes, in art and in real life, more than ever. And lucky for us, they're turning up worldwide in comic books, on movie and TV screens, splashed across canvasses, and shimmying up flagpoles just when we need them" (2015a).

While popular discourses have highlighted and celebrated the interventions from sports, films, music, social media, and television in the fight for Black lives, in giving voice to the voices of protest marching throughout the nation, video games are rarely part of the discussion. The long-standing place of gaming as a site for the production and dissemination of White-supremacist ideologies, alongside those discourses that see games as "kid's stuff," as the purview of White men, and otherwise reactionary, contributes to gaming's exclusion from these broader cultural discourses.

In an effort to highlight progressive games as a mainstream enterprise, as both having a message and offering the aesthetics, story lines, and game playability that are commonplace within hegemonic gaming culture, this chapter looks at how mainstream video games are becoming a site of dissent and opposition. This chapter looks at two games that point to both the mainstreaming of antiracist / #BLM / social justice gaming and the increased possibility and power in these virtual interventions. First, I examine *Mafia III*, a revenge fantasy chronicling the efforts of a Black veteran seeking to regain control of his life, all while liberating his community from those racist crime families that are profiting off, exploiting, and abusing Black people. Second, I offer analysis of *Watch Dogs 2*, a game that chronicles the efforts of Marcus Holloway, a Black hacker battling the injustices of the state and corporate America.

These games offer a political intervention, a site for the articulation of counternarratives and education about racism, inequality, state violence, and resistance. While their efforts to diversify the landscape of virtual reality are important, it is their centering of racism, their demand that Black lives matter, their narrative construction of resistance to the structures and manifestations of racism, their remixing of violence as a source of justice, and the moment of representation/ consumption that produce virtual stories that remix the conventions of video games with the pedagogies of antiracist social justice.

Mafia III: Antiracism

Mafia III transports players back to 1968 New Bordeaux (a virtual incarnation of New Orleans), bringing to life the usual video-game staples of violence, crime, and spectacle alongside the realities of racism, injustice, and segregation, facets of American life then, now, and into the foreseeable future. *Mafia III* was refreshing not only given the video-game industry's history of "undiversity" and new (and more explicit) racism (Malkowski and Russworm 2017; Gray 2014, 2012b; Williams et al. 2009; Leonard 2006) but because in the moment of daily reminders that Black lives do not matter and calcifying systemic racism, these games not only provided counternarratives and visibility for marginalized voices but created spaces of opposition, dissent, and justice. On NPR.com, Iman Smith described the game as creating a "cathartic alternate reality that directly confronts gamers of all walks of life with the reimagined raw trials of a protagonist rarely featured by the industry" (2017). Kahlief Adams described *Mafia III* as "the game of the decade" (Porter 2017). Shareef Jackson, who hosts the podcast *Spawn on Me* with Adams Cicero Holmes and Adams, similarly praised the game for its progressive politics and its resistance to the status quo: "The game is just so poignant"; it is "so in your face about the message that it's trying to deliver" (Porter 2017). For gamers and nongamers alike, *Mafia III* surprisingly provided spaces of progressive politics and antiracism within the traditional third-person-shooter ("shoot 'em up") mainstream gaming narrative (Kollar 2016).

Mafia III tells the story of Lincoln Clay, the son of a Dominican mother and a White father, who grew up in an orphanage run by Father James, a Black clergyman. After the city shuts down the orphanage, he finds a virtual and existential home with Sammy Robinson, a Black crime boss who runs various rackets in the city. Fast-forward to when Lincoln returns home after a tour in Vietnam; in an effort to help Robinson, Clay joins forces with members of the Marcano crime family to pull off a heist. Tragically, members of the Marcano family double-cross Lincoln, killing Robinson, burning down James's church, and ultimately unsuccessfully trying to kill Lincoln. The game starts here, as Clay seeks revenge against Robinson's killers and the White power structure that lifts and empowers them at the expense of the Black community.

Through violence directed at White supremacists and a narrative of antiracism, *Mafia III* creates a world not simply where revenge is imagined as good versus evil but where violence becomes a tool of punishment and retribution against White supremacy—it is a mechanism of the righteous in the struggle for justice. Creating a narrative centering around a fight against injustice, the game highlights the entrenched nature of American racism and the persistent struggle for Black life. "The game pulls no punches in depicting Lincoln's violent nature, and it does the same in showing players what it meant to be a black man in the Jim-Crow-era South. Some shopkeepers refuse you service and call you names," writes Justin Porter in the *New York Times* (2017). "Several police cars hunt you down if you commit a crime in a White, middle-class neighborhood. Do the same in a predominantly black neighborhood and one car will show up, if that. No matter where Lincoln is, the police are watching. He fights racist organizations, casual bias and the prejudice of friends" (Porter 2017). While the game provides diversity of story line and player-controlled characters that are rarely available within mainstream gaming, the power of *Mafia III* also emanates through its documenting of African American history and its centering of the fight against White supremacy. Its ability to bridge between past and present, to use history to tell a story about the moment, and to build from virtual reality into the headlines and daily realities speaks to the power and potential of the game.

While *Mafia III* is a story of criminal syndicates, revenge, corruption, and a nation in turmoil, it is a game about Blackness, about Black identity in the post-civil-rights/post-Vietnam world, about racism in 1968, about Black power, and about the history of Black organized crime. Blackness is at the game's core. And Lincoln represents the vehicle for the game's storytelling. In other words, Lincoln anchors not only the game's narrative but also its centering of Blackness. The game makes this clear, as his mixed racial identity matters little. In one instance, Father James remarks, "His mother, I heard she was Dominican. I always figured his father was White, maybe even Italian. Not that it mattered, back then if you looked Black, you Black. Same as today, I suppose." Making clear that racism is not simply a historical counterpoint to Obama's postracial America, *Mafia III* offers a clear link between past and present. The game centers Lincoln's Blackness and its meaning in America from the early moments of the game, with Whites in New Bordeaux regularly using the N-word. In one instance, a security guard tells Lincoln, "mind your manners," demanding that Lincoln go around back, as he could not be anything but "the help."

Mafia III tells a "robust and authentic story of the 1968 American South, when the Italian mafia's golden age was coming to a close. Focusing on the Black mafia provides a different lens for the series, rather than featuring another white member of the Italian mob," notes

Jessica Conditt (2016). Throughout the game, the importance of 1968, of American racism, of segregation in the South, and of White supremacy is made clear. This is not simply backstory or background to the commonplace crime game but central to understanding Lincoln Clay, Marcano, and the entire narrative. It is part of an effort to situate its story line about crime/gangs/violence—or simply a classic revenge plot of good against evil—as part of a larger struggle for Black freedom. The examples are endless: the nods to Angela Davis, the Black Panthers, and Malcolm X; the references to the 1968 Olympic protest and how Tommie Smith and John Carlos were "booed." In another instance, there is discussion about the assassination of Martin Luther King, with some characters questioning whether James Earl Ray was the only shooter. The implication is clear: America's racist power structure and White America were responsible for King's death, whether or not Ray acted alone.

Evident here, the game's staging of history is of primary importance; in many ways, 1968 is the main character as it allows for a narrative to deploy the language of 1960s racial justice even as it bridges between America's history books and the continuing struggle for Black freedom. According to Conditt, 1968 allows *Mafia III* to tell a story about American racism, about the Black mob, and so much more: "That history includes the Vietnam War, Creedence Clearwater Revival and other aspects of 1968 Americana. News stories air on the radio throughout the game, offering details about protests, pop culture phenomena and commentary on players' actions as they progress. And then there's the music" (2016). Bill Harms, the game's lead writer, similarly notes the importance of history: "As you drive around in the car, we have radio stations. We wrote a lot of news stories reflecting real-world events. Character[s] in the game comment on real-world events. Three women have a conversation about James Earl Ray, who assassinated Dr. King. We use those things to ground the game and give it the feel of a specific time and place. We weave those things into the narrative to help support that, just reinforce where the game is set and who the characters are" (quoted in Takahasi 2016).

Lincoln's experiences with racism, a sobering reminder all too common to Black veterans throughout US history, embody the unfulfilled promises that greet Lincoln on his return home to New Bordeaux. Yet his path is not simply through the realities of racism. Suffering from PTSD, triggered by White supremacy and its manifested violence, Lincoln is abandoned by a nation. It is clear that he is looking for a place to belong. Despite "welcome home" signs, national elation, and parades, he is plagued by powerlessness, fear, and guilt. According to Harms, who is White, Lincoln returns from Vietnam in a perpetual state of terror: Dealing with the aftermath of the war and confronted with the realities of American racism, Lincoln lives in the absence of safety and security. He lives without peace and freedom. He lives in fear for his life in a society that refuses to see his humanity. "When Lincoln arrives home, he doesn't go back to his old bedroom. He sleeps in the basement," notes Harms. "That's because the basement is essentially a very large foxhole and that's where he feels safe" (quoted in Conditt 2016).

Hoping to find himself and also give back to his community, Lincoln joins forces with his brother, Ellis Richardson; Sammy, the head of the local Black mob organization; and members of the local Italian mob to pull off a successful robbery of the Federal Reserve. For Lincoln and Sammy, the power of the money transcends its financial value. "What you boys did tonight, this changes everything," Sammy tells Lincoln and others upon seeing hundreds of thousands of dollars. "This isn't just money. It's freedom. It's real freedom. Ain't no one standing over me again. Over any of us." The money does not represent access to luxury items or a newfound class status but freedom and the pleasures that result from living free. Yet, as in the United States itself, that power is fleeting. Sammy, Ellis, and Lincoln are all double-crossed by their "brothers in arms."

Amid a barrage of racial slurs ("Fucking N-words"), Ritchie Doucet, one of the members of the Marcano crime family, stabs Ellis multiple times, as Sal Marcano, the leader of the crime syndicate, shoots Sammy in the head. Before setting fire to Sammy's bar, which served as a place of refuge for Lincoln and a place of community for Black New Bordeaux, Georgi Marcano shoots Lincoln in the head. While setting the stage for a game about racial retribution, building on a history of Black popular culture that celebrates antiheroes who violently avenge White supremacy, this moment also centers anti-Black racism. Like the United States, and Whites throughout the history of the nation, the Marcanos find profit and power in using Black bodies to exact labor and riches, only to respond with violence and reassertion of White power and dominance. Only this time, Lincoln, who survives the fire and the shooting, strikes back against evil, exacting retribution and finding pleasure in the systematic destruction of the Marcano crime family and the racism that plagues the city.

Lincoln Clay finds purpose in avenging the murder of Sammy and Ellis; in joining forces with Cassandra (a Black Haitian woman who runs a local criminal syndicate) and Father James; in striking back against White supremacy, against the "Dixie mafia," and against those criminal elements and political structures that use racism as a source and instrument of power. He exacts revenge against Sammy's and Ellis's killers but also at the very fabric that aids and abets their reign of terror.

One of the game's early missions takes place in an amusement park, which is "a cheeky opportunity to comment on the perverse pleasures of the world in which a game is set" (Plante 2016). In other words, in the midst of a world of racial segregation, lynchings, dehumanization, police violence, and denied Black innocence, there are ironically still places of play and pleasure. The staging here feels purposeful, in that for Blacks in this virtual reality and their "real" brethren, there are no places of play, of freedom from the brutality of American racism. The killing of Tamir Rice, a twelve-year-old boy who was shot by police while holding a toy gun, elucidates the ways that childhood and play have always been racially separate and unequal. Evident here, this becomes yet another instance when the game this virtual space to both history and our current moment, providing tools and connective tissue to the ongoing protests that define the struggle for Black lives.

But in this instance, the amusement park becomes a place where Lincoln Clay strikes back against racial terror. "The mission culminates with an intriguing and loaded cut scene. With his target cornered, Clay nooses the low-level mobster to a ferris-wheel cart, sending the ride in motion, until the lifeless body hangs high above the park for all to see. A Black man lynching a white man in the American South in 1968 is an arresting image" (Plante 2016). While the "game's pace" undercuts the power of this historical reversal, taking "no time to unpack what we're seeing, let alone acknowledge that, below the hanging man, fester dozens of other men murdered by Lincoln Clay" (Plante 2016), seemingly moving its (White) players away from the unpleasurable confrontation with history, this scene speaks to the game's investment in racial justice even as it imagines these politics through gruesome and horrific violence.

The centering of violence as a source of resistance, transformation, redemption, and freedom is in fact commonplace throughout *Mafia III*. This is of little surprise given the grammar of gaming, although rarely do these aesthetics, narratives, and normalization of violence come through story lines of antiracism. During one mission in which Lincoln kills Lou Marcano, Lincoln guts Lou and then proceeds to hang him from an Andrew Jackson memorial. In a moment when activists have fought to bring down the Confederate flag and other White-supremacist monument, Lincoln Clay repurposes them, reclaiming the symbolic and the material manifestations of racism as a monument to the destruction of racism.

In another mission, Lincoln kills Remy Doucet, who is concerned and outraged that an "N-word" is taking over the neighborhood. Remy uses the N-word on his deathbed. Unsatisfied with simply shooting him, Lincoln puts Remy on a cross and burns him to death. Throughout the game, when Lincoln kills the most virulent racist, the game breaks from a player-controlled mission, showing a video that seemingly remixes history for the sake of antiracism and racial retribution. When Lincoln ultimately kills Sal, he announces, "You tried to killed me because you thought you owned me." Whereas so many missions end with gun violence, Lincoln kills Sal slowly with a knife. The game fixates the camera to gaze at Sal, to celebrate his death, and to punctuate the righteousness of a knife penetrating his racist chest.

Mafia III goes beyond creating a story that centers on a Black hero. "As the game was developed, police shootings of Black men rose, the Black Lives Matter movement was born, and the development team realized they'd created a game that talked about race in ways that sometimes bridged the gap of history" (Porter 2017). The moment of reception and play is crucial, as the daily reminders of White supremacy and the evidence of its "victories" at the expense of Black pain are disrupted in a game that shows justice and destruction of White-supremacist enemies.

As much as *Mafia III* is about staging the past, it is just as invested in bringing to life twenty-first-century color lines and the ongoing resistance. For example, the game spotlights "black barbershop conversations" (Harris-Lacewell 2006), those conversations that take place apart from White surveillance and the power of the White gaze. Melissa Harris-Lacewell (now Harris-Perry) writes that the barbershop, beauty salon, and other Black communal spaces allow for Black conversations about everything from popular culture to everyday racism: "There were discussions of the relationships between black men and women. They talked about White power structures and the relationship of African-Americans to the state and to capitalism. They critiqued black leaders, discussed the political power of the black church, argued about reparations, and cheered on African American Olympic athletes" (2006, 172; see also P. Jones 2004). Eschewing narratives that privilege White voices within discourses around race, *Mafia III* works to elucidate beyond the spectacle, the protest, and televised speech. For example, while on a mission, you overhear someone talking: "Why White version of beauty; need to define for ourselves." Staging resistance while documenting the insidiousness of White supremacy in examples that persist after the Obama presidency, the game spotlights the impact of White supremacy on identity and the everyday efforts to resist and challenge its hold on the Black community and the American landscape.

While the game is clearly specific to 1968 and makes an effort to contextualize Lincoln's revenge within the racial and social landscape of the moment, it is hard not to see the connective tissue between the politics of White supremacy, White nationalism, and White resentment that defines the 1960s (and every other American decade) and our current moment, defined by the Black Lives Matter movement, Charlottesville, the 2016 election, and persistent racial and class inequality. The game does not shy away from spotlighting the specter of White supremacy—and its violence, insidiousness, and persistence in post-civil-rights America. The game includes the obvious references to signify White racism: the constant use of the N-word; the direct and indirect references to segregation / Jim Crow; the Confederate flag and the Klan. In one mission, members of the Dixie Mafia encourage Black teenagers to run so that the gang can sic dogs on the teens as if they were slave catchers. The game routinely makes clear that the police are instruments of racism and racist violence, dialoguing with and building on the protests of Black Lives Matter.

In chronicling the specter of White terror, of institutionalized and everyday racism and violence, *Mafia III* pushes the conversation deeper. While the player drives around, a discussion ensues on talk radio about the elimination of a scholarship as a result of the demands for equality. The show's host argues that even if the scholarship goes to only White students, they are not racist because they are going to the most deserving applications (yet another example of how the game is as much about 2016 as it is about 1968). Worse yet, those movements fighting for inclusion and those demanding diversity are antithetical to meritocracy in that less qualified and culturally backward people are provided rewards. In another instance, a news story on the radio references a White home owner shooting a Black person and how (White) property owners should have the right to defend themselves.

At the same time, *Mafia III* centers resistance and the fight for justice. Toward the end of the game, alongside clips of police deploying fire hoses, scenes of urban unrest, and clips of the assassination of Martin Luther King Jr., Father James (the game's moral compass and chief adherent of nonviolence) concludes that change results from incidents that strip a nation down to its "foundation." Out of that rubble and loss, there is potential for justice. In this regard, Lincoln Clay, in battling a known racist sin that is so often relegated to our textbooks, in exposing and rooting out White-supremacist evil, is breaking the city and the nation down to its foundation, a necessary step toward peace and equality. Defined by a refusal to center the White gaze or White pleasure, by a politics of Black humanity, love, and justice, and by an articulation of "freedom dreams," *Mafia III* builds on the work of activists and cultural producers who are challenging how we can use mediated space in transformative ways.

Watch Dogs 2: Resisting the 1 Percent

Released in 2016, *Watch Dogs 2*, a game on hacker culture, centers on Black characters. Of the five-member hacker crew, DedSec, a group that works to expose the evils of surveillance culture, two are Black men. The main character is Marcus Holloway. The game's wiki page describes him as follows:

> Marcus was born in Los Angeles, California in 1992 but moved to Oakland at a young age with his low-income family. Marcus was at one point placed into a community program where he would discover an affinity for computers. In 2012, rising crime rates would lead to the institution of the Home Domain Center, surveillance initiative, and in 2013, Marcus was falsely accused of being the primary suspect in a high tech robbery. With the only evidence being the HDC predictive software, he was merely sentenced to community service as punishment. However, because of the accusation made against him, Marcus was frequently discriminated against by the community. This disillusioned him to the system that put him in these circumstances, and under the alias "Retro," hacked local government officials and leak incriminating documents on HDC data gathering. (Watch Dogs Wiki, n.d.-b)

Despite Marcus having grown up in a world that saw him as a criminal, as someone destined for pathological behavior ("superpredator"), and despite a culture of discrimination, he was able to use his computer skills, his intellect, and his knowledge to produce freedom for himself and others suffering under the structures and technologies of violence and inequality. While he uses his gun and some other contraption that looks like a yo-yo to defeat enemies, the game is more about his (and your) intellect, creativity, and problem-solving ability. Throughout the game, the players have to figure out how to hack various "smart" devices, to infiltrate protected spaces, and to otherwise battle evil through their "nerd powers." Andrew Webster aptly describes this dimension of the game: "At its best, Watch Dogs 2 makes you feel like an all-powerful ghost. Often I was able to complete a mission while barely being physically present. I would remotely control cars, security cameras, and more, in order to create as much havoc as possible, all while sitting across the street, comfortably away from the violence. It's incredibly satisfying being able to casually stroll into a building and grab whatever you need, while the building's security force has already been defeated before you walk in the door" (2016). The other Black character is Horatio Carlin. He is described in the game's wiki page as follows:

Horatio was raised in a troubled household and found solace hiding on the internet and listening to music, whatever allowed him to escape into his own head and away from the shouting. As his home life spiraled out of control, Horatio regained control over his life by learning to code and hack. It felt good to him, exerting control over the Internet when everything else around him was falling apart. Fortunately, Horatio proved skilled and talented enough to apply for a job at Nudle, and got hired. It was something few people in his family had: a career with benefits and a retirement package. (Watch Dogs Wiki, n.d.-a)

In other words, Horatio is the American Dream, who succeeds because of his intellect and creativity; he is the living embodiment of his namesake, Horatio Alger. Given the confinement of such narratives for African Americans to sports and entertainment, the positioning of Horatio as the American Dream furthers the game's intervention approach.

In re-creating a world of hypersurveillance, technological intrusion, and the convergence of state and corporate interests, all of which disempower the people, the game's narrative embraces progressive politics. Its focus on police surveillance and state power waged against communities of color furthers its political intervention. This is evident in the game's description. "In 2016, ctOS 2.0, an advanced operating system networking city infrastructure, was implemented in several US cities to create a safer, more efficient metropolis."

While power rests in the hands of an increasingly powerful police state and its Silicon Valley partners, the game offers a narrative that centers hacker culture as both resistance to injustice and the means toward securing "freedom dreams" for all. The game's description makes its mission clear: using technology to undermine and ultimately destroy neoliberal transnational capitalism. "Play as Marcus Holloway, a brilliant young hacker living in the birthplace of the tech revolution, the San Francisco Bay Area. Team up with DedSec, a notorious group of hackers, and expose the hidden dangers of ctOS 2.0, which, in the hands of corrupt corporations, is being wrongfully used to monitor and manipulate citizens on a massive scale." In exploring surveillance culture and its impact on inequality, policing, and so much more, *Watch Dogs 2* offers a powerful companion to Simone Browne's *Dark Matters: On the Surveillance of Blackness* (2015). It also centers resistance. The progressive politics of the game can be found in its direct tackling of racial injustice as well. While violence surrounds the game and its characters, and while it too celebrates violence as necessary and even moral, *Watch Dogs 2* also imagines a world where creativity, technology, and intellect are the necessary tools to right societal wrong. In many instances, and in the game's conclusion, hacking and the critical thinking are the true antiseptics to societal violence and racial violence.

While *Watch Dogs 2* addresses racism through its narrative focus on surveillance, criminalization, and the dialectics between neoliberal capitalism and inequality, it also focuses on the realities of daily microaggressions and everyday racism. In one instance, Marcus laments how the smart car he has just stolen does not recognize his face because "his skin is too dark" (the game elucidates not only the ways that surveillance technology operates in relationship to race and skin color but also how popular culture imagines superheroes through Whiteness, since that car is from a superhero movie). In another moment, the game shines a spotlight on the Whiteness of Silicon Valley and the experiences of programmers of color in these historically and perpetually White industries. Tanya D perfectly summarizes this scene as follows:

> The true turning point that made me love this game was the following conversation between Marcus and Horatio, the only other brother on the team with a legit day job where he's also doubling up as a source of info for DedSec. When they are walking around the Nudle campus—Nudle being the game's satirical version of a huge technology company—there's a moment between them that many of us have had when working in corporate life:
>
> Marcus says to Horatio as they arrive at the campus, "Hey, Horatio man. I'm scared, bro."
>
> Horatio questions that with, "Scared? Of what?"
>
> For anyone who's been the only or one of a few black folks in a tech office, Marcus' answer is obvious. "Nobody looks like us," he says.
>
> Sometimes humor is our only option to keep cool in this situation, and that's how Horatio responds.

HORATIO: "Ha, man, welcome to Silicon Valley. Hey, what do you
   call a black man surrounded by thousands of white people?"
MARCUS: "What?"
HORATIO: "Mr. President."

The moment passes between them as they enter the cafeteria, and
Horatio gets his daily dose of microaggression from a white colleague
who's sure Horatio's up to no good. This coworker gives them both a
suspicious once over before casually threatening to take his "concerns"
to HR.
   Any person of color with a white colleague who's been convinced they
don't belong has had that same experience; the same sense of being guilty
until proven innocent . . . and then still maybe being called guilty. (2016)

In another instance, Horatio tells Marcus, "You haven't experienced
corporate life until you're the only brother in a meeting, and you have
to represent all of blackdom. If I had a nickel for every time somebody
complimented me on being well-spoken" (quoted in Porter 2017).
Throughout their conversation, yet another intimate moment when
two Black characters speak honestly about their experiences with racism, we bear witness to the power of community in the absence of
White intrusion; we are shown not only the nature of conversations in
the absence of the White gaze but also the power that emanates from
the expression of vulnerability, honesty, and truth. In other words, the
surveillance that often regulates African American behavior, language,
and interaction, that privileges White fragility (DiAngelo 2018), is for
a moment disrupted, allowing for a certain freedom in the game, all
while bridging to both everyday experiences with anti-Black racism
and the politics of resistance. The importance of this moment is evident
in how the game centers this truth-telling conversation about racism in
the workplace, microaggressions, and the lack of diversity within Silicon Valley. For Marcus and Horatio, this became a moment when they
share their experiences with each other and with other Black gamers.
This scene, and the game as a whole, also highlights the cultural power
and importance of code-switching, as each includes slang, demonstrat-
ing how freedom results in those moments when White judgment is
not operational. Reflecting on the power of this scene, Cicero Holmes

notes, "Code-switching is a survival tactic, especially for black men. It is our way of immediately disarming someone and letting them know that we are one of the good ones" (quoted in Porter 2017).

Yet the game's commentary is not limited to the everyday experiences of African Americans in Silicon Valley or how code-switching develops as a means of survival. It makes clear that the everyday and the individualized manifestations of anti-Black racism materialize in structural ways. The privileging of White masculinity not coincidentally leads to a culture that empowers companies to develop technologies that injure and harm communities of color. It is no coincidence that Silicon Valley is producing technologies that further the criminalization of Black and Brown bodies, which results in hypersurveillance and otherwise perpetuates racial inequality, given the demographic inequities on the ground. Like *Mafia III*, *Watch Dogs 2* spotlights White supremacy while centering resistance and the quest for social justice through the language of video games and the grammar of gaming that all too often uses, celebrates, and normalizes violence enacted by White male heroes. These games both reverse these narratives, repurposing violence, creativity, intellect, and heroism through Black male bodies, whose freedom is denied by those once-heroized White men. In a moment of powerlessness, it is no wonder these games have found an audience.

Conclusion: Can the Revolution Be Consoled?

Gil Scott-Heron, lamenting the corrupting influence of both television and materials, cautioned a passive public that "the revolution will not be televised." The fight for racial justice would come through organizing and activism. More than forty years later, the promise of racial justice remains elusive; the fight for a justice within virtual reality and the development of tools to realize "freedom dreams" in everyday lives remain just as tenuous. "As a child, I reveled in the power video games placed in my hands, especially since in my experience being young and being Black were oftentimes synonymous with being powerless. It's easy to feel in control when killing fake enemies leads to higher scores and, the prized goal, winning," writes Shonté Daniels in "Video Games, Violence, and the Black Lives Matter Movement: How My Hobby Became a Trigger" (2015). Despite this power and potential, games have failed to fulfill their promise, especially for gamers of color and for the struggle against anti-Black racism. "Over the years I've noticed games, specifically mainstream titles, haven't evolved. Game developers, more often than not, use violence as the primary source of conflict rather than in more productive ways such as to show its dangers. An almighty player is allowed to kill because it's assumed bloodshed is needed in order to win. And lately, that narrative has done nothing but remind me how real the violence in games can be" (S. Daniels 2015).

While the revolution may not be made into a game, played on a gaming console (consoled), or come as the result of the release of the latest virtual crime drama, games surely have a role to play in the fight for justice. They can educate; they can inspire our imaginations; they can educate and inform; they can build bridges to the past, provide language for understanding the present, and rethink the future; and they can provide the tools necessary in the larger fight against injustice. This was made clear in 2016. Noting the release of *Mafia III*, *Watch Dogs 2*, *Battlefield 1* (a game that allows players to participate as members of the Harlem Hellfighters, an all-Black regiment during World War I; Trickey 2018), and *Assassins Creed: Freedom Cry* (a game that provides the story of Adéwalé, "a former slave killing slave traders and plantation masters"; Gray, in press), Kishonna Gray writes about not only the visibility of Black heroes in gaming but also the power of their political narrative and its impact on Black gaming communities. "The year 2016 may go down as the year of the Black gamer. As many gaming blogs and forums raved, the number of titles featuring Black protagonists, in non-stereotypical positions dramatically increased" (Gray, in press). These possibilities are evident with Momo Pixel's *Hair Nah*, "a video game puts you in the shoes of a black woman traveling through three destinations—Osaka, Havana, and Santa Monica Pier—while frantically trying to swat away white hands touching your hair" (Payne 2018). Changes within the video-game industry and within virtual reality are because of organizations like Gameheads (Herold 2018), which has created games dealing with gentrification (*Here's Your Change*) and the model-minority myth (*Off Beat*) and another that gives voices to the experiences of GLBTQ youth (*Behind the Mask*). The company is also behind a game titled *Sneakers and an Oversized Hoodie*, a "video game that manages to simultaneously pay homage the Black Lives Matter movement, the classic arcade game 'Donkey Kong,' gospel music, and the Latin American aesthetic of magical realism" (Herold 2018) And as evident with *Mafia III* and *Watch Dogs 2*, there is an effort to mainstream these representations, voices, narratives, and politics within console games.

While video games continue to be the face of oppression—through the construction of hegemonic stereotypes; through creating the training ground for surveillance, rape culture, misogyny, and racism; through the maintenance of a toxic culture inside Silicon Valley, online, and within the gaming community—there is also a place and space for oppositional games, even in the mainstream.

Both *Watch Dogs 2* and *Mafia III*, through their embrace crime drama narratives, through their acceptance of virtual manifestations of violence, through their deployment of free-flowing open-exploration gaming, and through their use of graphics and music are so much more able to inform and entertain and to teach about racism and injustice, all while delivering a pleasurable experience. Their importance rests not simply with their offering of diverse games or offering lessons about racism. Their power extends beyond providing "positive" representations. In fact, each game's embrace of violence, revenge, and law breaking, all in the name of justice, has sparked some resistance, given the entrenched stereotypes about Black bodies. As noted by Gray, "the Black gaming community is divided to the extent that these in-game depictions capture the essence of Blackness as many express that Blackness is still consumed through traditional criminal narratives" (Gray, in press).

Yet the politics of the moment and the games' ideological intervention within both virtual reality and the broader body politics demonstrate that while there are no guarantees regarding politics or disrupting existing stereotypes (Hall and Jhally 1997), these games provide possibilities. The ability of these games to provide a platform to spark conversations about Jim Crow, about microaggressions, about White supremacy, about Hurricane Katrina, about hacker culture, and about so much more is central to their transformative power. Their ability to deploy and remix the violence of video games, to reimagine heroic violence, and to otherwise use entrenched gamer-language story lines as part of games about racial justice and racial reconciliation represents their ultimate intervention and source of power.

In a moment defined by retrenchment and preservation of White supremacy, misogyny, xenophobia, and homophobia, evident in both politics and culture, the messages of these games are that much more powerful. Both *Mafia III* and *Watch Dogs 2* follow in the footsteps of other Black popular-culture productions; they build on the work of video-game activists and those who are marching in the streets; they carry out the work of the gamers who spoke truth to power in what has been termed GamerGate, a moment that punctuated the long-standing resistance to diversity in game; they elucidate that toxicity and violence that circulate not only in games themselves but in gaming communities. Cherrie Todd, in "GamerGate and Resistance to the Diversification of Gaming Culture," writes, "Users of the hashtag #GamerGate have been the most vocal in their resistance to these changes. In 2014 reports of GamerGate activities started to circulate more widely, becoming a topical issue in the USA where news outlets began to describe the emergence of a 'culture war' over the diversification of gaming culture" (2015, 64). As such, these games, along with others, not only provide steps forward with the fight for diversity in gaming—a victory of sorts against those who bemoan "social justice warriors" and "PC culture," against those who express nostalgia for a moment in gaming when all the heroes were all White men and all the people of color were criminals (and athletes)—but also create a world that spotlights injustice and uses the language of ongoing racial justice movements. In other words, just as movies, music, sports, and television have provided spaces to document, to connect, and to build a community demanding change, these games are doing similar work, work that both finds power and breathes life into ongoing racial justice movements.

Note

1. This chapter represents a revision of a previously published essay entitled "Virtual Anti-Racism: Pleasure, Catharsis, and Hope in *Mafia III* and *Watch Dogs 2*," which appeared in "Extending Studies of Racialized Media beyond Racial Representation," a special issue of *Humanity and Society* (2019), edited by Emma Gonzalez-Lesser, Rhys Hall, and Matthew W. Hughey.

14

Decoding the Drug War

The Racial Politics of Digital Audience Reception

MICHAEL L. ROSINO

The War on Drugs is about a lot of things but only rarely is
it really about drugs.

— Dan Baum (1996, xi)

Mass incarceration, public health issues related to drug use, residential
segregation, police brutality, and police and government surveillance
are all widely recognized social problems with a common dominator.
These problems are all tied to a set of punitive drug-control policies
and militaristic policing practices commonly referred to as the "War
on Drugs" (Provine 2007; M. Alexander 2012). Moreover, these policies, practices, and consequences are intertwined with race, racism,
and racial inequality in US society (Provine 2007; M. Alexander 2012;
Rosino and Hughey 2018).

Policies and practices related to the War on Drugs reproduce barriers to essential social, economic, and symbolic resources for predominantly Black and Latinx individuals, families, and communities (see
Rosino and Hughey 2018). The War on Drugs has exacerbated family
and community disruption via racially targeted and militaristic policing and racialized hyperincarceration (M. Alexander 2012; Rosino and
Hughey 2018). It has introduced aggressive and violent forms of policing in majority-Black communities, producing greater levels of stress,
injury, and illness (Cooper 2015; Sewell and Jefferson 2016). In short,
drug policies and their enforcement are a significant mechanism for the
reproduction of structural racism.

A towering heap of studies suggest that US drug-control policies and practices are harmful, oppressive, or problematic, particularly for predominantly Black and Latinx communities (see Beckett et al. 2005; Beckett, Nyrop, and Pfingst 2006; Lurigio and Loose 2008; Radosh 2008; Lynch et al. 2013; Nicosia, MacDonald, and Arkes 2013; Ojmarrh and Caudy 2013; Schlesinger 2013; Ward, Hartley, and Tillyer 2016). However, these policies and practices are in constant flux and subject to heated debate. For example, many states in the United States have legalized or decriminalized forms of drug use and possession, particularly cannabis, in part because public support for legal reforms has skyrocketed (Ingram 2017).

However, lurking under the facade of this apparent agreement about drug policy are a number of contradictory narratives, arguments, and perspectives. People who support similar reforms may disagree about the impacts and function of drug laws and even why such changes in drug policies are important. And that is just the people who are in favor of reform. It is no surprise, then, that discussions about the War on Drugs are a constant fixture of all kinds of media including increasingly digital forms. And one of the central points of division within this debate is the place, role, and consequences of race and racism in relation to drug-prohibition policies and practices.

The debate over the War on Drugs in digital media allows us to think about an important aspect of racialized media: *audience reception*. Comment sections on digital news sites provide a platform for people to interpret and react to the stories, facts, and editorial views being reported. Comment sections afford people an opportunity to debate and discuss the causes and consequences of racism and racial inequality; political divides and partisan conflicts; the relationship between crime, police, and prisons; and lofty philosophical ideals such as equality and fairness.

"Don't read the comment section!" has become a common warning among those who share an article on social media platforms. This cautionary statement suggests that many of the comments in response to an article took an unreasonable stance or even communicated overtly racist or sexist messages. However, in this chapter, we will choose to ignore this warning in the name of advancing the sociological study of racialized media. Plunging ourselves into the treacherous terrain of digital-news-media comments also helps us better understand how audience members articulate reactions to news-media content about racialized social issues in these spaces. The ways that people participate in digital media spaces has important implications for racial politics and media.

Decoding the Digital Debate about the Drug War

Stuart Hall (1980, 130) wrote, "At a certain point . . . the broadcasting structures must yield encoded messages in the form of a meaningful discourse. . . . Before this message can have an 'effect' (however defined), satisfy a 'need' or be put to a 'use,' it must first be appropriated as a meaningful discourse and be meaningfully decoded. It is this set of decoded meanings which 'have an effect,' influence, entertain, instruct, or persuade, with very complex perceptual, cognitive, emotional, ideological or behavioural consequences." Following Hall, as a sociologist studying digital media, I think of media not just as a form of content, a means of communicating, or even a vehicle for distribution but as a social process. This process connects how information (including narratives, language, images, ideas, sounds, etc.) is produced, dispersed, consumed, interpreted, and reproduced by various social actors and institutions. Examining the things that people are collectively doing, both at each phase and throughout this process, provides fertile grounds for growing stronger and more fruitful understandings of the relationship between media and society.

A key set of actors within the media process is audiences. Especially in the age of digital media, consider how often audiences are implored by media content creators or companies to engage in the acts of "liking" and "sharing" on various social media platforms. Thinking of those who engage with media as active participants in a process of collective meaning-making (rather than passive receptacles of mass-mediated content) is an important innovation. This brings us back to "decoding." Again, Stuart Hall (1980) pointed out that each aspect of the media process is distinct yet interconnected. Moreover, at each stage, particular social conditions and power relations come to bear on practices relating to "meanings and messages in the form of sign-vehicles of a specific kind organized, like any form of communication or language, through the operation of codes within the syntagmatic chain of a discourse" (Hall 1980, 133).

It is important to present the general implications of Hall's concepts for the topic at hand. Media messages are encoded with particular interpretations during their production. Even more importantly, audience effects, including audience members' subsequent practices and awareness, are complicated. They do not straightforwardly reflect the messages encoded by producers. Instead, the audience effects of a media message are the product of an active set of interpretive practices that result in different ways of decoding media messages. Hall hypothesized that audiences may decode media information in three general ways: oppositional (deriving alternate or critical interpretations), negotiated (deriving both intended and alternate interpretations), or hegemonic/dominant (deriving intended interpretations). For a particularly "meta" example, consider that as part of the audience of this book, you are engaging in a form of decoding right now. I hope that you are, at least for the most part, interpreting the messages that I as the chapter's author have intentionally encoded here.

As noted by Henrik Bødker (2016, 420), Hall's "encoding/decoding" model remains extremely relevant to contemporary society, but it is "challenged by new mediated modes of circulation through social media." For instance, in the digital media landscape, "the medium and its mode of circulation/distribution became part of the decoding process" (Bødker 2016, 420). Digital technology has reshaped our routine, and even seemingly mundane, forms of engagement with media content. For an example, imagine the following scenario. You are leisurely browsing the internet on a rainy Sunday afternoon. You come across some content such as a news article, opinion essay, or even a meme that deeply resonates with you. Perhaps it speaks to something that you are concerned about, enlightens you to a new issue or worldview, or even puts forth a perspective that you find upsetting or reprehensible. For many of us, this feeling of resonance prompts an immediate next step: *sharing and commenting*. We may send the article to friends and family members via text message or email with a short commentary. We might post it to our social media accounts with our own editorializing or to invite others to engage with it. We might even scroll down to the comment section where the content is hosted and register our reactions or engage with the reactions of others.

Practices such as sharing and commenting, made fully possible by digital media technologies, raise new questions. For instance, what is your role in the digital media process? Are you simply an audience member in this scenario? Are you part of the distribution network? Are you, perhaps, a producer of your own original commentary that exists in relation to that media content? Maybe you are all three simultaneously. Or none. Or something completely different. The point is that the emergence of new forms of media requires new ways to understand the relationship between media, people, and society and the recontextualization of important concepts such as decoding.

New digital technologies offer new spaces where people do not simply consume and interpret media but also react and comment to mediated messages about events and issues. At the same time, the digital world, much like the material world, is shaped by divisions and unequal social relations. Digital inequalities (disparities in access to media technologies and influence over the production of content) structure the public debates that take place in these venues. Digital comment sections on news-media sites are not ideal spaces of inclusive and fair deliberation and public spheres where people propose rational arguments, listen to each other, or work to understand each other and find the common good (Hughey and Daniels 2013). Dominant ideologies and systemic inequalities influence audiences' active and collective digital decoding practices.

In this chapter, I draw on online comments on news articles to analyze how everyday people participate in the public debate on the War on Drugs in the digital sphere to highlight the racial politics of audience reception. In comment sections, people not only engage in decoding of the message within an article but articulate their own responses to media content and other audience members and, in doing so, express, clarify, and construct identities (Hughey 2012a; Rosino and Hughey 2017). Before delving further into these issues, I cover a bit more background on the relationship between racialized media and digital audiences.

The Racial Politics of Digital Audience Reception

In this chapter, I bring into focus particular forms of decoding in contemporary society that intersect with the *racial politics of digital audience reception*. Before we discuss and define the racial politics of digital audience reception, it is essential to first clarify the unique properties of a "digital audience." An audience is a group of people that observe, use, and partake in media messages and their reproduction (Ross and Nightingale 2003). They are formed by "pre-existing social and cultural histories and conditions, and sometimes by a sense of shared interests that incline them to repeatedly use popular media vehicles" (Ross and Nightingale 2003, 4). Increasingly, digital media audiences can interact with media content and each other. In other words, digital audiences now have more opportunities to communicate their interpretations of media content (Ross and Nightingale 2003).

Racial politics describes the power dynamics, conflicts, changes, and outcomes regarding both the racial distribution of resources (material and nonmaterial) and organization of society and the meanings given to racial categories and their relationships (Omi and Winant 2015). It is important to point out, for our purposes, that the media process is deeply implicated in all of this. In a basic sense, racialized media content is a supplier of *social information* for audiences (Entman and Rojecki 2001). As such, it is an instrument whereby racial meanings are circulated on a large scale. These circulated meanings influence how people understand the world in racial terms and how they engage in struggles over the racialized allocation of power and resources.

Audiences use their interpretations of racialized media messages for all kinds of social and cognitive ends: to inform their perspectives on social conditions and events, to develop a sense of self and social position, and to decide what future social and political actions to take. For instance, consider truth or reality. Whether fictional or not, the messages, or codes, that appear in racialized media content influence, even if only indirectly, what audiences think of as real or true (Dixon 2007). However, going back to Hall's theory of *encoding/decoding*, we have to also remember that people receive, understand, and use media messages in various ways. Depending on their racial backgrounds, attitudes, and social position, audiences presented with similar messages may derive opposing interpretations.

A brief example of how racial inequalities influence this process may be helpful. Due to centuries of racial segregation by law and practice, Whites tend to be socially isolated from people of color, and moreover, they generally see this isolation as normal (Bonilla-Silva 2014). At the same time, they have perspectives and act in response to the racial conditions in society, such as the oppression of people of color and the continuance of racial inequality. Whites who lack actual social experiences with people of color in their daily lives are much more likely to rely on the media for social information about racialized events and issues (Entman and Rojecki 2001; Mastro and Tropp 2004). Because of this, media content that includes racial stereotypes or White-supremacist messages are often used by Whites to justify racial inequality. For example, Robert M. Entman and Andrew Rojecki (2001, 9) write that that "the racial stereotyping of Blacks encouraged by the images and implicit comparisons to Whites on local news reduces the latter's empathy and heightens animosity."

So focusing on the racial politics of digital audience reception means acknowledging that there is a powerful connection between digital media, audiences, and the continuation of racial oppression. Importantly, this relationship is distinct from its nondigital counterparts. Hence, in this chapter, we are looking at internet comments and not some other form of media.

One of the major implications of digital media is that people have more ways to share commentary on media content. Especially on popular news sites, comment sections are often active and interactive arenas where people engage each other over racial issues. This raises important questions: What happens when audiences are not just consuming media but also participating in collective processes of definition and interpretation? Are audiences just interpreting racialized media content when they respond to it within online spaces that allow people to provide commentary? Or are they are making sense of themselves, others, and the world around them in racial terms? To further explore these questions, let us look at a case study: digital audience reception to media content on the War on Drugs.

Example: The Comment Sections of Articles on Racial Bias in the War on Drugs

To understand digital audience reception, I collected data from a source that can provide information about how audiences respond to media messages about the role of race in the War on Drugs in the media—online comments. The larger study that these findings draw from analyzed 3,145 internet comments on articles on the War on Drugs from 2009 to 2014. I focus here on how people interpreted messages within news media that were critical of the War on Drugs from a perspective of its role in reproducing racial inequality. The full study (see Rosino and Hughey 2017) includes coverage of the many ways in which commenters emphasized ostensibly nonracial components and the implications. However, in this chapter, in the spirit of its topic and theme, I instead center some clearer and more direct examples of racialized decoding.

Decoding is more complex than simply producing dominant or critical interpretations of media messages. Critiques that center the relationship between drug policy and racism and racial inequality have been surprisingly rare in news-media content on the War on Drugs (Rosino and Hughey 2017). Most of these critiques centered on pointing out that a disparity exists whereby Black and Latino men are disproportionately more likely to be arrested and incarcerated for drug-related charges. Yet how audience members respond to such media messages in comment sections can tell us a lot about how audiences engage in active interpretive practices.

Racial Bias or Racial Oppression? Dominant Decoding of Racialized Social Critiques

Let us consider the ways that commenters articulated agreement on articles centered on critiques of the racial unfairness of the War on Drugs. In such comments, people communicated that they understood that the policies and practices of the War on Drugs contribute to unequal outcomes between racial groups in the United States. For instance, commenters drew on the outcomes of the War on Drugs as depicted within the news articles themselves to demonstrate this point: "Regardless of anyone's opinions on this topic, can we at least agree that the racial numbers (1 out of 15 blacks versus 1 out of 106 whites incarcerated) tell us that something is definitely wrong with this picture?" (April 8, 2013, *Washington Post*).

However, this decoding of the intended meanings of the critiques also lent itself to audience members making claims about themselves and others: "Unfortunately, for one group of people, this is pure hyperbole while for another group of people this is a harsh reality. 'Race-baiters' are not the problem. It's being naive that hinders us from becoming a post-racial society" (October 5, 2013, *Huffington Post*); "Whites don't understand getting arrested for nothing because it simply doesn't happen to them. I'm a black university student nerd, who wouldn't commit any sort of crime, but I get questioned and cuffed way before my white or asian friends" (October 5, 2013, *Huffington Post*).

Although critical arguments that focused on the racist intentions and actions of powerful social actors were extremely rare in media content over the past thirty years on the War on Drugs (Rosino and Hughey 2017), other audience members decoded a more critical interpretation of the claims or statistics that are routinely presented about the racial inequities of the War on Drugs. That is, they interpreted these claims as support for the stance that the War on Drugs was explicitly motivated by racism against people of color (for which there is abundant scholarly evidence but scarce articulation in mass media): "Sounds like a war on black youth, not a war on drugs" (April 15, 2013, *Washington Post*); "Marijuana was made illegal because of racism" (April 8, 2013, *Washington Post*).

Yet the causes and consequences of racial bias or unequal outcomes was contested. For instance, the meaning of the racial discrepancies in arrest and incarceration was decoded by other audience members as produced by the characteristics of Black communities in relation to drugs and crime: "Given that crack is sold mostly in the ghetto—although often to white users—the result of the policy was to flood federal prisons with young black men" (April 8, 2013, *Washington Post*); "[These outcomes are caused by] the way drugs are sold in black areas open in the streets while in the white and other areas it's done in secret behind closed doors" (April 8, 2013, *Washington Post*).

Finally, commenters argued that the War on Drugs reflects structural racism and the continuation of racist institutions and White supremacy in US society: "The white man's 'War On Drugs' is merely an extension of the white man's 'War On Non-Whites' which the white man began in October of 1492" (October 8, 2013, *Huffington Post*); "[The War on Drugs] was designed to do exactly what it did, incarcerate as many black males as possible" (April 8, 2013, *Washington Post*); "Prisons are the new plantations" (October 8, 2013, *Huffington Post*).

Perhaps one of the most interesting aspects of these overall responses is the fixation on the overall disparity, rather than the social processes that occur as a result and catalyst of the racial inequality. That is, while these forms of decoding were critical of the War on Drugs, they were also reflections of the dominant messages prevalent in mass media that fail to illuminate the ways in which the policies and practices of the War on Drugs cause racial inequality and maintain structural racism (see Rosino and Hughey 2017).

In an analysis of 394 newspaper manuscripts, only 59 articles, op-eds, and letters to the editor criticized the War on Drugs on the grounds of racial unfairness. Of those, only 17 percent framed the War on Drugs as a cause of racial inequality. Only 8 percent (just five articles) discussed the War on Drugs as a set of policies and practices linked to either structural or intentional forms of racism. The remaining majority either pointed out that Black communities are uniquely susceptible to drug crimes or policing or simply noted that a disparity existed, both without thorough context on why these conditions exist. Thus, as the debate has played out in mass and digital media, the causes and consequences of racial disparities in criminalization have remained open to a host of interpretations and assertions.

Even explanations that hinged on ideas about the nature of drug use and sales in racialized communities did so without context or downplayed the role of racially targeted enforcement by the legal system and policing. As I and my coauthor, Matthew Hughey, argue, "The WOD [War on Drugs] and its contribution to racialized mass incarceration must be understood as more than an institution of state social control or a source of social problems. It is ultimately a mechanism of racialized social reproduction through its contribution to an ongoing connection between racial categories and the distribution of capital. In other words, the policing practices and incarceration related to the WOD help destroy access to valuable resources in poor black neighborhoods" (Rosino and Hughey 2018, 866). While the racialized outcomes of the War on Drugs are worth noting, they are only one part of the overall picture. Zooming out to the larger social structural level, the War on Drugs and its relationship with various forms of racial inequality or "bias" are most accurately explained and characterized as an ongoing process of racial oppression.

Criminalization or Criminality? Oppositional Decoding as Racialized Othering

The process of decoding media messages and the process of making claims about oneself and others are often interconnected in the context of digital media. This trend can be seen even more explicitly in the ways in which people engaged in certain forms of critical decoding of the media messages focusing on racial critiques of the War on Drugs. Whites are just as likely as other racial groups, if not more so, to commit drug crimes (Fellner 2009). However, Blackness was routinely equated with criminality in comment sections in response to claims about the racial unfairness of the War on Drugs. These forms of decoding interpreted media messages about racial disparities in arrest or mass incarceration as an outcome of inherent differences in traits between Whites and Blacks: "Lots of Black People Sell'n Dope, Lots of Black People In Prison" (April 8, 2013, *Huffington Post*).

As a parallel to making claims that equate Whiteness with innocence and Blackness or Latinidad with criminality, messages about disparate incarceration and arrest rates were thus decoded as a direct product of crime. Reported crime rates are skewed by whether groups are targeted by the criminal justice system and therefore more likely to be arrested and charged (Hall et al. 1978). Moreover, the immensely disproportionate rate at which Blacks and Latinxs are imprisoned, stigmatized, and targeted by the criminal justice system in comparison to Whites is magnitudes larger than disparities in reported rates of crime (Western 2007; Armaline 2011).

However, one commenter wrote, "the fact of the matter is, and the article 'discourages' us from paying attention to that cold, hard fact, but blacks and Latinos commit a higher proportion of crimes than whites" (October 4, 2013, *Huffington Post*). Another commenter wrote, "Quit the liberal hype! . . . They forgot to mention that *the* blacks are more likely to be the ones selling the drugs. More blind reverse discrimination" (April 8, 2013, *Huffington Post*; emphasis added). As Lynne Murphy (2016) argues, "'The' makes the group seem like it's a large, uniform mass, rather than a diverse group of individuals. This is the key to 'othering': treating people from another group as less human than one's own group."

Mass media is encoded with dominant narratives about the War on Drugs as simultaneously deracialized and producing racialized outcomes. Yet the framing of racial inequities of the criminal justice system as an overt consequence of the relative pathologies and criminality of racial groups was near nonexistent among narratives in newspapers that supported the War on Drugs. However, this interpretation arose commonly in comments reacting to media content about the racial bias in the War on Drugs. It is, therefore, an oppositional form of decoding.

This critical mode of decoding that interpreted messages about racial inequality in the criminal justice system as evidence of the assumed criminality of Blackness was further expressed through claims about Whiteness: "White kids are not more likely to become drug users. . . . There is a reason why 50% of the prison is blacks" (April 8, 2013, *Huffington Post*); "How many white kids you know selling drugs out front of a liquor store? How many white kids are smuggling drugs across the border?" (July 24, 2013, *Huffington Post*).

More broadly, media messages about racially disparate rates of drug arrest and incarceration were decoded as evidence of a correlation between Blackness, Latinidad, and general pathology, reflecting a "widespread narrative that black and Hispanic people possess an array of dysfunctional traits" (Hughey 2012b, 62). This form of decoding pulls from the logic of cultural racism that depicts racially unequal outcomes in society as an artifact of the cultural traits and collective choices of people of color (see Steinberg 1989; Bonilla-Silva 2014): "[The racial disparity in the War on Drugs is a result of] disparity in the CULTURAL systems . . . one parent families, third generation welfare families, hip hop music, ghetto unemployment and lack of economic investment in their communities, high crime in lower class communities, poor educations, lack of home discipline and love" (October 5, 2013, *Huffington Post*). Other comments of this same ilk were "It's behavior. Period" (October 4, 2013, *Huffington Post*) and "Young black boys and men need more self discipline. . . . There's way too much emphasis on fast money and a lifestyle that supports this" (October 5, 2013, *Huffington Post*). These forms of decoding not only rationalize the disparities in arrest and incarceration created by the racist policies and practices of the War on Drugs but also enable dominant-group members (Whites) to construct an idealized moral identity by defining racial "others" as less than human, criminal, deviant, or morally wrong (Schwalbe 2008; Hughey 2012b).

Additionally, these often overtly racialized claims did not appear in newspaper content that promoted support for punitive drug policies. The combined avoidance of naming racial categories within claims that supported the War on Drugs and articulation of the connection between racism, the War on Drugs, and racial oppression thus presented audiences with a discursive opening. Through decoding, commenters synthesized these themes and applied their own racial logic and meanings.

Dysfunctional Deviance: Dominant Decoding as Racialized Othering

Examining another form of dominant decoding reveals further limits of the persistent fixation on the racialized outcomes of criminalization and incarceration without attention to the processes that produce them. Unlike the previously presented theme, this form of decoding sustains critiques of the War on Drugs. Yet it still decodes claims about the racial implications of drug policy and enforcement practices in ways that nonetheless function as a form of racialized othering. A common argument against current US drug policy is that it fails to address, or even perhaps amplifies, the very social ills of crime and drug use that it purports to curtail. Due to the prevalence of such critiques being encoded into mass-media messages, this form of decoding represents a dominant/hegemonic perspective.

One of the most revealing findings of the analysis of newspaper articles is that a whopping 51 percent of critiques of the War on Drugs focused on how it was in some way dysfunctional. Of those claims, 35 percent focused on how the issues of drug-related crimes and drug misuse either remained steady or increased despite the stated intention of the War on Drugs to eradicate these social ills. Accordingly, a sizable share of responding comments argued that the War on Drugs was criminogenic (or that it produces crime and criminals) and therefore dysfunctional.

Moreover, racial meanings and the conflation of criminality with racial-group traits were often implicit, if not explicit, dimensions of these comments. The deviant and threatening others discussed within such remarks were often simply talked about as "they" or "them": "we put them in little cages and wonder why they want to kill each other" (April 8, 2013, *Washington Post*). Claims that were peopled with actual named subjects included such phrases as "thugs and criminal empires," "common thugs," "illegal invaders," "the Taliban and the terrorists of al Qaeda," and "terrorists as well as drug cartels."

At times, the logic behind the production of a racialized criminal threat to discredit the War on Drugs became quasi-conspiratorial in nature. One comment writer proposed the collusion of various racialized groups to destroy public order: "With social demographics changing within the country this will lead to serious civil unrest. The Muslim extremists are recruiting Latino and black men" (October 4, 2014, *Huffington Post*). Similarly, another commenter remarked that the War on Drugs developed "local gangs into transnational enterprises with intricate power structures that reach into every corner of society, controlling vast swaths of territory with significant social and military resources at their disposal" (2012, *Forbes*).

Comments in this vein also critiqued the presumed inexperience of those who emphasized the human rights, public health, or racial justice implications over the War on Drugs' contribution to racialized criminality. As one commenter wrote, "Come out of your ivory tower and get down to crack alley" (2012, *Forbes*). From this vantage point, the assertion that most drug-related criminal activities are committed by racially marginalized groups is merely a harsh truth. Ironically, this supposed truth is actually rooted in the racialized ways that criminals are represented in dominant culture and produced by targeted law enforcement rather than the empirical evidence.

This form of decoding interprets the production of incarceration as an aspect of the reproduction of racialized criminality. Drawing on critiques of these policies and practices and a vague awareness of their racial character, it enables commenters to deride the War on Drugs as problematic. But this form of decoding ignores the harmful consequences for vulnerable communities that are unjustly ensnared in the legal system and centers claims that it fails to protect an idealized racialized in-group ("us") from a dangerous, criminal, and pathological racialized out-group ("them"). Moreover, while claims focusing on the War on Drugs as dysfunctional within newspapers at times did contain subtler racial codewords or insinuations, comments often articulated the racist connotations of these insinuations in much clearer and more direct terms. Thus, part of the function of this form of decoding is that it allows audiences that are opposed to criminalization of drugs but not racial justice to explicitly say what is implied by the colorblind claims made in print and digital mass-media platforms.

Discussion and Conclusion: Digital Decoding and Racial Oppression

Through exploring modes of racial discourse that take place in online comments on news articles on the War on Drugs, I have brought to light three context-specific forms of decoding. Moreover, I have placed these findings in the context of trends within the larger media ecosystem, such as the overall framing of the debate over the War on Drugs within news media and the implications of the rise of digital media. I have placed the findings about digital comments in conversation with overall patterns in how the War on Drugs has been presented in news-media content over the past three decades. In general, I have categorized the forms of decoding highlighted in this chapter as *dominant* when they corresponded with overall trends in the news media content on the War on Drugs and *oppositional* when they did not.

The first of these forms of decoding is *dominant decoding of racialized social critiques*. This form of decoding entails an emphasis on two components of the racialized inequities produced by the War on Drugs: (unintentional) bias and unequal rates of arrest and incarceration. In doing so, it deemphasizes essential components of understanding the War on Drugs as part and parcel of an ongoing process of racial oppression, particularly the way that it contributes to racial inequality and flows from an array of racist practices that are both strategic and habitual.

Second, I identified *oppositional decoding as racialized othering*. This mode of decoding builds to the conclusion among audiences that punitive drug laws and practices are defensible and just. Yet it also does not dispute the evidence that those who are ensnared in the legal and carceral system due to punitive drug policies are more likely to be Black or Latinx. To marry evidence of unequal outcomes and support for the War on Drugs, audience members decode unequal rates of arrest and incarceration among racial groups as representative of relative rates of criminality, superior and inferior cultural practices, and fundamental moral and behavioral differences.

The third and final form of decoding that this analysis discovered is *dominant decoding as racialized othering*. Here, people emphasize critiques of the War on Drugs as criminogenic, as a catalyst for crime and violence through its production of opportunities and perverse incentives for illicit activities. By itself, this logic does not necessarily result in racialized othering or racist depictions of people of color. However, the common imagery and narratives around the production of dangerous and deviant drug criminals within audience responses was nonetheless deeply racialized. Paradoxically, it mirrors the logic of racial threat that underlies the racist application of drug-law enforcement policies and practices.

Implications for Racial Inequality and the War on Drugs

The growing normativity of media communication via interactive digital technologies such as computers, smart phones, and tablets presents analysts of digital media and social inequalities with obstacles and opportunities. People's processes of decoding media content in the era of digital technology have become more complexly and deeply embedded in daily life. Yet they are also more generative of tangible data for in-depth content and discursive analysis. In this chapter, I have seized the opportunity for analysis afforded by this trove of digital data. And in concluding, I want to apply insights from this analysis to better engage the relationship between racial oppression, racialized media content, and the processes of decoding within digital audience reception.

There is a value for both researchers and practitioners in focusing on the interpretive relationship between audiences and media content about racialized and contested social issues. Within the debates and dialogues that play out in these venues, this interpretive relationship appears as a site where people articulate and defend support for racial inequality, particularly in the face of the paucity of critical and racial-justice-oriented mass-media content. This concern is only heightened with the introduction of social media platforms that have the impact of amplifying or silencing the content that audiences engage. For instance, White social media users are much less likely than their Black counterparts to encounter, engage with, and share media content about racial inequality in the United States, although engaging such media content can lead to increased awareness (M. Anderson 2016).

In this particular case, the logics that are communicated and used in these forms of decoding bolster a consensus among large swaths of the population that the racialized outcomes of drug policies and their enforcement in the United States are either natural, just, legitimate, or not important. For example, a 2015 poll of those who support legalizing cannabis found that only 12 percent justified this position on the basis of the problematic nature of drug-law enforcement (Pew Research Center 2015). This consensus is counterintuitive in the context of the resounding evidence linking the War on Drugs to racial oppression. Thus, these forms of decoding, in tandem, contribute to the lack of focus placed on racial justice concerns among drug-policy reformers (see Provine 2007). Moreover, they strengthen the ability of politicians, advocates, and interest groups making claims about drug laws to subtly and implicitly draw on racial animus or racialized moral panics (see Haney López 2007, 2014).

Beyond the Debate: Revealing Cultural Logics

The import of these findings extends beyond just the "debate" over the War on Drugs. This analysis can also aid in unearthing insights about the dominant cultural logics that facilitate the maintenance and racially oppressive impacts of its policies and practices. So it is as important to examine the function of these modes of decoding in relation to enduring systems of racial oppression as it is to identify them. These three decoding processes affect collective awareness and actions in response to the War on Drugs and its racially oppressive consequences in two major ways.

The first way is that it maintains a norm of *antistructuralist reduction*. These forms of decoding bolster a heightened sense of focus on outcomes of inequality instead of processes of oppression or a focus on individual bias rather than systemic discrimination. This implication delimits the possibility for structural change, accountability for powerful actors within the state and criminal justice system, and restorative or reparative forms of justice.

Second is *racist rearticulation*, whereby expressions that critique racial inequality, prejudice, or discrimination are decoded in ways that implicitly support racial discrimination, surveillance, and stigmatization of racially marginalized groups. This function works through both influential critiques and supportive claims for the War on Drugs. Ultimately, by defining Black and Latinx people as inherently criminal, pathological, or deviant populations, these forms of decoding inherently prop up racialized systems of social control.

The rise of digital media entails both new decoding practices and a need to better understand those practices and their relationships to ongoing processes of racial oppression. The digital decoding of news media is intimately entwined with the stories that people tell about themselves and others as audience members. Decoding media messages about the War on Drugs provides opportunities for people to communicate contested and consequential racialized definitions of themselves, other people, and the way society works. Audience members are probably not developing their sense of self or their perspectives on racial issues and groups for the first time. Rather, audience members articulate, clarify, and redefine their identities and worldviews while actively interpreting racialized media messages in these settings.

Toward the Racial Politics of Meaning

How digital audiences decode news-media messages on the racial implications of the War on Drugs suggests what I call the *racial politics of meaning*. This framework has two interconnected components. On the one hand, people strategically use meaning-making practices to perceive and act on the racialized structure of society. These practices include forming and protecting a racial identity and ontology, rationalizing a set of actions, subverting dominant meanings, and imagining opportunities for social transformation and reproduction. On the other hand, the contexts of collective meaning-making that people inhabit are shaped by the ways that racialized messages are circulated, amplified, and silenced by institutions such as increasingly digital forms of mass media, the state, and the political sphere.

Audience reception and digital decoding are embedded within these micro and macro processes of collective racial meaning-making. While the ideas and narratives articulated in the current debate over the War on Drugs may not necessarily be new, the mode of communication whereby it takes place includes global diffusion, instant interaction, and inclusion of broader segments of the public. For these reasons, developing an in-depth sociological understanding of racial politics in contemporary society depends on the continued examination of the digital media practices that unfold around the decoding of racist events and evidence of racial oppression.

15

Dear White People

Using Film as a Catalyst for Racial Activism against
Institutional Racism in the College Classroom

TINA M. HARRIS, ANNA M. DUDNEY DEEB, AND ALYSEN WADE

The current racial climate in the United States has revealed what many scholars believe was an inevitable shift in societal attitudes about race. On the heels of the election of Senator Barack Hussein Obama to two terms as US president, many saw this moment as a triumph and that "racism is no longer a big problem" (Flores and Sims 2016, 206). The election did not result in a "postracial America"; rather, Obama's legitimacy, citizenship, and qualifications were questioned (Pham 2015). He was subjected to "unrelenting opposition from Congress, and the US public," as well as "horrifying racial attacks" on himself, "his wife Michelle, and his daughters that went largely ignored and dismissed" (Harris and Steiner 2018, 33). According to Lisa Flores and Christy-Dale Sims (2016), the presidency was perceived as an "entirely white institution" (206), and Obama's presence was interpreted as a threat to Whiteness and democracy.

The nation responded to this cognitive dissonance by electing the businessman and reality-television star Donald Trump to the presidency in 2016, despite his lack of political experience or acumen. The "Age of Trumpism" reflected a resurgence of an explicit pro-White rhetoric throughout the country and ignited a "rise in public displays of various formations of White supremacy, including the emergence of a loose group of disgruntled pro-white, far-right reactionaries who have strategically adopted the label of 'alt-right'" (Hartzell 2018, 6). This shift revealed an undercurrent in racial tensions that many people believed had significantly improved since the civil rights movement of the 1960s.

Despite the need for more discussion of race, many people remain resistant to engaging in authentic conversations about systemic racism. It has been the authors' experience as university instructors that the college classroom is one site, however, where members of society are afforded the unique opportunity to have these very conversations. College students enrolled in race-focused courses are in a structured environment where they can face issues of race and racism. According to Angela Putnam (2017), the classroom is where students gain an understanding of Whiteness, White privilege, and institutionalized racism.

However, White students will very likely experience feelings of guilt, shame, and anger. Similarly, students of color (SOC) will go through other emotions such as sadness, anger, and excitement as they either reflect on or share with classmates their own experiences with racism. We acknowledge that the emotional aspect of this classroom experience is inevitable. To create an optimal learning environment, we strategically devise ways for students to engage in self-reflexivity in a way that allows them to process those emotions and understand the pervasive nature of racism. Through course work, class discussions, and self-reflection, we believe that we achieve the larger goal of increasing students' level of cultural competence and understanding when it comes to interracial and intercultural communication.

A significant part of that learning comes from an awareness of the extent to which systemic racism affects everyone and not just people of color (POC). It is understood at the outset of the course that White students and students of color are very likely to have different racialized experiences. SOC have been cognizant of their "otherness" for most, if not all, of their lives. These divergent experiences are best understood when SOC share stories about the racial microaggressions to which they have been subjected at the university and beyond. Scholars have studied these realities by giving voice to SOC's racialized experiences in the classroom, on campus, and in the surrounding community (Harris et al. 2018; Sue 2010; Sue, Capodilupo, and Holder 2008; Sue et al. 2007). In addition to White students understanding or at least recognizing that their peers of color are penalized for their "otherness," per se, they become aware of the privileges they experience as a result of being in the majority group (Constantine and Sue 2007; T. Harris 2001). They have many opportunities to engage with the class and reflect on their Whiteness and how that translates to a qualitatively different life when compared to each other and to POC at their institution and in larger society. All students are encouraged to seize opportunities to become more knowledgeable about societal privilege and power and how they work together to create racial disparities in every area of life (T. Harris 2001).

Critical Communication Pedagogy and Film in the Classroom

As a communication scholar, the first author often uses critical communication pedagogy (CCP). This is the practice of studying the relationships between power and communication in educational contexts (Harris and Murphy 2017). I use it to understand the relationship between intersectional identities and media use or consumption in the college classroom. I demonstrate how a film can help achieve the goal of teaching students about how communication between racially different groups is used to perpetuate power differences, which sometimes result in systemic racism. Toward that end, my coauthors and I chose to analyze student reactions to watching the movie *Dear White People* (2014).

Inspired by the work of Tara Yosso (2002), who advocated for the use of a media curriculum to raise the social consciousness of audiences, we argue that educators can use film to deconstruct understandings of racial, gender, and class subordination in addition to discuss observations from films that explicitly tackle race and racism. While SOC are most likely aware of the salience of racism, White students and other students with less awareness are provided an opportunity not only to better understand its pervasiveness but also to identify ways in which they can engage more critically with each other and with visual texts that have been designed to entertain and educate their audiences on the issue of race (T. Harris 2001). Despite not being direct victims of racism, White students become more keenly aware of how they are knowingly or unknowingly benefactors and perpetuators of systemic racism.

These students are able to enroll in classes and experience college as a "typical" college student, facing few obstacles to their educational and professional aspirations. Often unbeknownst to them, their classmates of color deal with racial microaggressions (RMAs) (Chen and Simmons 2015; Harris et al. 2018). SOC become very aware of their racial identities and systemic racism early in life. Thus, when they arrive on college campuses, they anticipate that racism will occur but experience myriad other emotions when they are confronted with RMAs at their institution (Harris et al. 2018). In some instances, they enter college with the assumption that, due to the liberal and supposedly progressive nature of college campuses, their White peers and professors will be open-minded about racial differences. However, those hopes are soon dashed when they are ostracized, called a racial slur, or pointedly told that they do not deserve to be enrolled at the university. These experiences collectively produce a negative racial climate that tells SOC that they do not belong and that they do not matter. That might not be the sentiment of the entire university, but those RMAs become significant barriers to the academic success and feelings of belonging that SOC are seeking as they matriculate at a predominantly White institution (PWI). There is a considerable amount of research by scholars such as Lindsay Pérez Huber and Daniel Solorzano (2015, 2018) Derald Wing Sue (2010), Sue, Christina Capudulino, and Aisha Holder (2008), and Sue and colleagues (2007) supporting the contention that PWIs are replete with issues of race and are an important site for further scholarly inquiry.

The Film: *Dear White People*

Dear White People (2014) was directed by Justin Simien. It artfully captures the complex dynamics of racism at "Winthrop University" (a fictional PWI) from the vantage point of both White and Black students. It received twenty-six award nominations and fourteen wins from 2014 to 2015, including the Sundance Film Festival's Special Jury Award for Breakthrough Talent. Simien tells the story of the mounting racial tensions between Black and White students, tensions that fester and eventually explode when SOC tire of the covert and overt racism they are subjected to by their peers and administrators. The White students appear threatened by the presence of the proverbial "Other" on campus and orchestrate their annual blackface party to reflect and express their hatred for their Black peers. The party is thwarted by several Black students who crash the party and confront the White students about their racism. The administration finally becomes involved, but little is done to resolve the problem of campus racism. Simien has been criticized for not offering a viable solution to institutional racism, a criticism that is unfair since there has not been a fail-safe solution offered in real life either. Instead of viewing the film as remedy for a systemic issue plaguing our society, it should be read as a visual narrative that successfully captures the complexity of racism and its effect on humanity. Additionally, *Dear White People* and other films about systemic oppression have potential as a pedagogical and motivational tool to act against this very important social issue, as we will address further.

Film and Critical Race Pedagogy

Societal racism is present in the everyday lives of people living on the margins. Some universities and professors have responded (and continue to respond) by changing their curriculum in an effort to work within these institutions where racism and other forms of oppression occur on a regular basis (Bartlett and Feiner 1996; F. Johnson 1992; Pennington 1997; Stier and Sandström 2018). Specifically, instructors have been encouraged to (1) create racially responsive pedagogy (to eradicate racism from the curriculum and teaching methods), (2) eliminate her or his personal racism, (3) identify racially responsive (course) objectives, (4) develop proactive pedagogical strategies (cultural sensitivity), and (5) develop reactive pedagogical strategies (address cultural insensitivity) (S. King 1994). In a study on this very issue (T. Harris 2001), the first author chose to use two films about race in two different interracial communication classrooms in an effort to provide students with visual narratives representing racism, discrimination, and privilege, among other concepts (see also Jorge 2019). The overarching goal was to provide students the opportunity to think critically about their newfound knowledge about the role of racism in shaping reality for both the powerful (i.e., Whites) and the less powerful (i.e., non-Whites). The findings were that, while some students minimized the significant effect of race on POC, most expressed a heightened sensitivity to and critical awareness of how racism as a form of systemic oppression was designed to benefit Whites markedly more than POC. Paulo Freire ([1970] 2005) refers to this as a cultivation of "conscientization"

(104), meaning critical awareness. This is also understood as a liberating process or experience for oppressed people that allows them to communicate about their oppression to others (Reid 2016). Thus, classroom dialogue between SOC and their White peers allows them all to have a greater understanding of institutionalized racism and its far-reaching effect on all members of society. This awareness is further enhanced when an instructor chooses to integrate film into a course replete with historical facts, theories, and other forms of supporting evidence relative to race and interracial communication. Such an approach fulfills many of the aims of critical race pedagogy, which will be discussed shortly.

Additional benefits of using film as a powerful pedagogical tool are its ability to address the diverse learning styles of students, encourage critical thinking, and engage students with sensitive and important course content (Jorge 2019). While cognitive goals such as intellectual mastery and understanding are important curricular objectives, courses designed to achieve social awareness place equal weight on the need to develop behavioral objectives (i.e., engage in action) and affective objectives (i.e., experiential outcomes) in their curricula. The first author has taught this upper-level interracial communication course at a PWI for nineteen years, and it remains not only a high-demand course but a popular one as well. This success is due in part to goals of (a) creating a supportive climate, (b) allowing students to communicate with one another in the classroom, and (c) challenging students to engage in intrapersonal and interpersonal communication. The instructor always attempts to maintain her role as instructor (Lederman 1992), or as the person whose responsibility it is to educate and empower through knowledge. She also has the fortune to witness students being able to better understand abstract concepts, theories, and phenomena through some form of visual aid. As a critical communication pedagogy scholar, she has used the interracial communication classroom as a way to reposition race as a nontaboo topic for discussion. Naturally, the topic of race and race relations is at the center of this course, which challenges students to examine their willingness and openness to communicate honestly about race within and outside the classroom.

Critical Race Pedagogy

Critical race pedagogy (CRP) "encompasses the liberatory teaching practices of critical pedagogy with the tenets of critical race theory" (Lac 2017, 3). Critical race theory (CRT) (Crenshaw et al. 1995) is built on six themes: (1) a recognition that racism is endemic to (North) American life; (2) an express skepticism of dominant legal claims of neutrality, objectivity, colorblindness, and meritocracy; (3) a challenge to ahistoricism in the law; (4) a recognition of the experiential knowledge of POC; (5) an interdisciplinary theory; and (6) elimination of racial oppression. When applied to education, CRT evolves into CRP. "CRP is a combination of CRT and critical pedagogy. Therefore, CRP is aimed at cultivating critical awareness about structural oppressions with specific focus on race by providing a framework to identify, analyze and transform structural racial oppressions" (Shimomura 2015, 258). As Yosso (2002) notes, more critical awareness can be achieved through the use of "media [that] involve moving images and sounds in addition to written text" (54). Thus, when facilitated properly, film may be used as a pedagogical tool for social justice.

Paolo Freire's three-stage model of critical pedagogy describes how educators can move students to a level of critical consciousness where they are potentially compelled to look "toward changing the system as a response to experiencing inequities" (Yosso 2002, 54). The three stages are the magical stage, naïve stage, and critical stage. Progression through these stages should result in students looking "beyond fatalistic or cultural reasons for inequality to focus on structural, systemic explanation" and, hopefully, achieving "a critical level of consciousness" (Yosso 2002, 54). These stages are critical, as Harris and Weber (2010) have argued, when film is used in the classroom. "The onscreen images, interactions, and storylines serve the communicative function of creating meaning and progressive possibility" for students as they gain understanding of racism as a form of systemic oppression (Harris and Weber 2010, 55) and follow a character who is a member of a fictive community existing in larger society where mounting racial tensions abound. We have chosen a fictional story because it is a visual narrative that both educates and entertains ("edutainment") students about racism, discrimination, and prejudice through a scripted story line.

The director and producer as storyteller have creative license over what messages are being communicated to their audiences, as is the case with *Dear White People*; therefore, we have chosen this film for its storytelling potential and relatability.

I am the first author on this study, and I believe it is important that I offer a testimony about the salience of intersectionality when it comes to teaching, especially at a predominantly White institution (PWI). As an African American professor, I am profoundly aware of the impact that my race and gender might have on my students and their experience with the class in general and the film specifically. While some might view my intersectionality as a subjective identity that clouds my ability to effectively teach such a course, others may perceive it as a constant reminder of their Whiteness or a unique perspective on an issue with which they have limited experience. Each of these scenarios speaks to the difficult position or space that a professor of color is forced to occupy at a PWI. Much like White women, female professors of color are subjected to the conscious and subconscious gendered and raced biases of our students in our classrooms and at our institutions. This can translate into resistance to our teaching in general and even more so when we opt to center race in our curricula. I do not assume that all of my pedagogical strategies, classroom expectations, and instructional expertise will be welcomed with open arms; however, I acknowledge that resistance has been and will continue to be a part of this intellectual territory. Nevertheless, I remain hopeful that any and all efforts to advance discourse regarding race in my classes will encourage critical engagement by all students, particularly those who are ignorant to the reality of institutional racism.

Dear White People as a Visual Text

The movie *Dear White People* (2014) was shown in my interracial communication classroom in the spring of 2016. It was chosen because it tells the story of various forms of racism thriving on a university campus, similar to what is happening on real campuses throughout the United States. Racism and marginalization dominate at fictional Winchester University. SOC are marginalized and subjected to various forms of racial microaggressions on a fairly consistent basis. Winchester shares many qualities with a vast majority of universities and colleges in our country, thus making it (plausibly) relatable for my students. I chose this film in hopes that a visual representation of an educational institution fraught with racism, heteronormativism, and racialized sexism would help students better understand the role that film plays in facilitating social justice (Gillborn 2006a).

Winthrop University is an Ivy League university that prides itself on providing its students with a premier educational experience; however, it completely ignores and minimizes the fact that racism is present on campus. The administration and students are eventually forced to confront the institution's troubled past and present when everyone becomes aware of the plans of the "white-run humor/satire magazine publication" *Pastiche* to host a blackface-themed Halloween party (Dear White People Wiki, n.d.). Viewers watch as multiple student coalitions form to fight over whether the racist party should happen. The White students are committed to preserving this racist ritual, while SOC are diligently working to expose their peers and university for the racists that they are. The SOC are also responding with an array of emotions, as they have reached their limit for how much racism they will tolerate at this point in their lives. In short, "*Dear White People* adds a welcome new voice to cinema's oft-neglected discussion of race, tackling its timely themes with intelligence, honesty, and gratifyingly sharp wit" (Rotten Tomatoes, n.d.). The data that we collected of students' responses to the film show that the film allowed me to make racism relatable for students while also helping them not only to develop "a racial consciousness but [to] become full participants in the struggle to end racism on multiple fronts" (Lynn et al. 2006, 22).

The Study

There were four primary goals of this study: (1) to observe any recurring clusters in the data; (2) to understand the influence of standpoint on perceptions of the film and issues of race; (3) to aid instructors in how to best educate their students about the realities of racism; and (4) to illustrate the effectiveness of using film to facilitate self-reflexive analysis. The college classroom was selected as a site for cultural critique because it is a context where critical thinking and exposure to diverse worldviews are expected.

COMM 3820: Interracial Communication

This class is an upper-level, high-demand elective. The semester from which data were collected included forty-three students, twenty-eight of whom allowed their paper to be used in the study. The class comprised one biracial male (Filipino/White), one biracial female (Black/White), one Asian woman, one Black male, one African American female, two Black American females, one Jewish female, thirteen White males, and twenty-two White females. All of the non-White students and twenty-three (eight males and fifteen females) of the thirty-five self-identified White students consented to participate. Students did not receive credit for participating; their incentive was contributing to social science research. It is important to note that, because of their various standpoints (i.e., raced, gendered, privilege), the students most likely had qualitatively different experiences with the film.

A three- to four-page reaction-paper assignment aimed to elicit students' honest reactions to the film and its impact (or not) on their perceptions of race or race-related issues as per the assignment guidelines. Students were specifically asked to apply concepts to the film, identify the most important lesson(s) learned from the film, describe their perception of how real the film is in reflecting race and race relations on a university campus and/or society, and identify the primary lesson that they believe the director intended for the audience to learn. They were also asked to provide their final or overall thoughts about the film. Students were encouraged to be honest in their responses and reminded that they would be evaluated on the quality of their written communication.

Methodology: Cluster Analysis

For this study, my coauthors and I used Sonja Foss's (1989) cluster analysis to analyze our data. Cluster analysis is a methodology that allows one to gain knowledge of a rhetor's interpretation or understanding of an artifact. In this instance, the rhetor is the student. As per the meth-odology, we identified our research question guiding our analysis (i.e., "What is the experience that students have with a race-centered film, and what role do they believe it plays in addressing the issue of race in the lives of the characters in the film?"), selected our unit of analy-sis (i.e., student reaction papers), analyzed the artifacts, and wrote our analysis. For several months, we mined through 140 pages of data. We independently read each paper (Lincoln and Guba 1985) and high-lighted specific themes and/or concepts that students either directly or indirectly referenced when discussing specific aspects of the film.

Coding schemes were developed, tested, and revised, which resulted in major clusters or categories of observations and experiences that stu-dents had after watching the film. Several key terms were discovered that represented these recurring clusters within the texts. A total of five clusters were identified, along with eighty-eight subterms. The clusters and the number of subterms within each are as follows: (1) *theory to practice* (*n* = 39); (2) *introspection* (*n* = 22); (3) *cultural critique* (*n* = 13); (4) *cinematic critique* (*n* = 9), and (5) *neologism* (*n* = 5). Subterms are included that contextualize the meanings associated with the primary terms or clusters. In this chapter, a few exemplars are provided of sub-terms that best capture the larger clusters and that exemplify how stu-dents are recognizing and applying course concepts through the film.

Emerging Themes

Theory to Practice

The cluster of *theory to practice* refers to a student's identification of a concept learned in class that was observed as being present or cap-tured in the film. In general, when students identify course concepts at work in a text, they demonstrate that they have comprehended course instruction. In this case, students offered analyses of how the film illustrated interracial communication concepts. Twelve subterms illustrated this connection-making through *Dear White People*: (1) *assimilation*; (2) *code-switching*; (3) *colorblindness*; (4) *colorism*; (5) *cul-tural appropriation*; (6) *identity management and negotiation*; (7) *insti-tutionalized racism*; (8) *racial ambiguity*; (9) *racial self-segregation*; (10) *self-improvement*; (11) *self-awareness*; and (12) *White privilege*. Space limitations prevent us from providing examples of each subterm; however, we highlight important student observations of race issues in the film.

The subterm *assimilation* appeared frequently in the students' essays. Assimilation refers to efforts to adapt to the dominant culture and distance oneself from one's microcultural group to survive and belong. Students' statements were coded as *assimilation* when they recognized how characters in the film assimilated because of their status at a PWI. An African female student, for example, identified *assimilation* as a dominant theme or subtheme of the film. She wrote,

> The most important lesson the movie dealt with was whether people assimilate or acculturate themselves in environments. I really liked that that movie talked about this by using four black students that had different experiences in dealing with acculturation and assimilation. For example, one of the main characters, Coco, was more willing to assimilate. This was highlighted through her physical appearance and her actions. She wore her hair in a weave and talked differently with her white friends than she did with her black friends. She also offered to host a party that had a theme of blackface. These actions showed her separating herself from her black identity in order to take on a white identity. In contrast, Sam was more willing to acculturate. For example in the university she hung out with a majority of black people and she wore her hair natural, but she was still able to communicate with white people within the school. Even while having a white boyfriend, she was able to keep her identity as a black woman.

This student identified and appreciated multiple representations of African Americans' experience with assimilation. She recognized the nuances between two different strategies of belonging: assimilation and acculturation. Her sophisticated description of examples of assimilation in the film shows that she was able to put theory to practice. In other words, she was able to identify course theories at work in the text. There is also the possibility that she found Coco's experiences relatable given their shared intersectional identities (i.e., African American, female) and status as SOC at a PWI.

A student identified *code-switching* as an important theme. Code-switching refers to an individual's ability to alternate between speaking two different language systems. This was observed by a biracial male as being a main quality of the character named Troy, an African American man trying very hard to fit in with the White students at Winthrop. The student described a scene in which the men are playing poker and Troy is code-switching with the goal of being accepted:

> Troy's character is seen performing fluid code switching throughout the film. In contrast to the Armstrong-Parker election, Troy is seen adapting his Black identity to a group of European-American students during the poker game at Garmin Club House. Here, he maintains elements of Black community speech, but adjusts his demeanor to make the other students comfortable. He demonstrates awareness of and pokes fun at racial characterizations when he adopts the "white voice" in the line "Who the fuck is T-Bone Walker?" Later in the film, Troy is required by his father to interact with the wealthy attendees of a donor event. Though only a snippet of conversation is heard, it could be assumed that Troy must switch codes once again to adapt to a group where dominant culture is pervasive.

The student identified code-switching as an effort by Troy to distance himself from his Blackness in order to be accepted by his White peers. He also noted how this creates tension in Troy's relationship with his father, who expects his son to assimilate to White culture. Identifying this theme demonstrates the student's ability to observe an important educational moment within the subtext of the film.

Other students recognized and reflected on concepts such as *institutionalized racism* in the film. The most significant message that a White female learned from the film was the reality that institutionalized racism is a very common occurrence. The film ends with visual images of news reports on real White Greek organizations that hosted racist parties similar to the one in *Dear White People*. The student reflected,

> I also think [highlighting institutional racism] was the director's main purpose in producing this film. The rolling credits at the end of the film

are probably the most important aspects of the film because it showcases actual colleges battling this issue in recent years. I believe it makes it more believable and palpable. It puts the issue of institutionalized racism in the forefront of our minds and personifies it with concrete examples. I can honestly say I have never thought about the diversity, or lack thereof, before this film on my university's campus. From this class, I have learned that is most likely because I have white privilege, but now I recognize it everywhere I walk.

In this instance, the student recognized that particular scenes, specifically the end, were purposely created by the director to illustrate the reality of systemic racism currently occurring on college campuses. What is more, the student internalized the message and applied it to her own experience. While she may not directly be responsible for racial discrimination, she was able to identify how it is made possible by members of her racial group due to White privilege. In applying these concepts to her own life, this student revealed how she was putting theory into practice.

In still more instances of putting theory into practice, students reported moments of *self-awareness* and recognized areas for *self-improvement* in response to watching the film. Self-awareness and self-improvement moments are occasions when students are prompted by a scene or concept to engage in self-reflection regarding racial, ethnic, and/or gendered identity. For example, a White male shared about *Dear White People*, "This film challenged me to look within myself and when an issue of race is brought up to not just see my side or the other side, but try and see the commonalities we share in our desires for how to improve race relations in any aspect, but especially on a college campus where social groups normally work against each other instead of with each other to try and reach their own group's goals." Another White male expressed similar moments of self-reflection when he stated, "Part of the reason as to why I took this class was to make myself more aware about racial issues in today's society. From the concepts learned, the class has really opened my eyes to racial issues. I think the film does an excellent job at capturing race and race relations on a college campus. . . . There were a number of lessons to be learned from *Dear White People*, like acceptance and appreciating differences, but the one that stood out to me was not let any one thing define, and more so, confine you." These students, along with many others, appear to have looked inward and felt motivated to improve their behavior to prevent racial inequity. In short, these students expressed a desire to apply theories they learned and lessons they gleaned from the film to improve inter-racial communication.

A key takeaway from the *theory to practice* theme is that students were able to identify examples of course concepts in this film, which is useful in several ways: media represents and reinforces course concepts, provides additional sources of representation and understanding, and encourages students to identify their own role in fostering positive interracial communication. Presumably, students will now be able to recognize examples of these concepts at work in their everyday lives and other media beyond this initial film. This serves as a window into student comprehension for instructors, as well, who see their students understanding the material and identifying how it works beyond classroom instruction and in texts that represent the larger world.

Applied Introspection

The cluster of *applied introspection* is defined as any content from the film that prompted the student to identify race-related themes and to actively engage in efforts to combat racism. This cluster differs from the *self-reflection* and *self-awareness* subterms in the *theory to practice* cluster in that it looks specifically at concepts within the film and the film's ability to challenge students to identify ways that they can actively fight against racism in real-world contexts. An example of that is when students identified White privilege as a dominant theme in the film and then concluded that they must use this newfound knowledge to identify ways they can fight systemic oppression, which could include educating other White people about their privilege and encouraging them to become involved in the fight by addressing this issue with other White people in their interpersonal networks. A total of nine subterms reflect this overarching theme: (1) *personal history/narrative*; (2) *increased awareness*; (3) *unfortunate relatability*; (4) *catalyst for change (White guilt)*; (5) *self-awareness*; (6) *forced self-awareness*; (7) *introspection*; (8) *educational activism*; and (9) *racism is real*.

A White male's reflection illustrates the subterm *increased awareness* when he referenced the dominant themes of White privilege and racial segregation in the film. He began by acknowledging an awareness of White privilege before taking the class and watching *Dear White People*; however, he added that the racial tensions between the film's Black and White students is quite similar to what is happening on university campuses across the nation. More importantly, he viewed the film's message as an opportunity for him to be more aware about his Whiteness and privilege. Consider the following quote: "I also know, for example, that there is a sort of self-perpetuating segregation that occurs in universities as illustrated by there seeming to be 'white' cliques and 'black' cliques in the film (particularly at lunch). But my reaction, to be quite honest, was less of, 'Wow, this really captures the state of race relations at my university,' and more of 'Wow, I need to be less ignorant of race relations at my university.'" The student saw the film as a reminder of how he rarely, if ever, has to think about race. Another White male student expressed similar feelings of identifying his privilege through viewing the film. He claimed, "This film as a white male makes me really look within and think about the white privilege that I sometimes can overlook." He expressed how his awareness increased in direct response to viewing the film. Still another student, a White female, shared, "Prior to the film I feel that I was unaware of many race related issues ranging from issues having to do with which students live in certain on campus houses, to which students eat at certain on campus dining halls. This film definitely opened my eyes to think big picture, made me realize how many race related issues are involved with so many aspects of campus, and impacted my perceptions of race through being able to relate to college campus examples."

Another White female garnered lessons from the film that served to motivate her into action. She shared how it inspired her to be a *catalyst for change*: "This movie really sparked something in me that made me want to improve race relations at [my university]. I was appalled with my own cultural group in this film. The way in which White people were portrayed was horrific, however, I do know that there are still White people that act in such manners. I would hope audience members would not think differently about all White people from this film." She went on to explain that the movie does reflect the most racist and negative qualities of the majority group; however, there are White people who do not espouse these racist ideologies and behaviors. Nevertheless, she came to the realization that positive interracial communication is possible. She concluded, "We just need to have open, honest dialogue and be accepting of one another" to improve race relations. While this student was optimistic, her statement glossed over the pervasiveness of structural White supremacy and the fact that race relations require much more that "honest dialogue." Thus, students still have work to do to unpack the nuances of structural racism. In the course, as the author who taught the class, I attend to this issue by reminding students of the reality of racism and how it is ingrained in society on a systemic level; however, the students' ability to self-reflect in response to the lessons in the film should not be discounted, as it demonstrates that students were deriving meaningful information from the film. They were also thinking through ways to ameliorate troubling racial issues represented in the film. These students were able to identify the dominant messages of the film and learned larger lessons about the need to be more informed about race issues on campus and to examine their own privilege in the real world.

Cultural Critique

This next theme examines how students unpacked race issues explored in the film more critically. The *cultural critique* cluster refers to the idea that the film is a critique of society and bears the larger message of society's responsibility to improve race relations and address race issues. The thirteen subterms reflect the lessons that people are supposed to learn as a result of having watched the film: (1) *do not discriminate*; (2) *respect and appreciate differences*; (3) *hopefulness for change*; (4) *edutainment (i.e., education and entertainment)*; (5) *appreciation for education about race*; (6) *societal denial of racism*; (7) *edutainment and social responsibility*; (8) *fallacy of stereotyping*; (9) *racial realism*; (10) *need for dialogue*; (11) *disciplining racism*; (12) *self-acceptance*; (13) and *White guilt*.

Many students picked up on the idea of *Dear White People* as a form of *edutainment*, which refers to the notion that entertainment can be educational. Student comments revealed the educational value of social commentaries like *Dear White People* to educate audiences about societal ills like racism. A White female student claimed, "Overall, I think there was a bigger message that was made throughout this movie. That everyone is struggling with his or her own racial issues and race is still a major issue going on today. There is a lot of internalized racism because people are not talking to the right people. People are sticking together and forming segregations to find comfort [with people who share the same identity], which in turn is causing race to still [be] an issue. We need more diversity, we need more interaction, we need more dialogue to deal with the issues of how people are feeling and why they are acting and reacting the way they do. That is what this movie is trying to get across; it is time to talk!" Another White female expressed the following sentiment: "This movie was highly entertaining and I enjoyed it as entertainment. However, it had a much deeper meaning when I stopped and thought about it. This movie really sparked something in me that made me want to improve race relations." To these students, as well as many others, the film is a tool that provides a "bigger message" and has a greater purpose to inform and educate beyond just entertaining its audience.

The ability of entertainment to educate is related to the idea that that media reflects reality—a reality that some students found rings true in the film. The subterm *racial realism* is defined as exposure to a sobering reality of racism and an awareness of the myth of a postracial society. It is an observation made only by White male and female students in their papers. A statement from a White male captures the essence of this subterm. He wrote about how the film is a real and accurate reflection of racism on university campuses in the United States, using an incident at the University of Oklahoma to make his point. The video-recorded incident involved a busload of White fraternity members doing an aggressively racist chant, which was widely circulated on social media and received national news coverage. While the student did not believe such blatantly racist acts occur on his campus, it is the personal accounts of racial microaggressions that resonated for him in a very important way. He has heard "countless stories of blacks being pulled over by the police for doing nothing wrong and having storeowners watch them shop to make sure they are not stealing. The bottom line is that racism is not over, and we do not live in a 'post-racial' world." Similarly, another White male student shared how *Dear White People* is very realistic, and, he said, "[It] is one of the most interesting films I have ever seen." He then stated, "My major takeaway from this movie is that racism is very real and must be acknowledged in order for any progress to be made in terms of race relations." These students' recognition of the film reflecting real-life racism evinces how students found the film relevant and informative. They derived valuable meaning from the film, which is more than mere entertainment and reinforces the value of film in educating students about serious racial issues.

Cinematic Critique

This cluster attends to students' critique of *Dear White People* as a cinematic, artistic work. It accounts for how the artistic quality of the film may or may not affect the value of the film to educate students. Specifically, it attends to the believability of the story and whether the events depicted in the film are realistic or exaggerated and whether this interferes with students' ability to learn from the film. The subterms include (1) *overexaggeration* and (2) *realism*. The consensus among the students was that they were largely supportive of the film but also could look at it critically and find fault with it. This is important because it means that even if a film is not perfectly believable and if it has flaws in production and the like, it can still carry a powerful, believable message. A White female argued that overexaggeration in the film actually contributes to a more powerful message from the film:

> While I felt that some aspects of the movie were a little exaggerated and could come off as demeaning, I do believe there were many positive takeaways. Because of the prevalence of white privilege in our society, many white people are unaware that such racial issues still exist. By highlighting this fact with exaggeration and humor, the movie revealed to its white audience that such racial issues are not over and are still very real even today. There were multiple times during the film that such a point was made and I was able to connect it to something I had personally witnessed or experienced, not even realizing the implications it had on members of the other race at the time. Things in my life that I take for granted are not necessarily available to members of the microculture within our society. As a member of the majority group, it is easy

to overlook these privileges and not acknowledge the injustice experienced by members of the minority group.

Another White female found the film to be realistic and added, "I enjoyed this movie because it was realistic and it spoke to the heart of the issues that some of us college students are oblivious to. Now when I walk around campus, I do see how separated we are as a community. We all share many commonalities such as same location, same football team, same language, etcetera, yet we remain closer friends with people of our own racial and ethnic groups."

A White male stated that, "I really felt like the film captures the reality of race relations today. The issues in this movie are real life issues that go on every day on college campuses, and unfortunately, even our campus. Just as we have discussed in class, there have been many complaints about [our school] not being diverse, and we definitely need to do better." For this student, the film was also realistic and highly applicable to the state of race relations at his own university. Another White female expressed initially disbelieving some of the events in the film but then realizing that they reflect reality to an extent:

> Overall, the film made me think about whether the conflict and the reactions were realistic, or is it an exaggeration, because it's a movie? I don't want to sound naïve to think that it's not realistic, and I don't want to discount the fact that it is a movie. Either way, I liked the movie because it was not just focused on one problem but a range, from race stereotypes to institutional diversity to internalized racism. In conclusion, watching *Dear White People* intensified my awareness and understanding of racism in America today. Violence like in Ferguson and with Eric Garner make movies of this sort that much more pressing for American society to confront and discuss these issues.

This student initially questioned whether the film was realistic but ultimately compared it to real-life violence against people of color. From these examples, it appears that the film does communicate a sense of urgency about real-life racial issues, despite some moments that initially seem overexaggerated or unrealistic.

Neologism

Students demonstrate mastery of material and critical thinking when they can expand on course concepts and apply them to generate new knowledge (Anderson, Krathwohl, and Bloom 2001). Students contributed to their own learning when they thought of *neologisms*, or original labels that describe unnamed phenomena that were not directly covered in class but that they identified as related and relevant to the discussion of race through *Dear White People* and the interracial communication class. One student recognized the value of the film in increasing awareness of racial issues, or contributing to the "amplification of race." This student, who identifies as a Jewish female, stated, "In terms of representing the reality of racism and racial issues on campuses, this movie portrays a very public, very racist, race war of sorts. While I only have [my experience at my university] to compare this representation to, the movie still amplifies the racism on the campus in order to make a point for the movie. At the end of the film they show real life examples of incredibly racist parties that have happened at campuses." The student identified the strategy in *Dear White People* of depicting racist behavior to prove a larger point. The party depicted in the film is depicted almost to the point of exaggeration, according to several students' papers, but the final images of actual racist parties drives home with viewers that racism is alive and well. The student just quoted deemed this strategy "racial amplification," thereby describing for herself a way to inform others about the scourge of racism on college campuses. This student was deriving meaning from the film in a way that built on classroom instruction and the interracial communication curriculum.

Discussion and Conclusion

These students' experiences with *Dear White People* are examples of how film can be a very important tool for educating students about the significance of race as a social issue (Lynn et al. 2006). When used as an educational tool, this film functioned as a narrative text whose purpose was to demonstrate the reality of racism and its presence on college campuses. Many students shared in the postviewing class discussion that they were unaware of the fact that there were so many instances of White students hosting blackface- and cultural-appropriation-themed parties at PWIs throughout the United States. Their initial impression was that the depiction of these racist incidents was fictional; however, the newspaper headlines highlighted at the end of the film dispelled that misconception. They also became more aware of the racist experiences (i.e., racial microaggressions) that their peers of color are facing that are similar to those of the characters at the fictional Winthrop University. The students recognized the value and importance of film as a pedagogical tool designed to educate them about the important issue of race. As the instructor of this course, I chose *Dear White People* because it is a film that I believe is relatable for the students. That might not have been the case for all students, but it was hoped that this pedagogical tool would challenge students to engage critically with their course material, which involved understanding concepts and theories related to race and applying them to the characters and different subtexts embedded in the film. While the participating students were able to recognize both the educational and entertainment value of the film, they were also able to identify the dominant meanings embedded throughout the film, which may be attributed to in-class discussions of multiple race-related topics and issues and expectations of regular self-reflexivity along the way. Thus, they were better positioned to identify the realism of *Dear White People* through its capturing of the complex nuances of racism in an allegedly progressive environment.

The fact that students were able to make the aforementioned connections between course material and the film supports the argument by Marvin Lynn et al. (2006) that the interracial communication course is integral to students "becom[ing] full participants in the struggle to end racism on multiple fronts" (22). I have designed my course with the hope that students are equipped with the knowledge and communication skills necessary to dismantle racism on an individual and institutional level, where they might witness or experience it. While it is not guaranteed, the course is designed with the spirit that societal change will come as a result of students engaging critically with the issue of race in very complex ways. The class is an elective, and, on a very basic level, because students are taking it voluntarily, we believe it helps them achieve the personal goals of (1) becoming more knowledgeable about interracial communication, (2) developing a higher level of cultural competency, and (3) adopting communication strategies designed to fight racism, racial prejudice, stereotyping, and racial discrimination within and outside the classroom. Moreover, it is our contention that the use of film in such courses is vital to educating students about racial and social injustices occurring in society and on university campuses throughout the country.

This study further illuminates how film has the potential to prompt students to critically engage with the topic of race in a safe space and environment. Anecdotally, as the instructor of the course, I observed students referencing different scenes in the film throughout the rest of the semester when trying to demonstrate their understanding of certain concepts or relate to their classmates from racial standpoints different from their own. While the film is not solely responsible for any type of transformation that may have occurred, it is but one pedagogical tool used to prompt critical thinking about a very real social issue. Students were able to appreciate both the educational and entertainment value of *Dear White People* in a way that they otherwise might not have if they were not required to watch it for class. They may have dismissed the accounts of racism as being isolated incidents or exaggerations for the sake of entertainment; however, this in-class viewing of and responses to the film demonstrate that students are a great audience for understanding the power that lies within this type of narrative text. My coauthors and I acknowledge that this study does not resolve the issue of racism at PWIs, but it does offer support for our position that teacher-scholars should be committed to actively integrating film into their classrooms as the preparation of students to be global citizens in an increasingly diverse world.

Conclusion

Next Steps for Media Studies

EMMA GONZÁLEZ-LESSER AND MATTHEW W. HUGHEY

When Stuart Hall passed away in 2014, the *Guardian* called him the "godfather of multiculturalism," and Henry Louis Gates Jr. referred to him as "the Du Bois of Britain" (quoted in Loudis 2017). Yet, even as a founder of cultural studies as we know it, Hall's work was surprisingly underpublished, with most of his scholarly contributions put in the limelight posthumously. In the years that followed Hall's death, academic outlets began to pay tribute to the vast knowledge base that Hall spent his career developing. In 2016, the *International Journal of Cultural Studies* published a special issue titled "The Worldliness of Stuart Hall," and *African and Black Diaspora* published a special issue, "Hybridizing and Decolonizing the Metropole: Stuart Hall, Caribbean Routes and Diasporic Identity," in 2018. Also in 2018, the journal *Identities: Global Studies in Culture and Power* published a special issue on the life and work of Stuart Hall, in which Marcus Anthony Hunter penned the essay "The Sociology of Stuart Hall" (2018). Hunter wrote, "That Stuart Hall performed great acts of sociology is indisputable. . . . Such facts, however, do not mean that when the great conclave of the social sciences meet that his name will make it into the canon or even receive some version of disciplinary sainthood. . . . Over his career, Hall was often noted as a 'cultural theorist' and though a longtime faculty in a sociology department his work has not yet made its way into as much of the curriculum as ought to be. . . . Hall offers critique of sociology while illustrating the crucial role of the nexus of race, media analysis and popular culture" (30–31).

We hope that this book has taken an important step, albeit a humble one, in both rectifying this canonical omission and amplifying the import of his work. As mentioned in the introduction and within several of the chapters, Hall's pivotal "encoding/decoding" (1973) approach is the thread that binds this volume. Inspired by Hall's work, we hope to have afforded a look at current and innovative scholarship that examines the making, distributing, and consuming of racialized media. In particular, we hope to have moved the meter beyond the already well-researched sights, sounds, and texts of "racial representations" (so common in sociological investigations of the media) toward an analysis of our three prongs of design, delivery, and decoding. In this conclusion, we provide a short overview of sociological media studies, chart the broader theoretical insights from the substantive chapters of each section, and then consider how the framework of design, delivery, and decoding can move studies of racialized media forward from here.

A Brief Primer on Sociology (and the Larger Scholarship) of the Media

Sociology was once a leader in the study of media, especially considering the stronghold that was "mass communications" in the 1940s, coupled with public fears about the power of the media to facilitate fascism. After World War II, the field slowly moved away from the "hypodermic model" of media's "direct effects" and began to explore media representations by comparing observed political events (such as political rallies) and their corresponding media reports. Kurt Lang and Gladys Lang (1953), for example, showed that participants in political rallies did not recognize the media coverage of those same rallies. Moreover, scholars of the time found that people do not watch media randomly but focus on particular messages. For instance, in a now-classic study of the 1940 US presidential election, Paul Lazarsfeld, Bernard Berelson, and Hazel Gaudet (1948) found that people seek out political content that reinforces their existing belief structure. This led to the "uses-and-gratifications" approach to media, a subfield that continues to resonate with how contemporary cable news functions (J. Jones 2012).

Yet others were optimistic about the possibilities for mass media to inform and educate. Scholars began to investigate "what people do with the media" rather than "what media does to people" (Katz 1959, 2). This approach, known as the "selectivity paradigm," makes media users (rather than media) the focus, thereby emphasizing how people use media as a form of social and political resistance (Valkenburg, Peter, and Walther 2016, 320). But by the 1960s, counterculture and the growth of neo-Marxist paradigms foregrounded how media facilitates or distracts from inequality, alienation, and the encroachment of commodity fetishism; research shifted to examine what influences and sets "media agendas" (McCombs and Shaw 1972), what frames events (Palmerton 1988), and what shapes public understandings (Gamson and Modigliani 1989) toward either growing diversity or homogenization of ideas and content in media forms (cf. Curran, Gurevitch, and Woollacott 1985).

By the 1980s, the once somewhat cohesive "sociology of the media" was replaced by an interdisciplinary research concerned more with latent (rather than explicit) meanings of media content: what media representation *means* to audiences rather than a simple view of how media *affects* them. Inspired by earlier Durkheimian approaches that see media's role as "upholding and reaffirming at regular intervals the collective sentiments and the collective ideas which make its unity and its personality" (Durkheim [1912] 1965, 474–75), the "ritual communication approach" (cf. Carey 1989) was thus born; media was viewed as a mechanism that reproduces ideas of community and solidarity in broadcasting civic rituals (Chaney 1996), spectacles (Elliott 1981; Matthews 2017), and the social construction of reality itself (Dayan and Katz 1992).

Today we see less of a cohesive paradigm; there are now more segmented and specific reviews of mass-media effects (Felson 1996), the "social implications of the internet" (DiMaggio et al. 2001), the promotion of "television sociology" in the "new TV" age (Grindstaff and Turow 2006), and "online social research" (Golder and Macy 2014), to name just a few. Some of this shift can be attributed to the development of niche interdisciplinary studies (and their accompanying journals) or to the multiplicity of media types (e.g., studies of the internet or social media are vastly different from, and have distinct implications compared to, television or news media) that do not necessarily fit under the umbrella of "media studies."

Out of this disciplinary diversity, Stuart Hall emerged. His grounding in "cultural studies" and his adamant stance that rejected much of the "value-free" orientation of armchair theorizing made him a somewhat unwelcome guest in the house of Comte. Yet this own marginalization reveals the depth of Hall's commitment to his own sociological imagination. Hence, while grounded in sociology, we have explicitly turned toward an interdisciplinary approach in this book (a Hallsian [anti]sociology?). Such an approach is necessary not only to better empirically map where we have been (avoiding a sole sociology bias or sociological reductionism) but also to perhaps give readers insights on the current heading of social scientific analyses of media.

What Is Next for Race and Media Scholarship?

No text is the final word. While we are invigorated by the vibrancy of scholarship at the crossroads of race and media, some signposts alert us to both the dilemmas and the dividends that lie down the path. Here we list some of these areas (certainly not exhaustive!), as reflections of our excitement for the innovations and discoveries but also as recommendations for both scholarly pursuit and pragmatic (whether lawmaking, policy crafting, or direct-action activism) avenues for social change.

Racial and Ethnic Bias in the Media Labor Circuit

While some biases in the media are hypervisible—even embraced, as in the case of extreme reporting by Fox News (J. Jones 2012)—it can be difficult to pinpoint media bias. Tim Groeling (2013) indicates two main problems in identifying and studying media bias. The first is the problem of unobserved populations: potential stories die on the cutting-room floor owing to bias. The second is the problem of subjectivity, whereby selected content is portrayed in biased ways. Scholars have devised methodologies and techniques to address these problems, and many of the chapters in this book have taken such approaches; but several areas for study require illumination of the reasons for, and effects of, media bias.

Extreme racial bias characterizes mass media. Thomas Eisensee and David Strömberg (2007) estimate that forty-six times as many people must die in an African disaster to achieve the same news coverage of a similar disaster in eastern Europe. Whites remain significantly overrepresented as victims and officers in television news, while people of color are often overrepresented as criminals (Dixon 2017a, 2017b). This bias is well entrenched historically. In a study of the *New York Times*'s coverage of Puerto Ricans and Puerto Rico from 1948 to 1958 (the period just before and after Puerto Rican "independence"), Bianca Gonzalez-Sobrino and Matthew Hughey (2015) found a preponderance of nationalist and racist language that rationalized White paternalism over the island owing to the supposed cultural dysfunctions of the Puerto Rican diaspora. Such biases in depicting different racial and ethnic groups persist even as newspapers have moved into the digital era and extend to what issues are deemed "newsworthy."

These biases are also reflected in digitally downloadable content, via on-demand media. In an investigation of the Netflix series *House of Cards*, *Orange Is the New Black*, and *Hemlock Grove*, Bianca Gonzalez-Sobrino, Emma Lesser, and Matthew Hughey (2018, 323–24) found that these shows engage in high levels of either "racial exclusion" or "whitewashing," which is part and parcel of "the contemporary era in which such programming is produced—a moment of increasing racial inequality coupled with an increasing commitment to a post-racial or 'color-blind' mantra."

Similar patterns are emerging in social media, with evidence suggesting strong racial biases. Priyanga Gunarathne, Huaxia Rui, and Abraham Seidmann (2018) found that African American customers are less likely to receive brand responses to their complaints on social media relative to non–African American customers. Moreover, because of these biases, White populations are more likely to gain access to, and have confidence in, mass-mediated messages than are people of color, leading to an overrepresentation of White people's interests in media and an increased likelihood that their political needs will be met. As David Strömberg (2015, 187) notes, "The most direct evidence of this is perhaps provided by Reinikka and Svensson (2005), who find that schools to which it was cheaper to deliver newspapers, because they were closer to a newspaper outlet, received more government funds. Newspaper provision of news may, in this way, produce a political bias disfavoring remote and rural areas."

Overall, while we continue to document the existence of bias and the unbalanced variations of racial and ethnic representations, we must perhaps better emphasize the *mechanisms* that drive exclusion and White dominance in how media is designed, delivered, and decoded. How is racial bias influencing design and production choices, and how are these choices creating a ripple effect of bias? What skewed ideologies are undergirding gatekeepers' decisions regarding which media content we do and do not receive, and what are the impacts of the continuing stream of biased reviews, marketing, and accessible content? We must not only study the more readily observable behavioral patterns but—using the example of how audiences engage media—bring sociologically informed methodology and reasoning to bear on how audiences come to think about, feel, and create interpretive schemata that affect their media engagement. "Audience reception and 'use' cannot be understood in simple behavioral terms. The typical processes identified in positivistic research—effects, uses, 'gratifications'—are themselves framed by structures of understanding, as well as being produced by social and economic relations, which shape their 'realizations'" (Hall [1973] 1991, 95). Hall's nuanced understanding of the relationship of media and consumers allowed him to analyze the media world in ways that may otherwise have been ignored. Hall (1980, 130) later articulated, "Before the message can have an 'effect' (however defined), satisfy a 'need' or be put to a 'use,' it must first be appropriated as a meaningful discourse and be meaningfully decoded."

Media Advocacy in Design and Delivery

The recognition that media can set ideological programs, pragmatic timetables, and the contours of particular issues has never been far from its scholarly dissection. Importantly, for those who wish to intercede in, rather than solely understand, the strategic use of media making, the topic of media advocacy is key. Especially aligned with our sections on media design and delivery, media advocates attempt to influence decision-makers through what they produce and how it is marketed. Of import here are the half-century-old notions of "agenda setting" and "framing." As Lori Dorfman and Ingrid Krasnow (2014, 293) assert, "Media advocacy's blend of science, politics, and advocacy means that it draws on several theoretical foundations and disciplines, including political science, communications, and cognitive linguistics.

Agenda setting and framing have been the core concepts informing media advocacy strategy." In agenda setting, successful advocates study news media because these information brokers largely determine what issues we collectively engage, how that engagement takes place, and the terms of debate within the public sphere. Framing is the process by which people make meaning from media content. How people reconcile new information with existing and dominant understandings is key for advocates, as the power to set or appeal to what Dorfman and Krasnow (2014, 296) call the "default frame" (as either the new or the established way of thinking) is crucial for one to accept information as legitimate or spurious.

Sociology in particular and the social sciences writ large would be well served by outlining what makes and breaks successful media advocacy. Hall frequently reminded us that, simply put, media matters. Especially when examining how media has largely come to constitute much of what is "popular culture," which is often dismissed as superfluous to "real" problems in the world or fetishized as the keystone for liberation, Hall (1981, 229) understood the "popular" qua media as worthy of investigation for what it could mean for human emancipation and the establishment of rules for more equitable treatment:

> Popular culture is one of the sites where this struggle for and against a culture of the powerful is engaged: it is the stake to be won or lost in that struggle. It is the arena of consent and resistance. It is partly where hegemony arises, and where it is secured. It is not a sphere where socialism, a socialist culture—already fully formed—might be simply "expressed." But it is one of the places where socialism might be constituted. That is why "popular culture" matters. Otherwise, to tell you the truth, I don't give a damn about it.

Media Effects and Consumer Decoding

What media supposedly *does to* people has been a long-standing concern. We see a need for continued study of this question, with an emphasis on the social context, not simply as possible statistical "noise" to be eliminated from clean causal claims but as constituting (or, in the parlance of positivist science, as interaction effects of) the relationships observed. As Patti Valkenburg, Jochen Peter, and Joseph Walther (2016, 321–22) point out, there is a need to

> recognize the importance of social context at the micro, meso, and macro level in encouraging or discouraging media use. . . . Social influences can occur deliberately and overtly, when institutions, schools, or parents restrict or regulate media use. . . . On the macro level, structural aspects of the media system (e.g., channel availability) can affect media choices, . . . whereas on the micro level, adults can forbid children to watch violent content and encourage them to use educational media. . . . Social influences can also occur more covertly, through an individual's perception of the prevailing norms in the groups to which they belong (e.g., family, peer clique, subcultures).

The more covert aspects have received less scholarly attention. While the lion's share of scholarly attention focuses on either individual antecedents or larger structural constraints of media use, we must recognize the place of social identity in media usage and effects. That is, our self-concept often derives from our membership in a racial or ethnic group and shapes how we engage in which types of media and to what effect. This connects to part 3 of this book, on how consumers decode racialized media, in which authors demonstrated the salience of racial identity, and marginalization or power, for the experience of media consumption. Another example of this phenomenon is the racialization of Myspace and Facebook, in which White teens practiced a form of digital White flight toward Facebook and away from what they labeled the "ghetto" network of Myspace (Boyd 2011). As Hall ([1973] 1991, 93–94) noted, "The codes of encoding and decoding may not be perfectly symmetrical," and "what are called distortions or misunderstandings arise precisely from the lack of equivalence between the two sides in the communication exchange." Thus, what are commonly translated as misuses of, failures to understand, or overly emotional reactions to media—particularly from people who are racially marginalized—are not missteps but rather the consequences of inequality grounded in the asymmetrical relations of power between social groups.

The Design and Delivery of Journalism and News Making

The authors in the parts of the book on design and delivery have attested to the power that media creators and gatekeepers have to shape our racialized media realities. In a time of increased accusations of "fake news" and public distrust in scholarly knowledge and institutions meant to be trustworthy gatekeepers of verifiable information, the study of journalistic practices is taking on a new level of importance. The relevance of such scholarship is not new, especially within sociology. Max Weber ([1909] 1998) urged that sociological research should focus on the institutions of journalism and examine who owns and controls them and the political and commercial influences on how they operate. However, sociologists have been slow to take up Weber's charge, particularly in relation to how the "dominant cultural order" (Hall 1980, 123) has been inscribed within the news item through the "professional code [of] journalism" (Hall 1980, 126).

From one perspective, given the growth of virtual networks, it is more difficult for both mainstream local and national media to maintain credibility with the public at large. "Gone are the days of a fact-driven, source-verified news story" (Brown 2013, 817–18). Yet, simultaneously, this skepticism can be seen as neither new nor irrational but grounded in savvy takes by communities of color that biases of the "dominant cultural order" have long cast as outlandish claims rooted in irrational paranoia. In the context of the media's influence on public perception, distrust of the media in favor of trustworthy social networks is a common occurrence. Thus, Thaddeus Hoffmeister and Ann Watts (2018, 261) state, "Today, some like-minded people purportedly trust one another more than professional outsiders (journalists) to deliver news and information of import to them. Peer-to-peer networks dominate the media landscape and wield responsibility for screening and disseminating content for public consumption." It is therefore important to examine not only the "power elite" (C. Wright Mills 1956) at the intersection of corporate media and state influence but also how racialized communities are now some of the primary stakeholders, and content providers, for the creation of multiplicative "newses" and even "truths" that structure relationships far beyond domains we commonly think of as journalism or news making. Audiences are today enacting roles as both producer and consumer—what Axel Bruns (2008) calls the "prosumer or produser"—as well as sometimes bypassing gatekeepers, as some of the authors herein have discussed.

Blurring the lines between production, distribution, and consumption creates new challenges for how we understand "new, new media" and its role in informing or even constituting "the public." That is, media is not "new" in terms of an objective chronology but rather is about "sociomaterial practices" (Gershon 2017, 16), such as reaching a new audience or "enabl[ing] people to circulate knowledge in new ways" (Gershon 2017, 15).

Decoding Politics and Political Polarization

Weber (2015, 136) famously defined politics as "the pursuit for a portion of power or for influencing the division of power whether it is between states, or between groups of people which the state encompasses." While some people may read this definition as too Machiavellian, the fit of Weber's definition in current conditions tempers such an interpretation. If we consider media as a form of traditional, charismatic, or legal authority, the urgency for examining media's effect on politics (particularly political polarization) is ever more pressing. Empirical examinations of media and the political realm offer some context: "The more important empirical finding that emerges consistently in these studies is that most large media outlets are centrist compared to members of [US] Congress. . . . Most large US media outlets are politically centrist and provide a balance of competing viewpoints. But the first condition for growing mass polarization through increasingly partisan media is partially met: some talk radio shows, cable news channels, and websites do offer more ideologically extreme packages of news and opinion" (Prior 2013, 103–4).

But has the mass public become more politically polarized because of the authority of increasingly emergent partisan media? The answer appears to be yes—and no. Scholars note that partisan electoral behavior (that is, voting for parties and candidates that take more extreme conservative and liberal positions) occurs at greater rates with high cable penetration (controlling for a host of other variables). It is tempting to interpret cable news, particularly the commonly identified culprits MSNBC and Fox News, as driving this political divide. However, researchers first observed the impact of cable access on increased political partisanship in the 1970s, long before cable systems carried news channels. It appears that the glory days of broadcast television in the 1960s and 1980s helped to moderate political behavior. "Even people with little interest in news and politics watched network newscasts because they were glued to the set and there were no real alternatives to news in many markets during the dinner hour" (Prior 2013, 103–4).

Beginning in the 1970s, and cemented with the proliferation of both liberal and conservative twenty-four-hour cable news stations in the 1990s, cable television and internet both provided an escape from broadcast television news: "If the goal was to find a connection between media and more partisan elections, we can stop looking. The culprit turns out to be not Fox News, but ESPN, HBO, and other early cable channels that lured moderates away from the news—and away from the polls. Polarization without persuasion—through technology-induced compositional change of the voting public and elite-induced clarification of electoral choices—is sufficient to explain why elections have become more partisan and moderates have all but disappeared in Congress" (Prior 2013, 107–8).

Today's social media trends create different means of decoding news media. Although younger generations do not adhere to standard practices found relevant for political participation, namely, viewing the news, young people are gaining their news content not from single-source news corporations but from the variety of news content they encounter on social media sites like Facebook and Twitter (Sveningsson 2015). However, the existence of nonpartisan local media seems to drive less partisan politics and voting behavior. For instance, James Snyder and David Strömberg's (2010) analysis of roll-call voting, committee assignments, and witness appearances for US congresspersons between 1982 and 2004 shows that when US congresspersons represent districts with high media coverage, they operate as less ideologically extreme, vote more frequently against party leaders, and more frequently stand witness in congressional hearings. As for voting behavior, Claudio Ferraz and Frederico Finan (2008) find that local radio broadcasts in Brazil increased voters' likelihood to vote out mayors where malfeasance and corruption were uncovered (and reelect mayors who were either praised or at least less corrupt than average). Additionally, Horacio Larreguy, John Marshall, and James Snyder (2014) found that Mexican voters are particularly responsive to local radio and television reports about municipal audit reports. The effect of media here is strong, given that voters punish the party of corrupt mayors, but only in electoral precincts with local media stations. Similar results are reported by Abhijit Banerjee et al. (2014), who discovered that when residents in large Indian slums receive newspapers that cover the performance of the incumbent legislator and the qualifications of challengers, elections are characterized by higher voter turnout, less vote buying, and more votes for better-performing incumbents (cf. Strömberg 2015).

Given these contradictory forces, and the development of models that emphasize the power of either grassroots local media or top-down corporate media, we urge readers to revisit Stuart Hall's influential analysis of "authoritarian-populism" (1988), a shorthand term for how the structures of media design, delivery, and decoding aligned "the people" with socially conservative, free-market, elite interests and against the progressive social and Keynesian economic movements of the 1960s. Hall's approach would be particularly fruitful given the fragmentation of media into niche-oriented content, the collapse of meaningful boundaries between news and entertainment, and the rise of interactive digital media platforms (cf. Ouellete and Banet-Weiser 2018).

***

The intersection of race and media is important for people's lived existence. The making, sharing, and using of media about ourselves shape both the length and quality of our lives. As Stuart Hall (2017, 208) wrote, "I still think the best way to analyse the ideological dimensions of a media statement is not only in terms of the so-called bias of its overt content, or the material interests which it serves, but also in terms of the deep propositional structure, inner logics, structures of inference and interpretive schemas which ground the discourse."

Yet some people perceive research on racialized media as extending the longevity of racial issues. Either we have talked too much about race (and thus are part of the problem), or we have already reached "color-blindness" by and large; and thus it is irrelevant to continue such conversations. The first mistakes the remedy with the illness and minimizes the relevance of historical forms of racial inequality, as well as the extent to which those historical forms matter and have also shifted to still function today. This rendering can give people in dominant groups implicit social permission to silence and dismiss people of color and to play the "anything but racism" game in explaining why people of color still face inequality. The second is either willfully ignorant or simply misinformed and deluded. As Charles W. Mills (2007) reminds us, robust epistemologies of ignorance structure White perceptions of the end of racism.

Both of these fictions, and the pace and ease with which they are taken up as supposed facts, are disturbing not only because of their intentions but also because of their consequences: to stir up disdain, if not outright hostility, toward any person or group that would engage in overtly analyzing and proposing remedies for racial bias, exclusion, narrowcasting, discrimination, or trafficking of racist narratives in media, without distilling or reducing them to some other "nonracial" (e.g., class) phenomenon. Moreover, the turn away from studying race and media can distract from recognizing the pressing weight of reality that is unequally borne and threatens a new era of "benign neglect" (to appropriate the phrase once used by the senator [and sociologist] Daniel Patrick Moynihan to advise the Nixon White House): "The time may have come when the issue of race could benefit from a period of 'benign neglect.' The subject has been too much talked about. The forum has been too much taken over to hysterics, paranoids, and boodlers on all sides. We need a period in which Negro progress continues and racial rhetoric fades" (Frankel 1970). Contemporary "benign neglect," for which Obama's 2008 election was the cherry on top, has begun to shift to some extent as outwardly racial rhetoric rises to the surface in mainstream contexts. Nevertheless, many facets of colorblindness, such as the minimization of systemic racism's effects, continue to abound.

Of issue is the artificial distinction between material "progress" and "rhetoric" (often mapped onto discussions of "race" and "media," respectively), as if the two are easily or naturally distinguishable. In concert, we highlight the power of racial-media narratives in constituting the social world. We do not gesture toward the finished product of racial-media narratives but rather emphasize the questions implicit in the process of narrative making: who writes the story, with what language, grounding what characters, approved by which gatekeepers, told in what medium, delivered by what parties, to whom, and with what costs. This book is not the final answer but a humble attempt at clarifying some of those questions and answering a few. We hope that Stuart Hall would approve.

ACKNOWLEDGMENTS

We are grateful to the friends and colleagues who informally helped with the research and for the germinal ideas for this book. Our many conversations about race and media with Sheena Gardner, Bianca Gonzalez-Sobrino, Menaka Kannan, Daina Harvey, Michael Rosino, and Bandana Purkayastha helped us shape the idea of the text before a word was written. Your time, energy, and dedication helped extend both our reach and our sight.

The book came to New York University Press through the keen insight of acquisitions editor Ilene R. Kalish. She convinced us that the press was the right place for the text, and she was right. Assistant editor Sonia Tsuruoka also provided a great deal of support and served as an invaluable knowledge base for many of the authors. Thank you both for all your work and your unwavering belief in this project. To all at New York University Press who contributed time and effort to the production of this volume, its editorial board, its support staff, and the anonymous reviewers, we are most grateful for your assistance and professionalism.

We owe a rather large epistemological debt to the authors of various articles, chapters, and books that helped us to wrestle down, shape, and employ myriad ideas and debates in the intersecting fields of race and media: David L. Altheide, Shyonn Baumann, Howard Becker, Eduardo Bonilla-Silva, Ronald E. Chennault, Peter Chow-White, David Croteau, Troy Duster, Robert M. Entman, Elizabeth Ewen, Stuart Ewen, Robert Ferguson, John Fiske, William Gamson, Roxanne Gay, Henry Giroux, Juan González, Andrew M. Gordon, Herman Gray, Lawrence Grossberg, Doug Hartmann, bell hooks, Marcus A. Hunter, Vincent Hutchings, Michèle Lamont, Amanda Lewis, George Lipsitz, Alan A. Marcus, Dana Mastro, Lisa Nakamura, Diane Negra, Alondra Nelson, Sheridan Prasso, Jane Rhodes, Vincent F. Rocchio, Clara E. Rodríguez, Andrew Rojecki, Michael Schudson, Jeremy D. Stoddard, Joseph Torres, Nicholas Valentino, Jenny Walker, Stephen Walsh, and Howard Winant.

This book would not exist without the giant contributions of Stuart Hall, who paved the foundation on which the book stands. You are missed, and our words remain obliged to yours.

Thank you to the librarians at the University of Connecticut. Your knowledge and acumen were welcome aids in our research. We are extremely grateful to the Department of Sociology at the University of Connecticut for providing an institutional space for bringing this project home. Matthew Hughey wishes to acknowledge the Media Studies faculty at the University of Virginia, namely, Hector Amaya, Aniko Bodroghkozy, Siva Vaidhyanathan, and especially David Golumbia (now at Virginia Commonwealth University)—thank you for setting me on a path of media investigation, scrutiny, and analysis.

To the authors herein, your labors are the lion's share of this text. We thank you for your contributions and for your trust in our editorial eye. We are honored to be together in this project.

To Sherrill and Michael Hughey, thank you for instilling a critical eye for injustice and inequality, regardless of its overt or subtle manifestation. For Menaka Kannan, thank you for being a true and loyal friend.

To Bianca Gonzalez-Sobrino, your unwavering support through this process and so much more has made everything possible.

REFERENCES

ABC News. 2018. "Serena Williams: Cartoonist Mark Knight Defends Depiction of US Open Tantrum amid Accusations of Racism." *Australian Broadcasting Corporation,* September 11, 2018. www.abc.net.au.

Adkins Covert, Tawnya J., and Philo C. Wasburn. 2007. "Measuring Media Bias: A Content Analysis of *Time* and *Newsweek* Coverage of Domestic Social Issues, 1975–2000." *Social Science Quarterly* 88 (3): 690–706.

Adorno, Theodor W. 1945. "A Social Critique of Radio Music." *Kenyon Review* 18:229–35.

Ahmed, Sara. 2004. "Affective Economies." *Social Text* 22 (2): 117–39.

———. 2017. *Living a Feminist Life.* Durham, NC: Duke University Press.

Akinyemi, Aaron. 2014. "Samuel L. Jackson: Hollywood Avoids Real Issues of Racism." *International Business Times,* February 1, 2014. www.ibtimes.co.uk.

Alamo-Pastrana, Carlos, and William Hoynes. 2018. "Racialization of News: Constructing and Challenging Professional Journalism as 'White Media.'" *Humanity and Society,* December 20, 2018. https://doi.org/10.1177/0160597618820071.

Alexander, Elizabeth. 1994. "'Can You Be Black and Look at This?' Reading the Rodney King Video(s)." *Public Culture* 7 (1): 77–94. https://doi.org/10.1215/08992363-7-1-77.

Alexander, George. 2000. "Fade to Black." *Black Enterprise,* December 2000, 107–15.

Alexander, Jeffrey C. 2006. "Cultural Pragmatics: Social Performance between Ritual and Strategy." In *Social Performance: Symbolic Action, Cultural Pragmatics and Ritual,* edited by Jeffrey C. Alexander, Bernhard Giesen, and Jason L. Mast, 29–90. New York: Cambridge University Press.

Alexander, Michelle. 2012. *The New Jim Crow: Mass Incarceration in the Age of Colorblindness.* New York: New Press.

Alfred, Taiaiake, and Jeff Corntassel. 2005. "Being Indigenous: Resurgences against Contemporary Colonialism." *Government and Opposition* 40 (4): 597–614.

Allen, Ricky Lee. 2001. "The Globalization of White Supremacy: Toward a Critical Discourse on the Racialization of the World." *Educational Theory* 51 (4): 467–85. https://doi.org/10.1111/j.1741-5446.2001.00467.x.

Alterman, Eric. 2003. *What Liberal Media? The Truth about Bias and the News.* New York: Basic Books.

Alverson, Bridget. 2017. "The People's Comics: Using the Graphic Format to Teach about Current Events." *School Library Journal,* August 1, 2017. www.slj.com.

American Council for Better Broadcasts (ACBB). 1955. *Better Broadcasts, Better World* 8 (January 1, 1955): 4.

Anderson, Benedict. (1983) 2006. *Imagined Communities: Reflections on the Origin and Spread of Nationalism*. New York: Verso.

Anderson, Kim. 2000. *A Recognition of Being: Reconstructing Native Womanhood*. Toronto: Sumach.

Anderson, Lorin W., David R. Krathwohl, and Benjamin Samuel Bloom. 2001. *A Taxonomy for Learning, Teaching, and Assessing: A Revision of Bloom's Taxonomy of Educational Objectives*. New York: Longman.

Anderson, Monica. 2016. "Social Media Conversations about Race." Pew Research Center, August 15, 2016. www.pewresearch.org.

Anderson, Stuart. 2018. "Tariffs Are Costing Jobs: A Look at How Many." *Forbes*, September 24, 2018. www.forbes.com.

Anderson, Wendy K. Z. 2018. "Classifying Whiteness: Unmasking White Nationalist Women's Digital Design through an Intersectional Analysis of Contained Agency." *Communication, Culture and Critique* 11 (1) : 116–32. https://doi.org/10.1093/ccc/tcy002.

Andreassen, Rikke. 2017. "Social Imaginaries, Sperm and Whiteness: Race and Reproduction in British Media." *Journal of Intercultural Studies* 38 (2): 123–38. https://doi.org/10.1080/07256868.2017.1289906.

Anglin, Andrew. 2016. *A Normie's Guide to the Alt-Right*. August 31, 2016. https://katana17.files.wordpress.com.

Appiah, Osei. 2018. "Cultural Voyeurism: A New Framework for Understanding Race, Ethnicity, and Mediated Intergroup Interaction." *Journal of Communication* 68 (2): 233–42. https://doi.org/10.1093/joc/jqx021.

Armaline, William T. 2011. "Caging Kids of Color: Juvenile Justice and Human Rights in the United States." In *Human Rights in Our Own Backyard: Injustice and Resistance in the US*, edited by William T. Armaline, Davita Glasberg, and Bandana Purkayastha, 189–98. Philadelphia: University of Pennsylvania Press.

Armenta, Amada. 2017. "Racializing Crimmigration: Structural Racism, Colorblindness, and the Institutional Production of Immigrant Criminality." *Sociology of Race and Ethnicity* 3 (1): 82–95. https://doi.org/10.1177/2332649216648714.

ASNE (American Society of News Editors). 1998. "ASNE Sets New Vision for Newsroom Diversity beyond 2000." *ASNE Blog*, February 19, 1998. www.asne.org.

———. 2017. "The ASNE Newsroom Diversity Survey 2017." October 10, 2017. www.asne.org.

Aufderheide, Patricia. 1993. *Media Literacy: A Report of the National Leadership Conference on Media Literacy*. Aspen, CO: Aspen Institute.

Azuma, Hiroki. 2009. *Otaku: Japan's Database Animals*. Translated by Jonathan Abel. Minneapolis: University of Minnesota Press.

Bahá'í Office of Social and Economic Development. 2012. *Social Action*. Haifa, Israel: Bahá'í World Centre, November 26, 2012.

Baldasty, Gerald J. 1992. *The Commercialization of News in the Nineteenth Century*. Madison: University of Wisconsin Press.

Bales, Fred. 1986. "Television Use and Confidence in Television by Blacks and Whites in Four Selected Years." *Journal of Black Studies* 16 (3): 283–91.

Bancel, Nicolas, Thomas David, and Dominic Thomas. 2014. *The Invention of Race: Scientific and Popular Representations*. Routledge Studies in Cultural History 28. New York: Routledge.

Banerjee, Abhijit, Donald Green, Jeffery McManus, and Rohini Pande. 2014. "Are Poor Voters Indifferent to Whether Elected Leaders Are Criminal or Corrupt? A Vignette Experiment in Rural India." *Political Communication* 31 (3): 391–407.

Banet-Weiser, Sarah. 2012. *Authentic™: The Politics of Ambivalence in a Brand Culture*. New York: NYU Press.

Barthel, Michael, and Amy Mitchell. 2017. "Americans' Attitudes about the News Media Deeply Divided along Partisan Lines." Pew Research Center. May 10, 2017.

Bartlett, Robin L., and Susan F. Feiner. 1996. "Balancing the Economics Curriculum: Content, Method, and Pedagogy." *Alternative Pedagogies and Economic Education*, May 1996, 559–64.

Bashi, Vilna. 2004. "Globalized Anti-Blackness: Transnationalizing Western Immigration Law, Policy, and Practice." *Ethnic and Racial Studies* 27 (4): 584–606. https://doi.org/10.1080/01491987042000216726.

Baum, Dan. 1996. *Smoke and Mirrors: The War on Drugs and the Politics of Failure*. Boston: Back Bay Books.

Becerra, David, David K. Androff, Cecilia Ayón, and Jason T. Castillo. 2012. "Fear vs. Facts: Examining the Economic Impact of Undocumented Immigrants in the U.S." *Journal of Sociology and Social Welfare* 39 (4): article 7. https://scholarworks.wmich.edu.

Becker, Howard S. 1963. *Outsiders: Studies in the Sociology of Deviance*. New York: Free Press.

Beckett, Katherine, Kris Nyrop, and Lori Pfingst. 2006. "Race, Drugs, and Policing: Understanding Disparities in Drug Delivery Arrests." *Criminology* 44 (1): 105–37.

Beckett, Katherine, Kris Nyrop, Lori Pfingst, and Melissa Bowen. 2005. "Drug Use, Drug Arrests, and the Question of Race: Lessons from Seattle." *Social Problems* 52 (3): 419–41.

Behnken, Brian D., and Gregory D. Smithers. 2015. *Racism in American Popular Media: From Aunt Jemima to the Frito Bandito*. Santa Barbara, CA: ABC-CLIO.

Beier, J. Marshall. 2005. *International Relations in Uncommon Places*. New York: Palgrave Macmillan.

Benford, Robert D., and Scott A. Hunt. 1992. "Dramaturgy and Social Movements: The Social Construction and Communication of Power." *Sociological Inquiry* 62 (1): 36–55.

Benjamin, Ruha. 2016. "Informed Refusal: Toward a Justice-Based Bioethics." *Science, Technology, and Human Values* 41 (6): 967–90. https://doi.org/10.1177/0162243916656059.

Bennett, W. Lance. 1990. "Toward a Theory of Press-State Relations in the United States." *Journal of Communication* 40 (2): 103–27.

Berg, Charles Ramírez. 2002. *Latino Images in Film: Stereotypes, Subversion, and Resistance.* Austin: University of Texas Press.

Berger, Peter L., and Thomas Luckmann. 1991. *The Social Construction of Reality: A Treatise in the Sociology of Knowledge.* Harmondsworth, UK: Penguin Books.

Berson, Ginny Z. 2014. *How Southern California Public Radio Opened Their Doors to Latinos and Became the Most Listened-To Public Station in Los Angeles: A Case Study.* Lake Mary, FL: Latino Public Radio Consortium. https://latinopublicradio consortium.org.

Bérubé, Michael. 2009. "What's the Matter with Cultural Studies?" *Chronicle of Higher Education,* September 14, 2009.

Binning, Kevin R., Miguel M. Unzueta, Yuen J. Huo, and Ludwin E. Molina. 2009. "The Interpretation of Multiracial Status and Its Relation to Social Engagement and Psychological Well-Being." *Journal of Social Issues* 65 (1): 35–49. https://doi.org/10.1111/j.1540-4560.2008.01586.x.

Bishoff, Tanya, and Jo Rankin, eds. 1997. *Seeds from a Silent Tree: An Anthology by Korean Adoptees.* Glendale, CA: Pandal Print.

Blackmon, Sha'Kema M., Laura D. Coyle, Sheron Davenport, Archandria C. Owens, and Christopher Sparrow. 2016. "Linking Racial-Ethnic Socialization to Culture and Race-Specific Coping among African American College Students." *Journal of Black Psychology* 42 (6): 549–76.

Bliss, Catherine. 2015. "Defining Health Justice in the Postgenomic Era." In *Postgenomics: Perspectives on Biology after the Genome,* edited by Sarah S. Richardson and Hallam Stevens, 174–91. Durham, NC: Duke University Press.

Blosser, Betsy J. 1988. "Ethnic Differences in Children's Media Use." *Journal of Broadcasting and Electronic Media* 32 (4): 453–70. https://doi.org/10.1080/08838158809386716.

Bødker, Henrik. 2016. "Stuart Hall's Encoding/Decoding Model and the Circulation of Journalism." *Critical Studies in Media Communication* 33 (5): 409–23.

Bogle, Donald. 2001. *Toms, Coons, Mulattoes, Mammies, and Bucks: An Interpretive History of Blacks in American Films.* 4th ed. New York: Continuum.

Bonilla, Yarimar, and Jonathan Rosa. 2015. "#Ferguson: Digital Protest, Hashtag Ethnography, and the Racial Politics of Social Media in the United States." *American Ethnologist* 42 (1): 4–17.

Bonilla-Silva, Eduardo. 1997. "Rethinking Racism: Toward a Structural Interpretation of Racism." *American Sociological Review* 62 (3): 465–80.

———. 1999. "The Essential Social Fact of Race." *American Sociological Review* 64 (6): 899–906.

———. 2014. *Racism without Racists: Color-Blind Racism and the Persistence of Racial Inequality in Contemporary America.* 4th ed. Lanham, MD: Rowman and Littlefield.

Bonilla-Silva, Eduardo, and Tyrone A. Forman. 2000. "'I Am Not a Racist but . . .': Mapping White College Students' Racial Ideology in the USA." *Discourse and Society* 11 (1): 50–85. https://doi.org/10.1177/0957926500011001003.

Borshay Liem, Deann. 2000. *First Person Plural*. PBS and Mu Films. Documentary film.

———. 2010. *In the Matter of Cha Jung Hee*. PBS and Mu Films. Documentary film.

———. Forthcoming. *Geographies of Kinship: The Korean Adoption Story*. Mu Films. Documentary film.

Bossenger, Alyssa. 2017. "A Taste for Brown Sugar: Black Women in Pornography." *Feminist Review* 115 (1): 191–92. https://doi.org/10.1057/s41305-017-0033-3.

Boyd, Danah. 2011. "White Flight in Networked Publics? How Race and Class Shaped American Teen Engagement with Myspace and Facebook." In *Race after the Internet*, edited by Lisa Nakamura and Peter A. Chow-White, 203–22. New York: Routledge.

Brady, Patricia. 2011. *A Being So Gentle: The Frontier Love Story of Rachel and Andrew Jackson*. New York: Palgrave Macmillan.

Brantley, Phillip J., Erin L. O'Hea, Glenn Jones, and Dan J. Mehan. 2002. "The Influence of Income Level and Ethnicity on Coping Strategies." *Journal of Psychopathology and Behavioral Assessment* 24 (1): 39–45. https://doi.org/10.1023/a:1014001208005.

Brian, Kristi. 2012. *Reframing Transracial Adoption: Adopted South Koreans, White Parents, and the Politics of Kinship*. Philadelphia: Temple University Press.

Brock, André. 2012. "From the Blackhand Side: Twitter as a Cultural Conversation." *Journal of Broadcasting and Electronic Media* 56 (4): 529–49.

Brooks, Daphne A. 2016. "How #BlackLivesMatter Started a Musical Revolution." *Guardian*, March 13, 2016. www.theguardian.com.

Brown, Joseph Epes, with Emily Cousins. 2001. "There Is No Word for Art: The Creative Process." Chap. 5 of *Teaching Spirits: Understanding Native American Religious Traditions*, 61–82. New York: Oxford University Press.

Brown, Kristin. 2013. "Somebody Poisoned the Jury Pool: Social Media's Effect on Jury Impartiality." *Texas Wesleyan Law Review* 19 (3): 809–35.

Brown, Michael K., Martin Carnoy, Elliott Currie, Troy Duster, and David B. Oppenheimer. 2003. *Whitewashing Race: The Myth of a Color-Blind Society*. Berkeley: University of California Press.

Browne, Simone. 2015. *Dark Matters: On the Surveillance of Blackness*. Durham, NC: Duke University Press.

Bruns, Axel. 2008. "The Future Is User-Led: The Path towards Widespread Produsage." *Fibreculture Journal* 11:1–9.

Byrd, W. Carson, Matthew W. Hughey, Tukufu Zuberi, Evelyn J. Patterson, and Quincy Thomas Stewart. 2015. "Race, Methodology, and Social Construction in the Genomic Era." *Annals of the American Academy of Political and Social Science* 661 (1): 109–27. https://doi.org/10.1177/0002716215589718.

Campbell, Christopher P. 2016. "Representation: Stuart Hall and the 'Politics of Signi-fication.'" In *The Routledge Companion to Media and Race*, edited by Christopher P. Campbell, 11–18. London: Routledge.

Carby, Hazel. 2009. "Becoming Modern Racialized Subjects: Detours through Our Pasts to Produce Ourselves Anew." *Cultural Studies* 23 (4): 624–57.

Carey, James. 1989. *Communication as Culture: Essays on Media and Society*. Crows Nest, Australia: Unwin Hyman.

Carlson, Elizabeth, Gladys Rowe, Teddy Zegeye-Gebrehiwot, and Sarah Story. 2017. "Decolonization through Collaborative Filmmaking." *Journal of Indigenous Social Development* 6 (2): 23–49.

Carney, Nikita. 2016. "All Lives Matter, but So Does Race." *Humanity and Society* 40 (2): 180–99.

Carson, Clayborne. 2005. "To Walk in Dignity: The Montgomery Bus Boycott." *OAH Magazine of History* 19 (1): 13–15.

Carter, Zach. 2016. "A GOP Congressman Wants to Defund the Harriet Tubman $20. Really." *Huffington Post*, June 20, 2016. www.huffingtonpost.com.

Casillas, Delores-Ines. 2014. *Sounds of Belonging: US Spanish-Language Radio and Public Advocacy*. New York: NYU Press.

Castells, Manuel. 2007. "Communication, Power and Counter-power in the Network Society." *International Journal of Communication* 1 (1): 238–66.

———. 2011. "A Network Theory of Power." *International Journal of Communication* 5:773–87.

Ceniza Choy, Catherine. 2013. *Global Families: A History of Asian International Adoption in America*. New York: NYU Press.

———. 2016. "A History of Asian International Adoption in the United States." In *The Oxford Handbook of Asian American History*, edited by David K. Yoo and Eiichiro Azuma, 205–21. New York: Oxford University Press.

Center for the Study of Hate and Extremism. 2017. "Final U.S. Status Report Hate Crime Analysis & Forecast for 2016/2017." College of Social and Behavioral Sciences, California State University, San Bernardino. https://csbs.csusb.edu.

Chambers, Jason. 2008. *Madison Avenue and the Color Line: African Americans in the Advertising Industry*. Philadelphia: University of Pennsylvania Press.

Chaney, David. 1996. *Lifestyles*. London: Routledge.

Charmaz, Kathy. 2014. *Constructing Grounded Theory*. Thousand Oaks, CA: Sage.

Chavez, Leo R. 2013. *The Latino Threat: Constructing Immigrants, Citizens, and the Nation*. Stanford, CA: Stanford University Press.

Cheathem, Mark R. 2011. "Andrew Jackson, Slavery and Historians." *History Compass* 9 (4): 326–38.

Chen, Yea-Wen, and Nathaniel Simmons. 2015. "'I Was "Fortunate" Enough to Have Been Born a White Male': Understanding a Cycle of White Consciousness in Inter-cultural Communication Education." *Intercultural Communication Studies* 24 (2): 155–73.

Cheung-Miaw, Kayan. 2016a. "Dear Brother." In "This Heartbreaking Comic Shows Exactly Why We Need Asian-Black Solidarity against Police Brutality," by Sameer Rao. *Colorlines*, March 16, 2016. www.colorlines.com.

———. 2016b. "Two Mothers (English Version)." Tumblr. Accessed October 1, 2018. http://kayancheung.tumblr.com/post/142908473809.

Chideya, Farai. 2018. "In the Shadow of Kerner: Fifty Years Later, Newsroom Diversity and Equity Stall." Shorenstein Center on Media, Politics and Public Policy, Harvard Kennedy School. May 2018.

Child, Ben. 2013. "Italian Posters for *12 Years a Slave* Herald Brad Pitt over Chiwetel Ejiofor." *Guardian*, December 24, 2013. Accessed December 20, 2017. www.the guardian.com.

———. 2015. "DreamWorks Accused of 'Whitewashing' Ghost in the Shell by Casting Scarlett Johansson." *Guardian*, January 16, 2015. www.theguardian.com.

Christian, Aymar Jean. 2016. "Video Stars: Marketing Queer Performance in Networked Television." In *The Intersectional Internet: Race, Sex, Class, and Culture Online*, edited by Safiya Umoja Noble and Brendesha M. Tynes, 95–114. New York: Peter Lang.

Chuang, Angie, and Robin Chin Roemer. 2015. "Beyond the Positive-Negative Paradigm of Latino/Latina News-Media Representations: DREAM Act Exemplars, Stereotypical Selection, and American Otherness." *Journalism* 16 (8): 1045–61.

Clawson, Rosalee A., and Rakyua Trice. 2000. "Poverty as We Know It—Media Portrayals of the Poor." *Public Opinion Quarterly* 64 (1): 53–64.

Clinton, Catherine. 2004. *Harriet Tubman: The Road to Freedom*. New York: Little, Brown.

Cohen, Stanley. 1972. *Folk Devils and Moral Panics: The Creation of the Mods and Rockers*. London: MacGibbon and Kee.

———. 2011. "Whose Side Were We On? The Undeclared Politics of Moral Panic Theory." *Crime, Media, Culture* 7 (3): 237–43. https://doi.org/10.1177/1741659011417603.

Coleman, Robin R. Means. (1998) 2014. *African American Viewers and the Black Situation Comedy: Situating Racial Humor*. New York: Routledge.

Collins, Ben, and Tim Mak. 2015. "Who Really Runs #BlackLivesMatter?" *Daily Beast*, July 12, 2015. www.thedailybeast.com.

Collins, Patricia Hill. 1986. "Learning from the Outsider Within: The Sociological Significance of Black Feminist Thought." *Social Problems* 33 (6): S14–S32.

———. (1990) 2000. *Black Feminist Thought: Knowledge, Consciousness, and the Politics of Empowerment*. 2nd ed. New York: Routledge.

———. 2004. *Black Sexual Politics: African Americans, Gender, and the New Racism*. New York: Routledge.

Collins, Sharon M. 1989. "The Marginalization of Black Executives." *Social Problems* 36 (4): 317–31. https://doi.org/10.2307/800818.

Comscore. 2008. "U.K. Traditional Media Brands Attract Online Audiences from Around the World." http://www.comscore.com.

Comscore. 2016. "Comscore Ranks the Top 50 U.S. Digital Media Properties for February 2016." http://www.comscore.com.

Conditt, Jessica. 2016. "The Historical Research behind the Biracial Antihero in 'Mafia III.'" Engadget, August 11, 2016. www.engadget.com.

Considine, Austin. 2011. "For Asian-American Stars, Many Web Fans." New York Times, July 29, 2011.

Constantine, Madonna G., and Derald Wing Sue. 2007. "Perceptions of Racial Microaggressions among Black Supervisees in Cross-Racial Dyads." Journal of Counseling Psychology 54 (2): 142–53. https://doi.org/10.1037/0022-0167.54.2.142.

Cooper, Hannah L. F. 2015. "War on Drugs Policing and Police Brutality." Substance Use and Misuse 50 (8–9): 1188–94.

Courbold, Clare. 2017. "Roots, the Legacy of Slavery, and Civil Right Backlash in 1970s America." In Reconsidering Roots: Race, Politics, and Memory, edited by Erica L. Ball and Kellie Carter Jackson, 25–46. Athens: University of Georgia Press.

Crenshaw, Kimberlé. 1991. "Mapping the Margins: Intersectionality, Identity Politics, and Violence against Women of Color." Stanford Law Review 43 (6): 1241–99. https://doi.org/10.2307/1229039.

Crenshaw, Kimberlé, Neil Gotanda, Gary Peller, and Kendall Thomas, eds. 1995. Critical Race Theory: The Key Writings That Formed the Movement. New York: New Press.

Cripps, Thomas. 1977. Slow Fade to Black: The Negro in American Film, 1900–1942. New York: Oxford University Press.

Croteau, David, and William Hoynes. 1994. By Invitation Only. Monroe, ME: Common Courage.

———. 2014. Media/Society: Industries, Images, and Audiences. Thousand Oaks, CA: Sage.

Curran, James, Michael Gurevitch, and Janette Woollacott. 1985. "The Study of the Media: Theoretical Approaches." In Culture, Society and the Media, edited by Michael Gurevitch, Tony Bennett, James Curran, and Janette Woollacott. London: Methuen.

Daily Stormer. n.d. Home page. Accessed January 20, 2020. https://dailystormer.name.

Daniels, J. Yolande. 2000. "Black Bodies, Black Space: A Waiting Spectacle." In White Papers, Black Marks: Architecture, Race, and Culture, edited by Lesley Naa Norle Lokko, 194–217. Minneapolis: University of Minnesota Press.

Daniels, Jessie. 2009. Cyber Racism: White Supremacy Online and the New Attack on Civil Rights. Lanham, MD: Rowman and Littlefield.

Daniels, Shonté. 2015. "Video Games, Violence, and the Black Lives Matter Movement: How My Hobby Became a Trigger." Rewire.News, June 3, 2015. https://rewire.news.

Dávila, Arlene. 2008. Latino Spin: Public Image and the Whitewashing of Race. New York: NYU Press.

Day, Iyko. 2016. Alien Capital: Asian Radicalization and the Logic of Settler Colonial Capitalism. Durham, NC: Duke University Press.

Dayan, Daniel, and Elihu Katz. 1992. Media Events: The Live Broadcasting of History. Cambridge, MA: Harvard University Press.

Dear White People Wiki. n.d. "Pastiche." Accessed January 16, 2020. https://dearwhite people.fandom.com.

De La Cruz, Sonia. 2017. "Latino Airwaves: Radio Bilingüe and Spanish-Language Public Radio." *Journal of Radio and Audio Media* 24:226–37.

Delgado, Richard, and Jean Stefancic. 2012. *Critical Race Theory: An Introduction.* New York: NYU Press.

Deloria, Philip J. 1999. *Playing Indian.* New Haven, CT: Yale University Press.

Denzin, Norman. 2001. "Symbolic Interactionism, Poststructuralism, and the Racial Subject." *Symbolic Interaction* 24 (2): 243–49.

DiAngelo, Robin. 2018. *White Fragility: Why It's So Hard for White People to Talk about Racism.* Boston: Beacon.

Dillard, Cynthia. 2000. "The Substance of Things Hoped For, the Evidence of Things Not Seen: Examining an Endarkened Feminist Epistemology in Educational Research and Leadership." *International Journal of Qualitative Studies in Education* 13 (6): 661–81.

DiMaggio, Paul, Eszter Hargittai, W. Russell Neuman, and John P. Robinson. 2001. "Social Implications of the Internet." *Annual Review of Sociology* 27:307–36.

Dixon, Travis L. 2007. "Black Criminals and White Officers: The Effects of Racially Misrepresenting Law Breakers and Law Defenders on Television News." *Media Psychology* 10 (2): 270–91.

———. 2017a. "A Dangerous Distortion of Our Families: Representations of Families, by Race, in News and Opinion Media." Color of Change. January 2017. https://colorof change.org.

———. 2017b. "Good Guys Are Still Always in White? Positive Change and Continued Misrepresentation of Race and Crime on Local Television News." *Communication Research* 44 (6): 775–92.

Docan-Morgan, Sara. 2010. "Korean Adoptees' Retrospective Reports of Intrusive Interactions: Exploring Boundary Management in Adoptive Families." *Journal of Family Communication* 10 (3): 137–57.

Dorfman, Lori, and Ingrid Daffner Krasnow. 2014. "Public Health and Media Advocacy." *Annual Review of Public Health* 35 (1): 293–306.

Downing, John, and Charles Husband. 2005. *Representing "Race": Racisms, Ethnicities and Media.* London: Sage.

Du Bois, W. E. B. (1903) 1994. *The Souls of Black Folk.* New York: Dover.

———. 1926. "Criteria of Negro Art." *Crisis* 32 (6): 290–97.

Duffett, Mark. 2013. "Ghetto Voyeurism? Cross-Racial Listening and the Attribution of Sociocultural Distance in Popular Music." *Volume! La Revue des Musiques Populai-res* 10 (1) : 111–25. https://doi.org/10.4000/volume.3820.

du Gay, Paul, Stuart Hall, Linda Janes, Anders Koed Madsen, Hugh Mackay, and Keith Negus. 1997. *Doing Cultural Studies: The Story of the Sony Walkman.* Thousand Oaks, CA: Sage.

Durkheim, Emile. (1912) 1965. *The Elementary Forms of Religious Life.* New York: Free Press.

Dyer, Richard. 1997. *White*. London: Routledge.

Dyer-Witheford, Nick, and Greig de Peuter. *Games of Empire: Global Capitalism and Video Games*. Minneapolis: University of Minnesota Press, 2009.

Earl, Jennifer, and Katrina Kimport. 2011. *Digitally Enabled Social Change: Activism in the Internet Age*. Cambridge, MA: MIT Press.

Ebiri, Bilge. 2013. "A Tale Twice Told: Comparing *12 Years a Slave* to 1984's TV Movie *Solomon Northup's Odyssey*." *Vulture*, November 11, 2013. www.vulture.com.

Eisensee, Thomas, and David Strömberg. 2007. "News Droughts, News Floods, and U.S. Disaster Relief." *Quarterly Journal of Economics* 122 (2): 693–728.

Elliott, Philip. 1981. "Press Performance as Political Ritual." *Sociological Review* 29 (1): 141–77.

Engelman, Ralph. 1996. *Public Radio and Television in America: A Political History*. Thousand Oaks, CA: Sage.

Enloe, Cynthia. 2004. *The Curious Feminist*. Berkeley: University of California Press.

Entman, Robert M. 1994. "Representation and Reality in the Portrayal of Blacks on Network Television News." *Journalism and Mass Communication Quarterly* 71 (3): 509.

———. 2004. *Projections of Power: Framing News, Public Opinion, and U.S. Foreign Policy*. Chicago: University of Chicago Press.

———. 2007. "Framing Bias: Media in the Distribution of Power." *Journal of Communication* 57 (1): 163–73.

Entman, Robert M., and Andrew Rojecki. 2001. *The Black Image in the White Mind*. Chicago: University of Chicago Press.

Erigha, Maryann. 2019. *The Hollywood Jim Crow: The Racial Politics of the Movie Industry*. New York: NYU Press.

Everbach, Tracy, Meredith Clark, and Gwendelyn S. Nisbett. 2017. "#IfTheyGunnedMeDown: An Analysis of Mainstream and Social Media in the Ferguson, Missouri, Shooting of Michael Brown." *Electronic News* 12 (1): 23–41.

Ewen, Elizabeth, and Stuart Ewen. 2011. *Typecasting: On the Arts and Sciences of Human Inequality*. New York: Seven Stories.

Ewen, Stuart. 1996. *PR! A Social History of Spin*. New York: Basic Books.

Falk, Tyler. 2015. "Drop in Younger Listeners Makes Dent in NPR News Audience." *Current*, October 16, 2015. https://current.org.

Farhi, Paul. 2015. "NPR Is Graying, and Public Radio Is Worried about It." *Washington Post*, November 22, 2015.

Feagin, Joe R. 2013. *The White Racial Frame: Centuries of Racial Framing and Counter Framing*. 2nd ed. New York: Routledge.

Fellner, Jamie. 2009. "Race, Drugs, and Law Enforcement in the United States." *Stanford Law and Policy Review* 20 (2): 257–91.

Felson, Richard B. 1996. "Mass Media Effects on Violent Behavior." *Annual Review of Sociology* 22:103–28.

Fernandez, John P. 1981. *Racism and Sexism in Corporate Life: Changing Values in American Business*. Lexington, MA: Lexington Books.

Ferraz, Claudio, and Frederico Finan. 2008. "Exposing Corrupt Politicians: The Effects of Brazil's Publicly Released Audits on Electoral Outcomes." *Quarterly Journal of Economics*, May 2008, 703–45.

Ferree, Myra Marx, William Anthony Gamson, Jurgen Gerhards, and Dieter Rucht. 2002. *Shaping Abortion Discourse: Democracy and the Public Sphere in Germany and the United States*. New York: Cambridge University Press.

Fields, Karen E., and Barbara Fields. 1994. *Racecraft: The Soul of Inequality in American Life*. New York: Verso.

Flores, Lisa A., and Christy-Dale L. Sims. 2016. "The Zero-Sum Game of Race and the Familiar Strangeness of President Obama." *Southern Communication Journal* 81 (4): 206–22.

Flores-Yeffal, Nadia Y., Guadalupe Vidales, and Girsea Martinez. 2017. "#WakeUp-America, #IllegalsAreCriminals: The Role of the Cyber Public Sphere in the Perpetuation of the Latino Cyber-Moral Panic in the US." *Information, Communication and Society* 22 (3): 402–19.

Flores-Yeffal, Nadia Y., Guadalupe Vidales, and April Plemons. 2011. "The Latino Cyber-Moral Panic Process in the United States." *Information, Communication and Society* 14 (4): 568–89.

Folkenflik, David. 2015. "Univision Anchor Jorge Ramos Removed from Trump Press Conference." NPR, August 26, 2015. www.npr.org.

Foner, Nancy. 2000. *From Ellis Island to JFK: New York's Two Great Waves of Immigration*. New Haven, CT: Yale University Press.

Foss, Sonja. 1989. *Rhetorical Criticism: Exploration and Practice*. Long Grove, IL: Waveland.

Foucault, Michel. 1978. *The History of Sexuality, Volume 1: An Introduction*. Translated by Robert Hurley. New York: Vintage Books.

———. 1984. "The Order of Discourse." In *Language and Politics*, edited by Michael Shapiro, 108–38. Oxford: Oxford University Press.

———. 2012. "Discipline and Punish (from *Discipline and Punish: The Birth of the Prison*)." In *Contemporary Sociological Theory*, edited by Craig Calhoun, Joseph Gerteis, James Moody, Steven Pfaff, and Indermohan Virk, 3rd ed., 314–22. Chichester, UK: Wiley.

Frankel, Max. 1970. "Is 'Benign Neglect' the Real Nixon Approach?" *New York Times*, March 8, 1970.

Frasca, Gozalo. 2006. "Video Games of the Oppressed: Critical Thinking, Education, Tolerance, and Other Trivial Issues." In *First Person: New Media as Story, Performance, and Game*, edited by Noah Wardrip-Fruin and Pat Harrigan, 85–94. Cambridge, MA: MIT Press.

Freelon, Deen, Charlton McIlwain, and Meredith Clark. 2018. "Quantifying the Power and Consequences of Social Media Protest." *New Media and Society* 20 (3): 990–1011.

Freeman, Jo. 2015. "The Tyranny of Structurelessness." *Women's Studies Quarterly* 41 (3): 231–46.

Freire, Paulo. (1970) 2005. *Pedagogy of the Oppressed*. Translated by Myra Bergman Ramos. 30th Anniversary Edition. New York: Continuum.

Fresh Air. 2013. "'12 Years a Slave' Was a Film That 'No One Was Making.'" NPR, October 24, 2013. www.npr.org.

Frissell, Peregrine, Ala'a Ibrahim, Sheila Raghavendran, and Avery Yang. 2017. "Missed Deadline: The Delayed Promise of Newsroom Diversity." *AAJA Voices*, July 25, 2017. https://voices.aaja.org/index/2017/7/25/missed-deadlines.

Fujikane, Candace, and Jonathan Y. Okamura. 2008. *Asian Settler Colonialism: From Local Governance to the Habits of Everyday Life in Hawai'i*. Honolulu: University of Hawai'i Press.

Fujioka, Yuki. 1999. "Television Portrayals and African-American Stereotypes: Examination of Television Effects When Direct Contact Is Lacking." *Journalism and Mass Communication Quarterly* 76 (1): 52–75.

Futerman, Samantha, and Ryan Miyamoto, dirs. 2015. *Twinsters*. Netflix. Documentary film.

Gaines, Jane M. 1999. "Political Mimesis." In *Collecting Visible Evidence*, edited by Jane M. Gaines and Michael Renov, 84–102. Minneapolis: University of Minnesota Press.

Gallagher, Ryan J., Andrew J. Reagan, Christopher M. Danforth, and Peter Sheridan Dodds. 2018. "Divergent Discourse between Protests and Counter-protests: #BlackLivesMatter and #AllLivesMatter." *PLoS One* 13 (4): 1–23.

Gamson, William A., David Croteau, William Hoynes, and Theodore Sasson. 1992. "Media Images and the Social Construction of Reality." *Annual Review of Sociology* 18:373–93.

Gamson, William A., and Andre Modigliani. 1989. "Media Discourse and Public Opinion on Nuclear Power." *American Journal of Sociology* 95 (1): 1–37.

Gamson, William A., and Gadi Wolfsfeld. 1993. "Movements and Media as Interacting Systems." *Annals of the American Academy of Political and Social Science* 528 (1): 114–25.

Gao, Cindy. 2012. "The Virtuosic Virtuality of Asian American YouTube Stars." *Scholar and Feminist Online* 10 (3). http://sfonline.barnard.edu.

Gardner, Sheena K., and Matthew W. Hughey. 2017. "Still the Tragic Mulatto? Manufacturing Multiracialization in Magazine Media, 1961–2011." *Ethnic and Racial Studies* 42 (4): 645–65. https://doi.org/10.1080/01419870.2017.1380212.

Garrahan, Matthew, and Henry Sender. 2016. "Chinese Investors Flood into Hollywood." *Financial Times*, June 7, 2016. www.ft.com.

Garza, Alicia. 2014. "A Herstory of the Black Lives Matter Movement." Accessed January 29, 2019, at Black Lives Matter. www.blacklivesmatter.com.

Gay, Roxanne. 2013. "Justine Sacco's Aftermath: The Cost of Twitter Outrage." *Salon*, December 23, 2013. www.salon.com.

Gerbaudo, Paolo. 2012. *Tweets and the Streets: Social Media and Contemporary Activism*. London: Pluto.

Gershon, Ilana. 2017. "Language and the Newness of Media." *Annual Review of Anthropology* 46 (1): 15–31.

Giddings, Paula. 1985. *When and Where I Enter*. New York: Bantam Books.

Gilens, Martin. 1996. "Race and Poverty in America: Public Misperceptions and the American News Media." *Public Opinion Quarterly* 60:515–41.

———. 1999. *Why Americans Hate Welfare: Race, Media, and the Politics of Antipoverty Policy*. Chicago: University of Chicago Press.

———. 2000. "The Black Poor and the 'Liberal Press.'" *Civil Rights Journal* 5 (1): 18–26.

———. 2004. "Poor People in the News: Images from the Journalistic Subconscious." In *Class and News*, edited by Don Heider, 44–60. Lanham, MD: Rowman and Littlefield.

Gillborn, David. 2006a. "Critical Race Theory and Education: Racism and Anti-racism in Educational Theory and Praxis." *Discourse: Studies in the Cultural Politics of Education* 27:11–32.

———. 2006b. "Rethinking White Supremacy: Who Counts in 'White World.'" *Ethnicities* 6 (3): 318–40. https://doi.org/10.1177/1468796806068323.

Gilliam, Franklin D., Jr., and Shanto Iyengar. 2000. "Prime Suspects: The Influence of Local Television News on the Viewing Public." *American Journal of Political Science*: 44 (3): 560–73.

Gilmore, Ruth. 2007. *Golden Gulag: Prisons, Surplus, Crisis, and Opposition in Globalizing California*. Berkeley: University of California Press.

Glasser, Theodore L. 1984. "Objectivity Precludes Responsibility." *Quill*, February 1984, 13–16.

Glenn, Evelyn Nakano. 2002. *Unequal Freedom*. Cambridge, MA: Harvard University Press.

Goffman, Erving. 1959. *The Presentation of Self in Everyday Life*. New York: Anchor Doubleday.

———. 1986. "The Frame Analysis of Talk." In *Frame Analysis: An Essay on the Organization of Experience*, 496–60. Boston: Northeastern University Press.

Goldberg, Bernard. 2002. *Bias: A CBS Insider Exposes How the Media Distort the News*. Washington, DC: Regnery.

Golder, Scott A., and Michael W. Macy. 2014. "Digital Footprints: Opportunities and Challenges for Online Social Research." *Annual Review of Sociology* 40:129–52.

Golding, Peter, and Graham Murdock. 1991. "Culture, Communications, and Political Economy." In *Mass Media and Society*, edited by James Curran and Michael Gurevitch, 15–32. London: Edward Arnold.

Gonzalez-Sobrino, Bianca, and Matthew W. Hughey. 2015. "All the *Puertorriqueñidad* That's Fit to Print: UnAmerican Racial Citizens in *The New York Times* (1948–1958)." *Critical Sociology* 43 (7–8): 1009–28.

Gonzalez-Sobrino, Bianca, Emma Lesser, and Matthew W. Hughey. 2018. "On-Demand Diversity? The Meanings of Racial Diversity in Netflix Productions." In *Challenging the Status-Quo: Diversity, Democracy, and Equality in the 21st Century*, edited by David G. Embrick, Sharon M. Collins, and Michelle S. Dodson, 321–24. Leiden, Netherlands: Brill.

Goode, Erich, and Nachman Ben-Yehuda. 1994. *Moral Panics: The Social Construction of Deviance*. Chichester, UK: Wiley-Blackwell.

Goodman, Ronald. 1992. *Lakota Star Knowledge: Studies in Lakota Stellar Theology*. Mission, SD: Sinte Gleska University.

Gordon, Avery. 2011. "Some Thoughts on Haunting and Futurity." *Borderlands* 10 (2): 1–21.

Goslett, Miles. 2009. "Race Row as Black Stars Are Left Out of *Couples Retreat* Film Poster." *Daily Mail*, November 15, 2009. www.dailymail.co.uk.

Grabe, Maria Elizabeth, Shuhua Zhou, and Brooke Barnett. 2001. "Explicating Sensationalism in Television News: Content and the Bells and Whistles of Form." *Journal of Broadcasting and Electronic Media* 45 (4): 635–55.

Grady, Constance. 2018. "Daniel Mallory Ortberg Talks The Toast, The Merry Spinster, and the Joys of Peanut Butter." *Vox*, March 13, 2018. www.vox.com.

Gramsci, Antonio. 1992. *Prison Notebooks*. Vol. 1. Translated by J. A. Buttigieg. New York: Columbia University Press.

Grande, Sandy. 2015. *Red Pedagogy: Native American Social and Political Thought*. Lanham, MD: Rowman and Littlefield.

Graves, Sherryl Browne. 1999. "Television and Prejudice Reduction: When Does Television as a Vicarious Experience Make a Difference?" *Journal of Social Issues* 55 (4): 707–27. https://doi.org/10.1111/0022-4537.00143.

Gray, Kishonna L. 2012a. "Deviant Bodies, Stigmatized Identities, and Racist Acts: Examining the Experiences of African-American Gamers in Xbox Live." *New Review of Hypermedia and Multimedia* 18 (4): 261–76. https://doi.org/10.1080/13614568.2012.746740.

———. 2012b. "Intersecting Oppressions and Online Communities." *Information, Communication and Society* 15 (3): 411–28. https://doi.org/10.1080/1369118x.2011.642401.

———. 2014. *Race, Gender, and Deviance in Xbox Live: Theoretical Perspectives from the Virtual Margins*. New York: Routledge.

———. In press. *Intersectional Tech: Black Users in Digital Gaming*. Baton Rouge: Louisiana State University Press.

Gray, Kishonna L., and David J. Leonard, eds. 2018. *Woke Gaming: Digital Challenges to Oppression and Social Injustice*. Seattle: University of Washington Press.

Greenberg, Bradley S. 1972. "Children's Reactions to TV Blacks." *Journalism Quarterly* 49 (1): 5–14. https://doi.org/10.1177/107769907204900101.

Grieco, Elizabeth. 2018. "Newsroom Employees Are Less Diverse than U.S. Workers Overall." Pew Research Center. November 2, 2018. www.pewresearch.org.

Grindstaff, Laura, and Joseph Turow. 2006. "Video Cultures: Television Sociology in the 'New TV' Age." *Annual Review of Sociology* 32:103–25.

Groeling, Tim. 2013. "Media Bias by the Numbers: Challenges and Opportunities in the Empirical Study of Partisan News." *Annual Review of Political Science* 16:129–51.

Grossberg, Lawrence. 2006. "Does Cultural Studies Have Futures? Should It? (Or What's the Matter with New York?)." *Cultural Studies* 20 (1): 1–32.

Grynbaum, Michael M. 2017. "Trump Calls the News Media the 'Enemy of the American People.'" *New York Times*, February 18, 2017, A15.

Guinier, Lani. 2004. "From Racial Liberalism to Racial Literacy: *Brown v. Board of Education* and the Interest-Divergence Dilemma." *Journal of American History* 91 (1): 92–118.

Gunarathne, Priyanga, Huaxia Rui, and Abraham Seidmann. 2018. "Racial Bias in Social Media Customer Service: Evidence from Twitter." Paper presented at the Thirty-Ninth International Conference on Information Systems, San Francisco.

Habermas, Jürgen. 1970. "Towards a Theory of Communicative Competence." *Inquiry: An Interdisciplinary Journal of Philosophy* 13:360–75.

———. 1989. *The Structural Transformation of the Public Sphere*. Cambridge, MA: MIT Press.

Habermas, Tilmann, and Susan Bluck. 2000. "Getting a Life: The Emergence of the Life Story in Adolescence." *Psychological Bulletin* 126 (5): 748–69.

Habermas, Tilmann, and Cybèle de Silveira. 20008. "The Development of Global Coherence in Life Narratives across Adolescence: Temporal, Causal, and Thematic Aspects." *Developmental Psychology* 44 (3): 707–21.

Hall, Stuart. (1973) 1991. "Encoding and Decoding in the Television Discourse." In *The Cultural Studies Reader*, edited by Simon During, 90–103. London: Routledge.

———. 1980. "Encoding/Decoding." In *Culture, Media, Language—Working Papers in Cultural Studies, 1972–79*, edited by Stuart Hall, Dorothy Hobson, Andrew Lowe, and Paul Willis, 128–38. London: Routledge.

———. 1981. "Notes on Deconstructing 'the Popular.'" In *People's History and Socialist Theory*, edited by Raphael Samuel, 227–39. London: Routledge.

———. 1988. *The Hard Road to Renewal: Thatcherism and the Crisis of the Left*. New York: Verso.

———. 1992. "New Ethnicities." In *Race, Culture and Difference*, edited by James Donald and Ali Rattansi, 252–59. London: Sage.

———. 1993a. "Encoding, Decoding." In *The Cultural Studies Reader*, edited by Simon During, 90–103. London: Routledge.

———. 1993b. "What Is This 'Black' in Black Popular Culture?" *Social Justice* 20 (1–2): 104–14.

———. 2013. "The Spectacle of the Other." In *Representation: Cultural Representations and Signifying Practices*, 2nd ed., edited by Stuart Hall, Jessica Evans, and Sean Nixon, 215–70. London: Sage.

———. 2017. *Familiar Stranger: A Life between Two Islands*. Durham, NC: Duke University Press.

Hall, Stuart, Chas Critcher, Tony Jefferson, John Clarke, and Brian Roberts. 1978. *Policing the Crisis: Mugging, the State, and Law and Order*. London: Palgrave.

Hall, Stuart, and Sut Jhally. 1997. "Race—the Floating Signifier." Media Education Foundation. https://msu.edu.

Haney López, Ian F. 2007. "Post-racial Racism: Racial Stratification and Mass Incarceration in the Age of Obama." *California Law Review* 98 (3): 1023–74.

Haney López, Ian F. 2014. *Dog Whistle Politics: How Coded Racial Appeals Have Reinvented Racism and Wrecked the Middle Class*. Oxford: Oxford University Press.

Harper, Hilliard. 1988. "Latinos Protest NPR Move to Ax 'Enfoque.'" *Los Angeles Times*, March 3, 1988.

Harris, Cheryl I. 1993. "Whiteness as Property." *Harvard Law Review* 106 (8): 1709–91.

Harris, Tina M. 2001. "Student Reactions to the Visual Texts *The Color of Fear* and *Rosewood* in the Interracial Classroom." *Howard Journal of Communications* 12 (2): 101–17.

Harris, Tina M., Anastacia Janovec, Steven Murray, Sneha Gubbala, and Aspen Robinson. 2018. "Communicating Racism: A Study of Racial Microaggressions in a Southern University and the Local Community." *Southern Communication Journal*, September 2018, 1–13. https://doi.org/10.1080/1041794X.2018_1492008.

Harris, Tina M., and Mollie Murphy. 2017. "Race/Ethnicity in the Classroom." In *Handbook of Instructional Communication, Rhetorical and Relational Perspectives*, 2nd ed., edited by Marian L. Houser and Angela M. Hosek. London: Taylor and Francis.

Harris, Tina M., and Rebecca J. Steiner. 2018. "Beyond the Veil: A Critique of White Christian Rhetoric and Racism in the Age of Trump." *Journal of Communication and Religion* 41 (1): 33–45.

Harris, Tina M., and Kirsten Weber. 2010. "Reversal of Privilege: Deconstructing Privilege and Power in the Film *White Man's Burden*." *Communication Law Review* 10 (1): 54–74.

Harris-Lacewell, Melissa. 2006. *Barbershops, Bibles, and BET: Everyday Talk and Black Political Thought*. Princeton, NJ: Princeton University Press.

Hartnell, Anna. 2009. "Katrina Tourism and a Tale of Two Cities: Visualizing Race and Class in New Orleans." *American Quarterly* 61 (3): 723–47.

Hartzell, Stephanie L. 2018. "Alt-White: Conceptualizing the 'Alt-Right' as a Rhetorical Bridge between White Nationalism and Mainstream Public Discourse." *Journal of Contemporary Rhetoric* 8 (1–2): 6–25.

Haynes, Chris, Jennifer Merolla, and S. Karthick Ramakrishnan. 2016. *Framing Immigrants: News Coverage, Public Opinion, and Policy*. New York: Russell Sage Foundation.

Herman, Edward S., and Noam Chomsky. 1988. *Manufacturing Consent: The Political Economy of Mass Media*. New York: Pantheon.

Herold, Benjamin. 2018. "Video Game Design Meets Black Lives Matter and #MeToo." *Education Week*, August 30, 2018. https://blogs.edweek.org.

Hess, Amanda. 2016. "Asian-American Actors Are Fighting for Visibility: They Will Not Be Ignored." *New York Times*, May 25, 2016. www.nytimes.com.

Hesse-Biber, Sharlene Nagy. 2017. *The Practice of Qualitative Research: Engaging Students in the Research Process*. Thousand Oaks, CA: Sage.

Higgin, Tanner. 2009. "Blackless Fantasy: The Disappearance of Race in Massively Multiplayer Online Role-Playing Games." *Games and Culture* 4 (1): 3–26. https://doi.org/10.1177/1555412008325477.

———. 2010. "'Turn the Game Console Off Right Now!' War, Subjectivity, and Control in *Metal Gear Solid 2*." In *Joystick Soldiers: The Politics of Play in Military Video Games*, edited by Nina B. Huntemann and Matthew Thomas Payne, 252–71. New York: Routledge.

Hitlin, Paul, and Nancy Vogt. 2014. "Cable, Twitter Picked Up Ferguson Story at a Similar Clip." Pew Research Center, August 20, 2014. www.pewresearch.org.

Hobson, Janell. 2005. *Venus in the Dark: Blackness and Beauty in Popular Culture*. New York: Routledge.

———. 2014. "Harriet Tubman: A Legacy of Resistance." *Meridians* 12 (2): 1–8.

Hoffmeister, Thaddeus, and Ann Charles Watts. 2018. "Social Media, the Internet, and Trial by Jury." *Annual Review of Law and Social Science* 14:259–70.

Holder, Judith C., and Alan Vaux. 1998. "African American Professionals: Coping with Occupational Stress in Predominantly White Work Environments." *Journal of Vocational Behavior* 53 (3): 315–33. https://doi.org/https://doi.org/10.1006/jvbe.1998.1640.

Holland, Jesse J. 2014. "Black Twitter Flexing Muscles On and Offline." Associated Press, March 10, 2014. http://bigstory.ap.org.

Holmes, Chuck. 2017. "A Message from WBHM Chuck Holmes." WBHM: Public Radio for the Heart of Alabama, January 25, 2017. https://wbhm.org.

Hong, Caroline Kyungah. 2017. "Reframing Police Brutality and Black-Asian Relations through Comics." *Building Asian American Studies*, August 16, 2017. CUNY Academic Commons. https://buildingaas.commons.gc.cuny.edu.

Hooker, Juliet. 2016. "Black Lives Matter and the Paradoxes of U.S. Black Politics: From Democratic Sacrifice to Democratic Repair." *Political Theory* 44 (4): 448–69.

hooks, bell. 1992. "Eating the Other: Desire and Resistance." In *Black Looks: Race and Representation*, 21–39. Boston: South End.

Horn, John, Nicole Sperling, and Doug Smith. 2012. "Unmasking Oscar: Academy Voters Are Overwhelmingly White and Male." *Los Angeles Times*, February 19, 2012. www.latimes.com.

Horton, James Oliver, and Lois Horton, eds. 2006. *Slavery and Public History: The Tough Stuff of American Memory*. New York: New Press.

Howard, Philip N, Aiden Duffy, Deen Freelon, Muzammil Hussain, Will Mari, and Marwa Mazaid. 2011. "Opening Closed Regimes: What Was the Role of Social Media during the Arab Spring?" SSRN. www.ssrn.org.

Howard, Philip N., and Muzammil M. Hussain. 2013. *Democracy's Fourth Wave? Digital Media and the Arab Spring*. Oxford: Oxford University Press.

Hughey, Matthew W. 2009. "Cinethetic Racism: White Redemption and Black Stereotypes in 'Magical Negro' Films." *Social Problems* 56 (3): 543–77.

———. 2012a. "'Show Me Your Papers!' Obama's Birth and the Whiteness of Belonging." *Qualitative Sociology* 35 (2): 163–81.

———. 2012b. *White Bound: Nationalists, Antiracists, and the Shared Meanings of Race*. Stanford, CA: Stanford University Press.

———. 2014. *The White Savior Film: Content, Critics, and Consumption*. Philadelphia: Temple University Press.

Hughey, Matthew W. 2015. "The Five I's of Five-O: Racial Ideologies, Institutions, Interests, Identities, and Interactions of Police Violence." *Critical Sociology* 41 (6): 857–71.

———. 2017. "Race and Racism: Perspectives from Bahá'í Theology and Critical Sociology." *Journal of Bahá'í Studies* 27 (3): 7–56.

———. 2018. "Can Hollywood Separate Gold from White?" *Contexts Blog*, February 8, 2018. https://contexts.org/blog/2018-oscars.

Hughey, Matthew W., and Jessie Daniels. 2013. "Racist Comments at Online News Sites: A Methodological Dilemma for Discourse Analysis." *Media, Culture and Society* 35 (3): 332–47.

Hughey, Matthew W., and Sahara Muradi. 2009. "Laughing Matters: Economies of Hyper-Irony and Manic-Satire in *South Park* and *Family Guy*." *Humanity and Society* 33 (3): 206–37.

Hunt, Darnell. 1997. *Screening the Los Angeles "Riots": Race, Seeing, and Resistance.* Cambridge: Cambridge University Press.

———. 2017. *Race in the Writers' Room: How Hollywood Whitewashes the Stories That Shape America.* Color of Change. http://hollyowwd.colorofchange.org.

Hunt, Darnell, Ana-Christina Ramón, and Michael Tran. 2019. *Hollywood Diversity Report 2019: Old Story, New Beginning.* Los Angeles: UCLA College of Social Sciences.

Hunter, Marcus Anthony. 2017. "Racial Physics or a Theory for Everything That Happened." *Ethnic and Racial Studies* 40 (8): 1173–83. https://doi.org/10.1080/01419870.2017.1285040.

———. 2018. "The Sociology of Stuart Hall." *Identities* 25 (1): 29–34.

Huntington, Samuel P. 1996. *The Clash of Civilizations and the Remaking of World Order.* New York: Simon and Schuster.

———. 2009. "The Hispanic Challenge." *Foreign Policy*, October 28, 2009. Originally published in 2004. https://foreignpolicy.com.

Huynh, Mai Anh. 2004. "Double-A." In *Asian American X: An Intersection of Twenty-First Century Asian American Voices*, edited by Han Arar and Hsu John, 70–75. Ann Arbor: University of Michigan Press.

Ingram, Christopher. 2017. "Public Support for Marijuana Legalization Surged in 2016." *Washington Post*, March 29, 2017. www.washingtonpost.com.

James, Joy. 1999. *Shadowboxing: Representations of Black Feminist Politics.* New York: St. Martin's.

Jameson, Fredric. 2015. "The Aesthetics of Singularity." *New Left Review* 92:101–32.

Jenkins, Cheryl D., and Donyale R. Griffin Padgett. 2012. "Race and Objectivity." In *Race and News: Critical Perspectives*, edited by Christopher P. Campbell, Kim M. LeDuff, Cheryl D. Jenkins, and Rockell A. Brown, 232–51. New York: Routledge.

Jhally, Sut, and Justin Lewis. 1992. *Enlightened Racism: "The Cosby Show," Audiences and the Myth of the American Dream.* London: Routledge.

Johnson, Fern. 1992. "Continuities and Imperatives in Communication Education." In *Communication Pedagogy: Approaches to Teaching Undergraduate Courses in Communication*, edited by Linda Costigan Lederman, 39–54. Norwood, NJ: Ablex.

Johnson, Walter. 2013. *River of Dark Dreams: Slavery and Empire in the Cotton King-dom*. Cambridge, MA: Harvard University Press.

Johnston, Hank. 2014. *What Is a Social Movement?* New York: Polity.

Johnston, Jenny. 2010. "Our Blue-Eyed and Blonde-Haired Gift from God." *Daily Mail Online*, July 30, 2010. www.dailymail.co.uk.

Jones, Feminista. 2013. "Is Twitter the Underground Railroad of Activism?" *Salon*, July 17, 2013. www.salon.com.

———. 2015. "Why Harriet Tubman on the $20 Might Not Be the Best Idea." *Ebony*, July 2015. www.ebony.com.

Jones, Jeffrey. 2012. "Fox News and the Performance of Ideology." *Cinema Journal* 51 (4): 178–85.

Jones, Maggie. 2015. "Adam Crapser's Bizarre Deportation Odyssey." *New York Times Magazine*, April 1, 2015.

Jones, Patrice M. 2004. "Not Just Idle Chitchat." *Chicago Tribune*, April 20, 2004. www.chicagotribune.com.

Jordan, William G. 2001. *Black Newspapers and America's War for Democracy, 1914–1920*. Chapel Hill: University of North Carolina Press.

Jorge, Tamara Moya. 2019. "Towards a Film Literacy Canon: Identification and Multi-cultural Analysis of the Contents Used in Film Education with Pre-University Students in Spain." *Communication and Society* 32 (1): 235–49. https://doi.org/10.15581/003.32.1.235-249.

Joseph, Justine, and Ben C. H. Kuo. 2009. "Black Canadians' Coping Responses to Racial Discrimination." *Journal of Black Psychology* 35 (1): 78–101. https://doi.org/10.1177/0095798408323384.

Joseph, Miranda. 2002. *Against the Romance of Community*. Minneapolis: University of Minnesota Press.

Joseph, Ralina L. 2013. *Transcending Blackness: From the New Millennium Mulatta to the Exceptional Multiracial*. Durham, NC: Duke University Press.

Kaleem, Jaweed. 2017. "Federal Judge Blocks Arizona from Banning Mexican American Studies." *Los Angeles Times*, December 27, 2017. www.latimes.com.

Kapoor, Nisha. 2013. "The Advancement of Racial Neoliberalism in Britain." *Ethnic and Racial Studies* 36 (6): 1028–46. https://doi.org/10.1080/01419870.2011.629002.

Katz, Elihu. 1959. "Mass Communication Research and the Study of Culture." *Studies in Public Communications* 2:1–6.

Kaufman, Will. 2006. *The Civil War in American Culture*. Edinburgh: Edinburgh University Press.

Kelley, Robin D. G. 2002. *Freedom Dreams: The Black Radical Imagination*. Boston: Beacon.

———. 2015. "Beyond Black Lives Matter." *Kalfou* 2 (2): 330–37.

Kelly, Heather. 2013. "Zimmerman Book Dies after Twitter Campaign." *CNN*, July 17, 2013. www.cnn.com.

Kendi, Ibram X. 2016. *Stamped from the Beginning: The Definitive History of Racist Ideas in America*. New York: PublicAffairs.

Kettrey, Heather Hensman, and Whitney Nicole Laster. 2014. "Staking Territory in the 'World White Web': An Exploration of the Roles of Overt and Color-Blind Racism in Maintaining Racial Boundaries on a Popular Web Site." *Social Currents* 1 (3): 257–74. https://doi.org/10.1177/2329496514540134.

Khor, Shing Yin. 2014a. "Just Eat It: A Comic about Food and Cultural Appropriation." *Bitch Media*, February 14, 2014. www.bitchmedia.org.

———. 2014b. "What Would Yellow Ranger Do?" *Toast* (blog), January 10, 2014. http://the-toast.net.

Kim, Eleana. 2008. "The Origins of Korean Adoption: Cold War Geopolitics and Intimate Diplomacy." WP 09-09. US-Korea Institute at SAIS, Washington, DC.

———. 2010. *Adopted Territory: Transnational Korean Adoptees and the Politics of Belonging*. Durham, NC: Duke University Press.

Kimmel, Michael. 2015. *Angry White Men: American Masculinity at the End of an Era*. New York: Nation Books.

King, Hayden. 2019. "'I Regret It': Hayden King on Writing Ryerson University's Territorial Acknowledgement." Canadian Broadcasting Corporation Radio, January 20, 2019.

King, Susan E. 1994. "Winning the Race against Racism." *Journal of Physical Education, Recreation and Dance* 65 (9): 69–74. https://doi.org/10.1080/07303084.1994.10607003.

Kiser, Laurel J., Barbara Baumgardner, and Joyce Dorado. 2010. "Who Are We, but for the Stories We Tell: Family Stories and Healing." *Psychological Trauma* 2 (3): 243–49.

Kline, Susan L., Amanda I. Karel, and Karishma Chatterjee. 2006. "Covering Adoption: General Depictions in Broadcast News." *Family Relations* 55 (4): 487–98.

Kollar, Philip. 2016. "*Mafia 3* Confronts Players with the Horror of Racism, but I'm Not Sure It Will Last." *Polygon*, October 7, 2016. www.polygon.com.

Koltay, Tibor. 2011. "The Media and the Literacies: Media Literacy, Information Literacy, Digital Literacy." *Media, Culture and Society* 33 (2): 211–21.

Koopmans, Ruud. 2004. "Movements and Media: Selection Processes and Evolutionary Dynamics in the Public Sphere." *Theory and Society* 33 (3–4): 367–91.

Kovach, Margaret. 2010. "Conversational Method in Indigenous Research." *First Peoples Child and Family Review* 5 (1): 40–48.

Krijnen, Tony, and Sofie Van Bauwel. 2015. *Gender and Media: Representing, Producing, Consuming*. New York: Routledge.

Lac, Van T. 2017. "In Real Time: From Theory to Practice in a Critical Race Pedagogy Classroom." *I.E.: Inquiry in Education* 9 (1): 1–21. https://digitalcommons.nl.edu/ie/vol9/iss1/3.

Lamarre, Carl. 2018. "11 Celebrities Who Treated Kids to Free Screenings of 'Black Panther.'" *Billboard*, February 26, 2018. www.billboard.com.

Lang, Kurt, and Gladys Engel Lang. 1953. "The Unique Perspective of Television and Its Effect: A Pilot Study." *American Sociological Review* 18 (1): 3–12.

Larreguy, Horacio, John Marshall, and James Snyder. 2014. "Revealing Malfeasance: How Local Media Facilitates Electoral Sanctioning of Mayors in Mexico." NBER Working Paper 20697. National Bureau of Economic Research, Cambridge, MA.

Larson, Stephanie Greco. 2005. *Media and Minorities: The Politics of Race in News and Entertainment*. Lanham, MD: Rowman and Littlefield.

Lavin, Talia. 2018. "The Neo-Nazis of the Daily Stormer Wander the Digital Wilderness." *New Yorker*, January 7, 2018. www.newyorker.com.

Laybourn, Wendy Marie. 2017. "Korean Transracial Adoptee Identity Formation." *Sociology Compass* 11 (1): e12444.

———. 2018. "Beyond Honorary Whiteness: Ideologies of Belonging and Korean Adoptee Identities." PhD diss., University of Maryland.

Lazarsfeld, Paul, Bernard Berelson, and Hazel Gaudet. 1948. *The People's Choice: How the Voter Makes Up His Mind in a Presidential Campaign*. New York: Columbia University Press.

Leavitt, Peter A., Rebecca Covarrubias, Yvonne A. Perez, and Stephanie A. Fryberg. 2015. "'Frozen in Time': The Impact of Native American Media Representations on Identity and Self-Understanding." *Journal of Social Issues* 71 (1): 39–53.

Lederman, Linda Costigan, ed. 1992. *Communication Pedagogy: Approaches to Teaching Undergraduate Courses in Communication*. Norwood, NJ: Ablex.

Lee, Benjamin. 2016. "Paramount Sued by Chinese Company for Failed Transformers Product Placement." *Guardian*, April 27, 2016. www.theguardian.com.

Lee, Dan P. 2013. "Where It Hurts: Steve McQueen on Why *12 Years a Slave* Isn't Just about Slavery." *Vulture*, December 8, 2013. www.vulture.com.

Lee, Martin A., and Norman Solomon. 1992. *Unreliable Sources: A Guide to Detecting Bias in News Media*. New York: Carol.

Lee, Richard M. 2003. "The Transracial Adoption Paradox: History, Research, and Counseling Implications of Cultural Socialization." *Counseling Psychology* 31 (6): 711–44.

Leonard, David. 2006. "Not a Hater, Just Keepin' It Real: The Importance of Race and Gender Based Game Studies." *Games and Culture* 1 (1): 83–88.

Levy, Emanuel. 2003. *All about Oscar: The History and Politics of the Academy Awards*. New York: Continuum.

Lewis, Jioni A., Ruby Mendenhall, Stacy A. Harwood, and Margaret Browne Huntt. 2013. "Coping with Gendered Racial Microaggressions among Black Women College Students." *Journal of African American Studies* 17 (1): 51–73.

Lewis, Jon. 2003. "Following the Money in America's Sunniest Company Town: Some Notes on the Political Economy of the Hollywood Blockbuster." In *Movie Blockbusters*, edited by Julian Stringer, 61–71. New York: Routledge.

Lichter, S. Robert, Stanley Rothman, and Linda S. Lichter. 1986. *The Media Elite*. Bethesda, MD: Adler and Adler.

Lightfoot, Sheryl. 2016. *Global Indigenous Politics: A Subtle Revolution*. London: Routledge.

Lincoln, Yvonna S., and Egon G. Guba. 1985. *Naturalistic Inquiry*. Newbury Park, CA: Sage.

Lindfors, Bernth. 1999. *Africans on Stage: Studies in Ethnological Show Business*. Bloomington: Indiana University Press.

Little, John, and Kenn Little, dirs. 2017. *More than a Word*. Media Education Foundation. DVD.

Littlefield, Marci Bounds. 2008. "The Media as a System of Racialization: Exploring Images of African American Women and the New Racism." *American Behavioral Scientist* 51 (5): 675–85.

Livingstone, Sonia, and Shenja van der Graaf. 2010. "Media Literacy." In *The International Encyclopedia of Communication*, edited by Wolfgang Donsbach, 360–61. Oxford, UK: Blackwell.

Logue, Larry M., and Peter Blanck. 2008. "'Benefit of the Doubt': African-American Civil War Veterans and Pensions." *Journal of Interdisciplinary History* 38 (3): 377–99.

Lopez, Lori Kido. 2016. *Asian American Media Activism: Fighting for Cultural Citizenship*. New York: NYU Press.

Lorde, Audre. (1981) 1984a. *Sister Outsider: Essays and Speeches*. Trumansburg, NY: Crossing.

———. (1981) 1984b. "The Uses of Anger: Women Responding to Racism." In *Sister Outsider: Essays and Speeches*, 124–33. Trumansburg, NY: Crossing.

Loudis, Jessica. 2017. "Why We Need Stuart Hall's Imaginative Left." *New Republic*, September 27, 2017. https://newrepublic.com.

Lunch, Nick, and Chris Lunch. 2006. *Insights into Participatory Video: A Handbook for the Field*. Oxford, UK: Insight.

Lurigio, Arthur J., and Pamela Loose. 2008. "The Disproportionate Incarceration of African Americans for Drug Offenses: The National and Illinois Perspective." *Journal of Ethnicity in Criminal Justice* 6 (3): 223–47.

Lynch, Mona, Marisa Omori, Aaron Roussell, and Matthew Valasik. 2013. "Policing the 'Progressive' City: The Racialized Geography of Drug Law Enforcement." *Theoretical Criminology* 17 (3): 335–57.

Lynn, Marvin, Grace Benigno, A. Dee Williams, Gloria Park, and Colleen Mitchell. 2006. "Critical Theories of Race, Class and Gender in Urban Education." *Encounter: Education for Meaning and Social Justice* 19 (2): 17–25.

MacCabe, Colin. 2008. "An Interview with Stuart Hall, December 2007." *Critical Quarterly* 50 (1–2): 12–42.

Macedo, Donaldo Pereira, and Panayota Gounari. 2006. *The Globalization of Racism*. New York: Routledge.

Madison, Kelly J. 1999. "Legitimation Crisis and Containment: The 'Anti-Racist-White Hero' Film." *Critical Studies in Media Communication* 16 (4): 399–416.

Mai-Duc, Christine. 2015. "In Taking on Jorge Ramos, Donald Trump May Have Tussled with the Wrong Media Star." *Los Angeles Times*, August 26, 2015. www.latimes.com.

Malcolm X. (1964) 1965. "Speech at the Audubon Ballroom in Harlem." In *Malcolm X Speaks: Selected Speeches and Statements*, edited by George Breitman, 88–104. London: Pathfinder Books.

Malkowski, Jennifer, and TreaAndrea M. Russworm. 2017. *Gaming Representation: Race, Gender, and Sexuality in Video Games*. Bloomington: Indiana University Press.

Manovich, Lev. 2001. *The Language of New Media*. Boston: MIT Press.

Marshall, Joseph M., III. 2001. *The Lakota Way: Stories and Lessons for Living*. New York: Viking Compass.

———. 2007. "Introduction: Where Are You From?" In *The Day the World Ended at Little Bighorn: A Lakota History*, xiii–xxii. New York: Penguin Books.

Marx, Karl. (1939) 1993. *Grundrisse: Foundations of the Critique of Political Economy*. Translated by Martin Nicolaus. London: Penguin.

Mask, Mia. 2012. *Contemporary Black American Cinema: Race, Gender and Sexuality at the Movies*. New York: Routledge.

Massey, Douglas S., Karen A. Pren, and Jorge Durand. 2016. "Why Border Enforcement Backfired." *American Journal of Sociology* 121 (5): 1557–1600.

Mastro, Dana. 2009. "Effects of Racial and Ethnic Stereotyping." In *Media Effects: Advances in Theory and Research*, 3rd ed., edited by Jennings Bryant and Mary Beth Oliver, 325–341. Hillsdale, NJ: Lawrence Erlbaum.

———. 2015. "Why the Media's Role in Issues of Race and Ethnicity Should Be in the Spotlight." *Journal of Social Issues* 71 (1): 1–16.

———. 2017. "Race and Ethnicity in U.S. Media Content and Effects." In *Oxford Research Encyclopedia, Communication*. Oxford: Oxford University Press. http://oxfordre.com.

Mastro, Dana E., and Bradley S. Greenberg. 2000. "The Portrayal of Racial Minorities on Prime Time Television." *Journal of Broadcasting and Electronic Media* 44 (4): 690–703.

Mastro, Dana E., and Maria A. Kopacz. 2006. "Media Representations of Race, Protypicality, and Policy Reasoning: An Application of Self-Categorization Theory." *Journal of Broadcasting and Electronic Media* 50 (2): 305–22.

Mastro, Dana E., and Linda R. Tropp. 2004. "The Effects of Interracial Contacts, Attitudes, and Stereotypical Portrayals on Evaluations of Black Sitcom Characters." *Communication Research Reports* 21 (2): 119–29.

Matthews, Julian. 2017. "The Sociology of Mass Media." In *The Cambridge Handbook of Sociology*, vol. 1, *Core Areas in Sociology and the Development of the Discipline*, edited by Kathleen Odell Korgen. Cambridge: Cambridge University Press.

Maxwell, Jon. 2014. *aka Dan*. YouTube. www.youtube.com/playlist?list=PL2T8s_i7PmAEYOiss64MnSQwsv6EwlymD.

———, dir. 2016. *aka SEOUL*. NBC Asian America and International Secret Agents. Documentary film.

May, Vivian M. 2014. "Under-theorized and Under-taught: Re-examining Harriet Tubman's Place in Women's Studies." *Meridians* 12 (2): 28–49.

McCauley, Mary Carole. 2016. "Harriet Tubman's Image." *Baltimore Sun*, April 21, 2016. www.baltimoresun.com.

McCauley, Michael. 2005. *NPR: The Trials and Tribulations of National Public Radio*. New York: Columbia University Press.

McChesney, Robert. 2008. *The Political Economy of Media: Enduring Issues, Emerging Dilemmas*. New York: Monthly Review Press.

McClintock, Pamela. 2014. "$200 Million and Rising: Hollywood Struggles with Soaring Marketing Costs." *Hollywood Reporter*, July 31, 2014. www.hollywoodreporter .com.

McCombs, Maxwell E., and Donald L. Shaw. 1972. "The Agenda-Setting Function of Mass Media." *Public Opinion Quarterly* 36 (2): 176–87.

McDonald, Steve. 2011. "What's in the 'Old Boys' Network? Accessing Social Capital in Gendered and Racialized Networks." *Social Networks* 33 (4): 317–30. https://doi.org/ https://doi.org/10.1016/j.socnet.2011.10.002.

McKenzie, Jordi. 2010. "Do 'African-American' Films Perform Better or Worse at the Box Office? An Empirical Analysis of Motion Picture Revenues and Profits." *Applied Economics Letters* 17:1559–64.

McLeod, Douglas M., and Benjamin H. Detenber. 1999. "Framing Effects of Television News Coverage of Social Protest." *Journal of Communication* 49 (3): 3–23.

McLuhan, Marshall. (1964) 1994. *Understanding Media: The Extensions of Man*. Cambridge, MA: MIT Press.

McNair, Brian. 2017. *Fake News: Falsehood, Fabrication, and Fantasy in Journalism*. New York: Routledge.

Melamed, Jodi. 2011a. "Reading Tehran in *Lolita*: Making Racialized and Gendered Difference Work for Neoliberal Multiculturalism." In *Strange Affinities: The Gender and Sexual Politics of Comparative Racialization*, edited by Grace Kyungwon Hong and Roderick A. Ferguson, 76–112. Durham, NC: Duke University Press.

———. 2011b. *Represent and Destroy: Rationalizing Violence in the New Racial Capitalism*. Minneapolis: University of Minnesota Press.

Mellinger, Gwyneth. 2013. *Chasing Newsroom Diversity*. Urbana: University of Illinois Press.

Mettler, Suzanne. 2018. *The Government-Citizen Disconnect*. New York: Russell Sage Foundation.

Miller, Robin. 2004. "Wikimedia Founder Jimmy Wales Responds." *Slashdot*, July 28, 2004. https://slashdot.org.

Miller, Toby, Nitin Govil, John McMurria, and Richard Maxwell. 2001. *Global Hollywood*. London: British Film Institute.

Mills, C. Wright. 1956. *The Power Elite*. New York: Oxford University Press.

Mills, Charles W. 1997. *The Racial Contract*. Ithaca, NY: Cornell University Press.

———. 2007. "White Ignorance." In *Race and Epistemologies of Ignorance*, edited by Shannon Sullivan and Nancy Tuana, 13–38. Albany: SUNY Press.

Mindich, David T. Z. 2000. *Just the Facts*. New York: NYU Press.

Mohanty, Jayashree, and Christina Newhill. 2006. "Adjustment of International Adoptees: Implications for Practice and a Future Research Agenda." *Children and Youth Services Review* 28 (4): 384–95.

Morning, Ann. 2014. "Does Genomics Challenge the Social Construction of Race?" *Sociological Theory* 32 (3): 189–207.

———. 2017. "Kaleidoscope: Contested Identities and New Forms of Race Membership." *Ethnic and Racial Studies* 41 (6): 1–19.

Moss, Sonita R. 2016. "Beyoncé & Blue: Black Motherhood and the Binds of Racialized Sexism." In *The Beyoncé Effect: Essays on Sexuality, Race and Feminism*, edited by Adrienne Trier-Bieniek, 155–76. Jefferson, NC: McFarland.

MPAA (Motion Picture Association of America). 2016. *Theatrical Market Statistics*. www.mpaa.org.

Murphy, Lynne. 2016. "Linguistics Explains Why Trump Sounds Racist When He Says 'the' African Americans." *Quartz*, October 11.

Nabizadeh, Golnar. 2016. "Comics Online: Detention and Space in 'A Guard's Story.'" *Ariel: A Review of International English Literature* 47 (1–2): 337–57.

Nakamura, Lisa. 2001. "Cybertyping and the Work of Race in the Age of Digital Reproduction." In *Cybertypes: Race, Ethnicity, and Identity on the Internet*, 1–30. New York: Routledge.

———. 2008. *Digitizing Race: Visual Cultures of the Internet*. Minneapolis: University of Minnesota Press.

Nakamura, Lisa, and Peter Chow-White. 2012. *Race after the Internet*. New York: Routledge.

National Advisory Commission on Civil Disorders. 1968. *Report of the National Advisory Commission on Civil Disorders*. New York: Bantam Books.

National Communication Association. 1998. "K–12 Speaking, Listening, and Media Literacy Standards and Competency Statements." January 12, 1998. www.natcom.org.

National Public Media. 2017. "NPR Audience Profile." NPR. www.nationalpublicmedia.com.

Newsweek. 1982. "The Hard-Luck Christmas of '82." December 27, 1982.

Ngai, Sianne. 2015. "Visceral Abstractions." *GLQ* 21 (1): 33–63.

———. 2017. "Theory of the Gimmick." *Critical Inquiry* 43:466–505.

Nicosia, Nancy, John MacDonald, and Jeremy Arkes. 2013. "Disparities in Criminal Court Referrals to Drug Treatment and Prison for Minority Men." *American Journal of Public Health* 103 (6): e77–e84.

Nielsen. 2016. "Report: The Latino Listener: How Do Hispanics Tune into the Radio." January 25, 2016. www.nielsen.com.

Norman, Greg. 2018. "Caravan Showdown: Crowds Reach Guatemalan Border Town as Mexico Prepares for Potential Mass Crossing." *Fox News*, October 19, 2018. www.foxnews.com.

North, Michael. 2008. *Machine-Age Comedy*. Oxford: Oxford University Press.

NPR. 2012. "Six National Leaders and Experts Look at Diversity at NPR." April 30, 2012. www.npr.org.

———. 2014. "NPR: A Strategic Plan." www.npr.org.

———. 2018. "NPR's Staff Diversity Numbers, 2018." November 12, 2018. www.npr.org.

Obasogie, Osagie K. 2013. *Blinded by Sight: Seeing Race through the Eyes of the Blind.* Stanford, CA: Stanford University Press.

Obasogie, Osagie K., and Zachary Newman. 2016. "Black Lives Matter and Respectability Politics in Local News Accounts of Officer-Involved Civilian Deaths: An Early Empirical Assessment." *Wisconsin Law Review* 3:541.

Obenson, Tambay A. 2013. "About That Popular 'Black Films Don't Sell Overseas' Industry Belief . . . Reality, or Just Laziness?" *IndieWire*, April 28, 2013. www.indiewire.com.

O'Brien, Luke. 2017. "The Making of an American Nazi." *Atlantic*, December 2017.

O'Connell, Jenniger. 2018. "Serena Williams Cartoon: Outrage-Mongering or Old-Fashioned Racism?" *Irish Times*, September 11, 2018. www.irishtimes.com.

Oeur, Freeden. 2016. "Recognizing Dignity: Young Black Men Growing Up in an Era of Surveillance." *Socius: Sociological Research for a Dynamic World* 2. https://doi.org/10.1177/2378023116633712.

Oh, Arissa H. 2015. *To Save the Children of Korea: The Cold War Origins of International Adoption.* Stanford, CA: Stanford University Press.

Ohito, Esther Oganda. 2016. "Refusing Curriculum as a Space of Death for Black Female Subjects: A Black Feminist Reparative Reading of Jamaica Kincaid's *Girl.*" *Curriculum Inquiry* 46 (5): 436–54.

Ohlheiser, Abby. 2015. "Harriet Tubman Is Your Possible Replacement for Andrew Jackson on the $20." *Washington Post*, May 15, 2015. www.washingtonpost.com.

Ojmarrh, Mitchell, and Michael S. Caudy. 2013. "Examining Racial Disparities in Drug Arrests." *Justice Quarterly* 32 (2): 288–313.

Omi, Michael, and Howard Winant. 2015. *Racial Formation in the United States: From the 1960s to the 1990s.* 3rd ed. New York: Routledge.

Ono, Kent A., and Derek T. Buescher. 2001. "Deciphering Pocahontas: Unpacking the Commodification of a Native American Woman." *Critical Studies in Media Communication* 18 (1): 23–43.

Opam, Kwame. 2013. "Black Twitter's Not Just a Group—It's a Movement." *Salon*, September 3, 2013. www.salon.com.

Ouellette, Laurie, and Sarah Banet-Weiser. 2018. Editors' introduction to "Media and the Extreme Right." Special issue, *Communication, Culture, and Critique* 11 (1): 1–6.

Palmerton, Patricia. 1988. "The Rhetoric of Terrorism and Media Response to the 'Crisis in Iran.'" *Western Journal of Speech Communication* 52 (2): 105–21.

Park, Robert. 1922. *The Immigrant Press and Its Control.* New York: Harper Brothers.

Park Nelson, Kim. 2009. "Mapping Multiple Histories of Korean American Transnational Adoption." WP 09-01. US Korean Institute at SAIS, Washington, DC.

———. 2016. *Invisible Asians: Korean American Adoptees, Asian American Experiences, and Racial Exceptionalism.* New Brunswick, NJ: Rutgers University Press.

Pate, SooJin. 2014. *From Orphan to Adoptee: U.S. Empire and Genealogies of Korean Adoption*. Minneapolis: University of Minnesota Press.

Patton, Michael Quinn. 2002. *Qualitative Research and Evaluation Methods*. Thousand Oaks, CA: Sage.

Patton, Venetria K. 2000. *Women in Chains: The Legacy of Slavery in Black Women's Fiction*. Albany: SUNY Press.

Payne, Teryn. 2018. "Momo Pixel 'Hair Nah' Video Game Interview." *Teen Vogue*, January 5, 2018. www.teenvogue.com.

PBS. 2018. "Separated: Children at the Border." *Frontline*, July 31, 2018. www.pbs.org.

Peeters, Rens, and Jacco van Sterkenburg. 2017. "Making Sense of Race/Ethnicity and Gender in Televised Football: Reception Research among British Students." *Sport in Society* 20 (5–6): 701–15.

Penney, Joel, and Caroline Dadas. 2014. "(Re)Tweeting in the Service of Protest: Digital Composition and Circulation in the Occupy Wall Street Movement." *New Media and Society* 16 (1): 74–90.

Pennington, Dorthy L. 1997. "Mainstreaming Interracial Communication." *Speech Communication Teacher* 11 (2): 11–13.

Pérez Huber, Lindsay, and Daniel G. Solorzano. 2015. "Racial Microaggressions as a Tool for Critical Race Research." *Race Ethnicity and Education* 18 (3): 297–320.

———. 2018. "Teaching Racial Microaggressions: Implications of Critical Race Hypos for Social Work Praxis." *Journal of Ethnic and Cultural Diversity in Social Work* 27 (1): 54–71. https://doi.org/10.1080/15313204.2017.1417944.

Perry, Imani. 2011. *More Beautiful and More Terrible: The Embrace and Transcendence of Racial Inequality in the United States*. New York: NYU Press.

Pew Research Center. 2015. "In Debate over Legalizing Marijuana, Disagreement over Drug's Dangers." April 14, 2015. www.people-press.org.

———. 2016a. "The Changing Latino Electorate." January 19, 2016. www.pewhispanic.org.

———. 2016b. "The Nation's Latino Population Is Defined by Its Youth." April, 20, 2016. www.pewhispanic.org.

Pham, Vincent N. 2015. "Our Foreign President Barack Obama: The Racial Logics of Birther Discourses." *Journal of International and Intercultural Communication* 8 (2): 86–107. https://doi.org/10.1080/17513057.2015.1025327.

Phoenix, Aisha. 2014. "Colourism and the Politics of Beauty." *Feminist Review* 108: 97–105.

Pillow, Wanda S. 2012. "Sacajawea: Witnessing, Remembrance and Ignorance." *Power and Education* 4 (1): 45–56.

Plante, Chris. 2016. "*Mafia 3*'s Commentary on Racism Is Undercut by Shooter Tropes." *Verge*, October 13, 2016. www.theverge.com.

Porter, Justin. 2017. "A Fresh Narrative in Gaming." *New York Times*, February 25, 2017.

Potter W. James. 2010. "The State of Media Literacy." *Journal of Broadcasting and Electronic Media* 54 (4): 675–96.

Powell, Gloria Johnson. 1982. "The Impact of Television on the Self-Concept Development of Minority Group Children." In *Television and the Socialization of the Minority Child*, edited by Gordon L. Berry and Claudia Mitchell-Kernan, 110–30. New York: Academic.

Powell, Malea. 2002. "Rhetorics of Survivance: How American Indians Use Writing." *College Composition and Communication* 53 (3): 396–434.

Pretsky, Holly. 2017. "NPR in Spanish: Approaching Content for a Bilingual Audience." NPR, December 14, 2017. www.npr.org.

Prior, Markus. 2013. "Media and Political Polarization." *Annual Review of Political Science* 16 (1): 101–27.

Prokop, Andrew. 2018. "7 Questions about the Government Shutdown You Were Too Embarrassed to Ask: Why Did the Government Shut Down?" *Vox*, January 22, 2018. www.vox.com.

Provine, Doris Marie. 2007. *Unequal under Law: Race in the War on Drugs*. Chicago: University of Chicago Press.

Pulido, Laura. 2015. "Geographies of Race and Ethnicity I: White Supremacy vs. White Privilege in Environmental Racism Research." *Progress in Human Geography* 39 (6): 809–17.

Putnam, Angela L. 2017. "Perpetuation of Whiteness Ideologies in U.S. College Student Discourse." *Journal of Intercultural Communication Research* 46 (6): 497–517. https://doi.org/10.1080/17475759.2017.1380068.

Quarry, Wendy. 1994. "The Fogo Process." Master's thesis, University of Guelph, Canada.

Quinn, Annalisa. 2016. "A Toast to The Toast, the Site That Was Just for You. Yes, Even You." NPR, June 27, 2016. www.npr.org.

Radosh, Polly F. 2008. "War on Drugs: Gender and Race Inequities in Crime Control Strategies." *Criminal Justice Studies* 21 (2): 167–78.

Raheja, Michelle H. 2007. "Reading Nanook's Smile: Visual Sovereignty, Indigenous Revisions of Ethnography, and *Atanarjuat (The Fast Runner)*." *American Quarterly* 59 (4): 1159–85.

——. 2015. "Visual Sovereignty." In *Native American Key Words*, edited by Stephanie N. Teves, Andrea Smith, and Michelle H. Raheja, 25–34. Tucson: University of Arizona Press.

Raleigh, Elizabeth. 2018. *Selling Transracial Adoption: Families, Markets, and the Color Line*. Philadelphia: Temple University Press.

Rao, Sameer. 2016. "This Heartbreaking Comic Shows Exactly Why We Need Asian-Black Solidarity against Police Brutality." *Colorlines*, March 15, 2016. www.colorlines.com.

Ray, Rashawn, Melissa Brown, Neil Fraistat, and Edward Summers. 2017. "Ferguson and the Death of Michael Brown on Twitter: #BlackLivesMatter, #TCOT, and the Evolution of Collective Identities." *Ethnic and Racial Studies* 40 (11): 1797–1813.

Reese, Stephen D., Oscar H. Gandy Jr., and August E. Grant, eds. 2003. *Framing Public Life*. Mahwah, NJ: Lawrence Erlbaum.

Regan, Paulette. 2010. *Unsettling the Settler Within: Indian Residential Schools, Truth Telling, and Reconciliation in Canada.* Vancouver: University of British Columbia Press.

Reid, Alyssa. 2016. "Traversing the Terrain: Paths and Roadblocks to Conscientization in Forensic Competition." *National Forensic Journal* 34 (1): 48–56.

Reinikka, Ritva, and Jakob Svensson. 2005. "Fighting Corruption to Improve Schooling: Evidence from a Newspaper Campaign in Uganda." *Journal of the European Economic Association* 3(2–3): 259–67.

Reyes, Angela. 2016. "The Voicing of Asian American Figures: Korean Linguistic Styles at an Asian American Cram School." In *Raciolinguistics: How Language Shapes Our Ideas about Race*, edited by H. Samy Alim, John R. Rickford, and Arnetha F. Ball, 309–26. New York: Oxford University Press.

Reynolds, Barbara. 2015. "I Was a Civil Rights Activist in the 1960s. But It's Hard for Me to Get behind Black Lives Matter." *Washington Post*, August 24, 2015. www.washingtonpost.com.

Reynolds, Jason D., Joseph G. Ponterotto, Jennie Park-Taylor, and Harold Takooshian. 2017. "Transracial Identities: The Meaning of Names and the Process of Name Reclamation for Korean American Adoptees." *Qualitative Psychology*, November 2017.

Rhines, Jesse Algeron. 1996. *Black Film / White Money.* New Brunswick, NJ: Rutgers University Press.

Rhodes, Jesse. 2017. *Ballot Blocked: The Political Erosion of the Voting Rights Act.* Stanford, CA: Stanford University Press.

Roberts, Dorothy E. 1997. *Killing the Black Body: Race, Reproduction, and the Meaning of Liberty.* New York: Knopf Doubleday.

———. 2011. *Fatal Invention: How Science, Politics, and Big Business Re-create Race in the Twenty-First Century.* New York: New Press.

———. 2012. "Prison, Foster Care, and the Systemic Punishment of Black Mothers." *UCLA Law Review* 59:1474–1500.

Rocchio, Vincent F. 2018. *Reel Racism: Confronting Hollywood's Construction of Afro-American Culture.* New York: Routledge.

Rogers, Katie. 2016. "John Cho, Starring in Every Movie Ever Made? A Diversity Hashtag is Born." *New York Times*, May 10, 2016. www.nytimes.com.

Root, Jay. 2018. "Caravans Help Migrants Travel Safely. But Recent Attention from Trump Might Change That." *Time*, October 30, 2018. http://time.com.

Roscigno, Vincent J., and William F. Danaher. 2001. "Media and Mobilization: The Case of Radio and Southern Textile Worker Insurgency, 1929 to 1934." *American Sociological Review* 66 (1): 21–48.

Rosino, Michael L., and Matthew W. Hughey. 2017. "Speaking through Silence: Racial Discourse and Identity Construction in Mass Mediated Debates on the 'War on Drugs.'" *Social Currents* 4 (3): 246–64.

———. 2018. "The War on Drugs, Racial Meanings, and Structural Racism: A Holistic and Reproductive Approach." *American Journal of Economics and Sociology* 77 (3–4): 849–92.

Ross, Karen, and Virginia Nightingale. 2003. *Media and Audiences: New Perspectives*. New York: McGraw-Hill.

Roth, Wendy D. 2016. "The Multiple Dimensions of Race." *Ethnic and Racial Studies* 39 (8): 1310–38.

Rotten Tomatoes. n.d. "Dear White People." Accessed October 10, 2018. www.rotten tomatoes.com.

Ryan, Charlotte. 1991. *Prime Time Activism*. Boston: South End.

Said, Edward. 1978. *Orientalism*. New York: Pantheon Books.

Sangweni, Yolanda. 2013. "The 9 Most Memorable 'Black Twitter' Hashtags of 2013." *Essence*, December 11, 2013. www.essence.com.

San Juan, E., Jr. 1994. "The Predicament of Filipinos in the United States: 'Where Are You From? When Are You Going Back?'" In *The State of Asian America: Activism and Resistance in the 1990s*, edited by Karin Aguilar-San Juan, 205–19. Boston: South End.

Santa Ana, Otto. 2013. *Juan in a Hundred: The Representation of Latinos on Network News*. Austin: University of Texas Press, 2013.

Santos, Jody. 2009. *Daring to Feel: Violence, the News Media, and Their Emotions*. Lanham, MD: Lexington Books.

Scherr, Rebecca. 2013. "Framing Human Rights: Comics Form and the Politics of Recognition in Joe Sacco's *Footnotes in Gaza*." *Textual Practice* 29 (1): 111–31.

Schilling, Vincent. 2015. "DOI Issues Determination." *Indian Country Today*, July 2, 2015. http://newsmaven.io.

Schlesinger, Traci. 2013. "Racial Disparities in Pretrial Diversion: An Analysis of Outcomes among Men Charged with Felonies and Processed in State Courts." *Race and Justice* 3 (3): 210–38.

Schneider, David J. 2004. *The Psychology of Stereotyping*. New York: Guilford.

Schudson, Michael. 1978. *Discovering the News*. New York: Basic Books.

Schudson, Michael, and Chris Anderson. 2009. "Objectivity, Professionalism, and Truth Seeking in Journalism." In *The Handbook of Journalism Studies*, edited by Karin Wahl-Jorgensen and Thomas Hanitzsch, 88–101. New York: Routledge.

Schwalbe, Michael. 2008. *Rigging the Game: How Inequality Is Reproduced in Everyday Life*. New York: Oxford University Press.

Schwartz-Shea, Peregrine, and Dvora Yanow. 2012. *Interpretive Research Design: Concepts and Processes*. New York: Routledge.

Scroggs, Patricia Hanigan, and Heather Heitfield. 2001. "International Adopters and Their Children: Birth Culture Ties." *Gender Issues* 19 (4): 3–30.

Sedgewick, Eve. 1997. *Novel Gazing: Queer Readings in Fiction*. Durham, NC: Duke University Press.

Sender, Katherine. 2004. *Business, Not Politics: The Making of the Gay Market*. New York: Columbia University Press.

Sewell, Abigail A., and Kevin A. Jefferson. 2016. "Collateral Damage: The Health Effects of Invasive Police Encounters in New York City." *Journal of Urban Health* 93 (S1): 42–67.

Sexton, Jared. 2010. "Proprieties of Coalition: Blacks, Asians, and the Politics of Policing." *Critical Sociology* 36 (1): 87–108.

Shaw, Clifford R., and Henry D. McKay. 1942. *Juvenile Delinquency and Urban Areas.* Chicago: University of Chicago Press.

Shimomura, Fuyu. 2015. "Can Critical Race Pedagogy Break through the Perpetuation of Racial Inequity? Exploring What Is Behind the Structural Racism and Potential Intervention." *International Journal of Sociology and Anthropology* 7 (12): 254–60. https://doi.org/10.5897/IJSA2015.0560.

Shohat, Ella. 2001. Introduction to *Talking Visions: Multicultural Feminism in a Transnational Age,* edited by Ella Shohat, 1–63. Cambridge, MA: MIT Press.

Sidanius, Jim, and Felicia Pratto. 1999. *Social Dominance: An Intergroup Theory of Social Hierarchy and Oppression.* New York: Cambridge University Press.

Sides, John, Michael Tesler, and Lynn Vavreck. 2018. *Identity Crisis: The 2016 Presidential Campaign and the Battle for the Meaning of America.* Princeton, NJ: Princeton University Press.

Silverstein, Michael. 1976. "Shifters, Linguistic Categories, and Cultural Description." In *Meaning in Anthropology,* edited by Henry Selby and Keith Basso, 11–55. Albuquerque: University of New Mexico Press.

———. 2003. "Indexical Order and the Dialectics of Sociolinguistic Life." *Language and Communication* 23:193–229.

Silvey, Rachel. 2010. "Envisioning Justice: The Politics and Possibilities of Transnational Feminist Film." In *Critical Transnational Feminist Praxis,* edited by Amanda Lock Swarr and Richa Nagar, 192–218. Albany: SUNY Press.

Silvio, Teri. 2010. "Animation: The New Performance?" *Journal of Linguistic Anthropology* 20 (2): 422–38.

Simon, Roger. 2000. "The Paradoxical Practice of Zakhor: Memories of 'What Has Never Been My Fault or My Deed.'" In *Between Hope and Despair: Pedagogy and the Remembrance of Historical Trauma,* edited by Roger Simon, Sharon Rosenberg, and Claudia Eppert, 9–26. Lanham, MD: Rowman and Littlefield.

Singleton, John. 2013. "Can a White Director Make a Great Black Movie?" *Hollywood Reporter,* September 19, 2013. www.hollywoodreporter.com.

Slap, Gail, Elizabeth Goodman, and Bin Huang. 2001. "Adoption as a Risk Factor for Attempted Suicide during Adolescence." *Pediatrics* 108 (2): e30.

Small, Stephen. 2018. "Theorizing Visibility and Vulnerability in Black Europe and the African Diaspora." *Ethnic and Racial Studies* 41 (6): 1182–97. https://doi.org/10.1080/01419870.2018.1417619.

Smith, Andrea. 2012. "Indigeneity, Settler Colonialism, White Supremacy." In *Racial Formation in the Twenty-First Century,* edited by Daniel Martinez HoSang, Oneka LaBennett, and Laura Pulido, 66–90. Berkeley: University of California Press.

Smith, Iman. 2017. "How One Video Game Unflinchingly Tackles Racism with History and Raw Interactions." NPR, January 3, 2017. www.npr.org.

Smith, Linda Tuhiwai. 2012. *Decolonizing Methodologies: Research and Indigenous Peoples.* 2nd ed. London: Zed Books.

Smith Squire, Alison. 2017. "Mother Becomes Only Black Woman in the World to Have Two White Babies." *Daily Mail Online*, January 29, 2017. www.dailymail.co.uk.

Snyder, James, and David Strömberg. 2010. "Press Coverage and Political Accountability." *Journal of Political Economy* 118 (2): 355–408.

Squires, Catherine R. 2014. *The Post-racial Mystique: Media and Race in the Twenty-First Century.* New York: NYU Press.

Squires, Catherine R., and Aisha Upton. 2018. "The Color of Money, or How to Redesign a 'Monument in Your Pocket.'" *Humanity and Society*, December 6, 2018.

Staples, Brent. 2015. "What the Country Owes Harriet Tubman." *Taking Note* (blog), *New York Times*, July 17, 2015. https://takingnote.blogs.nytimes.com.

Statista. n.d. "Combined Market Share of the 'Big Six' Major Film Studios in North America from 2000 to 2017." Accessed January 10, 2019. www.statista.com.

Stavitsky, Alan. 1995. "Guys in Suits with Charts: Audience Research in US Public Radio." *Journal of Broadcasting and Electronic Media* 39:177–89.

Steinberg, Stephen. 1989. *The Ethnic Myth: Race, Ethnicity, and Class in America.* New York: Atheneum.

Stier, Jonas, and Margareta Sandström. 2018. "Managing the Unmanageable: Curriculum Challenges and Teacher Strategies in Multicultural Preschools in Sweden." *Journal of Intercultural Communication* 48 (November 2018). http://immi.se/intercultural.

Stoddart, Mark C. J. 2007. "Ideology, Hegemony, Discourse: A Critical Review of Theories of Knowledge and Power." *Social Thought and Research* 28:191–225.

Strömberg, David. 2015. "Media and Politics." *Annual Review of Economics* 7 (1): 173–205.

Stuart, Tessa. 2012a. "A. Martinez Hired at KPCC: The Madeleine Brand Show Goes National." *LA Weekly*, August 17, 2012. www.laweekly.com.

———. 2012b. "How KPCC's Quest for Latino Listeners Doomed the Madeleine Brand Show." *LA Weekly*, November 1, 2012. www.laweekly.com.

Sue, Derald Wing. 2010. *Microaggressions in Everyday Life: Race, Gender, and Sexual Orientation.* Hoboken, NJ: Wiley.

Sue, Derald Wing, Christina M. Capodilupo, and Aisha M. B. Holder. 2008. "Racial Microaggressions in the Life Experience of Black Americans." *Professional Psychology: Research and Practice* 39 (3): 329–36. https://doi.org/10.1037/0735-7028.39.3.329.

Sue, Derald Wing, Christina M. Capodilupo, Gina C. Torino, Jennifer M. Bucceri, Aisha M. B. Holder, Kevin L. Nadal, and Marta Esquilin. 2007. "Microaggressions in Everyday Life: Implications for Clinical Practice." *American Psychologist* 62:271–86. https://doi.org/10.1037/0003-066X.62.4.271.

Sullivan, Shannon. 2014. *Good White People.* Albany: SUNY Press.

Sullivan, Shannon, and Nancy Tuana. 2012. *Race and Epistemologies of Ignorance.* Albany: SUNY Press.

Sumner, Rachel, Maclen J. Stanley, and Anthony L. Burrow. 2015. "Room for Debate (and Derogation): Negativity of Readers' Comments on Black Authors' Online Content." *Psychology of Popular Media Culture* 6 (January). https://doi.org/10.1037/ppm0000090.

Sun, Chyng, Rachael Liberman, Allison Butler, Sun Young Lee, and Rachel Webb. 2015. "Shifting Receptions: Asian American Stereotypes and the Exploration of Comprehensive Media Literacy." *Communication Review* 18 (4): 294–314.

Sveningsson, Malin. 2015. "'It's Only a Pastime, Really': Young People's Experiences of Social Media as a Source of News about Public Affairs." *Social Media + Society* 1 (2): 1–11.

Sylvie, George. 2011. "The Call and Challenge for Diversity." In *Changing the News: The Forces Shaping Journalism in Uncertain Times*, edited by Wilson Lowrey and Peter J. Gade, 83–101. New York: Routledge.

Takahashi, Dean. "How Developers Created the Story behind *Mafia III* and Its Lead Character Lincoln Clay." *VentureBeat*, September 16, 2016. https://venturebeat.com.

Takezawa, Yasuko. 2011. "Toward a New Approach to Race and Racial Representations: Perspectives from Asia." In *Racial Representations in Asia*, edited by Yasuko Takezawa, 7–19. Kyoto: Kyoto University Press.

Tanya D. 2016. "Racism in *Watch Dogs 2* Is Subtle, and That's How It Won Me Over." *Polygon*, December 22, 2016. www.polygon.com.

Tavlin, Noah. n.d. "How False News Can Spread." TED-Ed. Accessed December 7, 2020. http://ed.ted.com.

Taylor, Keeanga-Yamahtta. 2016. *From #BlackLivesMatter to Black Liberation*. Chicago: Haymarket Books.

Taylor, Shelley E., and Annette L. Stanton. 2007. "Coping Resources, Coping Processes, and Mental Health." *Annual Review of Clinical Psychology* 3 (1): 377–401. https://doi.org/10.1146/annurev.clinpsy.3.022806.091520.

Terry, Neil, Michael Butler, and De'Arno De'Armond. 2005. "The Determinants of Domestic Box Office Performance in the Motion Picture Industry." *Southwestern Economic Review* 32:137–48.

Thomas, James M. 2014. "Medicalizing Racism." *Contexts* 13 (4): 24–29. https://doi.org/10.1177/1536504214558213.

Thomas, Robina Anne. 2005. "Honouring the Oral Traditions of My Ancestors through Storytelling." In *Research as Resistance: Critical, Indigenous, and Anti-oppressive Approaches*, edited by Leslie Brown and Susan Strega, 237–54. Toronto: Canadian Scholars.

Thomas, Thomas J., and Theresa R. Clifford. 1988. *Audience 88: Issues and Implications*. Washington, DC: Corporation for Public Broadcasting.

Thrasher, Steven W. 2015a. "Pop Culture's Black Lives Matter Moment Couldn't Come at a Better Time." *Guardian*, July 1, 2015. www.theguardian.com.

———. 2015b. "To Put Harriet Tubman on the $20 Bill Would Be an Insult to Her Legacy: I Don't Want to See the Abolitionist Commodified with a Price, as She Once Was as a Slave." *Guardian*, May 15, 2015.

Tickner, J. Ann. 2005. "What Is Your Research Program? Some Feminist Answers to IR's Methodological Questions." *International Studies Quarterly* 49 (1): 1–22.

Todd, Cherie. 2015. "GamerGate and Resistance to the Diversification of Gaming Culture." *Women's Studies Journal* 29 (1): 64–67.

Trenka, Jane Jeong, Julia Chinyere Oparah, and Sun Yung Shin. 2006. *Outsiders Within: Writing on Transracial Adoption*. Boston: South End.

Trickey, Erick. 2018. "One Hundred Years Ago, the Harlem Hellfighters Bravely Led the U.S. into WWI." Smithsonian.com, May 14, 2018. www.smithsonianmag.com.

Tuan, Mia. 1998. *Forever Foreigners or Honorary Whites? The Asian Ethnic Experience Today*. New Brunswick, NJ: Rutgers University Press.

Tuan, Mia, and Jiannbin Lee Shiao. 2011. *Choosing Ethnicity, Negotiating Race: Korean Adoptees in America*. New York: Russell Sage Foundation.

Tuchman, Gaye. 1972. "Objectivity as Strategic Ritual." *American Journal of Sociology* 77 (4): 660–79.

Tuck, Eve. 2009. "Suspending Damage: A Letter to Communities." *Harvard Educational Review* 79 (3): 409–27.

Tukachinsky, Riva. 2015. "Where We Have Been and Where We Can Go from Here: Looking to the Future in Research on Media, Race and Ethnicity." *Journal of Social Issues* 71 (1): 186–97.

Tukachinsky, Riva, Dana Mastro, and Moran Yarchi. 2015. "Documenting Portrayals of Race/Ethnicity on Primetime Television over a 20-Year Span and Their Association with National-Level Racial/Ethnic Attitudes." *Journal of Social Issues* 71 (1): 17–38.

US Bureau of the Census. 1971. *General Demographic Trends for Metropolitan Areas, 1960 to 1970*. PHC(2)-1. Table 10, "Population Change inside and outside Central Cities, by Race: 1960 to 1970." Washington, DC: US Bureau of the Census.

———. 2018a. "Demographic Turning Points for the United States: Population Projections for 2020 to 2060." March 2018. www.census.gov.

———. 2018b. "Historical Poverty Tables." Table 2, "Poverty Status of People by Family Relationship, Race, and Hispanic Origin: 1959 to 2017." www.census.gov.

———. 2018c. "Income and Poverty in the United States, 2017." Report no. P60-263. Table 3, "People and Families in Poverty by Selected Characteristics." www.census .gov/data/tables/2018/demo/income-poverty/p60-263.html.

Valkenburg, Patti, Jochen Peter, and Joseph Walther. 2016. "Media Effects: Theory and Research." *Annual Review of Psychology* 67:315–38.

Van De Donk, Wim, Brian D. Loader, Paul G. Nixon, and Dieter Rucht. 2004. *Cyberprotest: New Media, Citizens, and Social Movements*. London: Routledge.

van Dijk, Teun A. 1993. "Principles of Critical Discourse Analysis." *Discourse and Society* 4 (2): 249–83. https://doi.org/10.1177/0957926593004002006.

van Doorn, Bas W. 2015. "Pre- and Post-Welfare Reform Media Portrayals of Poverty in the United States: The Continuing Importance of Race and Ethnicity." *Politics and Policy* 43 (1): 142–62. https://doi.org/10.1111/polp.12107.

Waldman, Diane, and Janet Walker. 1999. *Feminism and Documentary*. Minneapolis: University of Minnesota Press.

Walker, Grady. 2018. *Movie Making as Critical Pedagogy: Conscientization through Visual Storytelling*. New York: Palgrave Macmillan.

Wang, Ami A., and Paul Farhi. 2018. "White House Suspends Acosta after His Testy Exchange with Trump." *Washington Post*, November 8, 2018. www.washingtonpost.com.

Wang, Tai-Li. 2012. "Presentation and Impact of Market-Driven Journalism on Sensationalism in Global TV News." *International Communication Gazette* 74 (8): 711–27.

Ward, Jeffrey T., Richard D. Hartley, and Rob Tillyer. 2016. "Unpacking Gender and Racial/Ethnic Biases in the Federal Sentencing of Drug Offenders: A Causal Mediation Approach." *Journal of Criminal Justice* 46:196–206.

Ward, L. Monique. 2004. "Wading through the Stereotypes: Positive and Negative Associations between Media Use and Black Adolescents' Conceptions of Self." *Developmental Psychology* 40 (2): 284–94.

Warrior, Robert Allen. 1992. "Intellectual Sovereignty and the Struggle for an American Indian Future." *Wicazo Sa Review* 8 (1): 1–20.

Washburn, Patrick. 2006. *The African American Newspaper: Voice of Freedom*. Evanston, IL: Northwestern University Press.

Washington Post. 2017. "Ed Gillespie Campaign Ad." September 28, 2017. www.washingtonpost.com.

Watch Dogs Wiki. n.d.-a. "Horatio Carlin." Accessed January 6, 2020. http://watchdogs.wikia.com.

———. n.d.-b. "Marcus Holloway." Accessed January 6, 2020. http://watchdogs.wikia.com.

Weaver, Andrew J. 2011. "The Role of Actors' Race in White Audiences' Selective Exposure to Movies." *Journal of Communication* 61:369–85.

Webb, Jim. 2016. "We Can Celebrate Harriet Tubman without Disparaging Andrew Jackson." *Washington Post*, April 24, 2016.

Weber, Max. (1909) 1998. "Preliminary Report on a Proposed Survey for a Sociology of the Press." *History of the Human Sciences* 11 (2): 111–20.

———. 2015. *Weber's Rationalism and Modern Society*. Translated and edited by T. Waters and D. Waters. New York: Palgrave Macmillan.

Weber-Pillwax, Cora. 2001. "What Is Indigenous Research?" *Canadian Journal of Native Education* 25 (2): 166–74.

Webster, Andrew. 2016. "*Watch Dogs 2* Is Exactly What the Original Game Should Have Been." *Verge*, November 14, 2016. www.theverge.com.

Weiner, Albert. 1980. "The Function of the Tragic Greek Chorus." *Theatre Journal* 32 (2): 205–12.

Weiss, Rick, and Justin Gillis. 2000. "Teams Finish Mapping Human DNA." *Washington Post*, June 27, 2000, A1.

Wells-Barnett, Ida B. 1991. "The Case Stated." In *Selected Works of Ida B. Wells-Barnett*, 140–50. New York: Oxford University Press.

We Need Diverse Books. n.d. "About WNDB." Accessed June 12, 2017. https://diversebooks.org.

Western, Bruce. 2007. *Punishment and Inequality in America*. New York: Russell Sage Foundation.

White Bird, Francis. 2008. "Levels of Lakota Language." *Lakota Country Times*, March 18, 2008.

Wilder, JeffriAnne. 2015. *Color Stories: Black Women and Colorism in the 21st Century*. Santa Barbara, CA: ABC-CLIO.

Williams, Dmitri, Nicole Martins, Mia Consalvo, and James D. Ivory. 2009. "The Virtual Census: Representations of Gender, Race and Age in Video Games." *New Media and Society* 11 (5): 815–34. https://doi.org/10.1177/1461444809105354.

Williams, Patricia J. 2016. *Seeing a Color-Blind Future: The Paradox of Race*. New York: Farrar, Straus and Giroux.

Wilson, Clint C., II, Felix Gutierrez, and Lena M. Chao. 2013. *Racism, Sexism, and the Media*. 4th ed. Thousand Oaks, CA: Sage.

Winant, Howard. 2001. *The World Is a Ghetto: Race and Democracy since World War II*. New York: Basic Books.

Wolfe, Patrick. 2006. "Settler Colonialism and the Elimination of the Native." *Journal of Genocide Research* 8 (4): 387–409.

Workneh, Lily. 2016. "Meet April Reign, the Activist Who Started #OscarsSoWhite." *HuffPost*, February 2, 2016. www.huffpost.com.

Wright, David. 2016. "Trump: Tubman on the $20 Bill Is 'Pure Political Correctness.'" CNN.com, April 21, 2016. www.cnn.com.

Wu, Frank. 2002. "Where Are You Really From? Asian Americans and the Perpetual Foreigner Syndrome." *Civil Rights Journal* 6 (1): 14–22.

Wurzburger, Andrea. 2018. "These Are the Celebrities Who Are Donating Money and Movie Theaters So That Kids Can See Black Panther." *VH1 News*, February 16, 2018. www.vh1.com.

Wuthnow, Robert. 2005. "Democratic Renewal and Cultural Inertia: Why Our Best Efforts Fall Short." *Sociological Forum* 20 (3): 343–67.

Wynne, Kelly. 2018. "Ann Coulter Slams 'Pretty White Girl' Taylor Swift for Democratic Endorsement." *Newsweek*, October 8, 2018.

Xing, Jun. 1998. *Asian America through the Lens: History, Representations, and Identity*. Walnut Creek, CA: AltaMira.

Yang-Stevens, Kat, and Alex Quan-Pham. 2016. "Akai Gurley the 'Thug,' Peter Liang the 'Rookie Cop' and the Model Minority Myth." *Truthout*, February 26, 2016. www.truth-out.org.

Yearwood, Gladstone L. 2000. *Black Film as a Signifying Practice: Cinema, Narration and the African American Aesthetic Tradition*. Trenton, NJ: Africa World.

Yosso, Tara J. 2002. "Critical Race Media: Challenging Deficit Discourse about Chicanas/os." *Journal of Popular Film and Television* 30 (1): 52–62.

Younge, Gary. 2013. "The Misremembering of 'I Have a Dream.'" *Nation*, August 14, 2013. www.thenation.com.

Yuen, Nancy Wang. 2017. *Reel Inequality: Hollywood Actors and Racism*. New Brunswick, NJ: Rutgers University Press.

Zimmer, Carl. 2018. *She Has Her Mother's Laugh: The Powers, Perversions, and Potential of Heredity*. New York: Penguin.

Zirin, Dave. 2013. "A Review of '42': Jackie Robinson's Bitter Pill." *Nation*, April 17, 2013. www.thenation.com.

Zubiaga, Arkaitz, and Heng Ji. 2014. "Tweet, but Verify: Epistemic Study of Information Verification on Twitter." *Social Network Analysis and Mining* 4 (1): art. 163.

Zubiaga, Arkaitz, Maria Liakata, Rob Procter, Geraldine Wong Sak Hoi, and Peter Tolmie. 2016. "Analysing How People Orient to and Spread Rumours in Social Media by Looking at Conversational Threads." *PLOS One* 11 (3): e0150989.

ABOUT THE EDITORS

Matthew W. Hughey holds a BA (sociology, UNCG), MEd (cultural studies, Ohio University), and PhD (sociology, University of Virginia) and is Associate Professor of Sociology at the University of Connecticut, where he also serves as Affiliate Faculty in the Africana Studies Institute; the American Studies Program; the Institute for Collaboration on Health, Intervention, and Policy (InCHIP); and the Graduate Certificate Program in Race, Ethnicity, and Politics (REP). He concurrently serves as Research Associate for Critical Studies in Higher Education Transformation at Nelson Mandela University (South Africa); International Collaborator with the Research Group on Gender, Identity, and Diversity at the University of Barcelona (Spain); and Affiliate Member of Culture, Politics, and Global Justice at the University of Cambridge (England). He has held visiting academic appointments at University of Kent Law School (England), Trinity College Dublin (Ireland), University of Warwick (England), Columbia University (USA), and University of the Free State (South Africa).

Emma González-Lesser holds a BA in women's and gender studies from Simmons College and an MA in sociology from the University of Connecticut. She is a PhD candidate in sociology at the University of Connecticut, focusing on the area of race and ethnicity. Her primary research focuses on understanding constructions of Jewishness as they are situated within the contemporary ethno-racial schema of the United States, emphasizing social, cultural, identity-based, ethnic, and racial claims surrounding definitions of Jews, with particular consideration of Jews of color. She has published an article on microaggressions in *Sociological Inquiry*, as well as book chapters and multiple encyclopedia articles, and has presented her research at the annual meetings of the Southern Sociological Society and the Eastern Sociological Society and organized panels for these conferences as well. She is the managing editor for *Humanity and Society* and guest editor of a special issue of the same journal. She has received grants from El Instituto at the University of Connecticut and a predoctoral fellowship from the Sociology Department at the University of Connecticut.

Carlos Alamo-Pastrana holds a PhD in sociology from the University of California, Santa Barbara, and is Associate Professor of Sociology and Latin American and Latina/o Studies at Vassar College, where his teaching interests focus on comparative racial formations, Latinx studies, Afro-Latinx intellectual history, popular culture, and prison studies.

Rachelle J. Brunn-Bevel is Associate Professor of Sociology and Anthropology at Fairfield University. Brunn-Bevel received a bachelor of arts degree, with distinction, in sociology and political science at the University of Delaware and her master of arts and PhD in sociology with a graduate certificate in urban studies from the University of Pennsylvania. Her research examines how students' race, ethnicity, class, gender, and immigrant status intersect to influence their educational experiences and outcomes.

Christopher Chávez (PhD, University of Southern California) is Associate Professor and Doctoral Program Director at the School of Journalism and Communication at the University of Oregon. Chávez's research lies at the intersection of globalization, media, and culture. Before his doctoral research, he worked as an advertising executive at several advertising agencies, including TBWA\Chiat\Day, Goodby, Silverstein & Partners, and Publicis & Hal Riney.

Niamh Costello is a PhD student in social welfare at the University of California, Los Angeles. Niamh holds an MSc in public policy and human development from Maastricht University. Her research addresses attitudes to welfare and poverty in the global South.

Justin de Leon, PhD, is a researcher with the Global Feminism Research Collaborative at Vanderbilt University. He was formerly Lecturer at the

University of California, San Diego, teaching courses on race, gender, indigeneity, and critical media production. He received his doctorate in international relations at University of Delaware with a focus on feminist theory and indigeneity. De Leon served as Director of the Native Film and Storytelling Institute 2018 Pilot Program at UC, San Diego, a residential program that combines feminist and Indigenous approaches to storytelling and representation with professional filmmaking training.

Anna M. Dudney Deeb holds a BA (communication studies / French, Loyola Marymount University), an MA (communication studies, Colorado State University), and a PhD (communication studies, University of Georgia). She holds graduate certificates in women's studies and university teaching. She is an adjunct professor at Brenau University in Gainesville, Georgia. Her recent research examines African Americans' and women's rhetorical activist strategies at the 1893 World's Columbian Exposition through the public addresses of Frederick Douglass, Ida B. Wells, and the exposition's Congress of Women.

David Elkins is a master's student in the Department of Sociology, Anthropology and Social Work at Texas Tech University. Elkins's research focuses on the anti-immigrant sentiment and how current immigrant legislation is affecting the lives and educational trajectories of undocumented youth in the United States.

Nadia Y. Flores-Yeffal is Associate Professor in the Department of Sociology, Anthropology and Social Work at Texas Tech University. She received her doctorate in sociology from the University of Pennsylvania. Flores-Yeffal's research focuses on the causes, social processes, and consequences of undocumented migration from Mexico and Central America to the United States. She has also written extensively about the criminalization of immigrants through the use of media.

Martin Gilens is Professor of Public Policy at the UCLA Luskin School of Public Affairs. He earned a PhD in sociology at the University of California, Berkeley, and has held fellowships at the Institute for Advanced Study in Princeton, the Center for Advanced Study in the Behavioral

Sciences at Stanford, and the Russell Sage Foundation. Gilens is a member of the American Academy of Arts and Sciences and taught at Yale and Princeton before joining the Luskin School at UCLA in 2018. His research examines representation, public opinion, and mass media, especially in relation to inequality and public policy.

Tina M. Harris is Professor in the Department of Communication Studies at the University of Georgia. Her expertise is in the area of interracial communication, where she explores the ways in which individuals communicate about race. Her research addresses how racial identities play a critical role in how people choose to communicate with others from a different race and the strategies that are used to navigate those difficult conversations.

William Hoynes holds a BA (history and political science, Tufts University) and a PhD (sociology, Boston College) and is Professor of Sociology at Vassar College, where he teaches courses on media, culture, research methods, and social theory. During his twenty-five years at Vassar, Hoynes has served as Chair of the Sociology Department and Director of both the Media Studies Program and the American Studies Program.

Leslie Kay Jones earned her PhD in sociology from the University of Pennsylvania and during 2017–18 was Mellon Doctoral Fellow in the Price Lab for Digital Humanities at the University of Pennsylvania. She is Assistant Professor in the Department of Sociology at Rutgers–New Brunswick. She specializes in the study of race and gender, critical race theory, online social media, and collective mobilization.

Minjeong Kim is Associate Professor of Sociology at San Diego State University. Her research areas include gender and family in the context of international migration, as well as race, gender, and sexuality in the media. She has published works on media representations of Asian Americans.

Rachel Kuo is a PhD candidate at New York University in the Department of Media, Culture, and Communication, researching digital technologies and racial justice movements. She is a founding member and current affiliate of the Center for Critical Race and Digital Studies.

SunAh M. Laybourn is Assistant Professor of Sociology at the University of Memphis. She received her PhD from the University of Maryland in 2018. Her areas of interest include race and ethnicity, social psychology, identity, and media/culture. Laybourn is pursuing two lines of research: immigration, citizenship, and belonging through the case of Korean transnational transracial adoptees and citizenship rights advocacy; and media and racialized meaning-making and its effects on identity development.

David J. Leonard is Professor at Washington State University, Pullman. He regularly writes about issues of anti-Black racism, media culture, inequality, and the criminal justice system. Leonard is a past contributor to *Undefeated*, *NewBlackMan*, *Feminist Wire*, *Huffington Post*, *Chronicle of Higher Education*, and *Urban Cusp*.

Maretta McDonald is a Louisiana BOR/SREB doctoral fellow and PhD candidate in sociology at Louisiana State University. Her primary research interests are race/ethnicity, crime, intersectionality, and public policy. She earned her master's degree from Southeastern Louisiana University in applied sociology. Her master's thesis examined the relationship between race and child-support enforcement system outcomes. She is currently researching the impact of race on various topics such as support for child-support enforcement policy, representation in mass media, and intimate-partner homicide.

Sonita R. Moss is a PhD candidate in the Sociology Department at the University of Pennsylvania. Her master's thesis examined an alternative food site using ethnographic methods. She is the recipient of a 2017–18 Fulbright US Student Program Research Grant to conduct her dissertation research in Paris, France. Her dissertation study is an eighteen-month ethnography of the contemporary Black American immigrant community.

Dorothy E. Roberts is the fourteenth Penn Integrates Knowledge Professor and George A. Weiss University Professor of Law and Sociology at University of Pennsylvania, with joint appointments in the Departments of Africana Studies and Sociology and the Law School, where she is the inaugural Raymond Pace and Sadie Tanner Mossell Alexander Professor of Civil Rights. She is also Founding Director of the Penn Program on Race, Science and Society. An internationally recognized scholar, public intellectual, and social justice advocate, Roberts has written and lectured extensively on the interplay of race and gender in US institutions and has been a leader in transforming thinking on reproductive health, child welfare, and bioethics.

Michael L. Rosino is a doctoral candidate in sociology at the University of Connecticut. His areas of focus include racism and racial inequality, political sociology, collective action, mass media, and human rights. His research covers the racial politics of political parties, racialized dynamics of political power, the racial politics of mass-media debates over drug policy, the role of the human rights framework in collective action against racial injustice in the United States, the relationship between racial oppression and grassroots democracy, and the reproduction and contestation of racial oppression in daily social interactions.

Catherine R. Squires is Professor of Communication Studies at the University of Minnesota. She earned her PhD from Northwestern University. When she is not reading or writing, she is always on the lookout for interesting birds that might be visiting the Midwest.

Aisha Upton holds a BA and an MA (African American studies and sociology, Ohio University). She is a doctoral candidate at the University of Minnesota. Her research focuses on race, gender, social movements, and civic engagement. More specifically, her research centers on Black women's voluntary associations and Black radical movements.

Alysen Wade earned her MA from the University of Georgia in 2016, focusing on mid-eighteenth-century women's literacy groups known as the Blue Stockings. She works in the corporate world, helping women and injured workers access benefits under the Family Medical Leave Act. She is also a freelance writer engaging with topics such as critical race theory, current events, radical feminism, and historical funerary practices.

INDEX

Page numbers in italics refer to tables and illustrations.